Awakening

THE STORY OF THE BENGAL RENAISSANCE

SUBRATA DASGUPTA

PENGUIN BOOKS
An imprint of Penguin Random House

PENGUIN BOOKS

USA | Canada | UK | Ireland | Australia
New Zealand | India | South Africa | China | Singapore

Penguin Books is part of the Penguin Random House group of companies
whose addresses can be found at global.penguinrandomhouse.com

Published by Penguin Random House India Pvt. Ltd
4th Floor, Capital Tower 1, MG Road,
Gurugram 122 002, Haryana, India

Penguin Random House India

First published by Random House India 2011
This edition published in Penguin Books by Penguin Random House India 2019

Copyright © Subrata Dasgupta 2010

All rights reserved

10 9 8 7 6 5 4 3 2

The views and opinions expressed in this book are the author's own and the
facts are as reported by him which have been verified to the extent possible,
and the publishers are not in any way liable for the same.

ISBN 9788184001839

Typeset in Adobe Caslon by InoSoft Systems, Noida
Printed at Manipal Technologies Limited, India

This book is sold subject to the condition that it shall not, by way of trade
or otherwise, be lent, resold, hired out, or otherwise circulated without the
publisher's prior consent in any form of binding or cover other than that in
which it is published and without a similar condition including this condition
being imposed on the subsequent purchaser.

www.penguin.co.in

MIX
Paper | Supporting
responsible forestry
FSC® C043100

This is a legitimate digitally printed version of the book and therefore might not
have certain extra finishing on the cover.

Contents

Acknowledgements	v
A Chronology	ix
Prologue	1
'In the Midst of So Noble an Amphitheatre'	7
A City of Two Towns	47
Translators, Printers, Teachers, Preachers	67
Warrior-Raja	99
Bhadralok in Class, English in Taste	145
Enfant Terrible	164
Humanist by Creed, Humanist in Deed	200
A 'Jolly Christian Rhymer' of 'Exquisite Graces'	234
Voices of Their Own	277
'Where the Intellect May Safely Speculate…'	327
Bachelor of Arts, Master of Letters	340
The Sound of Monistic Music	373
Breaking the Wall of Western Contempt	396
Epilogue: The Most Impossibly Gifted of Them All	431
Bibliography	451
Index	476

To
Shome, Tabby
&
Deep

Acknowledgements

In writing this book I have felt rather like a lawyer marshalling the evidence and then preparing a coherent narrative to present to judge and jury. That evidence lies quite explicitly in the notes and the bibliography that accompany this narrative. But the story I have told here does not reveal the influences of the thoughts, conversations, remarks, and commentaries of and by various persons I have encountered over many years.

Sometimes, I was merely an eavesdropper on their conversations; other times I would listen to them in those sessions of sweet but unsilent thought that Bengalis call 'adda'; or over lunch and dinner at people's homes and restaurants; or in coffee breaks at conferences; or in the aftermath of lectures and seminars. And, in more recent times, there have been the emails.

This is then the time to acknowledge my debt in one way or another to: Rukun Advani, Robert Anderson, Amiya Bagchi, Jasodhara Bagchi, Tirthankar Bose, Donald Cardwell, B. Chandrasekaran, Dhritiman Chatterji, Rosinka Chaudhuri, Sarbananda Chaudhuri, Sukanta Chaudhuri, Supriya Chaudhuri, Sisir Kumar Das, Deepanwita Dasgupta, Malay Dasgupta, Barun De, Jonathan Feinstein, John Gero, Wenceslao Gonzales, S. Irfan Habib, Richard Hills, Norman

Holland, Rajesh Kochhar, Deepak Kumar, Bimal Matilal, John Meriwether, Thomas Nickles, Lewis Pyenson, William Radice, Burton Raffel, Dhruv Raina, Tapan Raychaudhuri, Herbert A. Simon, Alan Smith, Abha Sur, and Robert Weber.

I must mention three other persons in particular, all now deceased.

It was impossible to write about the Asiatic Society, Hindu/Presidency College, and nineteenth-century Indian science without thinking of Jatis Chandra (J.C.) Sengupta. His image—complete with cigar and robust voice—would intrude insistently into my consciousness.

The spirit of Rabindra Kumar (R.K.) Dasgupta permeated my entire mental space while I was engaged in the writing of this book. Over almost forty years I have been privy to his profound knowledge, and learning on and insight into all things pertaining to the intellectual history of nineteenth-century Bengal (and more). I was also fortunate to have access to his remarkable library.

Long before my awareness of the Bengal Renaissance, I have been listening to its music, as rabindra-sangeet, in the voice of Pratima Dasgupta from as far back as I can remember.

Jasodhara Bagchi and Rosinka Chaudhuri read certain chapters in preliminary form and responded with valuable comments. I thank them. Needless to say, I alone am responsible for the content of this book.

Writing, as writers of all persuasions know, necessitates a critic other than the one within the writer. That critic for this book was my editor Chiki Sarkar. The book evolved through multiple drafts in which she goaded me to add this, delete that, and forced me again and again to reconsider the text just when I thought it was all done. I thank her for her editorial acumen.

I thank Anton Rippon, my schoolmate from over half a century ago. From across the Atlantic and via cyberspace he has been a sympathetic witness to the evolution of this book.

For almost three decades, the University of Louisiana at Lafayette has offered me a liberal environment to freely live the interdisciplinary and cross-cultural life. I thank, in particular, Ray Authement, Steve Landry, Bradd Clark, and David Barry for affording me the liberty to cross at will the boundaries between the sciences and the humanities, and between the cultures of East and West. My colleagues in the Institute of Cognitive Science—Claude Cech, Michael Kalish, Anthony Maida, Michele Feist, Istvan Berkeley, and Clay Rice—helped create a multidisciplinary academic unit rare in this age of hyper-specialization.

I first embarked on what is now called cognitive history during my time at the University of Manchester Institute of Science and Technology. In telling this story of the awakening of the nineteenth-century Indian mind to new creative possibilities I remembered, with much affection, that pivotal period spent in Manchester.

Every effort was made to secure permission from publishers to quote passages from their copyrighted works. I thank in particular the following publishers.

Advaita Ashrama, for permission to quote from Swami Vivekananda, *Complete Works*, 2001.

Cambridge University Press, for permission to quote from P.J. Marshall (ed.), *The British Discovery of Hinduism in the Eighteenth Century*, 1970.

Macmillan Publishers India, for permission to quote from Rabindranath Tagore, *Glimpses of Bengal*, 1997 and Rabindranath Tagore, *Reminiscences*, 2001.

Oxford University Press India, for permission to quote from: E.J. Thompson, *Rabindranath Tagore: Poet and Dramatist*, 1989; Sukanta Chaudhuri (ed.), *Calcutta. The Living City*. Volume 1, 1990. Ghulam Murshid, *Lured by Hope: A Biography of Michael Madhusudan Dutt*, 2003; Ghulam Murshid (ed.), *The Heart of a Rebel Poet: Letters of Michael Madhusudan Dutt*, 2004; C. Lokugé (ed.) *Toru Dutt: Collected Prose and Poetry*, 2006.

Sadharan Brahmo Samaj, for permission to quote from S.D. Collett, *The Life and Letters of Raja Rammohun Roy*, D.K. Biswas and P.C. Ganguli (ed.), 1988.

Sahitya Samsad, for permission to quote from J.C. Bagal (ed.), *Bankim Rachanabali, Volume III: English Works*, 1969.

Writers Workshop Calcutta, for permission to quote from Rassundari Debi, *Amar Jiban*, Enakshi Chatterjee, (trans.), 1999.

Finally, a note of gratitude to my family: To Mithu, who as always, bore with phlegmatic forbearance my preoccupations and obsessions while this work was in progress. To Shome, who in the midst of his own writing, frequently rescued me from the vagaries of my laptop software and Deep who kept a quizzical filmmaker's eye on my progress.

A Chronology

1750	Warren Hastings arrives in India.
1761	William Carey is born.
1772	Hastings is appointed governor of Bengal. Nathaniel Halhed arrives in India. Rammohun Roy is born.
1773	Fort William completed by Hastings. James Mill is born.
1774	Warren Hastings becomes first governor-general of India.
1775	David Hare is born.
1776	Halhed's *A Code of Gentoo Law* is published.
1778	Halhed's *A Grammar of the Bengali Language* is published. The Bengali type font is invented by Panchanan.
1781	Calcutta Madrasa is established by Warren Hastings.
1783	William Jones arrives in Calcutta. Henry Colebrooke arrives in India.
1784	Formation of the Asiatic Society with William Jones as President.
1785	Warren Hastings leaves India. Charles Wilkins's translation of *Bhagvada Gita* is published. Nathaniel

	Halhed leaves India. Jones delivers his second annual anniversary discourse at the Asiatic Society. David Drummond is born.
1786	Jones delivers his third annual anniversary discourse at the Asiatic Society.
1788	Warren Hastings's impeachment trial begins. Volume I of *Asiatick Researches* published. Lord Wellesley is appointed governor-general.
1789	Jones's translation of *Sakuntala* is published.
1793	William Carey arrives in India.
1794	Jones delivers his eleventh and last annual anniversary discourse at the Asiatic Society. The death of William Jones. Dwarakanath Tagore is born.
1795	Warren Hastings's impeachment trial ends. Henry Colebrooke's 'On the Duties of a Faithful Hindoo Widow' is published in *Asiatick Researches*.
1799	Joshua Marshman and William Ward arrive in India.
1800	Formation of the College of Fort William, Calcutta. The Baptist Mission is established by Carey, Marshman, and Ward in Serampore. The Serampore Mission Press is established. Ramram Basu is appointed a pandit in the College of Fort William. Carey's translation of the Bible into Bengali is published.
1801	Tarinicharan Mitra and Mrtyunjay Vidyalankar appointed pandits in the College of Fort William. Carey's Bengali-English bilingual *Kathopaketan* is published by Serampore Press.
1802	John Gilchrist founds the Hindustanee Press.

A Chronology • xi

1803–4	Rammohun Roy's *Tuhfat-ul-Muwahhdin* is published.
1805	Lord Wellesley's tenure as governor-general ends. The Sanskrit Press is established. Rammohun Roy becomes John Digby's munshi. Henry Colebrooke's 'On the Vedas or Sacred Writings of the Hindoos' is published in *Asiatick Researches*.
1806	Henry Colebrooke is elected president of the Asiatic Society. William Carey is elected a member of the Asiatic Society.
1806–10	The *Ramayana* is translated from Sanskrit to Bengali by Carey and Marshman and published by the Asiatic Society.
1807	Carey is appointed professor of Sanskrit in the College of Fort William.
1809	Henry Louis Vivian Derozio is born.
1813	Ramtanu Lahiri is born. Radhanath Sikdar is born. Krishna Mohun Banerji is born.
1814	Peary Chand Mittra is born.
1815	Rammohun Roy's *Vedanta Grantha* (in Bengali) is published. Rammohun founds the Atmiya Sabha.
1816	Rammohun's 'Abridgement of the *Vedant*' is published.
1817	Hindu College is founded. Rammohun's 'A Defence of Hindoo Theism' is published. His 'A Second Defence of the Monotheistic System of the Veds' is published. James Mill's *History of British India* is published. Debendranath Tagore is born.
1818	Serampore College is founded. The Marquess of Hastings issues orders against the practice of sati.

	The Calcutta Book Society is established. Robert May establishes the first girls' school in Chinsurah. Calcutta School Society is established.
1819	The Female Juvenile Society for the Establishment and Support of Bengali Female Schools is established.
1820	Ishwar Chandra Vidyasagar is born.
1823	Formation of the Royal Asiatic Society of Great Britain and Ireland with Henry Colebrooke as president. Rammohun Roy, William Adam, and Dwarakanath Tagore establish the Calcutta Unitarian Committee. The Unitarian Press is established. Rammohun writes his 'memorial' on education to Lord Amherst. The General Committee for Public Instruction is established by the government.
1824	Sanskrit College is founded. Madhusudan Datta is born.
1826	Sanskrit College moves to its own building.
1828	The Brahmo Samaj is founded by Rammohun Roy and his associates. Henry Derozio joins Hindu College as a teacher.
1829	Lord William Bentinck abolishes sati. Ishwar Chandra Vidyasagar is admitted to Sanskrit College.
1830	The Trust Deed of the Brahmo Samaj is executed. Rammohun Roy leaves for England. The Dharma Sabha is established.
1831	Henry Derozio resigns from Hindu College. He founds *The East Indian*. Derozio dies.

A Chronology • xiii

1833	Rammohun Roy dies in England. Ramtanu Lahiri joins Hindu College as a teacher. Mahendralal Sircar is born.
1834	Thomas Babington Macaulay arrives in India.
1835	St Xavier's founded by Belgium Jesuits. Macaulay writes his 'Minute on Education'. The 'Anglicist-Orientalist controversy' ends. Calcutta Medical College is founded.
1836	La Martiniere is founded by Major-General Claude Martin. Ramakrishna (Gadadhar Chattopadhyay) is born. Madhusudan Gupta performs human dissection.
1837	Madhusudan Datta enters Hindu College. Eugene Lafont is born.
1838	The Society for the Acquisition of General Knowledge is established by the Derozians. Bankimchandra Chattopadhyay is born.
1840	D.L. Richardson's *Selections from the British Poets* is published. Madhusudan Gupta receives a medical diploma from Calcutta Medical College. Dwijendranath Tagore is born.
1841	Vidyasagar completes education and leaves Sanskrit College. He is appointed head pandit in the College of Fort William.
1841–2	Madhusudan Datta's first English poems are published.
1842	David Hare dies. Satyendranath Tagore is born.
1843	David Drummond dies. Madhusudan Datta converts to Christianity. He is turned away from Hindu College.

1844	Madhusudan enrolls in Bishop's College.
1846	Vidyasagar is appointed assistant secretary in Sanskrit College. Dwarakanath Tagore dies.
1847	Vidyasagar resigns from Sanskrit College. Madhusudan Datta leaves Bishop's College and leaves Calcutta for Madras.
1848	Madhusudan arrives in Madras. He marries Rebecca Thompson McTavish. *The Captive Ladie* is published in a periodical.
1849	J.E.D. Bethune founds the Hindu Balika Vidyalaya (later renamed Bethune School). Vidyasagar is appointed head writer and treasurer in Fort William College. Madhusudan's *The Captive Ladie* is published in book form. Madhusudan adopts the Christian name 'Michael'. Bankimchandra Chattopadhyay enters Hooghly College. Jyotirindranath Tagore is born.
1850	Vidyasagar is appointed professor of Sanskrit in Sanskrit College.
1851	Vidyasagar becomes principal of Sanskrit College.
1852	Hannah Catherine Mullens publishes the first Bengali novel *Phulmoni o Karunar Bibaran*.
1854	The College of Fort William is dissolved by Lord Dalhousie. Charles Wood's Education Despatch arrives in India. Madhusudan Datta publishes his essay *The Anglo-Saxon and the Hindu*. The Government School of Art is established.
1855	Vidyasagar is appointed an assistant inspector of schools for Bengal. He writes pamphlets advocating widow remarriage. Hindu College becomes

A Chronology • xv

	Presidency College. Vidyasagar's *Barnaparichay* is published. Pramatha Nath Bose is born.
1855–6	Vidyasagar submits petitions against kulin polygamy to the government.
1856	The Civil Engineering College, Calcutta (later Bengal Engineering College), India's second oldest engineering college, is founded. The Widow Remarriage Act is passed. First widow remarriage amongst upper-caste Hindus takes place. Madhusudan Datta returns to Calcutta. Toru Dutt is born. Swarnamkumari Tagore is born.
1857	The Universities of Calcutta, Bombay, and Madras are founded. Presidency College is affiliated with the University of Calcutta. The Civil Engineering College and Calcutta Medical College are affiliated with the University of Calcutta. The law faculty of the University of Calcutta is established.
1858	Peary Chand Mittra's novel *Alaler Gharer Dulal* is published. Vidyasagar resigns principalship of Sanskrit College. Henrietta White comes to Calcutta from Madras to live with Madhusudan. Madhusudan's first original Bengali work, a play called *Sermistha*, is completed. Jadunath Bose and Bankimchandra Chattopadhyay are first graduates of the University of Calcutta. Jagadish Chandra Bose is born.
1859	Madhusudan's first child Sarmistha is born. Kadambari Devi is born.
1860	St Xavier's is relocated to Park Street. Vidyasagar's *Sitar Banabas* is published. Madhusudan begins

	writing *Meghnadabadh Kabya*. His first sonnet *Kabi-Matribhasa* is published. The 'age of consent' for girls is established at ten. Sanskrit College is affiliated with the University of Calcutta.
1861	First part of *Meghnadabadh Kabya* is completed. Prafulla Chandra Ray is born. Rabindranath Tagore is born.
1862	Kaliprassana Sinha's *Hutom Pachar Naksa* is published. Madhusudan Datta leaves for England. St Xavier's College is affiliated with the University of Calcutta.
1863	Henrietta and two children join Madhusudan in London. Madhusudan and family go to Versailles. Vivekananda (Narendranath Dutta) is born.
1864	Bankimchandra's first novel *Rajmohan's Wife*, the first 'Indian novel in English', is published. Eugene Lafont arrives in Calcutta as a teacher in St Xavier's.
1865	Bankimchandra's first Bengali novel *Durgeshnandini* is published.
1866	Madhusudan is called to the Bar. Haimabati Sen is born.
1867	Madhusudan returns to Calcutta. Margaret Noble (Nivedita) is born.
1868	Mahendralal Sircar founds the *Calcutta Journal of Medicine*.
1869	Toru Dutt and her family moves to France. Mahendralal Sircar publishes article proposing an institution for experimental science. Jagadish Chandra Bose enters St Xavier's.

1870	*The Dutt Family Album* is published. Toru Dutt and her family move from France to England. Campbell Medical School is established. Eugene Lafont is appointed rector of St Xavier's.
1871	Toru Dutt meets Mary Martin.
1872	Bankimchandra writes the first part of *Vande Mataram*. He launches the literary journal *Bangadarshan*.
1873	Madhusudan Datta and Henrietta White die. Annette Akroyd's Hindu Mahila Vidyalaya is established. Toru Dutt and her family return to Calcutta. Eugene Lafont meets Mahendralal Sircar.
1875	Haimabati Sen marries.
1876	The Indian Association for the Cultivation of Science is founded by Mahendralal Sircar and others. The first part of Rassundari's *Amar Jiban* is completed. Mary Carpenter and Annette Ackroyd establish the Banga Mahila Vidyalaya, the first women's college in India. Toru Dutt's *A Sheaf Gleaned in French Fields* is published. Haimabati Sen is widowed. The University of Calcutta awards its first honorary degrees. The Indian Association is founded.
1877	Toru Dutt dies. Jyotirindranath Tagore launches the literary magazine *Bharati*. Rabindranath's first poem is published. Rabindranath's 'Bhanu Singha' poems are published.
1878	Toru Dutt's novel *Bianca* is published posthumously. A second edition of *A Sheaf* is published. Rabindranath goes to England. Banga Mahila

	Vidyalaya and Bethune School merge to form Bethune College, India's first women's college.
1880	Pramatha Nath Bose is appointed to the Geological Survey of India. Jagadish Chandra obtains a BA degree from Calcutta University. He leaves for England. Rabindranath returns to India.
1881	Vivekananda meets Ramakrishna. Rabindranath's first musical drama *Valmiki Pratibha* is composed.
1882	Ramakrishna visits Vidyasagar. Toru Dutt's *Ancient Ballads and Legends* is published. Bankimchandra's novel *Anandamath* is published. The full version of 'Vande Mataram' is completed by Bankimchandra. Jagadish Chandra is admitted to Christ's College, Cambridge, as an undergraduate. Prafulla Chandra Ray is admitted to Edinburgh University as an undergraduate. Rabindranath's *Sandhya Sangeet* is published.
1883	Kadambini Bose and Chandramukhi Basu become India's and the British Empire's first university graduates. Rabindranath's *Prabhat Sangeet* is published.
1884	Jagadish Chandra receives the BA degree in the natural science tripos from Cambridge University. Rabindranath's *Bhanu Singha Thakurer Padabali* is composed. Kadambari Devi commits suicide. Rabindranath's first short story, *Ghater Katha*, is published.
1885	Prafulla Chandra writes his *Essay on India* in Edinburgh. The Indian National Congress is established. Prafulla Chandra receives the BSc

	degree in chemistry from Edinburgh University. Jagadish Chandra is appointed a professor of physics in Presidency College.
1886	Ramakrishna dies.
1887	Prafulla Chandra is awarded the doctor of science (DSc) degree in inorganic chemistry from Edinburgh University.
1888	Women are first admitted to Campbell Medical School. Prafulla Chandra returns to India.
1889	Prafulla Chandra is appointed a professor of chemistry in Presidency College.
1890	Haimabati Sen's second marriage takes place. Rabindranath's *Meghaduta* is published.
1891	Vidyasagar writes his autobiographical fragment. He dies. The 'age of consent' is raised to twelve. Haimabati Sen enters Campbell Medical School. Rabindranath's Selidah period begins.
1893	Bankimchandra's last novel *Rajsingha* is published. Vivekananda delivers address at the World's Parliament of Religions in Chicago.
1894	Haimabati completes studies in Campbell Medical School and enters Calcutta Medical College. Bankimchandra Chattopadhyay dies. Jagadish Chandra begins research in physics. Prafulla Chandra's first scientific paper is published.
1895	Vivekananda visits England. Margaret Noble meets Vivekananda. Jagadish Chandra's first paper on radio wave physics is published.
1896	Rabindranath Tagore sings 'Vande Mataram' in the 12th session of the Indian National Congress.

	Vivekananda returns to India from American tour. Prafulla Chandra's first paper on mercurous nitrite is published.
1897	Vivekananda founds the Ramakrishna Mission. Jagadish Chandra returns to India from his first European lecture tour.
1898	Margaret Noble arrives in India, is initiated into the Order of Ramakrishna, and is named Nivedita by Vivekananda.
1899	Vivekananda embarks on second visit to the West.
1900	Vivekananda returns to India from Western visit. Jagadish Chandra delivers a lecture at the International Physics Conference in Paris.
1902	Vivekananda dies. Prafulla Chandra's *A History of Hindu Chemistry* is published.
1904	Mahendralal Sircar dies.
1905	Debendranath Tagore dies.
1906	Second part of Rassundari's *Amar Jiban* is completed.
1908	Eugene Lafont dies.
1911	Nivedita dies.
1912	Rabindranath Tagore's *Gitanjali* is published.

Prologue

There is properly no history; only biography.
Ralph Waldo Emerson

IN THE SUMMER of 1912 the Irish poet W.B. Yeats was handed a manuscript of poems by his friend William Rothenstein, an English artist. The poems were English translations of Bengali originals written by another of Rothenstein's friends, the Indian poet Rabindranath Tagore.

At a party held that same summer in Rothenstein's London home, Yeats gave a reading from the manuscript to a gathering of friends. They decided to publish a selection of the poems. In autumn, a slender volume titled *Gitanjali (Song-Offerings)* was printed privately, in limited edition, by the India Society, an organization formed two years before in London to promote the study of Indian art, literature, music, and culture. The volume, edited by Yeats, included an introduction by him.

The next year, 1913, the British publishing house of Macmillan issued a 'trade' edition of *Gitanjali*, and in November, Rabindranath Tagore was awarded the Nobel Prize for literature for this collection. Thus came to pass a very public and symbolic climax to the phenomenon known as the Bengal Renaissance:

a fitting way to celebrate and recognize this phenomenon by bestowing a glittering prize on the person who was its very epitome.

FOR MOST PEOPLE, the mention of the word renaissance conjures up visions of the Italy of the fifteenth and sixteenth centuries. It takes them to that land's fabled towns and city republics, and makes them think of popes and princes, kings and cardinals, merchants and bankers. They might even sense, uneasily, shadowy images of blood and gore, war and assassinations, intrigue and murder—for that Italy was a violent land. Above all else, though, the word renaissance is linked irrevocably with the creative spirit in its most profuse richness and diversity.

Was the Bengal Renaissance anything like the Italian one? Many eminent Indian (and some Western) thinkers have pondered and debated this question. But really, the answer does not matter. What matters is that there came into being in Bengal, beginning sometime in the waning years of the eighteenth century and flowering to fullness through the nineteenth century, an awakening of the Indian mind of such a nature that we can call it a revolution. The 'Bengal Renaissance' was the name given to this revolutionary awakening of the Indian mind.

This book tells a story of this awakening.

The dramatis personae were not all Bengalis or even all Indians but they were all *of* Bengal. Some were concerned with the discovery of the Indian past. Some invented prose as a literary style in the Bengali language, and some new forms of poetry and story telling. Some were religious reformers, and some social reformers. Some created new modes of education. Some fought on behalf of women's rights and against injustice to women. Some argued for a more humanistic, secular, and rational society. Some created a scientific ethos for the country. And some stirred within their fellow countrymen a new nationalist consciousness.

But what connected them all was that they shared in the creation and formation, in one way or another, of a mentality which straddled two cultures, Western and Indian. This cross-cultural mentality, let us call it the *Indo-Western mind*, was the ultimate and supreme product of the Bengal Renaissance. Yet this mentality was as much the means to that awakening as its product. This is why the story told here turns its gaze again and again to the West. Without the West this awakening would not have happened. Without the West there would not have been a Bengal Renaissance.

OUR STORY BEGINS in the last quarter of the eighteenth century with Warren Hastings, India's first governor-general, a hard-headed empire builder, yet a man of cultivation and sensibility who wished to know the languages and culture of the people he ruled. Following him came a band of earnest men from the British Isles led by William Jones and Henry Colebrooke, scholars extraordinaire, who dug into the Indian past with missionary passion, a passion shared by some who really *were* missionaries, of whom the most notable was the indefatigable William Carey, an Englishman who pioneered the writing of Bengali prose.

There was the enigmatic and contradictory Rammohun Roy, a veritable Renaissance Man who (amongst other things) invented a reformed, almost Protestant Hindu church and, as a result, was detested by his conservative compatriots; and his friend David Hare, a liberal, enlightened Scot who conjured up the idea of a college where the youth of Bengal could be taught Western thought. There was the astonishingly precocious Henry Louis Vivian Derozio of Portuguese descent, English in taste but Indian bred, who appeared briefly and brilliantly, like a meteor in the sky, just long enough to initiate a new Indian literary tradition and goad pupils scarcely younger than him to question the very foundations of their Hindu manners and mores.

We come upon a woman named Rassundari Devi who taught herself to read and write in the teeth of hostility against female literacy so that she could read the scriptures for herself, and then went on to write an autobiography and create a literary genre virtually unknown in her country. We encounter another woman, Toru Dutt, who like Derozio died brutally young yet lived long enough to write poems and novels in English and French when few Indian women could read at all; and a spirited woman named Haimabati, a child widow at ten who battled for her independence and identity and became a 'lady doctor'.

Then there was an Englishman named Thomas Babington Macaulay who set Indians' teeth on edge with his sneers at all things Indian but who, all the same, wrote a document that played a seminal role in the Indian awakening. And the tempestuous Madhusudan Datta who defied convention, became Christian, turned his back on his Bengalihood, then returned to it and created new forms of Bengali verse on European lines. And his benefactor, Ishwar Chandra

Vidyasagar, scholar, humanist, social and educational reformist, feminist, head of a college created for traditional Sanskrit learning who, inspired by European Enlightenment thought, ushered in humanism and secularism through the portals of his college and caused consternation amongst the orthodoxy.

We come across a physician named Mahendralal Sircar, a visionary who dreamt of a scientific India and converted his dream into reality; and his friend Eugene Lafont, a Belgian priest who in a Jesuit school in Calcutta made science a living subject for his wards. We will find in our story the redoubtable Bankimchandra Chattopadhyay, Bengal's first man of letters, a civil servant in the service of the Raj, creator of the novel in Indian literature, and composer of a song that became a national hymn. There was Father Lafont's onetime pupil Jagadish Chandra Bose and his contemporary and friend Prafulla Chandra Ray, two lonely workers in laughably primitive laboratories who rose to be the frontiersmen of modern science in India and who silenced the voice of Western disbelief that Indians had the capacity to think scientific thought.

A barely literate mystic, Ramakrishna's homespun Hindu philosophy inspired an intellectual named Narendranath Dutta to metamorphose into a monk called Vivekananda who preached at home and abroad a new form of Vedantism, who in turn inspired an Irish woman, Margaret Noble to adopt his faith and become a Hindu nun named Nivedita.

And finally, we come upon the impossibly gifted Rabindranath, poet, songster, dramatist, story teller, philosopher, and educationist, the most brilliant of a bountifully endowed family of siblings, spouses, and friends, the Tagores of Jorasanko, who wove together a milieu of art and music and literature.

These were the foremost dramatis personae of this story though there were others, as we shall see, who flitted in and out.

Finally, the Bengal of *this* Renaissance did not only mean Calcutta, just as the Italy of *that* Renaissance did not only mean Florence. Yet we must look to Calcutta (now Kolkata), that much-maligned, chaotic, exhausted, yet irrepressible and effervescent city, for it was the locus classicus of this awakening just as Florence was the cradle of that other renaissance. Calcutta spawned institutions—the Asiatic Society, the College of Fort William, Sanskrit College, Hindu College, Calcutta Medical College, the University of Calcutta, Bethune School, amongst others—which were inextricably entwined in the unfolding of the Bengal Renaissance.

With that let the story begin.

One

'In the Midst of So Noble an Amphitheatre'

WARREN HASTINGS (1732–1818) came to India in 1750 at the age of seventeen. When he finally departed for his native England in 1785, he had lived on the subcontinent for most of his working life, save for an interlude in London from 1764–9.

Like so many of his countrymen he arrived in India fresh out of school recruited by the East India Company as a 'writer'. Writers were clerks, the lowest ranked officials in the Company hierarchy whose job was to maintain accounts of the Company's trades. They were poorly paid; yet in Britain, these were much coveted appointments.[1] For, these mostly callow young men came to India in search of wealth, and employment by the East India Company gave them ample opportunity to secure it: as well as serving the Company's commercial interests, its employees, from writers up, were allowed to trade on their own and thus could vastly enrich themselves, if they survived long enough on the subcontinent. For the more ambitious there was also the opportunity to rise through the ranks of the Company hierarchy, possibly to membership of its Council or even to that of the all-powerful position of governor in one or the other of the British presidencies in India.

Warren Hastings was fortunate in both respects. He came to India with not much money. He left India, at the age of fifty-two, a very wealthy man and, since 1774, as India's first governor-general, having served as Bengal's governor for two years before that. A portrait of Hastings by Joshua Reynolds, painted when he was living in London in the mid 1760s, shows a finely featured face and, though only in his mid thirties, with already receding hair. He is dressed elegantly and seated in a plush armchair with one hand resting on what looks like a scroll upon a table. The face, looking away from the viewer, is unsmiling, aloof, thoughtful; he is yet to become governor but the trappings of wealth and power are already in evidence—as befitting a person Reynolds would want to paint.

It is not easy to typecast Warren Hastings. He was, of course, an empire builder on behalf of the British government and the East India Company. It was his job to make profits for the Company and to extend his country's power, prestige, and jurisdiction over India. Towards these ends he did what he had to: wage war when necessary, play politics, wheel and deal, concoct strategies of statecraft, and, along the way, do exceedingly well financially.[2]

And at the end of it all, back in England, he would suffer the humiliation of impeachment in Parliament for 'high crimes and misdemeanours' against Indians, for bribery and corruption, and violating Company rules and acts of parliament[3]—charges from which, seven years after the impeachment trial began, he would be acquitted.

In the annals of British history Warren Hastings is probably best known because of his impeachment which, as told by a sympathetic nineteenth century biographer, was a tale of passion, politics, and personal animosities. Hastings had his friends in London but his enemies were more influential and they won the day.[4] Oratorial excess also played its part: by the playwright-politician Richard Brinsley Sheridan whose speech before Parliament in early 1787 decisively turned the tide against Hastings and persuaded Parliament that his impeachment was justified,[5] and who again spoke for four days in the course of the trial which began in February 1788.[6] But in the impeachment trial Hastings's name is inevitably linked, above all, with that of Edmund Burke, parliamentarian, historian, and orator, Hastings's implacable enemy and the man who brought the articles of impeachment before Parliament, whose thunderous speech at the trial would span no less than nine days.[7] Eventually, in 1795, seven years to the month since the impeachment trial began, the House of Lords, whose very composition had changed quite dramatically in the course of these years, and some of whose members had been schoolboys when the trial began, voted on the trial. They found Hastings, by a majority, not guilty on each of the sixteen charges of 'high crimes and misdemeanours' that had been brought against him.[8]

Hastings may or may not have deserved the impeachment; what is certain is that he secured a place in India's cultural and intellectual history as the unlikely begetter of what came to be called the Bengal Renaissance. If we must assign a year to mark its beginning let us choose 1772, the year Hastings was appointed by the East India Company's court of directors as governor of Bengal—from which, when the financially-stricken Company was subordinated to the authority of Parliament, he would be elevated in 1774 to governor-general of British India. The Raj began with Hastings in 1772.

Hastings believed that to rule India effectively one must know India and its culture. The Englishmen in India must learn to 'think and act like an Asian'.[9] This could only come about if one could communicate with Indians; and *that* meant learning India's languages.[10] Hastings himself had learnt Persian (the language of the Mughal courts), Hindustani, and some Bengali.[11] But then, he was no intellectual slouch though he called himself 'an unlettered man'.[12] Hastings had been educated at the public school Westminster (though his formal education had ended for financial reasons at the age of seventeen before he could complete his schooling), and in his time he was known as an outstanding student.[13]

Hastings's interest in Indian thought was not simply the result of empire-building pragmatism. In 1775, the year after his appointment as governor-general, he wrote from Calcutta to Samuel Johnson, England's pre-eminent man of letters, that it was one of his first wishes to free Indians from the 'reproach of barbarism' that had been cast upon them.[14]

> Although the situation in which I have been placed has... precluded me from gratifying my curiosity by research of my own into the history, traditions, arts, or natural productions of this country, yet I have not been inattentive to them, having esteemed it among the duties of my station to direct and encourage the pursuit of others to their discoveries, who were better qualified by their talents or leisure for the attainment of them.[15]

Amongst these 'others' were Indian Muslim and Hindu scholars:

> I have for some time past employed some of the most learned of the Mahometan and Gentoo inhabitants in forming a compilation of their respective laws and have had the satisfaction of receiving an abstract of the Gentoo law, completed under the most respectable authority.[16]

In fact, in pursuit of the practical need to understand the Hindu code of law—the 'Gentoo law'—Hastings had commissioned a group of pandits to put this code into written Sanskrit. The code was then translated into Persian (as none among the English bureaucrats apparently knew Sanskrit). He commissioned a further task: 'A translation of this work into the English language, executed by a young man of genius and ability, has been transmitted to the Court of Directors [of the East India Company, in London], and I hope will have their sanction for its publication.'[17]

THIS 'YOUNG MAN of genius and ability' was Nathaniel Halhed (1751–1830), alumnus of Harrow School and Christ Church College, Oxford, a highly gifted linguist who, according to a contemporary, 'knew so much of so many things' with 'so ready a command of all he knew'.[18] Apparently spurned by a girl who preferred his friend the playwright Richard Sheridan, Halhed chose to come to India in 1772 as a young writer of twenty.[19] It became Halhed's task, as a Persian speaker, to translate the Hindu code from its Persian version into English.[20] The result was *A Code of Gentoo Law*, published in 1776.

This work was never quite accepted as the ultimate legal authority in Hindu law for the purpose of administering civil law. However, it was hailed by many in England as a valuable literary document that revealed to Europeans in greater detail than ever before the nature of these ancient laws. Indeed, *A Code of Gentoo Law* was later translated into French and German.[21]

Halhed's next major accomplishment, once more with Hastings's support, was to learn Bengali and prepare *A Grammar of the Bengali Language*, published in 1778. To publish this work there had to be a Bengali printing press. In fact, there were none. Hastings was once more aided by the presence, in Calcutta, of another young gifted writer-scholar in the East India Company. Charles Wilkins (1749-1836), a friend of Halhed, with the help of a local blacksmith and Hastings's encouragement, was able to produce a Bengali typeface which was used to print Halhed's *Grammar*. This press was the first for the Bengali language.[22] Wilkins would later design typefaces for Persian and Devanagri (Sanskrit) scripts.[23]

Designing and crafting typefaces—an intricate skill—was not the kind of expertise that fell within the scope of most young eighteenth century Englishmen's education. Wilkins, it turned out, was the nephew of a noted British printer and engraver,[24] and (we presume) he had considerable training in his uncle's establishment. Later, Hastings would appoint him as the official printer to the East India Company.[25] However, Wilkins was no 'mere' printer-typographer. He was a linguist as well and, once again under Hastings's sponsorship but (by his own account[26]) persuaded by Halhed, he took to learning Sanskrit. The great fruit of this labour was his translation of the *Bhagavada Gita* into English, published in Britain in 1785.

THE TRANSLATOR'S ART is subtle, rich and complex. But when

translation is of a text from a little-studied culture it is also an act of discovery for the translator brings into light aspects of a culture or a literature that were scarcely known.

Here is what Nathaniel Halhed said in his preface to *A Code of Gentoo Laws*. Speaking of Hindu laws which were 'interwoven with the religion of the country and are thereby revered as of the highest authority', he told his (mainly British) readers that these laws will allow one to form 'a precise idea of these people which, to their great injury, have long been misrepresented in the Western world'.[27]

And here is Warren Hastings introducing to Nathaniel Smith, chairman of the East India Company, Charles Wilkins's translation of the *Bhagavada Gita*. The hard-headed empire builder admitted: 'Every accumulation of knowledge, and especially such as is obtained by social communication with people over whom we exercise a dominion founded on the right of conquest, is useful to the state…'[28] Yet, 'it attracts and conciliates distant affections; it lessens the weight of the chain by which the natives are held in subjection'.

> It is not very long since the inhabitants of India were considered by many as creatures scarce elevated above the degree of savage life… Every institution which brings their real character home to observation will impress us with a more generous sense of feeling for their natural rights and teaches us to estimate them by the measure of our own.[29]

There follows a surprising foretelling: '…these [writings] will survive when the British dominion in India shall have long ceased to exist…'[30]

These remarks signal the capacity of someone belonging to one culture to take a sympathetic view, or even *empathize*, with the manners and mores of another.

There is a striking passage in Halhed's long preface to *Gentoo Laws* which illustrates this empathy. Halhed was speaking of 'Ashumeed Jugg' (Asvamedha Yajna), the horse-sacrifice ceremony described in *Gentoo Laws*, which he compared to the goat-sacrifice (scapegoat) mentioned in the Old Testament. In the Biblical account, Aaron was commanded to 'lay both his hands' upon a goat's head and confess all the sins of the children of Israel; the goat, then sent away into the wilderness, took with it all these transgressions.[31] Halhed found a symbolic similarity between Asvamedha—the 'Gentoo sacrifice'—and the scapegoat ceremony; and he noted that perhaps his (Western) readers may find the 'hidden meaning' of the horse-sacrifice ritual by appealing to their understanding of the scapegoat ceremony. Here was an empathetic insight into an apparently strange and alien custom.[32]

Likewise, Charles Wilkins in his much briefer preface to his translation of the *Bhagavada Gita* invited his readers to note that though the 'most learned *Brahmans* of the present time' were Unitarians, believing in one 'Supreme Being' in accordance with Krishna's teachings, yet they performed such rituals as 'sacrifices, ablutions, &c' to satisfy the 'prejudices of the vulgar'. These performances were 'as much the bread of the *Brahmans*' as the superstitions of the 'vulgar' masses supported the priesthood in other countries.[33]

NATHANIEL HALHED BELONGED to the English upper class. His father was a director of the Bank of England,[34] and as befitting a son of a privileged family he was educated at Harrow School and Oxford.

In Oxford he met another old Harrovian, five years his senior, by the name of William Jones (1746–94). Jones too would land up in Calcutta, in 1783, and connect once more with Halhed who returned to England two years later in 1785, as did Warren Hastings. Unlike Halhed, however, Jones came to India not as a lowly writer but to take up a judgeship in the Supreme Court in Calcutta—an appointment which, he hoped, would earn him the wealth that had eluded him as a barrister in England.[35] He also came to India with a formidable reputation and a knighthood. By thirty-seven (the age at which he would arrive in Calcutta), Jones was considered the foremost Orientalist in the Continent (and by implication, the world) and a phenomenal linguist.

An Orientalist is an 'expert in or student of oriental languages, history, culture, etc.',[36] that is, a scholar of Asia. The *Oxford English Dictionary* tells us that the earliest use of this word appeared in a 1723 text and so by Jones's time (he was born in 1746) to be described as an Orientalist might not have seemed so exotic. In the eighteenth century, the term 'Oriental' referred to all aspects of the non-Christian civilizations of Asia. It is no coincidence that Orientology as a scholarly discipline came into existence in these times—in the age of empire. The 'Oriental' was, after all, the site of some of Europe's richest colonies. The opening up of these lands through colonization unveiled Oriental cultures whose antiquity, richness, and strangeness (their 'otherness') as objects of intellectual curiosity were as irresistible as Oriental lands were as sources of economic plunder.[37]

Jones was known to have mastered twenty-eight languages. He himself would one day list and categorize his knowledge of these languages: (a) 'Eight languages studied critically:— English, Latin, French, Italian, Greek, Arabic, Persian, Sanskrit.' (b) 'Eight studied less perfectly, but all intelligible with a dictionary: Spanish, Portugese, German, Runick, Hebrew, Bengali, Hindi, Turkish.' (c) 'Twelve studied less perfectly, but all attainable: Tibetan, Pali, Phalavi, Deri, Russian, Syriac, Ethiopic, Coptic, Welsh, Swedish, Dutch, Chinese.'[38]

He loved the classics, and his greatest heroes from antiquity were Demosthenes and, especially, Cicero.[39] Indeed, Cicero became the model for the conduct for his own professional life. Marcus Tullins Cicero who lived in the Rome of Julius Caesar and Pompey was a statesman, lawyer, philosopher, political writer, and one of Rome's fabled orators—a supreme intellectual on one hand but equally a man of public affairs who, in the turmoil of the waning Roman republic, would be murdered by his political enemies.[40] Such was Jones's reverence for the Roman, that according to one of his biographers, he read through a twenty-volume set of Cicero's writings once each year.[41]

Jones was enchanted by the classical world and its thinkers, but he also had other favourites. Milton was the 'most perfect scholar' and the 'sublimest poet'.[42] He studied and admired Euclid, Locke, and the influential jurist Blackstone.[43] Though fond of riding and swimming, his idea of a holiday was to devote it to reading law, the classics, and logic.[44] He was passionate about the idea of liberty, a love that led him to support the cause of American independence and befriend

Benjamin Franklin whom he visited in Paris.[45] In London, he moved in the circle of the redoubtable Samuel Johnson, and came to know such luminaries as Edmund Burke and Sir Joshua Reynolds (the most influential artist of the English establishment and founder of the Royal Academy), who would, one day, paint Jones.[46] The portrait showed him as a not-unhandsome young man bearing a pensive look.

Jones's career as an Orientalist began as an undergraduate at University College, Oxford, which he entered in 1764, aged seventeen. Here, in addition to his pursuit of the classics, he studied Arabic and Persian. Very soon Jones acquired a reputation as an Orientalist and by the age of nineteen, two years into his time at Oxford, he was offered a job as a nobleman's personal Persian interpreter (which he turned down).[47] In 1768, however, the year in which he obtained his BA from Oxford,[48] he took up the task, at the behest of the king of Denmark, of translating into French (another of his languages) a Persian manuscript of a history of the Persian ruler and conqueror Nader Shah.[49] The translation was published in 1770, and an English edition followed in 1773. In between, Jones wrote *A Grammar of the Persian Language*. By the age of twenty-six William Jones' European reputation as an Orientalist was established. In 1772, the Royal Society elected him a fellow for his accomplishments as a linguist and Orientalist, and the year after he was admitted to Samuel Johnson's exclusive Literary Club of which he would become the president in 1780.[50]

Warren Hastings was living in London from 1764–9—this was his English 'interregnum' between his two lives in India.[51] As we have seen, Samuel Johnson knew Hastings, and it was possibly through Johnson that Hastings met Joshua Reynolds. Did Hastings and Jones meet during this time? Whether they did or not, given Hastings's keen interest in Indian culture and languages and, especially, his attraction to the Persian language, he would most certainly come to know Jones by reputation by the time he was governor-general of Bengal in 1774. We know that Johnson sent Hastings a copy of *A Grammar of the Persian Language* with the assurance that Hastings's 'favourite language' was not being neglected.[52]

Jones's life as an Oriental scholar was at first paid for by employment as the tutor to the son of an earl. Such employment within the bosom of English aristocracy brought him patronage, security, and, of course, 'connections'. Yet he would eventually be weary of his 'domestic' situation and the lack of the personal liberty he so cherished. Besides, he was impatient for financial success. Partly because of this but also, no doubt, with one ambitious eye to his beloved Cicero, he decided, in 1770, to read for the Bar. Like his hero he too would make the law and politics his future life.[53]

Thus, for several years Jones led parallel lives: Oriental scholarship and the study of law. In 1774 he was called to the Bar and, for a few years, he practised as a lawyer. But (perhaps inevitably, given his scholarly disposition), his reputation in law would ultimately rest not in legal practice but in legal theory and philosophy. Books on jurisprudence by Jones would appear along with books in Oriental studies. He became almost as much an authority on English and comparative law as he was on Eastern languages, history, and cultures.[54]

Cicero continued to beckon—this time wearing his politician's hat: Jones stood for parliament in 1780 but lost.[55]

This must have disappointed him sorely, for a very different kind of love had entered his soul. As far back as 1766, as a twenty-two year old, he had met Anna Maria Shipley, daughter of the dean of Winchester Cathedral (and later a bishop), and had fallen in love.[56] But marriage was out of the question till he was financially independent and 'established'. It would be a long courtship. Eventually, his need for wealth (with its accompanying social status), triggered by his love for Anna Maria, and his passion for Oriental studies would all be nicely fulfilled by the offer of a judgeship in the Supreme Court in Calcutta. In 1783, finally married to Anna Maria, Sir William Jones, FRS—Orientalist, linguist extraordinaire, historian, legal scholar, political pamphleteer (for he was that too), and even one with a place 'among the minor eighteenth century poets',[57] still only in his mid thirties—set sail to take up his appointment as a judge in Calcutta.

OF THE COUNTLESS Europeans—the 'nabobs', rulers, adventurers, travellers, missionaries—who came to India in the late eighteenth century to seek careers, make fortunes, proselytize, 'civilize', it was truly fortuitous that there was this one man who could help advance, as much as anyone in the world, the Orientalist project begun by such persons as Halhed and Wilkins under Hastings's patronage. And it must have seemed equally fortuitous to William Jones to arrive in a land whose history, culture, and language cohered so exquisitely with his interests. Here was the Orientalist par excellence in the heart of the Orient. Jones would tell an audience of fellow 'Anglo-Indians' (as Englishmen who lived in India used to be called in England in those times) not long after his arrival in Calcutta:

When I was at sea last August, on my voyage to this country, which I had long and ardently desired to visit, I found one evening, on inspecting the observations of the day, that *India* lay before us, and *Persia* on our left, whilst a breeze from *Arabia* blew nearly on our stern. A situation so pleasing in itself, and to me so new, could not fail to awaken a train of reflection in a mind, which had early been accustomed to contemplate with delight the eventful histories and agreeable fictions of this eastern world. It gave me inexpressible pleasure to find myself in the midst of so noble an amphitheatre... [58]

It was undoubtedly a happy chance, for no person was intellectually and temperamentally better prepared to continue this creative encounter between the West and India. Jones's preparedness lay not just in the fact that he was an established Orientalist—after all, his publications in Oriental studies were almost entirely related to Persian history, language, and culture rather than to India. There was also the fact that since he was first approached in 1778 by a 'person of influence' about the possibility of a judgeship in India, he had given much attention to India. Very soon he came to be recognized as an authority on Indian laws and current political affairs.[59]

Politically and ideologically, Jones was a Whig—an English liberal. He was suspicious of authority, disliked the aristocracy, was willing to fight against tyranny and for tolerance and individual liberty.[60] If Cicero was his ultimate ideal, men like Locke, Milton, and Voltaire were his latter-day heroes because of their views on liberty, and he took a keen, sympathetic interest in the American cause, as we have seen. And so, though not particularly well disposed towards the Indian people—he thought of them as 'soft and voluptuous, but artful and insecure'—Jones's ideology prompted him to look forward to his move to India if it could help relieve some of the 'misery' of the Indian people.[61]

As an Orientalist, however, it was not so much contemporary India that interested him but the 'other', more unknown, 'mysterious' India. The six-month-long sea voyage to the subcontinent gave him ample time, when not 'in the sweet society and conversation of Anna Maria',[62] to devote to planning his Orientalist studies in India. He planned to stay only six years there, so he had much to do. By the middle of the voyage he had prepared a 'to do' list of projects:

Objects of enquiry during my residence in Asia.

1. The Laws of the Hindus and Mohammedans.
2. The History of the *Ancient* World.
3. Proofs and Illustrations of Scripture.
4. Traditions concerning the Deluge, &c.
5. Modern Politics and Geography of Hindustan.
6. Best mode of governing Bengal.
7. Arithmetic and Geometry, and mixed Sciences of the Asiatics.
8. Medicine, Chemistry, Surgery, and Anatomy of the Indians.
9. Natural Productions of India.
10. Poetry, Rhetoric, and Morality of Asia.
11. Music of the Eastern Nations.
12. The Shi-King, or 300 Chinese Odes.
13. The best accounts of Tibet and Cashmir.

14. Trade, Manufactures, Agriculture, and Commerce of India.
15. Moghul Constitution, contained in the *Defteri Alernghiri*, and *Ayein Acbari*.
16. Mahratta Constitution.
    To print and publish the *Gospel* of St. Luke in Arabic.
    To publish Law Tracts in Persian or Arabic.
    To print and publish the *Psalms* of *David* in Persian verse.
    To compose, if God grant me life,
    a) Elements of the Laws of England.
       Model—The Essay on Bailment—Aristotle.
    b) The History of the *American* War.
       Model—Thucydides and Polybus.
    c) Britain Discovered, an heroic Poem on the Constitution of England. Machinery. Hindu Gods.
       Model—Homer.
    d) Speeches, Political, and Forensic.
       Model—Demosthenes.
    e) Dialogues, Philosophical, and Historical.
       Model—Plato.
    f). Letters.
       Model—Demosthenes and Plato.
       12 JULY 1783—*Crocodile Frigate*.[63]

A breathtakingly encyclopaedic programme that encompassed not just the history of Asia but its sciences and arts, as well as practical affairs of governance.

As a child of the eighteenth century, Jones would have been shaped by the European Enlightenment ethos: we know that he admired Voltaire. We imagine that he would have been moved by the writings of the eighteenth century French philosophers—for whom the 'philosophical spirit is...a spirit of observation and exactness, which relates everything to true principles', who 'takes for true what is true, for false what is false, for doubtful what is doubtful, and for probable what is probable'.[64] He would have been stirred by the project of the French encyclopaedists such as Denis Diderot and Jean le Rond d'Alembert and their *Encyclopédie*, a twenty-eight-volume enterprise, published between 1751 and 1772,[65] dedicated to 'the interrelation of all knowledge'.[66]

As we have seen, Oriental studies in India began before Jones's arrival. In fact, it had begun even before the time of Warren Hastings's governorship.[67] In 1767, John Zephaniah Holwell's elaborately titled *Interesting Historical Events relating to the Provinces of Bengal and the Empire of Indostan* was published. (In the history of the Raj, Holwell will probably be best remembered for his account of the 'Black Hole' incident of 1756).[68] And in 1768, Alexander Dow's *The History of Hindustan* appeared. In Hastings's own time as governor-general and before Jones, there were, of course, Halhed and Wilkins (and others). But these works and their authors stood in relative isolation to one another (despite Halhed's and Wilkins's friendship), and this was the state of Oriental studies in India—till the arrival of William Jones.

Sir William and Lady Anna Maria Jones reached Calcutta in September 1783.[69] Whatever his immediate duties as a Supreme Court judge may have been, he must have been impatient to begin implementing his Asian 'objects of enquiry'; he must have also realized that such a far-reaching programme would require many hands to the deck. By January

1784, he was circulating a letter to all interested compatriots in the city about establishing a society for the promotion and pursuit of Oriental studies. In response, thirty men (none Indian) met in a room in the Supreme Court premises on January 15, 1784, where Jones outlined his plan for a 'Society to be established for the purpose of inquiring into the History, and Antiquities, Arts, Sciences and Literature of Asia'[70]—a society then named the Asiatick Society. (Eventually, the 'k' would disappear.) Later the name would change to 'Royal Asiatic Society of Bengal' and, finally, after Indian independence, it became, as it is now, the Asiatic Society of Bengal. It was his hope, Jones said, that this society would slowly but surely 'advance to maturity', as the Royal Society had, beginning from 'only a meeting of a few literary friends at *Oxford*...'[71]

The scope of this society, Jones told his audience, would be '*Man* and *Nature*; whatever is performed by one, or produced by the other'[72]—but 'Man and Nature' as it pertained to Asia, India in particular.

> ...you will...correct the geography of *Asia* by new observations and discoveries; will trace the annals, and even traditions, of those nations, who from time to time have peopled or desolated it; and will bring to light their various forms of government, with their institutions, civil and religious; you will examine their improvements and methods in arithmetick and geometry; in trigonometry, mensuration, mechanicks, opticks, astronomy, and general physicks; their system of morality, grammar, rhetorick, and dialectick; their skill in chirugery [that is, surgery] and medicine and their advancement, whatever it may

be in anatomy and chymistry. To this you will add researches into their agriculture, manufactures, trade; and whilst you inquire with pleasure into their musick, architecture, painting and poetry, will not neglect their inferior arts…[73]

[Y]ou will bring to light! Jones's project was nothing less than the European '(re)discovery of Asia', much as the Europeans of the Middle Ages and the Renaissance '(re)discovered' ancient Greece and Rome.

Yet, oddly enough, for this supreme polyglot, knower of twenty-eight tongues, languages were not part of the project, though 'the diversity and difficulty of…[these] are a sad obstacle to the progress of useful knowledge'.[74] For, Jones tells his listeners, 'I have ever considered language as the mere instrument of real learning, and think them improperly confounded with learning itself: the attainment of them is, however, indispensably necessary.'[75]

Warren Hastings was invited to accept the presidentship,[76] which he declined, suggesting instead that the position should be given to Jones.[77] Thus, William Jones was established as the Asiatic(k) Society's first president, a position he retained till his death in 1794. Thus it was that Indology, the study of Indian culture, history, and philosophy as a special branch of Oriental studies was born.

WILLIAM JONES IS not just a dramatis persona in our story here but one of its first personae. If the Bengal Renaissance was a revolution that created a new consciousness, that invented a new kind of Indian mind,[78] Jones must be seen as one of the progenitors of this revolution, a begetter of this mind.

He envisioned, created, and presided over the Asiatic Society from its inception till his death in 1794. If in these ten years he had done nothing more than simply 'act presidential' he would have still left his firm imprint on the cultural history of British India. The Asiatic Society was no fly-by-night association that faded a few years after or with its founder's death—as was the fate of several such associations formed in eighteenth-century England.[79] Indeed, membership in the Society rose from 89 in 1788 to 123 in 1795, the year after Jones's passing, to over 200 in the early years of the nineteenth century. Membership would wax and wane over the course of the nineteenth century, ranging from a low of 119 in 1845 to a peak of 446 in 1871.[80] The Asiatic Society would celebrate the bicentenary of its founder's birth in 1946, and it continues to flourish to this day.[81]

More relevant to our story here is that the founding of that Society, the scholars it attracted in its next two or three decades, and the fruits of their industry created a collective space of beliefs and knowledge concerning Indian antiquity; and along with it, a new consciousness in certain minds, both Indians and British. This new consciousness (and for the Indians, as we will see, *self*-consciousness) was one of the primary features of the Bengal Renaissance.

So what was the essence of this new consciousness?

Witness, first, an almost throwaway remark by Jones's old Oxford friend Nathaniel Halhed in his 1776 Preface to *A Code of Gentoo Laws*. He was speaking of the Code:

...proof of this antiquity may be drawn from every page of the present Code of Laws, in its wonderful correspondence with many parts of the Institutes of Moses, one of the first of known legislators; from whom we cannot possibly find grounds to suppose the Hindoos received the smallest article of their religion or jurisprudence, though it is not impossible, that the doctrine of Hindoostan might have been early transplanted into Egypt and thus become familiar to Moses.[82]

Here, then, was a new set of beliefs created by an English Orientalist about India: the recognition—the perception—of the antiquity of Hindu religion and law; its 'wonderful correspondence' with Mosaic law as enunciated in the Old Testament; the possibility that Hindu law may have antedated Mosaic law; and even the suspicion that Moses may have been influenced by Hindu doctrines that had come to him via Egypt.

In 1788, the first volume of *Asiatick Researches*, the Society's journal, appeared.[83] The launching of this publication was possibly as momentous an event as the founding of the Asiatic Society itself: a learned society counts for little without a journal as its mouthpiece. *Asiatick Researches*—later renamed the *Journal of the Asiatic Society of Bengal*, and still later, the *Journal of the Asiatic Society*—quickly became a vital forum for communicating the findings of the Orientalists. The second, third, fourth, and fifth volumes were published in 1790, 1793, 1795, and 1797 respectively and created 'quite a sensation in the literary world', especially in Europe. Such was the demand for these works in the West that over the next few years new editions had to be published to meet demands, and a French translation in two volumes was brought out in Paris.[84]

In one of the articles that appeared in this inaugural volume (though originally written as a first draft in 1784), William Jones compared the 'Gods of Greece, Italy [ancient Rome] and India'. And he tells his readers that

> ...when features of resemblance, too strong to have been accidental, are observable in different systems of polytheism... we can scarcely help believing that some connexion has immemorially subsisted between the several nations who have adopted them.[85]

The resemblances that most struck him were between the deities of the ancient Greeks, Romans, and Hindus; but he also related them to the gods of Egypt, China, Persia, Syria, and others of that part of Asia. Surely, he wrote, if these similarities can be shown, then '...we may infer a general union or affinity between the most distinguished inhabitants of the primitive world at the time when they deviated, as they did...deviate, from the rational adoration of the only true God'.[86]

Jones found a coherence between Janus, the Roman god of wisdom, of 'prudence and circumspection' (and also the god of gates), and Ganesa, 'the God of Wisdom in Hindustan', bearing an elephant's head, 'the symbol of sagacious discernment'. In ancient Rome, the name of Janus would be invoked 'before any other God', to him would be offered in rites and rituals, corn, wine, and incense. In Hindu rituals, ceremonies, sacrificial rites, 'all world affairs of moment' would begin with an invocation to Ganesa.[87] So also 'the mountain-born Goddess' Parvati, Siva's consort, resembles Jupiter's wife, Juno, 'the Olympian': 'her majestic deportment, high spirit, and general attributes are the same; and we find her both on Mount Cailasa and at the banquets of deities.'[88] Like Nathaniel Halhed, Jones came to the conclusion 'that a connexion subsisted between the old idolatrous nations of Egypt, India, Greece, and Italy, long before they migrated to their several settlements, and consequently before the birth of Moses'.[89]

In this same first volume of *Asiatick Researches* of 1788, Jones published the text of his third annual (or 'anniversary') discourse, delivered three years before, on February 2, 1786.[90] Perhaps no other of Jones's vast corpus of works (other than his translation of *Sakuntala*, on which more later) has attracted more attention from Indian readers—and (as we will see) for good reason.

But let us take a short diversion first. The Indian scholar Kapil Raj has offered a reconstruction of 'A Day in the Life of a Calcutta Judge', the judge being William Jones. This account is based on Jones's own description of such a day in a letter, except that Kapil Raj, with an appropriate sense of drama, places the day on February 2, 1786, the day of Jones's third anniversary lecture. It gives us a fascinating picture of the judge–scholar's daily life in Calcutta.[91]

It is, as we might expect, a packed day. Rising at the crack of dawn, Jones walks from his house in the fancy Calcutta suburb of Garden Reach to Fort William, the ultimate symbol of British authority in Bengal (and, indeed, in India), from where a palinquin ride delivers him at the building of the Supreme Court. Here, he bathes, dresses, breakfasts. Then he spends an hour with his Sanskrit pandit Ramlochan, and another hour on Persian with his munshi Bahaman. Come nine o'clock, he robes and becomes the judge. His duties in the Court end at three. He returns home to Anna Maria; he dresses for dinner (English customs must be maintained even in India). On other days they would cross the Hooghly river for a carriage drive through the sylvan environs of the Botanical Gardens located in the suburb of Sibpur. But on this particular day, he takes the palanquin back to the Court where, at seven in the evening, in the Grand Jury Room, he delivers his lecture before an audience of thirty-five.

This lecture (or 'discourse') contained certain passages that must have gladdened the hearts of Hindu Indians had they cared to read the printed article that followed. Its most famous (and most cited) paragraph began with a paean to Sanskrit: 'The Sanskrit language, whatever be its antiquity, is of a wonderful structure; more perfect than the Greek, more copious than Latin, and more exquisitely refined than either...'[92]

Jones's judgement was more than aesthetic. He also believed that Sanskrit had too much in common with Greek and Latin for the similarities to be accidental: '...no philologer could examine them all three without believing them to have sprung from some common source, which, perhaps, no longer exists.'[93]

This idea is consistent with Jones's earlier assertion of the common origin of some religions. He would extend it further, finding connections between Sanskrit and modern European languages: '...there is a similar reason, though not quite so forcible, for supposing that both the Gothick and the Celtick... had the same origin with the Sanskrit...'[94] And, by extension, 'the old Persian might be added to the same family'.[95] (Here, Jones was drawing on the belief held by eighteenth century philologists that such modern European languages as German, English, Dutch, and the Scandinavian ones all came from a common 'Gothic' source; while such languages as Welsh, Irish, and Cornish derived from a common 'Celtic' root.) [96]

The different scripts too seemed linked to him:

> ...nor can I help believing [that]...the polished and elegant *Devanagari* [and]...the square Chaldaic lettering in which most Hebrew books are copied, were originally the same, or derived from the same prototype, both with the Indian and Arab characters: that the Phenician, from which the Greek and Roman alphabet were formed by various changes and inversions had a similar origin, there can be little doubt...[97]

Later in the lecture, Jones returned to an earlier motif: 'Of the Indian religion...it will be sufficient...to assume, what might be proved beyond controversy, that we now live among the adorers of those very deities, who were worshipped under different names in old Greece and Italy...'[98]

As for Indian philosophy, here too Jones found a link to the Greeks:

> The six philosophical schools whose principles are explained in the *Dersana Sastra*, comprise all the metaphysicks of the old Academy, the Stoa, the Lyceum; nor is it possible to read the *Vedanta*...without believing that Pythagoras and Plato derived their sublime theories from the same fountain with the sages of India.[99]

These passages would become music to the ears of those Indian intellectuals who read them in the years to follow. But their pleasure would have been somewhat dampened had they heard what Jones had said the year before, in his second anniversary discourse delivered in February 1785.[100] This was Jones the imperious, imperial Englishman, who had no doubts about the intellectual superiority of the European. 'Whoever travels in *Asia*, especially if he be conversant with the literatures of the countries through which he passes, must naturally remark the superiority of *European* talents.'[101]

> ...although we must be conscious of our superior advancement in all kinds of useful knowledge, yet, we ought not therefore to contemn [*sic*] the people of *Asia*, from whose researches into nature, works of art, and inventions of fancy, many valuable hints may be derived for our own improvement and advantage.[102]

A stereotype of the Asian mentality and disposition that will become familiar to the Indian reader was then offered: '...we may decide on the whole, that reason and taste are the grand prerogatives of *European* minds, which [*sic*] the *Asiaticks* have soared to loftier heights in the sphere of imagination.'[103]

And while a glimpse of '*Sanscrit* poetry from the specimens already exhibited' may make 'us' 'thirst' for more, when it came to the '*Sciences*...it must be admitted that the *Asiaticks*, if compared with our Western notions, are mere children'.[104] In mathematics, 'let us not expect any new *methods*, or the analysis of new *curves* from the geometrician of *Iran, Turkistan* or *India*[italics in original]'.[105]

Jones's words constitute a virtual archetype of British views of the Indian mind: on the one hand a frank admiration of its imaginative and speculative powers, on the other a profound scepticism about its capacity for rational thought. This motif would prevail into and through the nineteenth century despite (as we shall see shortly) the discovery by yet another Orientologist of the originality and antiquity of Indian mathematics.

Jones decided to quench his personal thirst for Sanskrit poetry with appropriate action. We find him writing to an English friend in September 1787 from 'a delightful cottage' in 'Chrishna-nagar' (Krishnagar) that he could 'now converse familiarly in Sanscrit' with his Brahmin pandit associates. 'Sanscrit has engaged my vacations lately.'[106] About this time he wrote to a person in England (whose private tutor he had once been) of a Sanskrit play called 'Sacontala' [*Sakuntala*] by 'Calidas [Kalidasa]...the Indian Shakespeare...'[107] Soon after, he was reading a Bengali revised version of the drama with the assistance of his pandit teacher Ramlochun.[108] In 1789, Jones's translation into English of the play was published as *Sacontalá or The Fatal Ring, an Indian drama by Cálidása, translation from the original Sanscrit and Prácrit.* 'Pracrit' or (in modern spelling) Prakrit refers, generically, to the vernacular or 'natural' dialect, an evolutionary product of Sanskrit.[109] In fact, the languages spoken by the characters in the play are both Sanskrit and Prakrit, the former used by the high castes, the upper class, and ascetics, the latter by the lower castes and classes and—women.

Jones's friend, admirer, and early biographer Lord Teignmouth described *Sakuntala* as 'exhibiting a most pleasing and authentic picture of old Hindu manners, and one of the greatest curiosities that the literature of Asia has yet brought to light'.[110] 'One of the greatest curiosities'! A telling phrase—as if *Sakuntala* was an anthropological specimen, to be displayed and staged.

Two years later Georg Forster translated this translation into German[111] and presented a copy of the translation to Wolfgang Goethe[112] who was inspired enough to write of it:

> Woulds't thou the young year's blossoms and fruits
> of its decline
> And all by which the soul is charmed, enraptured,
> feasted, fed.
> Woulds't thou the earth and heaven itself in one name
> combine?
> I name thee, O Sakuntala, and all at once is said.[113]

Goethe's response is perhaps the best known but he was by no means the only nineteenth century German to be moved by *Sakuntala*.[114] Since that time, the play has been translated into most of the major European languages and performed widely on the stage.[115]

IN NOVEMBER 1793, Anna Maria Jones left for England for good, for reasons of poor health. The plan was that Jones would follow as soon as his translation of the complete 'digest' of Hindu and Muslim laws was completed. This was not to be. He completed his translation of the Laws of Manu (or 'Menu' as he and other British Orientalists spelt it) in the summer, and that was his last major book. In fact, Jones himself was not in the best of health: a portrait painted of him while in India shows him as gaunt and emaciated, far from the plump-faced man Joshua Reynolds had painted in England.[116]

On February 20, 1794, Jones delivered his eleventh annual discourse—'On the Philosophy of the Asiaticks'—before the Asiatic Society.[117] Two months later, on April 27, Jones passed away at home. Anna Maria would hear the news only in the later half of the year.[118] Amongst those who grieved his passing were the Hindu and Muslim scholars who had taught him, discussed and debated with him, and become his friends.[119]

William Jones had come to India in 1783 intending to stay for six years, long enough to accumulate £30,000 and become financially independent.[120] He would never leave the country. He was buried in the Old Park Street Cemetery in Calcutta, besides hundreds of his fellow Britons who also never returned, by accident or design, to their homeland. The epitaph on the monument erected over his grave was composed by Jones himself, apparently only a short time before his death.[121] It spoke of his love for 'parents, kindred, friends, country', his dedication of his life to their service and the 'improvement of his mind' before resigning it 'calmly, giving glory to his creator'. Nothing was said of his scholarly accomplishments.

AN ERA ENDED, the first decade of Indological studies. Many scholars would continue the Orientalist programme that Warren Hastings had, almost unconsciously, initiated and men like Holwell, Dow, Halhed, Wilkins, and, above all, Jones had pioneered. Their work and influence would spill over into the nineteenth century and ensure the continuing liveliness of the

Asiatic Society.[122] Indeed, the Society became a model for the formation of the Royal Asiatic Society of Great Britain and Ireland, in London in 1823.

The man who delivered the discourse at the first meeting of this new society in London was Henry Thomas Colebrooke (1765–1837), a former president (1806–15) of the 'parent' society in Calcutta.[123] Colebrooke was best known as a Sanskritist: an interpreter of the Vedantic and other Hindu texts on religion and philosophy. But he was also a mathematical sophisticate whose contribution was seminal to the history of ancient Indian mathematics. Both these aspects of his contributions as an Orientalist and Indologist have bearings on our story of the Bengal Renaissance.

Henry Colebrooke was of a scholarly disposition. When he arrived in Madras (now Chennai) in 1783, as an eighteen year old 'writer' in the East India Company, he brought with him a passion for mathematics, a deep love for the civilizations of Greece and Rome, and a mastery of the classical languages. In his early years in India he evinced little interest in Oriental studies; he expressed his contempt of Persian and Arabic literatures and was likewise ill disposed towards Hindu culture.[124] At some point in his tenure in India, however, he turned to Sanskrit; in 1794, he wrote to his father, 'I am now fairly entered among oriental researches, and…Sanskrit inquiries.'[125] Indeed, so thorough was his volte-face that by the time of Jones's death he was regarded as the great man's intellectual heir.[126] This assumption of Jones's mantle was virtually formalized when, in 1798, he completed the labour Jones had begun before his death: the translation of a complete 'digest' of Hindu law.[127]

Colebrooke's turn from the Greek and Latin classics to Sanskrit studies may well have been a result of the belief, born from the work of men like Jones, in the close affinity between the Greek and Latin languages and Sanskrit. To delve into Sanskrit, thus, would seem to a classically rooted European a natural route to furthering the study of the humanities.[128] Indeed, Colebrooke, in his Royal Asiatic Society discourse of 1823, corroborated this idea in a manner of speaking, when he spoke of 'The ancient language of India, the polished Sanskrit, *not unallied* to Greek and various other languages of Europe...'[129]

Like Nathaniel Halhed, Colebrooke was born into a wealthy family, the son of a banker who served as chairman of the East India Company.[130] Unlike Halhed but like the printer-scholar Charles Wilkins, Colebrooke had no university education: he was educated at home and left for India when others of his class and privilege were making their dutiful way to Oxford or Cambridge. As in the case of Wilkins, missing university proved to be of no disadvantage to either his official or scholarly career. He became a judge, first in the districts, then in the court of appeal in Calcutta, and then rose to be a member, in 1807, of the governor-general's Supreme Council during the tenure of Lord Minto, the highest position a British civilian could attain in India.[131] He would also be appointed a professor of Sanskrit at the College of Fort William, founded in 1800 by the then governor-general Lord Wellesley.[132]

Like his predecessors in Indology, Colebrooke added vital elements to the subject. In 1795, he directed readers' attention to the idea that according to Hindu scriptures the Hindu widow does not *have* to 'burn herself with a husband's corpse';

'she has the alternative' of living in austerity, in chastity, in 'acts of piety and mortification'. He quoted passages from the scriptures in support of this.[133] Ghastly though this alternative life was, at least she could still live. This evidence would have bearings on the later movement to abolish sati.

In 1805, he announced in a long essay, after an exhaustive exposition on the Vedic texts, that Hinduism, as developed in the Vedas, was monotheistic.[134] In effect, Colebrooke said, the precepts of the Vedas had been 'antiquated' by later practices, such as those found in the Puranas, or even 'worse', the Tantras.[135] Perhaps this article and its contents were Colebrooke's most significant contribution to Oriental studies.

But he was by no means done. We recall that Sir William Jones had once said that in the sciences the Indians were 'mere children'[136]; that one should not expect from Asian mathematicians any new 'methods'. Returning permanently to England in 1815, after thirty-two years in India, Colebrooke would roundly confound Jones's belief. In an article written in 1817, he announced, first, his intention of determining the antiquity of Indian algebra and of comparing its age to that of the algebra developed by the Alexandrian mathematician Diophantus and the Arabs. His Indian textual sources were the (now) famous treatises *Vijaganita* and *Lilabati* of Bhaskara (1114–85) and two far older algebraic texts composed by the astronomer Brahmagupta (598–670). Comparing these texts, and using commentaries by other scholars of those times, Colebrooke concluded that Brahmagupta's chapters on algebra and arithmetic preceded the beginning of Arab science.[137]

But there was an Indian who preceded even Brahmagupta: in Bhaskara's works, Colebrooke found a passage citing the astronomer Aryabhata (476–550 CE) that mentioned not just algebra but a particular class of sophisticated algebraic problems. Colebrooke concluded that Aryabhata was the earliest known Hindu author of algebraic works.[138] As to a comparison of Aryabhata and Diophantus, Colebrooke believed that the Indian was more advanced—and offered a compendium of features of Indian algebra as evidence.[139] And while he believed that the 'Greeks of Alexandria' had priority over the Indians (and both over the Arabs), he also concluded that the Greeks' algebra was 'imperfect' and that of the Indians more 'distinguished'.[140]

ULTIMATELY, WHAT JONES, Colebrooke, and their fellow scholars of the Asiatic Society created was a space for beliefs and knowledge about Indian antiquity. At its core was an idea of a 'golden age' in the Indian past. Modern day scholars are, of course, sceptical about the very concept of a golden age.[141] Perhaps they are right. But these are eighteenth- and early nineteenth-century minds, shaped by the beliefs of the European Enlightenment, these are the perceptions, beliefs, values *they* held.

What did this 'golden age' consist of? It referred to a period ranging from the Vedas (that reached back to some time in the 2nd millennium BCE) to about the seventh century CE. It had a complex and 'polished' language: Sanskrit. It produced an elaborate system of rules, moral precepts, customs, manners, rites, and laws; a rich literature; and a highly developed mathematics and astronomy.

This idea of a golden age was one facet of this new set of beliefs and knowledge about Indian antiquity. The other aspect that so excited the British Orientalists was the connection between the language and religion of the ancient Hindus and those of the classical culture of Greece and Rome: that Sanskrit possibly shared with Greek and Latin (and other ancient tongues) a common, still older origin; that the Hindu and other ancient polytheistic religions may have yet a common origin. Knowledge of the Sanskrit language and the Hindu gods had lain with the pandits for centuries. But the *comparative* knowledge of Eastern and Western tongues and religions was an achievement of the Orientalists.

The new consciousness engendered by these 'Asiatick' studies was not just a matter of new knowledge, new discoveries, new understandings. When William Jones wrote that he found Sanskrit to be 'more perfect than the Greek, more copious than Latin, and more exquisitely refined than either', we see glimpses of a perception that bordered on *admiration*. When he compared Kalidasa with Shakespeare (off-hand though this comment may have been), we see a new kind of gaze that had not been present before. We see this same new awareness in Henry Colebrooke's conclusion that Indian algebra was 'distinguished' in a way that Hellenistic algebra was not. And, we find this in Colebrooke's admission that 'we' (the Occident) may have something to learn from 'them' (the Orient): 'To those countries of Asia, in which civilization may be justly considered to have had its origins, or to have attained its earliest growth, the rest of the civilized world owes a large debt of gratitude...'[142]

Perhaps we might take this passage from Colebrooke's 1823 discourse before the Royal Asiatic Society as a kind of collective epitaph on the Orientalists' labours. This new awareness of some Englishmen was to have a profound impact on the minds of nineteenth-century Bengal.

Notes

1. Spear [1932] 1998, p. 7; Bernstein 2000, p. 7.
2. Gleig 1841.
3. Bernstein 2000, p. 264.
4. Gleig 1841, pp. 490 ff.
5. Bernstein 2000, p. 220.
6. Ibid., p. 240.
7. Ibid., p. 257.
8. Ibid., pp. 258, 264.
9. Kopf 1969, p. 18.
10. Ibid., pp. 17–18, 21.
11. Bernstein 2000, p. 39.
12. Warren Hastings to Nathaniel Smith, October 4, 1784, pp. 184–91 in Marshall 1970, p. 189.
13. Bernstein 2000, p. 39.
14. Warren Hastings to Samuel Johnson, August 7, 1775, pp. 17–20 in Gleig 1841, p. 18.
15. Gleig 1841, p. 18.
16. Ibid., p. 18.
17. Ibid., pp. 18–19.
18. Quoted in Marshall 1970, p. 9.
19. Stephen and Lee 1917b.
20. Das 2001, p. 35.
21. Marshall 1970, p. 11.
22. Das 1991, pp. 32–3.

23. Sarkar 1990, p. 129.
24. Kopf 1969, p. 20; Das 1991, p. 32.
25. Bernstein 2000, p. 144.
26. Marshall 1970, p. 11.
27. Halhed 1776, p. 147.
28. Warren Hastings to Nathaniel Smith, October 4, 1784, pp. 184–91 in Marshall 1970, p. 189.
29. Ibid., p. 189.
30. Ibid., p. 189.
31. *Leviticus*, 16, 21, 22.
32. Halhed 1776, pp 147–9.
33. Wilkins 1785, p. 194.
34. Stephen and Lee 1917b.
35. Mukherjee 1968, p. 73.
36. *The Oxford English Dictionary* (2nd Edition, 1988).
37. Said [1978] 1994. See also, Sahlins 2000.
38. Jones and Teignmouth 1835, pp. 167–8.
39. Mukherjee 1968, p. 20.
40. Everitt 2003.
41. Mukherjee 1968, pp. 30–1.
42. Quoted in Mukherjee 1968, p. 29.
43. Ibid., p. 25.
44. Ibid., p. 28.
45. Ibid., p. 27.
46. Ibid., p. 31.
47. Ibid., p. 27.
48. Chaudhuri 1980, p. 8.
49. Mukherjee 1968, p. 39.
50. Chaudhuri 1980, p. 8.
51. Bernstein 2000, pp. 55–6.

52. S.N. Mukherjee 1968, p. 31.
53. Ibid., p. 30.
54. Ibid., p. 37.
55. Ibid., p. 34.
56. Ibid., p. 27.
57. Ibid., p. 43. For discussions of William Jones as a poet, see Ray [1948] 2002; and Dasgupta [1948] 2002.
58. Jones 1784, p. 2.
59. Mukherjee 1968, pp. 46–7.
60. Ibid., pp. 31, 61.
61. Ibid., p. 48.
62. Quoted in Mukherjee 1968, p. 74.
63. Jones and Teignmouth 1835, pp. 7–8.
64. 'Definition of a *Philosophe*,' attributed to Cesar Chesnan Dumarsais (1676–1756). See Kramnick 1995, pp. 21–2.
65. Pyenson and Pyenson 1999, pp. 410–15.
66. '*Encyclopédie*,' attributed to Denis Diderot (1713–84). See Kramnick 1995, p. 17.
67. Marshall 1970, pp. 5–7.
68. Bernstein 2000, pp. 43–5.
69. Mukherjee 1968, p. 76.
70. Jones 1784, p. 2.
71. Ibid., p. 3.
72. Ibid., p. 4.
73. Ibid., pp. 4–5.
74. Ibid., pp. 4–5.
75. Ibid., pp. 4–5.
76. Letter to Warren Hastings, January 22, 1784, from John Hyde, William Jones, and eleven other founding members of the Asiatic Society, in Chaudhuri 1980, p. 7.

77. Letter from Warren Hastings to William Jones and other founding members of the Asiatic Society, January 30, 1784, in S. Chaudhuri 1980, p. 11.
78. See 'Prologue'.
79. Robinson 1953; Schofield 1963.
80. Mitra 1885, p. 83.
81. Anon [1948] 2002.
82. Halhed 1776, p. 162.
83. Mitra 1885, p. 47.
84. Ibid., pp. 47–8.
85. Jones 1789, p. 196. References are to the reprinted version.
86. Jones 1789, p. 196.
87. Ibid., p. 217.
88. Ibid., p. 223.
89. Ibid., p. 242.
90. Jones 1786, pp. 72–83. References are to the reprinted article.
91. Raj 2007, pp. 85–101.
92. Jones 1786, p. 77.
93. Ibid.
94. Ibid.
95. Ibid.
96. See footnote *b* in Marshall 1970, p. 252.
97. Jones 1786, p. 78.
98. Ibid., p. 78.
99. Ibid., pp. 78–9.
100. Jones 1785.
101. Ibid., p. 39.
102. Ibid.
103. Ibid.

104. Ibid., pp. 41–2.
105. Ibid.
106. W. Jones to T. Caldicott, September 27, 1787, in Jones and Teignmouth 1835, pp. 83–4.
107. Quoted in Mukherjee 1968, pp. 114–15.
108. Mukherjee 1968, p. 115.
109. Sen 1979, pp. 1–4.
110. Jones and Teignmouth 1835, p. 128.
111. Figueira 1991, p. 12.
112. Ibid., p. 12.
113. This translation from Goethe's German original is taken from Dasgupta 1995a, pp. 125–6.
114. Figueira 1991, pp. 11–24.
115. Johnson 1991, p. x.
116. See reproduction in Mukherjee 1968, following p. 122.
117. Jones 1794.
118. Mukherjee 1968, pp. 138–9.
119. Ibid., p. 139.
120. Ibid., p. 73.
121. Jones and Teignmouth 1835, p. 197.
122. Anon [1885] 1986.
123. Colebrooke 1823.
124. Stephen and Lee 1917a, pp. 738–42.
125. Quoted in Stephen and Lee 1917a, p. 739.
126. Kopf 1969, p. 28.
127. Stephen and Lee 1917a, p. 740.
128. S. Chaudhuri, n.d.
129. Colebrooke 1823, p. 4. Emphasis added.
130. Stephen and Lee 1917a, p. 738.
131. Ibid., pp. 740–1.

132. Kopf 1969, pp. 45–7.
133. Colebrooke 1795, p. 117.
134. Colebrooke 1805.
135. Ibid.
136. Jones, 1785, p. 42.
137. Colebrooke 1817, p. 631.
138. Ibid., p. 632.
139. Ibid.
140. Ibid., p. 640.
141. Thapar 2002, p. 280.
142. Colebrooke 1837, p. 2.

Two

A City of Two Towns

PARK STREET CEMETERY, where Sir William Jones was brought to his final rest, was perhaps what the poet Rupert Brooke meant when he wrote of 'some corner of a foreign field/that is forever England'.

For here lay, amidst tangled weeds and creepers, shrubs, bushes, and overgrown unkempt grass, a stone and marble jungle of tombstones, crosses, pyramids, follies, and other quite fantastic funerary monuments, all those from the Christian West, most from the British Isles, who had made Bengal (what turned out to be) their ultimate home. In his 'City of Dreadful Night' (1891), Rudyard Kipling described walking amidst the tombs: it was as if he was walking 'down the streets of a town, so tall are they, and so closely do they stand'.

Jones was a particularly eminent denizen of Park Street Cemetery. But there were others who had claims to fame in one fashion or another. Here lay, for instance, Rose Aylmour, age all of twenty, on whose tomb was carved an elegiac poem by one who had once loved her, the poet and writer Walter Savage Landor. And there was the grave of Lt Col. Robert Kyd, founder of the Indian Botanical Gardens across the Hooghly river, where Jones and his Anna Marie might have gone for evening carriage rides. Elsewhere lay Henry Vivian Louis Derozio, aged twenty-two, teacher, poet, and firebrand who will loom large in this story. There were others who must have been luminaries in the Raj, men like Charles Short and John Royd, for not far from where they were laid to rest there are streets named after them.

Park Street, on which the cemetery is situated, was so named after a nearby deer park that belonged to Sir Elijah Impey, chief justice of the Supreme Court in Sir William Jones's time; it belongs to what is colloquially called 'sahib-para' (literally, 'the locality of the sahibs'). One end runs into Chowringhee, and here one is well and truly in the heart of sahib-para, for as the term suggests, in the time of the Raj this was where the sahibs and their memsahibs lived, where the Raj had its seats of power and authority. Near the Chowringhee end of Park Street, the Asiatic Society would enjoy its first premises; and, indeed, this is where the Society resides to this day.

Yet, the Bengali word 'para' does not quite do justice to the spread of the sahib's habitat in British Calcutta. In truth, the sahib-para was a town of its own: the 'European Town' or, more evocatively, the 'White Town', to be distinguished from the 'Black Town', the habitat of the Indians. Thus, Calcutta in the age of the Raj was a city of two towns, and the people of the Bengal Renaissance were denizens of both White and Black Towns.

The descriptors 'white' and 'black' apply to more than the colour of skins: the White Town, as Sir William Jones recorded not long after reaching Calcutta in 1783, was 'large, airy and commodious', its houses generally 'well built', some almost 'palaces'.[1] The Black Town, in contrast, was overcrowded, its houses dingy and badly built.[2] This description of the Black Town, of course, overlooks, the opulence of the houses that belonged to the wealthiest of the Calcutta Indians which *were* situated in the Black Town. These were not 'almost palaces' but were, indeed, extravagantly palatial in character.

THAT THE LOCUS of the Bengal Renaissance was Bengal was, of course, a historical happenstance. Had Warren Hastings chosen Madras—where he had been posted before his appointment as governor of Bengal in 1772—as his capital we might be speaking of the Madras Renaissance. Yet it was Calcutta that became the capital city of the Raj; that became, in Hastings's imagination, the 'first city of Asia';[3] that was dubbed the 'second city of the British Empire'. And it remained so till the capital shifted to New Delhi in 1911.

As it turned out, many of the people who 'made' the Bengal Renaissance spent much of their lives outside Calcutta, in the provincial towns and districts of Bengal, or even outside Bengal.[4] Thus, to associate Calcutta with the Bengal Renaissance might seem misleading. Yet, if Florence is seen as the 'cradle of the Italian Renaissance',[5] despite the spread of creative wealth over Venice, Milan, and the other towns and cities of northern Italy,[6] then Calcutta's claim as the 'cradle' of the Bengal Renaissance is not unjustified. We have already seen, for instance, that the Orientalists, creators of a comparative consciousness about India's cultural past (its language, religion, mathematics) were inhabitants of Calcutta. The Asiatic Society was situated in Calcutta. Calcutta was where most of 'the action was'.

On a map of modern Calcutta (or Kolkata), a trace of the areas of what used to be the White or European Town looks absurdly miniscule compared to what was *not* the White Town. Yet in these acreages had lain the power, wealth, and glory of Britain's Indian Empire. Here had lain the ambitions and the visions of the empire builders.

Dalhousie Square was the nucleus of the White Town, the historical seat of British officialdom. Named after Lord Dalhousie (governor-general, 1848–56) it was originally known to the British in Calcutta as Tank Square and to Indians as Lal Dighi, because of the great 'tank', an artificial body of water that dominated it. The uncle–nephew artists Thomas and William Daniell, assiduous recorders in paint and print of late-eighteenth-century British India, especially of Calcutta, showed us in one of their works how Tank Square looked in their time. One sees a massive, steep embankment slope from the street level to the water level. A wide band of steps, a ghat in effect, interrupts the embankment and a crowd of people—'natives'—are at the water's edge. In the background, distanced carefully from the street, is a row of elegant buildings dominated by what is clearly St Andrew's Church, built in 1818. A resident of Calcutta visiting London's Trafalgar Square for the first time may experience a start of recognition on being confronted with the church of St Martin-in-the-Field—and with good reason. For, St Andrew's Church on Tank Square in Calcutta was modelled after St Martin-in-the-Field.[7]

Lined against one side of Tank Square is the Writer's Building, once the offices for the writers of the East India Company and now the headquarters of the West Bengal government. Halhed, Wilkins, and Colebrooke would have all worked there once. On Tank Square had also stood the original Fort William before Lord Clive began, after 1757, building the new Fort William, farther south down the river.

The full 'glory' of the White Town may have nucleated in Tank Square but it lay properly to its south. A part of the thoroughfare called Chowringhee appears in an engraving by the Daniells, and captures something of the paradox that was this imperial city: a row of majestic, 'almost palatial' buildings set well back from the thoroughfare itself with the latter peopled by Indians, on foot, on camelback, and in bullock cart. No European can be seen. But then, the sahibs and their memsahibs would take the air along Chowringhee in their carriages. Still, the engraving does not evoke Chowringhee in its full glory: despite the impressive buildings there is a touch of desolation about the scene. Only a few years later, in 1803, an English lord freshly landed in Calcutta would describe Chowringhee as 'an entire village of palaces' which presented 'the finest view I ever beheld in my life'.[8]

To the west of Chowringhee lay the great stretch of green called the Maidan. Farther southwest, flanking the westward curve of the Hooghly river (as the Ganga is called in this part of its long journey), was Garden Reach, the elegant suburb where Sir William Jones had his town residence. It was his habit to walk, early morning, a few miles up the road, northeast to Fort William.[9] In Fort William we are in that part of the White Town that perhaps had the largest place, from within the White Town, in the story of the Bengal Renaissance.

Fort William—the 'new' Fort which succeeded the 'old' Fort (of 'Black Hole' notoriety) that had stood on Tank

Square—was begun by Lord Clive after the Battle of Plassey in 1757 and completed in 1773 under Hastings's watch.[10] The Supreme Court, where Jones performed his judicial duties, in whose Grand Jury Room the Asiatic Society was conceived, was located inside the Fort.[11] In 1800, a college was founded within its boundaries: the College of Fort William.

The College *of* Fort William. It was almost as if Fort William was a town in itself and the College its own educational institution. Indeed, the Fort represented the seat of the Raj, the ultimate white town within the White Town, and the college was its very own place of higher learning. The College of Fort William was the brainchild of Lord Wellesley (governor-general, 1798–1805). In establishing the college, he was entirely shaped by imperial and colonial concerns. The French Revolution had rocked Europe. Wellesley was an aristocrat through and through (his brother was the Duke of Wellington, who became one of England's nineteenth-century heroes after defeating Napoleon in the Battle of Waterloo in 1815), and like most British aristocrats Wellesley loathed the French and their revolutionary doctrines. He feared the effect these 'erroneous principles' would have on the minds of the Company's employees.[12] Besides, there was the new danger posed by a Napoleon, fresh from his conquest of Egypt, casting a covetous eye on India.[13]

The time was at hand to 'fix and establish sound and correct principles of religion and government' in the minds of the young men, mostly absurdly young and untutored, who came to India as servants of the Company.[14] (Not all were of the intellectual quality of a Halhed, Wilkins, or Colebrooke, nor were they of the seriousness of a Colebrooke who despised the wantonness of the lives led by these young 'nabob' wannabes.[15]) This would be the 'best security' for the 'stability of the British power in India'.[16]

Thus the College of Fort William. Wellesley dreamed up the college as an 'Oxford of the East', an institution that would compare in size and intellectual scope to Cambridge and Oxford. Its purpose was to fill what Wellesley saw as a massive lacuna: the absence of a system of formal education necessary to the proper administration of India; to prepare all those who came to India as employees of the East India Company, and as representatives of Britain, to become the proper kind of civil servants fit not only to run the Company but also serve British sovereign interests in India, as magistrates, ambassadors, and governors of provinces.[17] As an institution for the proper education of civil servants, it was to ensure a 'sufficient correspondence' between the qualifications of its graduates and the duties they would have to carry out; to establish a 'just conformity' between their roles as public servants and the 'dignity and importance of their public status'.[18] Towards this end, their education should be based on the education of persons who would be similarly occupied in Britain; to which must be added knowledge of the history, culture, and laws of India.[19] Accordingly, the college would teach Arabic, Persian, and Sanskrit; modern Indian languages; English, Islamic, and Hindu laws; Latin and Greek; modern European languages; economics, geography, and mathematics; the natural sciences; and European and Indian history.[20]

Wellesley's project was thus driven far more explicitly and comprehensively by British self-interest than was Hastings' project a generation earlier. His ambition was not the pursuit of Orientology. In fact, Wellesley's ideas laid the foundation for future schemes for the training and education of the civil service officers in India half a century later.[21] Yet, interestingly (as we shall see), Wellesley's plans had a benign side effect no less than Warren Hastings' motivation had *its* benign side effect.[22]

In fact, there was a natural continuity between Warren Hastings's and Lord Wellesley's projects. If the British Orientalists spearheaded by Sir William Jones and the Asiatic Society were the first 'generation' of 'White Townsmen' who helped shape the Bengal Renaissance, then the scholars who became the teaching faculty of the College of Fort William formed the second such 'generation' from the White Town to add to this story. The difference lay in that Indians began to participate more directly in this endeavour. The Black Town made its appearance in our story via the College of Fort William.

THE REST OF Calcutta was, of course, mostly where the Indians, predominantly Bengalis, lived: the 'Native' or Black Town. 'Mostly', because like any other substantial commercial city, Calcutta was inhabited by people of many races and ethnicities. Armenians, Jews, Chinese, Greeks, Portuguese, people of mixed British and Indian parentage and other Eurasians also resided in the city, forming a sort of 'Grey Zone' between the Black and White Towns.[23] Calcutta's population in 1837 was about 229,700. Of these, Bengali Hindus accounted for about 120,300 and Bengali Muslims for 45,100; other Hindus and Muslims were, respectively, 17,300 and 13,700, approximately. 'Lower Castes' counted for 19,000. The English population was about 3,100, Eurasians 4,700, and the Portuguese, 3,200. The Chinese were some 360, Armenians 640, and Jews 300.[24]

The size of the Jewish community was, thus, quite small in nineteenth century Calcutta—there were only some 1,900 of them by the end of that century[25]—but they left their imprint on the city. In particular, the Ezra family, prominent traders and real-estate investors, built impressive mansions in the sahib-para, and a synagogue said to be the 'largest and most splendid in the Orient'.[26] They donated a hospital to Calcutta Medical College (on which more later), became sheriffs of Calcutta, and gave their name to a busy, lively commercial street.

The Armenians, once a large community of traders and merchants, were also assiduous builders of mansions in and around the Park Street area. A street aptly named Armenian Street commemorated their presence in the city, and their church, located on that street and named the Church of the Holy Nazareth, built in 1724, is said to be the oldest Christian house of worship in Calcutta.[27]

A stroller on Free School Street, off Park Street, if he is paying attention, may suddenly come to a halt before a plaque on a wall announcing that in that house, the English novelist William Makepeace Thackeray was born in 1811. Thackeray did not live in Calcutta for long, departing for England at the age of six. But, as the story goes, he retained a nostalgic memory of this house, for he would draw it for his grandmother complete with a monkey looking out of a window.[28] This building happens to house the Armenian College, an educational institution founded as the Armenian

Philanthropic Academy in 1821.[29] Free School Street and its nearby streets and lanes were also where the Anglo-Indian community made their homes. This, then, was part of the Grey Zone. The teacher, poet, and firebrand Henry Louis Vivian Derozio who, as we will see, has a large place in this story, was born in another part of this same area.

IF THE WHITE Town's nucleus was Tank Square, that of the Black Town was a short distance to its north, in Barabazar (Great Bazaar),[30] a wholesale market to behold, experience, and savour for the density of its layout and the diversity of its wares. Here is a British observer from 1850 describing its riches:

> ...jewels of Golkanda and Bundelkhand, the shawls of Cashmere, the broad cloths of England, silks of Murshidabad and Benares, muslins of Dacca, Calicoes, ginghams, Chintzes and beads of Coromondel, firs and fruits of Caubul, silk fabrics and brocades of Persia, spices and myrrh from Ceylon, Spice Islands and Arabia, shells from the eastern coast and straits, drugs, dried fruits and sweetmeats from Arabia and Turkey, cows' tails from Tibet, and ivory from Ceylon.[31]

Barabazar had long been peopled by traders and merchants from all over India, and the Bengalis had little or no presence in it, save as customers. In Barabazar, this same English observer said, one could find 'a diversified group of Persians, Arabs, Jews, Marwarees, Armenians, Madrasees, Sikhs, Turks, Parsees, Chinese, Burmese and Bengalees'[32]—a melding of the Black Town with the Grey Zone. In particular, Barabazar belonged most to the Marwaris, originally from Rajasthan, who had dominated it ever since the nineteenth century.[33] However, save its historical role as the original locus of Calcutta's Black Town, Barabazar has no further place in our story. We must turn, rather, farther north. To Chitpur Road, for instance.

In a painting of Chitpur Road, circa 1867, by the artist William Simpson,[34] we see a narrow, crowded road, bustling with people. There are vendors transporting their wares loaded onto baskets hanging at the ends of a bamboo pole on a man's shoulder, on push carts and on bullock carts. One or two women can be seen but men dominate the scene. Muslims and Hindus, they stand in deep conversation, perhaps negotiating deals, some sitting or reclining on porches familiar in Calcutta houses by the name roak (or colloquially, rok).

Chitpur is more than an exemplar of a Black Town para. It is more than the city's oldest designated road.[35] It has its own arresting history. In its Jorasanko location stands the palatial house of the Tagore (or, in Bengali, Thakur) family; today Chitpur Road is called Rabindra Sarani after the greatest of the Tagores, and the 'Jorasanko Thakurbari' is a university called Rabindra Bharati University.

The Tagores of Jorasanko were undoubtedly the preeminent of Chitpur's denizens in the time of the Bengal Renaissance but there were others. The poet Michael Madhusudan Datta, one of its major dramatis personae, lived in a house on Chitpur Road during his most creative period.[36] Jorasanko was also the site of the residence of Kaliprassana Sinha (or Singha), wealthy social reformer,[37] associated with the widows' remarriage movement of the 1850s and whose satirical sketches entered into the literary history of the Renaissance—and, indeed, the history of Indian literature.[38]

DENIZENS OF CHITPUR belonged to the uppermost stratum of the bhadralok class, an unwitting creation of the Raj. The British in India needed brokers, agents, revenue collectors, contractors, lawyers, and managers to help them in their transactions with Indian producers. They needed Indians as middlemen, in other words. These middlemen in Bengal became the core of the Bengali bhadralok. In helping the British make money they too amassed fortunes; in turn, they turned financiers—moneylenders—to British traders and investors. And they bought large estates in the rural areas and property in Calcutta. The opulent houses in the Black Town were evidence of their affluence. Where before, homes in Calcutta had been their temporary residences (basha) while their permanent homes (bari) had lain in their ancestral villages and towns, these Black Town houses became their new baris.[39] The Deb family of Shobhabazar, the Tagores (or Thakurs) of Pathurighata, the Tagores of Jorasanko, the Mallicks of Barabazar, the Deys of Simla, the Setts of Barabazar, and others formed the uppermost echelons (abhijat) of the bhadralok class. These were names that became part of nineteenth century Calcutta lore: families fabled for the extravagant opulence of their residences which were more mansions and palaces than simply houses.

We get a sense of the scale of these Bengali 'palaces' of the Black Town from an account recorded of one of the Deb family homes. In the second half of the eighteenth century, Raja Nabakrishna Deb of Shobhabazar built what was called a rajbari (the house of a raja). His grandson, Radhakanta Deb, described, in his will, how areas of this house should be used by his family after his death. And so we read of the thakurdalans (the part devoted to the family deity), of the 'confection room, store-houses and godowns (warehouses)', of the navaratna (temple), the natmandir (the area given to devotional singing, recitation, performance, etc.), the chak (a square) 'surrounded by buildings to the north thereof', and the cow house—all to be 'set apart and dedicated' to the worship of the family deity and the conduct of other religious rites and festivals; that the 'old and new' dewan khanas (reception rooms or halls) should be used by his sons and their heirs for dancing, music, and 'other amusements', to receive 'respectable persons', and for public meetings; that the daptar khana (office rooms) and the family 'cook rooms' should be used as before; that the garden 'called Govindabagan' containing the tank (artificial lake or pond)—also incorporated within the 'family dwelling house'—should continue to be used by his sons and heirs; that the baithak khana (sitting room or parlour) in Govindabagan along with 'all out-houses and appurtenances' should be used in turn, each year, by each of his sons and their heirs 'according to their respective seniority'; that the khabar ghar (dining room), the hall 'called Dhalaghar', the naba ghar (bathroom), and the halls of the rangmahal (inner rooms used by the women for relaxation) should continue to be used by the women of the family as before.[40]

Many of the nineteenth century abhijat bhadralok were born into wealth, while others began in quite humble circumstances. Dwarakanath Tagore, Rabindranath's grandfather, for example, inherited substantial zamindari estates. He built upon this wealth, buying many more estates, but he also served as a revenue agent for the East India Company, launched a bank (with others), and formed a partnership with an Englishman which invested in a variety of enterprises including coal, tea, indigo, salt, sugar, railways, and even river navigation.[41] In contrast, another eminent abhijat bhadralok, Dwarakanath's contemporary, Matilal Sheel was born into a small cloth merchant family and began life selling empty bottles and corks; before the age of thirty he had become one of Bengal's 'merchant princes',[42] with business interests in indigo, flour, and zamindari. Like Dwarakanath, he too entered into partnership with a European.[43]

The bhadralok class was not, of course, restricted to the aristocracy, the abhijat. Below them in wealth and status, though not necessarily in education, were the middle class (maddhyabitta): officers in commercial houses, practitioners of 'native' medicine (kavirajs), teachers, lawyers, writers, government bureaucrats, small traders, and the like. Though not as rich as the aristocratic bhadralok they were not poor.[44] Rammohun Roy, Michael Madhusudan Datta, Bankimchandra Chattopadhyay, Prafulla Chandra Ray, and Jagadish Bose, among the principal protagonists of the Bengal Renaissance, came from the maddhyabitta.

The Black Town is not important to our story simply as the home of the bhadralok and of some of the key players in the renaissance. It was also home to some of the most important educational establishments in the city.

As will become clear, formal education along Western lines—'English education', to use the conventional expression—was a fundamental agent in the creative encounter between West and East, between Anglo-Europe and India. As far as Calcutta was concerned, the locus of this education lay very much more in the Black than the White Town. In the latter area, the Park Street–Loudon Street part of sahib-para best represented this realm, in that both St Xavier's and La Martiniere had both school and college sections here. St Xavier's, a Catholic educational institution founded by Belgium Jesuits in 1835, came to Park Street in 1860, on the site of a burnt-out theatre called Sans Souci. It was intended to serve sons of Calcutta's Anglo-Indian Catholic families—'Anglo-Indian' in the nineteenth-century sense, meaning, broadly, any person of European, but usually British, origin living in India—though non-Catholics or even non-Christians were not excluded. It was one of the several Christian educational institutions that came into existence in the city, but perhaps only La Martiniere amongst the others had comparable stature.

La Martiniere was founded in 1836 by a Frenchman, Major-General Claude Martin, who had served in the East India Company and with the Nawab of Awadh (formerly Oudh) and amassed a massive fortune which was willed to found three schools, in Calcutta, Lucknow, and Lyons, in France. Like St Xavier's, La Martiniere was very much a sahib-para institution: it occupied majestic grounds and a building to match, on Loudon Street, not far from St Xavier's. Unlike St Xavier's however, La Martiniere was an all-denominational Christian institution.

But La Martiniere has no significant place in this story whereas St Xavier's very definitely does; and not because Rabindranath Tagore spent a characteristically listless spell in the school section of the institution, but because of the presence there, from 1864 through to the end of the century, of Father Eugene Lafont. This Jesuit man of God was also a man of science, and in this latter capacity has a substantial presence in the making of the Bengal Renaissance.

As for the Black Town, we must travel from Park Street northward along Lower Circular Road—passing along the way the intersection with Dharamtollah Street, on which had stood David Drummond's 'Durramtollah Academy' where young Henry Derozio was taught—to the congestion of Sealdah; we then turn westward into Harrison Road till we arrive at the intersection with College Street. We have entered the portals of what might be called Calcutta's college-para.

In a literal sense, this term may mislead, for Calcutta's colleges are actually spread throughout the city and its environs. Still, as far as *this* story goes, and as far as the nineteenth century pertains, this is the college-para. For here, within the perimeter of a few square miles, are located the principal educational 'players' in the story of the Bengal Renaissance. Here is located Presidency College which began as Hindu College in 1817, at the very vanguard of Western-style liberal arts education in Bengal, indeed, in India: Derozio taught here; Michael Madhusudhan Datta was expelled from here; indeed, most of the most prominent bhadralok reformers of the mid-and late-nineteenth century studied here. (Presidency College was also for a time the home of what was first called the Civil Engineering College, founded in 1856, later to be renamed and relocated as the Bengal Engineering College, the country's second oldest institution of engineering education.) Here is located Sanskrit College, the scene of a delicate balance between traditional

Sanskritic and European learning, where Vidyasagar both studied and taught. Here we see Calcutta Medical College and the beginning of Western (allopathic) medical education in India. Here stands Scottish Church College, founded by the Scottish clergyman Alexander Duff as the General Assembly's Institution, almost as celebrated, in the nineteenth century, as Presidency College in the dispensation of the liberal arts. Here stands David Hare's school. And if we are willing to extend the scope of college-para ever so slightly, we come to Bethune College, founded as Bethune School for the education of girls in 1849, becoming, in 1878, India's first women's college. And here is the location of the University of Calcutta, formed in 1857, created just before its sister universities of Bombay and Madras, and thereby laying smug claim to being India's first university by a few months.

The college-para, with the University of Calcutta at the fore, represented formal higher education in four broad areas, as recognized by the four faculties of the university: arts (meaning the humanities or liberal arts), law, science and civil engineering, and medicine.[45]

WE HAVE ALREADY seen the denizens of the 'official' White Town as patrons—for example, Warren Hastings's support of the early Orientalists. Another form of his patronage was his establishment of the Calcutta Madrasa (or 'Mohammedan College') in 1781 in response to the request of Muslims for the 'instruction of young students in Mohammedan learning'[46]— specifically, Islamic law. The madrasa was initially situated in the Sealdah area but later, in 1827, it was moved to Wellesley Square (in the Grey Zone) where it still resides.

In creating the College of Fort William in 1800, Lord Wellesley also afforded a certain kind of patronage. For though his aim was to educate the young employees of the East India Company—the means he envisioned was to gather together both British and Indian scholars for this purpose.[47] In fact this 'bicultural' gathering made the College of Fort William the first academic institution of its kind in India.[48]

As we shall see, the establishment of Hindu College in 1817 and the Indian Association for the Cultivation of Science in 1876 also entailed significant patronage—except that in these situations the patrons were a collective of wealthy Bengalis. They were the abhijat bhadralok of the Black Town.

A CITY HAS history. A city is also a witness *to* history. Its streets and buildings, parks, cemeteries, and waterways, schools and colleges, law courts and museums are repositories of events, occasions, and people from the past.

Thus Calcutta: which above all is a repository of the history of the awakening called the Bengal Renaissance. Let me reiterate that it would be wrong to say this awakening only happened in Calcutta. Yet the city, its Black Town, White Town, and the Grey Zone in between, laid out the prime geography in which the people who made the renaissance mostly lived and worked, where the events of the awakening mostly took place.

Notes

1. Quoted in Mukherjee 1968, p. 77.
2. Finch 1850. Cited in Mukherjee 1970, p. 36.
3. See Kopf 1969, p. 19.
4. Sarkar 1990, pp. 95–6.
5. Plumb 1964, pp. 118 ff.
6. See Burke 1999, Berenson 1968.
7. Chaudhuri 1990, p. 166.
8. Quoted in Moorehouse 1974, p. 73.
9. See Chapter 1. Also, Raj 2007, pp. 95 ff.
10. Chaudhuri 1990, p. 159.
11. Nair 1990, p. 13.
12. Quoted in Kopf 1969, p. 47.
13. Ibid., p. 46.
14. Ibid., p. 47.
15. For a fascinating account of the lives these nabobs led, see Spear [1932] 1998.
16. Quoted in Kopf 1969, p. 47.
17. Das 1978, p. 20.
18. Quoted in Das 1978, p. 22.
19. Das 1978, p. 22.
20. Kopf 1969, p. 48.
21. Das 1978, p. 23.
22. See Chapter one.
23. Sinha 1978, pp. 12, 39.
24. Mukherjee 1970, p. 37.
25. Chowdhury and Chaliha 1990.
26. Ibid., p. 53.
27. Chaliha and Gupta 1990, p. 54.

28. Dasgupta 1990, p. 124.
29. Chaliha and Gupta 1990, p. 55.
30. Sinha 1978, p. 54; Sinha 1990.
31. C. Grant, *Anglo-Indian Sketches* (1850). Quoted in S. Bhattacharya 1990, p. 204.
32. Ibid.
33. Sinha 1990, p. 42.
34. The Old Court House scene is reproduced in Sinha 1990, p. 33; the scene of Chitpur Road is reproduced in Gupta and Chaliha 1990, p. 29.
35. Gupta and Chaliha 1990, p. 27.
36. Sen 1979, p. 195.
37. Nair 1990, p. 17.
38. Das 1991, p. 168.
39. Mukherjee 1970, pp. 44–5.
40. This description is abstracted from Radhakanta Deb's will as quoted in Sinha 1978, pp. 160–2.
41. Dutta and Robinson 1995, pp. 20–2.
42. Bhattacharya 1990, p. 209.
43. Mukherjee 1970, p. 48.
44. Ibid., p. 50.
45. Ray and Gupta 1957, pp. 44, 61–2.
46. Ibid., p. 4.
47. Kopf 1969, p. 46.
48. Das 1978, p. 70.

Three

Translators, Printers, Teachers, Preachers

IN OCTOBER 1792, a gathering of fourteen Baptists assembled in Kettering, a small town in Northamptonshire, and formed the Baptist Missionary Society.[1] One of these men was a thirty-one-year-old by the name of William Carey (1761–1834), ordained a Baptist minister the previous year. Thus began an eventful, mostly tumultuous, and certainly remarkable, journey for this man. It would transport him to India, to a town called Serampore a few miles north along the Hooghly from Calcutta—a journey that would entangle him inextricably in ways he could never have imagined with the British Orientalists in Calcutta and with Bengalis; a journey that would lodge him firmly in the annals of the Bengal Renaissance.

The aim of the Baptist Missionary Society was 'to evangelize the poor dark idolatrous heathens by sending missionaries into different parts of the world where the light of the glorious Gospel was not at present published'[2] and to obey Christ's command to his apostles: 'Go ye therefore and teach all nations, baptizing them in the name of the Father, and of the Son, and of the Holy Ghost.'[3]

Its founders came, almost without exception, from the English lower classes: artisans, shopkeepers, tradesmen—the 'mechanics' class as the term was. Theirs was the society of tinkers, tailors, and candlestick makers. William Carey was a shoemaker before he became an ordained minister. Of the two Baptists who also appear in this story, Joshua Marshman (1769–1837) was a weaver's apprentice, while William Ward (1769–1823) trained as a printer. Needless to say, they had barely any formal education and were regarded as anti-establishment by the Anglican Church. Baptists in England belonged to an assortment of Protestant denominations known collectively as Dissenters: those who dissented against, and distanced themselves from, the Anglican faith, the Church of England. They looked to the apostles and to the latter's injunction to 'Repent and be baptized every one of you in the name of Jesus Christ for the remission of sins, and ye shall receive the gift of the Holy Ghost.'[4] The very essence of the Baptist belief system lay in repentance, and in being saved from one's sins by baptism, by immersion in water, as St John the Baptist had baptized sinners in the Jordan river.

FOR THE BAPTIST Missionary Society, India with its masses of 'poor, dark, idolatrous heathens' offered limitless opportunities for conversion. None among its members was more zealous in this aim than William Carey. Even before the founding of the society—in which he had played a prominent part[5]—Carey had published a tract titled *An Enquiry into the Obligations of Christians to use Means for the Conversion of the Heathens* (1792). Thus it was that the society elected to dispatch Carey to India, along with another member, the doctor-turned-missionary

John Thomas, who had already spent some time in India. In June 1793, Carey, accompanied by his wife, sister-in-law, and three children, set sail with John Thomas, and arrived in Bengal in November of the same year.[6]

This was scarcely a propitious time for missionary work in India. The official policy of the East India Company was to oppose all evangelical efforts—not because of an enlightened attitude to 'other' religions or cultures but out of a purely pragmatic, self-interested desire to not create unrest amongst the 'natives', which might undermine British control and authority. And since the Baptists were despised by the Anglican establishment and discriminated against (as were all Dissenters) in England, their prospects in India were even bleaker.

This makes the story of William Carey (and his later fellow missionaries, Joshua Marshman and William Ward) all the more interesting. Indeed, it offers many lessons. For one thing, it tells us that in the eighteenth and nineteenth centuries formal education *really* had little to do with becoming and being learned; indeed, this seems to be a motif during this period of British rule. For another thing, it tells us that even in the straitjacketed confines of a severely class-ridden people such as the English were, it *was* possible for one to break free and be eventually recognized and accepted by the elite, dominating class. William Carey, a one-time shoemaker and minister of a dissenting, marginalized church (as the Baptists then were), would one day become a professor in the College of Fort William, an institution founded by a peer of the realm—a marquess, no less.

Carey's story also offers a glimpse of the fascinating process called 'acculteration': how a person belonging to one culture assimilates, blends, and enters into a wholly foreign culture. What happened to Carey the Englishman through his interaction with Indian culture was the mirror image of what happened to many of the Indian elite through their interaction with English culture.

Most intriguing of all about Carey's story, and most pertinent to *our* story, is how the Baptist zeal to evangelize the Indian 'heathen' resulted in deeds having nothing to do with evangelism. Rather, these deeds, of a secular nature, found their remarkable way into the new consciousness that defined the Bengal Renaissance. This again is another motif that runs through this early part of the story.

IF CONVERSION IS taken as the sole measure of a missionary's success then Carey was a signal failure up to the end of the eighteenth century. Christianity was by no means unknown in India at the time, not even in Bengal. The Jesuits—members of the Catholic Society of Jesus founded by Ignatius of Loyola (1491–1556)[7] —from Portugal arrived in India in the time of Akbar (who reigned from 1560 to 1605), and the Mughal emperor, known for his tolerance of religious diversity,[8] had permitted Portuguese missionaries to preach Christianity in parts of India, including Bengal.[9] Indeed, the oldest church in Bengal was established in 1599 in Bandel, a small town not far from Calcutta.[10]

By and large, however, despite this considerable history, Portuguese success in the region was limited, in part because conversion to Christianity was often enforced upon unfortunate victims under the point of the sword; and in part because the Portuguese missionaries failed to understand the temperament of the Bengali Hindu, and were ignorant of the complex structure and diversity within the Hindu belief system.[11] Christianity, thus, did not have much of a track record in Bengal when Carey arrived in 1793. Constrained by the meagre resources offered by the Baptist Missionary Society and with the official antipathy of the East India Company hovering over his head, Carey and his family suffered considerable hardship in their first few years in India.

For seven years, Carey failed to make a single conversion—and even the first convert proved to be a disappointment, for he simply disappeared.[12] Carey and his family were on their own, living from hand to mouth. Eventually, he was offered a job as manager of an indigo factory in a small town called Malda which gave the family some relief.[13] But by then the stress and strain of their first years in Bengal had taken a toll on Carey's wife, Dorothy, who became psychotic.[14]

Yet Carey's missionary zeal never faltered. He understood that evangelization of the 'poor, dark, idolatrous heathen' and spreading the word of the Gospel would have to happen in terms that the 'heathens' would comprehend: in their vernacular rather than the Persian of officialdom or the Sanskrit of the priesthood. Perhaps Carey's working-class background and the Dissentors' inherent identification with the 'lower' English classes played a role in this.

Thus, while on the ship bringing him to India, Carey began to learn the Bengali language, guided by John Thomas.[15] Later, ensconced in Bengal, he strove to master the language under the tutelage of a paid munshi,[16] and even made an effort to understand the dialect spoken in Malda.[17] Like William Jones and his fellow Orientalists of the Asiatic Society, William

Carey possessed a gift for learning tongues and by the end of the eighteenth century he had mastered Bengali, translated the Bible into the language, and was very near to publishing it. He also installed a small printing press in Malda.[18]

At this time two events occurred that changed the course of Carey's life in a way he could not have anticipated. One was the arrival, in 1799, of two English Baptist missionaries, Joshua Marshman and William Ward. The other was the founding by Lord Wellesley of the College of Fort William a year later.

Marshman and Ward were also working class, like most of north England's Baptists. Like Carey they had scant formal education. And as in his case, this proved to be of little disadvantage to them. They were both gifted in their different ways, possessing talents and abilities that were symbiotic with each other's and with Carey's own abilities. Marshman, for instance, was an autodidact from a very early age, became an avid reader, worked with a bookseller, and served as a schoolmaster in Bristol.[19] Education would be his forté as a missionary in India. He brought with him his wife Hannah, very much the helpmate in his educational activities, as it would turn out, and son John Clark who would later write an important memoir of Carey, Marshman, and Ward. As for William Ward, a carpenter's son and a printer's assistant, he had had editorial experience in his youth and these particular skills were put to great use in India.[20]

As it happened, neither Marshman nor Ward possessed the necessary documents that would allow them to land on British territory in India and practise as missionaries. To avoid expulsion by the British authorities they travelled up the river to the Danish settlement of Serampore, some sixteen miles north of Calcutta on the opposite side of the Hooghly, and sought the protection of the Danish governor, who obliged. The governor also suggested—with a canny eye to the possible benefit for the settlement, no doubt—that Serampore be made the headquarters of the Baptist mission in Bengal. The offer was accepted by Carey, Marshman, and Ward, and the Baptist Mission was established in Serampore in 1800.[21]

THE COLLEGE OF Fort William also opened in the same year. Its campus was located in a section of the Writers' Building in Tank Square.[22] And while the students of this 'Oxford of the East' were all British, some Indian *scholars* would gain from it, for the College of Fort William was the first academic institution in India that assembled under one roof British and Indian scholars with a common purpose.[23]

As an institution established to match Cambridge and Oxford, the College of Fort William would fall ridiculously short. For one, it lasted for only half a century and was formally dissolved by Lord Dalhousie, governor-general, in January 1854.[24] Its academic range was also limited. The departments in the college were of Arabic and Bengali, comparative legal studies, European classics, European history, 'Hindu' languages, Hindustani (Urdu), history and antiquity of Hindustan and the Deccan, Persian, religious instruction, Sanskrit, and science and mathematics.[25]

The professors in charge of these departments were, of course, all British. But along with them, and assisting them, were Bengali scholars. From the first days of Oriental studies in the Warren Hastings era, the Orientalists had always depended on pandits and munshis. The employment by the College of

Fort William of such scholars formalized this tradition. One of them was Tarinicharan Mitra (1772–1838), a Calcutta native learned in Urdu and Persian, hired in 1801 by the college as a pandit in the Hindustani Department.[26] Tarinicharan became a protégé of John Gilchrist, a surgeon-turned-linguist and professor of Hindustani, and gained the modest historical distinction of being among India's first 'Western'-trained linguist.[27] Then there was Mrtyunjay Vidyalankar (1762–1819), appointed chief pandit in the Bengali department in 1801,[28] a reputed Sanskrit scholar and also adept in Oriya and Bengali, who ran a tol, a traditional Sanskrit school, before joining the College. And, perhaps the best known of the 'Fort William pandits' was Ramram Basu (1757–1813). Which brings us back to William Carey.

Carey completed his translation of the Bible (or at least some part of it) into Bengali in 1796 but its publication was delayed for lack of resources till 1800.[29] While the Bengali Bible raised curiosity in rural Bengal its immediate effect was negligible.[30] However, over the next thirty years the indefatigable Serampore Mission Press printed translations of the Bible into a large number of Indian languages and dialects.[31] Carey's munshi in the Bengali translation project was none other than Ramram Basu—and in this we see the foreshadow of the future network connecting the Orientalists of the Asiatic Society, the Serampore missionaries, and the College of Fort William. Ramram had worked from 1787 as munshi to John Thomas, Carey's fellow missionary (incognito, for like Carey later on, Thomas was 'officially' an indigo manufacturer in Malda).[32] With Carey's arrival in 1793, Ramram became his munshi. The Bengali taught the Englishman Bengali and Sanskrit, and assisted him in translating the Bible; the Englishman in turn taught the Bengali English (and, no doubt, the Gospel).

There was a period, from 1796 to 1800, when Carey distanced himself from his munshi for a moral transgression (in the Englishman's eyes) by Ramram: the latter apparently seduced a young widow, got her pregnant, and had the child aborted.[33] However, time and self-interest are both miraculous healers of differences. When the Serampore Mission opened in 1800, Ramram joined the missionaries. When the College of Fort William opened the same year, Carey, as a scholar and translator of the Bengali Bible, was appointed professor in charge of the Bengali department; the one-time shoemaker and itinerant preacher in a marginalized church had risen high. Ramram Basu became a member of the Bengali department.

Ramram, Mrityunjoy, and Tarinicharan were perhaps the most distinguished of the munshis of the College. But in the course of its relatively brief life it would have over 160 'native' members in its teaching staff.[34] Each of the departments of Arabic, Persian, Hindustani, and Sanskrit-Bengali were allotted a 'chief munshi', a 'second munshi', and several 'subordinate munshis'.[35] Many came from northern India, from places such as Benares, Lucknow, Delhi, and Awadh; some were from Bengal and Bihar, Murshidabad, Muzzaffurpur, Patna, and Midnapore; many were already in residence in Calcutta before the College opened its doors. They were all profoundly learned and widely respected as authorities in their respective fields, many proficient in more than one language. One munshi, named Allah Dad, appointed to the Persian department, was reputed not only as an Arabic and Persian scholar but also knew English, Greek, and Latin.[36]

Like his predecessors in Orientology such as Halhed, Wilkins, and Jones, and his contemporary Colebrooke (who was professor of Sanskrit in the college), William Carey now had two vocations. His primary vocation remained that of missionary/preacher/evangelist; he was first, foremost, and always, the spreader of the Word amongst the 'heathens'. His new vocation as translator and Bengali scholar—a very secular occupation—was the means to that end. Learning the vernacular, translating into the vernacular, expounding in the vernacular were but tools. But Carey, like all fine craftsmen, cared for his tools. Thus it was that Carey honed Bengali grammar and Bengali prose. This was indeed his secondary vocation—but the one that contributed to the shaping of the Bengal Renaissance.

WHAT HAPPENED TO make this so? There is no simple answer to this. Indeed, it would be grossly unfair, and simplistic, to give all credit to William Carey alone. Rather, the answer lies in a fascinating social and intellectual milieu—of institutions and personalities; of the beliefs and desires of some of these personalities; and of certain cultural circumstances. Carey happened to hold a critical position in this milieu.

Let us begin with beliefs, perceptions and desires, since these are where most actions and events in history begin.

We have already seen that Carey and his Baptist brethren, by virtue of their faith, were driven, even goaded, by an evangelical zeal to spread the Word amongst the 'heathens' and convert them to Christianity. In Carey's case there was the additional personal belief that for the 'heathen native' to receive the Word, the Word itself must be heard in the native's own tongue. As for the perceptions held by Carey and his Serampore brethren about the Bengalis and their Hindu practices, these too would have further strengthened their collective goal to evangelize. 'Bengal needed Christ desperately'—this from a letter written by Carey in March 1795.[37] William Ward too was unsparing in his disgust at what he saw:

> ...to form a just conception of the state of darkness in which so many minds are involved as are comprized[sic] in the heathen population of India, a person has need to become an inhabitant of the country, that he may read and see the production of these minds, and witness the effects of the institutions they have formed, as displayed in the manners, customs and moral circumstances of the inhabitants.[38]

The 'Hindoo', he despaired, were 'still walking amidst the thick darkness of a long long night, uncheered by the twinkling of a single star'.[39]

The 'manners, customs and moral circumstances' the missionaries abhorred most were idolatry, sati, the caste system, ritual infanticide, and 'ghat killings'[40], that is, leaving the dead or dying by the banks of the Ganga river, ostensibly as offerings to the Mother Ganga but in effect causing death by exposure. Idolatry, of course, horrified Christians whose Fourth Commandment told them that 'thou shalt not make unto thee any graven image, or any likeness of any thing that is in heaven above, or that is in the earth beneath, or that is in the water underneath the earth'.[41] To Carey, Kali was 'the most devil-like figure that could be thought of'.⁴² As for sati, William Ward recorded 'a horrible day' when three women were burnt with their dead husbands near his home.⁴³

Out of these beliefs and perceptions emerged a practical goal: the translation of the Bible into the vernacular, the Scripture in Bengali prose. But translation was not enough. The Good Book must be sent out to the masses; a vernacular Bible must be printed. Carey had set up a small press in Malda, but it was not till the Serampore Mission Press was launched very soon after the Mission itself was established that the printing of the Bible and other Christian tracts on a proper scale became possible.

The Mission Press was a profoundly significant technological as well as institutional element of Carey's overall milieu. It was fortuitous that William Ward, one of the Serampore trio, had trained as a printer in his youth, just as two decades earlier it was fortuitous that Charles Wilkins, the nephew of a prominent printer and engraver, had had experience in a press.[44] For, under Ward's management, the Serampore Mission Press flourished and, within a decade, grew into one of the major type foundries in Asia.[45]

There was, in fact, another striking link between Wilkins's setting up of the first Bengali press in Calcutta in the 1770s and the establishment of the Serampore Press. Wilkins had been fortunate in securing the blacksmith Panchanan who had cut and crafted the first Bengali type with which Nathaniel Halhed's *Grammar of the Bengal Language* was printed in 1778. Panchanan now transferred his skill to Serampore in 1800 and soon became an indispensable asset of the Serampore Mission Press.[46] Three years later, on his retirement, Panchanan's apprentice and, as it happened, son-in-law Manohar Karmakar took over his responsibilities.[47]

The skill and expertise in type cutting, metal casting, founding, and engraving that Panchanan and Manohar brought to the Serampore Mission Press formed yet another hugely significant component—a technological one—of the milieu in which Carey was embedded. Indeed, it held a yet larger significance.

We already know that the Serampore Mission Press was not the first press to print a book in India, nor the first to print a book in an Indian language. Wilkins and his press, set up under the aegis of the East India Company and Warren Hastings, had obvious precedence on both these counts. In fact, the moveable type, invented (or, rather, reinvented several centuries after the Chinese and the Koreans had already done so) by Johannes Gutenberg in Mainz (Germany) in the 1450s, had been brought to Goa a hundred years after Gutenberg by the Portuguese.[48] A Portuguese book written by St Francis Xavier (the founder of Jesuit schools in India in the sixteenth century, and whose name was given to the college founded much later, St Xavier's[49]) was printed in 1554.[50] The first book in an Indian language, Tamil, was printed in Lisbon in 1551, but the print was set in Roman type,[51] and the first book in Indian type, also Tamil, was printed by the Portuguese in 1578.[52]

As it turned out, the sixteenth century Portuguese in southern India printed primarily in Roman script, perhaps due to the difficulty of casting types for Indian scripts. Printed books in Arabic and Persian were apparently in circulation in India, but except for an enterprising man associated with the East India Company in the seventeenth century—Bhimiji

Parek, who endeavoured without success to cast types for the Devanagiri script—there is not much evidence that the Mughals, or the English or other Europeans in India, or the Indians themselves, were interested in establishing printing presses for Indian languages.[53]

Notwithstanding this history and the fact that Panchanan himself had pioneered the Bengali type in 1778, 1800—the year the Serampore Mission Press was established—was significant in the history of printing and publishing in India.[54] Over the next several decades, Panchanan and, upon his retirement, son-in-law Manohar produced not only different fonts for each of the Bengali and Devanagiri scripts, but also for some fifteen different Asian languages. These included a type for Chinese with its thousands of 'characters' for the benefit of Joshua Marshman[55] who translated the Bible into Chinese—which, being the autodidact that he was, he had taught himself with some encouragement from a Spanish Catholic priest who had lived in Peking (now Beijing).[56] (There is a wonderful, if apocryphal, tale that because the Spanish priest spoke no English and Marshman knew no Spanish, the two discussed the Chinese language in their lingua franca, Latin![57])

The Serampore Press became, in fact, a printing factory. Its products went beyond the printing of the Bible or other Christian tracts in Indian tongues. The mission of the Serampore Mission Press, if not of the Serampore Mission itself, extended its reach into the secular world. And *this* brings us back to another component of William Carey's evolving socio-cultural milieu: the College of Fort William.

WILLIAM CAREY'S APPOINTMENT in the Bengali department of the newly founded College of Fort William created a teacher out of the preacher. And much as the preacher needed what he preached to be available as Bengali text so also the new teacher needed what he taught to be available in the vernacular. Alas, when Carey delivered his first lecture in May 1801, 'not a single prose work was found to exist' in the Bengali language.[58]

Carey's task at Fort William College was to teach Bengali to the youthful, newly recruited Company officials. To achieve this he could simply select available Bengali texts describing the language itself and its literature, and use them to fit his pedagogic needs. Unfortunately the situation was never quite that simple. The fact was that in the eighteenth century, especially in its second half, Bengali language and literature had fallen into a state of disrepair[59]—a situation that had dismayed Nathaniel Halhed while writing his *Grammar of the Bengal Language* (1778). The principles of the language eluded him and the uncertain orthography—conventions of spelling—exasperated him. And, contrary to the impression he had been given about the richness of the Bengali literary tradition, he himself could find no more than half a dozen Bengali works.

At the turn of the century Carey reported a similar experience; in Nabadip, a place in Bengal highly reputed as a centre of Bengali learning, he found at most forty distinct works representing the whole of Bengali language and literature.[60] Corroborating these findings, several surveys conducted by the British in the early years of the nineteenth century depicted Bengali as literarily 'sterile'.[61] The problem lay not so much in the paucity of Bengali literary works but in the poverty of Bengali *prose* literature. If this sounds surprising, even more surprising is that the first prose works in Bengali, composed in the 1740s, were by Portuguese and Indian Christian writers who produced Bengali tracts on Christianity.[62] The reason for this was that till the beginning of the nineteenth century, prose was not the favoured literary form in India.[63] It was poetry and the poetic form that ruled—and this was certainly the case in Bengal.

From the fifteenth century up to the death of the poet Bharatchandra Ray (1712–60), Bengali literary production occurred in essentially three forms:[64] epic poems (maha kabya), telling stories from the *Ramayana* and *Mahabharata*; long narrative poems known as mangal kabya, telling stories about local or cult deities—Bharatchandra was a poet in this tradition—and compositions associated with the amorous play (lila) of Krishna and Radha, of which the *Srikrishna Kirtan*, attributed to Chandidas, is believed to be the oldest.

Halhed's and Carey's perplexity may be understood when we take into account two overarching features of these literary forms. First, the poems were mostly meant to be sung or recited: the literary tradition was fundamentally an oral tradition. The epic poems and the lila poems were only put into writing in the eighteenth century.[65] And second, this literature was in the form of verse: kabya. The two features were obviously connected, for we are speaking of an age in which reading and writing were confined mostly to scholars—and *their* interest was essentially in Sanskrit. The people of that age were 'verse-minded'.[66] The main metrical form used was a fourteen-syllable metre called payar and this form apparently sufficed for literary purposes.[67]

The possibility of prose as a literary form in Bengali was, thus, not realized. Indeed, what little Bengali prose had survived into the eighteenth century was largely limited to letters and legal documents. Apart from the 'verse-mindedness' of the Bengali people, another reason why Bengali prose may have had virtually no presence in literature—even though Bengali had wide usage as a spoken language—was that the language carried little prestige in either the world of practical affairs or amongst scholars. The 'superior' languages of affairs were English, Persian, and Portuguese, while to the pandits it was Sanskrit that mattered. Bengali was considered 'barbaric'.[68]

This, then, was William Carey's dilemma. Bengali literature abounded in the poetic form; in fact, there was an embarrassment of riches. But such riches were not for the students of Fort William College who needed practical knowledge of the language so that they could communicate in the vernacular in their imperial mission. They needed textbooks that taught them grammar, dictionaries that gave them the meaning of words, and 'readers' that showed them the spoken tongue and how to write in the language.

Thus began a fruitful symbiotic relationship between the College and Serampore Mission Press: each needed the other. From the College emerged grammatical works, translations of both prose and verse, and original works of prose. The press, under William Ward's watchful eye and using the skills of Panchanan and, then, Manohar Karmakar, printed them. Carey, of course, was the link between the College and the Press. Thus also began a collaboration, under the aegis of the College, between Carey and Bengali scholars-turned-writers, most notably Ramram Basu and Mrtyunjay Vidyalankar.

Here then was another of the ironies, one more paradox of British rule in India: for it was the work of a few Britons—the Halheds, the Wilkinses, the Careys—that elevated Bengali into a language that mattered. Here was an avowedly imperial institution, the College of Fort William, serving as a catalyst for what was, in effect, the *birth* of serious Bengali prose. Here were the first signs of an awakening of Indian minds in response to British stimulus.

There were yet other paradoxes.

ANYONE WHO HAS read, or at least knows of, the novels, essays, and stories written by Bankimchandra Chattopadhyay or Rabindranath Tagore, or the writers who followed them, might well be startled to realize that at the beginning of the same century in which Bankimchandra and Rabindranath would brilliantly ply their trade, William Carey was struggling to find a model of Bengali prose to build upon. When Carey began his translation of the Bible into Bengali, he could not draw upon existing texts of Bengali prose for there were none, as we have seen. What little prose there were—letters and legal documents—had barely any literary merit.[69] It is true that a few Portuguese missionaries had translated Christian texts into Bengali in the sixteenth century. However, these had no subsequent influence, and certainly not on Carey.[70]

And so, Carey's model for translating the Bible into Bengali was—English prose! Not surprisingly, the result was that Carey's Bengali acquired an English flavour in respect to sentence structuring.[71] For instance, the typical English sentence structure is 'subject + verb + object/adverbial adjunct', as in 'God created heaven and earth', whereas the typical sentence structure in Bengali is 'subject + object + verb'. Carey's Bengali translation followed the English structure, which made it rather awkward.[72]

When Ramram Basu, Mrtyunjay Vidyalankar, and other pandits of the College began their own work of creating Bengali prose texts, they too faced a similar dilemma. They knew only the Bengali poetry of the earlier ('medieval') period; as for colloquial Bengali, the language of everyday speech, that was deemed unseemly for literary purposes. What Ramram and his fellow munshis did have by then were Carey's biblical translations. Here was an unexpected side effect of Carey's translation of the Bible: regardless of whether the Bengali Bible was actually read by laypersons, his prose provided a model for their own creation of Bengali prose![73] The result was a prose that was often stilted, clumsy, and neither strictly conforming to the English model nor to idiomatic Bengali.

As an example, here is a Bengali sentence from Ramram and how it would read in English.[74]

rajara	patra	likhilen	tahardigake
the kings	letter	wrote	to them

The idiomatic Bengali version would be:

rajara	tahardigake	patra	likhilen
the kings	to them	letter	wrote

As another example of the influence of English prose, Carey translated the English sentence 'I am out of a job' as 'ami bekar achi', which though grammatically correct is unidiomatic, for the usual Bengali form would be, simply 'ami bekar'. Certain usages of the verb in English are omitted in idiomatic Bengali.[75] Again, in Carey's translation of the Bible, the English phrase 'break bread' becomes 'ruti bhangilen' (ruti=bread, bhangilen=breaks). The Bengali phrase sounds quite incongruous, even comical, since the act itself, of breaking bread in the Western sense, is something Bengalis do not perform.[76] And when the Bible tells of Judas approaching Jesus in Gethsemane and saying 'Hail master' and then kissing him,[77] Carey translated 'Hail' to 'namaskar', a Bengali word with a connotation, both verbal and gestural, that does not cohere with the word 'Hail'. The appropriate Bengali word, in the context of a disciple (an inferior) greeting his master (a superior)—albeit a disciple about to betray the master—would have been 'pronam'.[78]

But let us not forget that in performing these early exercises in prose the men in the Bengali Department of Fort William College were treading terra incognita. They were pioneers of a new literary form. And pioneers in any realm have to experiment. So also for Carey, Ramram, and Mrtyunjay.[79] Their goal was to create texts that could teach practical Bengali to their students. For this, they did not just have to experiment with the style but also the subjects. Thus in 1801, Carey's *Kathopaketan* (Dialogues), a bilingual text in English and Bengali, was published (by the Serampore Mission Press, let us not forget). This consisted of thirty-one imaginary conversations—between men and women, Bengalis and Europeans, involving different styles of speech from the bhadralok to the labouring class.[80] The idea was to demonstrate how people of different kinds speak, and here

Carey anticipated the realism and colloquialism of later Bengali writers. Carey was, in fact, a genuine pioneer of Bengali fiction in the sense that he was the first to create fictional characters in a work of Bengali prose.[81]

A pioneer of Bengali fiction! Yet another paradox of the Indo-British creative encounter: an Englishman pioneering, not just Bengali prose but Bengali prose fiction. And even if we do not accept the idea, it still puts the spotlight on the fact that at the beginning of the nineteenth century there was no such thing as fiction in Bengali literature, at least in the accepted sense of the term 'fiction'.

As for Ramram Basu, he too pioneered a genre of prose writing. On Carey's request he wrote a historical work called *Pratapaditya Charitra* (1801), the life of Pratapaditya, a chieftain in the time of Akbar. Later scholars would debate whether *Pratapaditya* really was a historical work. One verdict is that while the overall framework of the narrative was historical and parts of the story were supported by facts, other parts were fictive, and some even of 'the fairy tale type'.[82] Thus, *Pratapaditya Charitra* was 'an embryonic form of the historical novel'.[83]

In writing a Bengali narrative in prose, Ramram faced a problem that sounds strange to our ears. This was the problem of punctuation. At the time, the Bengali language had no punctuation marks save for the sign called 'dari', a vertical stroke (|), and the double dari (||). These were used to signify the ends of the first and second lines of a couplet. Here was another sort of literary experiment: Ramram had to play around with the dari and/or other means to punctuate his narrative prose. At first he used '|' to mark the end of a paragraph; he then left spaces between sentences, another form of punctuation; he then increased the frequency of '|' to signify the end of one or two sentences; and finally settled for it to mark the end of each sentence: the dari became a sentence marker.

Like Ramram, Mrtyunjay Vidyalankar, under the official blessings of Fort William College, also wrote a historical work, called *Rajabali* (1808), on the Indian kings up to the advent of the British in India. And like *Pratapaditya*, *Rajabali* mixed fact and fiction.[84] Mrtyunjay's book had some claims to being chronological, and in that sense, has been viewed as an early instance of a kind of history of India written in the vernacular.[85] Perhaps more significantly, it is not so much as 'real' history or historical biography or historical fiction that these two works would be remembered; rather, it is as experiments in narrative prose.[86] More interestingly, *Pratapaditya Charitra* and *Rajabali* marked the stirring of a sense of the past: a historical consciousness[87]—not only a consciousness à la the Orientalists of a 'glorious' ancient past but rather a broader desire to question and know what really happened in history. Indeed, *Pratapaditya Charitra* was regarded so highly as a historical work that it was translated from the Bengali into Marathi in 1816.[88]

The translation of the *Ramayana* from Sanskrit into Bengali prose was another kind of translation, a project undertaken by Carey and Joshua Marshman, and produced in three volumes between 1806 and 1810.[89] This work was published by the Asiatic Society.[90] As a teacher and scholar Carey must have felt fulfilled and happy at this time. Earlier in 1806 he was elected a member of the Asiatic Society.[91] Already the author of a Bengali grammar published in 1801, he completed a grammar of the Sanskrit language in 1806, a work praised later by distinguished Orientalist Horace Hayward Wilson as 'a singular monument of industrious application'.[92] The year after, following Colebrooke's resignation as professor of Sanskrit, and on his nomination, Carey was appointed to fill his position.[93]

Carey was now bestriding ancient and vernacular tongues though the vernaculars drew him most. To add to the grammars of Bengali and Sanskrit, he went on to produce a grammar and a dictionary of Marathi (1895 and 1810 respectively), and grammars of the Punjabi (1812), Telugu (1814), and Kannada (1814) languages.

THE WORD DOMINATED his daily life—the Word, and the multiple tongues in which the Word must be told. Here is a day in the life of Carey as he described in a letter written in 1806 to a Baptist friend in England.

> I rose this day at a quarter before six, read a chapter in the Hebrew Bible, and spent time till seven in private address to God and then attended family prayer with the servants in Bengalee. While tea was pouring out, I read a little Persian with a Moonshi… read also before breakfast a portion of the Scriptures in Hindoosthanee. The moment breakfast was over sat down to the translation of the Ramayana from Sangskrit with a Pundit…continued this translation till ten o clock at which time I went to [the] College [of Fort William] till between one and two o clock—when I returned home I examined a proof sheet of the Bengalee translation of Jeremiah which took till dinner time… After dinner translated…

greatest part of the 8th chap. of Matthew into Sangskrit... after six sat down with a Thilngua [Telegu] Pundit...to learn that Language... I began to collect a few thoughts into the form of Sermon...and preached in English at half past seven... the Congregation was gone by nine o clock. I then sat down to write to you, after this I conclude the evening by reading a chapter in the Greek Testament...and commending myself to God. I have never more time in a day than this, though the exercise vary.[94]

Amidst all this linguistic work he never forgot his Baptist mission. Carey must have revelled in the life of the mind but he and his Serampore brethren were fundamentally men of action: they had come to Bengal to spread the Word of the Gospels and to evangelize. Though it must have pleased him to teach the students of the College of Fort William the Bengali language so they too could communicate with the 'natives' in the vernacular, that kind of teaching could never meet his primary goal of evangelizing the native heathen; after all, the students of the College were all British. Hence the efforts of the Serampore missionaries—Joshua Marshman and his wife, especially—to establish boarding and vernacular schools.[95] So successful were their efforts that by 1813 the Serampore Mission was overseeing some twenty schools.[96] Indeed, the Mission was amongst the first to establish in India what came to be called 'missionary schools'. One of these was for impoverished and indigent children of the streets of Calcutta; this school melded humanitarian and missionary aims and taught its pupils not only the three Rs but also Christian values and moral principles.[97] By the end of 1812, the school had over three hundred boys and over a hundred girls. Marshman would even receive funds from the East India Company for his efforts.

IN A STRANGE sort of way the Serampore missionaries epitomized the cross-cultural mentality which (as we shall see progressively) would be the fundamental characteristic of the people who made the Bengal Renaissance. Carey was an exemplar of the 'acculturated Englishman':[98] '...I may indeed say that their [the Hindus'] manners, customs, habits and sentiments are as obvious to me as if I myself was a native,' he would remark.[99] The nature of Carey's (and his Serampore brethrens') cross-cultural mentality, of course, differed from that of the Indians, for it was shaped by their Christianity and their evangelizing instinct. This was manifested most explicitly in their educational projects and, ultimately, their most lasting educational endeavour, the establishment of Serampore College in 1818.

If the College of Fort William was designed to train future officials of the East India Company, Serampore College was intended to train Indian—'indigenous'—missionaries. The institution, according to its prospectus, would be the 'handmaid of evangelization'.[100] However, just as Lord Wellesley (and Warren Hastings before him) believed that future Company officials must know the languages and culture of the people they would officiate amongst, so also the Serampore trio believed that effective missionaries in India must not only be Indians, must not only be learned in the doctrines they would impart, but also be knowledgeable about the doctrines they would have to combat and replace. They would have to be mindful of the first maxim of warfare: 'know your enemy'—the enemy being the Hindu scriptures and associated dogmas, in their case. Towards this end the students must be well versed in both Eastern and Western learning; and the college would admit both Christians and non-Christians so that the potential missionaries could obtain directly 'that knowledge of the character, the feelings, and prejudices of the heathen among whom they were designed to labour'.[101]

How DID THE educational projects of the Serampore Mission connect to the story of the Bengal Renaissance? The answer is that they formed a small but integrative element of a much profounder phenomenon—some would even say the *fundamental* source of the new awakening—the advent of English (or Western) education.[102] As it turned out William Carey had a say in the debate on English/Western education—a tempestuous debate, to say the least, which we shall encounter soon enough.[103] But what about the other institutional face of William Carey's activities? What of Fort William College?

In its heyday, the College of Fort William became something of a crucible for collaboration between sahibs and Indian scholars,[104] in translating texts, creating grammars, and compiling dictionaries across a range of both classical and modern Asian languages: Arabic, Bengali, Burmese, Chinese, Hindustani (Hindi and Urdu), Kannada, Marathi, Oriya, Punjabi, Persian, Sanskrit, and Telugu.[105] As we have seen, the college, the Asiatic Society, and the Serampore Mission Press formed a fruitful partnership in these endeavours. (Other presses were established outside the Mission—the

Urdu scholar John Gilchrist's Hindustanee Press of 1802, a Persian press established in 1805, and, through the influence of Henry Colebrooke, the Sanskrit Press in 1807[106]—and they too involved themselves in this grand enterprise.)

It was natural that the College of Fort William and the Asiatic Society—firmly and physically institutionalized by 1805 in its own proud premises on Park Street—would embrace one another since their common ground was Orientology. The fact that certain individuals straddled both institutions—Colebrooke, for instance, was president both of the Asiatic Society and of the council of Fort William College in 1807[107]—no doubt helped in forging a close connection between the two.

The Asiatic Society survived off subscriptions, and its association with an official organization founded by a governor-general would no doubt have been of benefit. In this sense, then, Fort William College—its sahibs and munshis—contributed to the '(re)discovery of the Indian past', which was the whole point of Indology. The college also afforded to its Indian scholars and intellectuals, including its very significant Bengali contingent, an environment conducive for work. What might have been the fortunes of Ramram Basu and Mrtyunjay Vidyalankar if the college had not existed we will, of course, never know. We cannot say: 'no Fort William College, no Ramram or Mrtyunjay.' But what we *do* know is that the college gave them an environment in which they could express their intellectual and creative abilities in the writing of Bengali prose.

Likewise, what might have been the chief Urdu pandit Tarinicharan Mitra's fate had the college not been, we cannot say. Apparently well versed in Sanskrit, Persian, Arabic, and Urdu, and knowing English, Tarinicharan used his linguistic fluency to great effect under the mentorship of the professor of Hindustani, John Gilchrist.[108] Together, they produced a book, under the aegis of the college, called *Oriental Fabulist* (1803), a multilingual work in which popular fables such as Aesop's were translated from English into a number of languages: 'Hindustani', Persian, Arabic, Bengali, Urdu, and so on. One of the oddities of the book was that all the Asian texts were in Romanized script, based on principles invented by Gilchrist.[109]

The ultimate legacy of the College of Fort William was its contribution to the growth of Indian prose literature—in several languages.[110] And it was Carey (along with Ramram Basu and Mrtyunjay Vidyalankar) who pioneered Bengali prose in the college.[111] More so than the printing press, more than the schools and colleges he set up, it was this that was his legacy.

Notes

1. Elliott 2007, p. 6.
2. Marshman 1859, vol. I., p. 52. Quoted in Elliott 2007, p. 18.
3. *Matthew*, 28, 19.
4. *The Acts of the Apostles*, 2, 38.
5. Elliott 2007, p. 21.
6. Das 1974, p. 9; Elliott 2007 p. 56.
7. Armstrong 1993, p. 284.
8. Ibid., p. 263. See also Sen 2005, pp. 16–18.

9. Das 1974, p. 3.
10. Ibid., p. 4.
11. Ibid., pp. 6–9.
12. Elliott 2007, p. 76.
13. Ibid., p. 56.
14. Kopf 1969, p. 72; Das 1974, p. 9.
15. Elliott 2007, p. 56.
16. Ibid., p. 57.
17. Ibid.
18. Ibid., p. 58.
19. Ibid., p. 59.
20. Ibid., p. 62.
21. Ibid., p. 57.
22. Kopf 1969, p. 62.
23. Das 1991, p. 70.
24. Kopf 1969, p. 235.
25. Ibid., p. 64.
26. Das 1978, p. 34.
27. Kopf 1969, p. 112.
28. Ibid., pp. 112–13.
29. Das 1974, p. 11.
30. Ibid., p. 12.
31. Das 1991, p. 28.
32. Kopf 1969, p. 121.
33. Ibid., p. 122.
34. Das 1978, pp. 137–40.
35. Ibid., 31.
36. Das 1978, pp. 32–3.
37. Kopf 1969, p. 91.
38. Quoted in Das 1978, p. 11.

39. Ibid.
40. Elliott 2007, pp. 65, 67, 69.
41. *Exodus*, 20, 4.
42. Quoted in Elliott 2007, p. 66.
43. Ibid., p. 70.
44. See Chapter one.
45. Das 1991, p. 32.
46. Kopf 1969, p. 115.
47. Ibid., p. 116.
48. Quaisar [1982] 1998, p. 58.
49. Nambodiry 1995, pp. xx–xxiii. See also Chapter two.
50. Das 1991, p. 32.
51. Ibid.
52. Quaisar [1982] 1998, p. 58.
53. Ibid., pp. 58–64.
54. Das 1991, p. 33.
55. Kopf 1969, p. 116.
56. Elliott 2007, p. 61.
57. Ibid., p. 61.
58. Marshman 1859, vol. I, p. 147. Quoted in Das 1966, p. 23.
59. De 1961, p. 32.
60. Kopf 1969, p. 58.
61. Ibid., p. 58.
62. Das 1991, p. 71.
63. Ibid., p. 70.
64. Ibid., pp. 2–3.
65. Ibid., pp. 2–3.
66. Sen 2005, p. 23.
67. Ibid.
68. Das 1991, pp. 19–20.

69. Ibid., pp. 14–16.
70. Ibid., p. 16.
71. Ibid., p. 50.
72. Ibid., pp. 50–1.
73. Das 1991, p. 50.
74. Ibid., p. 51.
75. Ibid., p. 53.
76. Ibid., p. 59.
77. *Matthew*, 26, 49.
78. Das 1991, p. 59.
79. Ibid., pp. 26–7.
80. Ibid., pp. 68–9.
81. Ibid., p. 74.
82. Ibid., p. 80.
83. Ibid., p. 81.
84. Ibid., pp. 107–8.
85. Sen 2005, p. 166.
86. Ibid., pp. 165–7; Das 1991, pp. 70–4, 420, 427.
87. Das 1966, p. 108.
88. De 1961, p. 148.
89. Das 1978, p. 173.
90. Anon [1885] 1986, p. 105.
91. Kopf 1969, p. 81.
92. Quoted in Kopf 1969, p. 91.
93. Kopf 1969, p. 91.
94. W. Carey to John Ryland, Calcutta, June 12, 1896. Quoted in Elliott 2007, p. 62.
95. Elliott 2007, pp. 81–2.
96. Ibid., p. 83.
97. Ibid., p. 82.

98. Kopf 1969, p. 51.
99. Quoted in Kopf 1969, p. 80.
100. Ibid., p. 84.
101. Marshman 1859, Vol. II, p. 463. Quoted in Elliott 2007, p. 85.
102. Majumdar 1960, p. 21.
103. See Chapter four.
104. Kopf 1969, p. 67.
105. Das 1978, pp. 165–74.
106. Kopf 1969, pp. 82, 115.
107. Ibid., p. 70.
108. Ibid., p. 110.
109. Kopf 1969, p. 111.
110. Das 1978, p. 120.
111. Das 1966.

Four

Warrior-Raja

SOME TIME IN 1817 a notice appeared in a periodical of the Baptist Missionary Society in England.

> Rama-Mohana-Raya, a very rich...Brahmun of Calcutta, is a respectable Sanskrit scholar, and so well-versed in Persian, that he is called Moulvee-Rama-Mohana-Raya: he also writes English with correctness and reads with ease English, Mathematical and metaphysical works...[1]

So it began. This man was evidently not just another 'rich Brahmun of Calcutta' but a person of some standing amongst the denizens of the city's White Town, since 'Europeans breakfast at his house at a separate table, in the English fashion'.[2] The author of this notice was obviously one of the Serampore missionaries, for he notes, 'Rama-Mohana-Raya' 'has paid us a visit at Serampore'. And being a zealous Baptist writing for other zealous Baptists 'back home', the writer's interest in the man lies in the fact that 'He has published in Bengalee, one or two philosophical works from the Sanskrit which he hopes may be useful in leading his countrymen to renounce idolatry...'[3]

Yet the man was obdurate, apparently; a maverick, an enigma: '[He] admires Jesus Christ, but knows not his need of the atonement. He has not renounced his caste and this enables him to visit the richest families of Hindoos. He is said to be very moral; but is pronounced to be a most wicked man by the strict Hindoos.'[4]

There, in this brief notice published in an obscure journal, we have something of this man: 'Rama-Mohana-Raya' (a name usually spelt in English as 'Rammohun Roy'[5]), a wealthy Brahmin, well-versed in Persian, Sanskrit, Bengali, and English, consummate in mathematics and metaphysics, at ease with 'Europeans', abhorring certain Hindu rituals, admirer of Christ but not enough to convert, revered by some of his compatriots as a moral being, reviled by others for wickedness.

Rammohun Roy (1772–1833) was a lifelong warrior.[6] A warrior-raja, we may call him, for he was given the princely title near the end of his life. He fought major battles—in some cases entire wars, as we shall see. Indeed, some warred with him in absentia, in a ghostly sort of way, long after he was dead.[7] Even Mahatma Gandhi could not make up his mind about him. He once dismissed Rammohun as a 'pigmy' compared to the saints of an earlier time: Chaitanya, Kabir, Nanak, and the like. Later, he would call Rammohun a 'giant'.

LIKE SO MUCH about Rammohun, there is even controversy about the year of his birth.[8] Some accounts claim that he was born in 1774; the inscription on his tombstone at Arno's Vale Cemetery near Bristol, England, where he was buried, says so as well.[9] Others have his birth year as 1772, and this seems to be more accepted as the correct year. In his posthumously published *Autobiographical Sketch* (1833) Rammohun was coy about his birth year—indeed, coy about any mention of specific dates that might allow a reader to infer his age.[10]

For people fascinated by historical coincidences, both the years associated with his birth were perhaps portents of things to come, for they were also the years we associate with Warren Hastings: 1772 is when he was appointed governor of Bengal; 1774 is the year of his elevation to the position of India's first governor-general. Hastings, as we have seen, insisted that the young 'writers' of the East India Company should learn the vernacular languages and know something of the history and culture of the people his countrymen were to dominate. This insistence led to the emergence of Indology and the birth of a historical consciousness about India's cultural past:[11] harbingers (as we shall see) of a reinvention of the Indian mind, an awakening especially in Bengal. And no one had a larger role in this reinvention than Rammohun.

At any rate, less controversial is his birthplace: Rammohun was born in his paternal home in a village called Radhanagar which in his time was within the district of Burdwan.[12] By his own account, Rammohun came of a paternal lineage of 'Brahmins of a high order'—he was a 'kulin Brahmin'—who at some time in the past had abandoned the 'religious duties of their race' to which they had been formerly devoted, in exchange for 'worldly pursuits and aggrandizement'.[13] Such pursuits had apparently worked well for his immediate ancestors. Both his paternal grandfather and father had served under Mughal rulers,[14] and Rammohun was born into a wealthy zamindar family.

By the time he was nine he had been married off thrice. One of the wives died very young, and of the other two one bore his children and died in 1824 while the third outlived him.[15] Polygamy was a common practice amongst kulin Brahmins, a practice called kulinism, and Rammohun's father—himself with three wives, the second being Rammohun's mother[16]—merely enforced the tradition upon the child.[17] By all accounts, Rammohun's relations with his wives were not especially cordial. He would live apart from them, or they from him, because 'they were Hindus and he was considered an outcast by them',[18] for founding a reformed, monotheistic Hindu sect. In later years, Rammohun would express his abhorrence of polygamy and wrote forcefully against kulinism: 'this horrible polygamy amongst Brahmins is directly contrary to the law given by ancient authors.'[19]

From what we know about his early teens, he seemed to have possessed a startling precocity in matters of the mind. Obedient to his father's wishes, he went to Patna (at that time an important centre of Muslim learning) and studied Persian and Arabic, 'these being indispensable to those who attach themselves to the courts of the Mahommedan [*sic*] princes'.[20] There, he read the poetry and philosophy of the Persian Sufis, the Koran, and Euclid and Aristotle in Arabic[21]—perhaps as the Muslim scholars of Baghdad had done a thousand years before. Obedient also to the priestly tradition followed by his mother's family, he studied Sanskrit and the 'theological works written in it'.[22]

That was as far as filial deference went. His first battle was with his father. While still in his early teens he conducted theological disputes with his father, opposing the latter's orthodoxy with heretical counter-arguments.[23] By the age of sixteen he was writing a text questioning the practice of idolatry by Hindus.[24] It is possible that these early questionings of Hindu practices may have been kindled by his Persian, Arabic, and Islamic education.[25] Predictably, this produced 'a certain coolness' between the precocious boy and his orthodox Hindu relatives, and so he left the family nest and, for the next four years, travelled 'chiefly within but…[also] beyond the bounds of Hindoostan'.[26] His wanderings took him as far as Tibet[27] where he took time to study Buddhism and, apparently, dispute 'daily with the worshippers of the living Lama'.[28]

Four years later Rammohun was summoned back home by his father. The prodigal son returned to the parental fold, to a new house the father had built in Langulpara, a village adjacent to Radhanagar. But the return was short-lived. Rammohun's thinking was by now too far removed from that of his family. He left the family home once more, this time more or less for good, though he did not estrange himself from his family. He was then in his early twenties.

His whereabouts for the next several years is once more a matter of disagreement amongst scholars. Sophia Dobson Collet's memoir places Rammohun in Benares (now Varanasi) for the next several years.[29] The editors of her memoir believe this was almost certainly not the case. According to their research Rammohun left his two wives with his mother and moved to Calcutta in 1796. That same year he received a part of his share of his father's estate: a property in Jorasanko.[30]

In Calcutta, Rammohun began a money-lending business where his customers were officials of the East India Company, often hard-pressed for funds to sustain their lifestyles.[31] Here is a fine paradox, one of many characterizing the man: he chose a living (at least initially) in an arguably despised occupation even as he embarked on a life of the mind. Money-lending was a lucrative occupation. And (as we have seen[32]), it was one of the occupations that both produced the Bengali bhadralok and which the bhadralok of Calcutta resorted to for enhancing their wealth.

Within a few years of coming to Calcutta Rammohun was the owner of several landed estates or taluks, which would yield him a handsome regular income and make him financially independent.[33] One of the taluks was located in Serampore.[34] So, in a sense, he became a neighbour of the Serampore missionaries well before they communicated on theological topics of common interest. Over the years, he would sell the Jorasanko property and purchase three houses, one in the White Town (on Chowringhee), the others in the Black Town: one on what came to be called Amherst Street (now Rammohun Sarani), the other, most closely associated with him, on Upper Circular Road (now Acharya Prafulla Chandra Ray Road) in the Maniktala area,[35] where Rammohun would entertain both Indian and British friends.

But entertaining Indian and British luminaries was for the future. Some time in 1799 Rammohun left for Benares and other places in 'Upper India'.[36] What exactly he did for the next few years and his precise whereabouts are hazy.[37] Indeed, even the year of the birth of his first child, his eldest son Radhaprasad, has proved to be controversial. The general opinion seems to be that Radhaprasad was born in 1800, a few months after Rammohun's departure from Calcutta.[38] The only thing we know for certain about those years in

Rammohun's life is that he served as a 'writer' in one of the Company establishments in Benares for some months in early 1803.[39] It is possible but not definite that he resided in Benares for some three or four years, in which case we might assume that in Benares, a well-known centre of Sanskritic and Vedantic learning, he furthered his theological studies in Vedantic literature.

By the middle of 1803, Rammohun was back in Bengal. Official records show him as employed as munshi to Thomas Woodforde, registrar of the appellate court in Murshidabad.[40] By one of those curious situations that informed Rammohun's life, the year before he had lent Woodforde a substantial sum of money![41] Why would Rammohun, already a wealthy man, a member of the bhadralok, want to be employed as a munshi to an Englishman? By his own account, even in his twenties, his first acquaintance with Europeans had softened his 'prejudice' against them and, indeed, he had become 'inclined in their favour'.[42] Perhaps this employment was motivated by Rammohun's desire to know the English at close quarters and master their language. As he would admit much later, he had persuaded himself that 'their rule, though a foreign yoke, would lead more speedily to the amelioration of the native inhabitants'.[43] This was maybe why he desired to cultivate their friendship 'even in their public capacity'.[44] Let us not forget that Rammohun was inherently an intellectual maverick. This may have been another manifestation of his contrary nature.

Around this time, in May or June 1803, Rammohun's father passed away.[45] Theirs had been a strained relationship but, apparently, the son was present at the father's deathbed (though even *this* has been questioned by at least one commentator[46]).

The death was to be a watershed in Rammohun's life. In the years leading up to 1803–4, the young man—alongside the restless wandering, making money, and establishing himself as a bhadralok of consequence—had been preparing himself for a life of the mind. He had studied, met theologians of other religions, and his views against Brahmanical practices had intensified. By his own account, he had already engaged in 'continued controversy with the Brahmins on the subject of their idolatry and superstition, and my interference with their custom of burning widows and other pernicious practices, revived and increased their animosity against me'.[47]

His father and the family had been aware, of course, of this 'continued controversy' and the father's death released the son from any residual hesitancy he may have had. It was the signal for him to explicitly 'come out': 'After my father's death I opposed the advocates of idolatry with still greater boldness. Availing myself of the art of printing now established in India, I published various works and pamphlets against their errors in the native and foreign languages.'[48]

Within a year of his father's death Rammohun had published his first work, in two 'foreign languages': a treatise in Persian with an Arabic introduction called *Tuhfat-ul-Muwahhdin*. The English translation of the title is *A Gift to the Monotheists*, though the first actual English translation of the treatise, published in 1884, has it as *A Gift to Deists*.[49] In it, Rammohun rejected blind faith in the authority of religious leaders and advocated reason as a shield against religious dogmatism. He also argued against idolatry, and espoused monotheism, the doctrine that holds that there is one God.[50] In this he was influenced, by his own account, by a self-taught mix of Christian, Sunni Muslim, and certain Hindu belief systems.[51]

THE *TUHFAT* WAS a kind of trial run, a part of Rammohun's preparation for not only a life of the mind but a life as reformist, theologian, and writer—and above all as a warrior planning to wage fierce battles against Hindu orthodoxy. Over a decade would elapse before he published his next work. If his father's death had released him from caution in publicly expressing his opinions on Hinduism, it was apparently not till 1815 that his preparation was complete.

In 1815 the floodgates were finally raised: out poured, one after another, the 'various works and pamphlets' he mentioned in his *Autobiographical Sketch*. Between 1815 and 1820, the first significant phase of his writings, produced fourteen Bengali and ten English works on one or another aspect of the Hindu scriptures, and what the scriptures said (or did not say) about the practices of idolatry, polytheism—the doctrine of many gods—and sati.[52]

So what transpired in the long interregnum between the appearance of *Tuhfat* in 1803–4 and the Bengali work *Vedanta Grantha* in 1815? For one thing, Rammohun became an intermittent employee of the East India Company. We have already seen that by the time of publishing *Tuhfat* he was involved quite directly with British officialdom: as a 'writer' in Benares and then as a munshi to Thomas Woodruffe in Murshidabad. In 1805 began his association with a Company official named John Digby who employed Rammohun as his private munshi. Rammohun accompanied the Englishman in the latter's various capacities as a Company civil servant throughout Bengal and Bihar.[53] At various times Digby appointed Rammohun 'sheristadar' (a registrar or record keeper, usually the head 'native' officer of a court of law or collector's office)[54] and, temporarily, as 'dewan' (the highest 'native' officer in the revenue department under a district collector and, indeed, the highest position an Indian could hold in the East India Company's administrative structure).[55] Rammohun also accompanied John Digby to the Bhutan–Cooch Behar border and served as an envoy of the British government to Bhutan to help settle some border disputes between the two independent kingdoms of Bhutan and Cooch Behar.[56]

This was clearly a period in which Rammohun's 'European' connections were consolidated. Perhaps, he became a munshi once more in order to strengthen his European connections in Calcutta. In any case, John Digby seemed one of those unusual Company servants whom we have been sporadically encountering in this story: for he, sahib employer to Rammohun's munshi employee, soon became the latter's friend, admirer, and supporter. It was also a period in which, by way of his various employments, Rammohun consolidated his personal wealth.

This period also culminated in Rammohun finally moving permanently to Calcutta and setting up residence there,[57] most prominently in his 'garden house' in the Maniktala area of the Black Town, the house furnished in 'English style', where he would entertain both Indian and British friends, where—as the Serampore missionary reported to the Baptist Missionary Society—he would indulge in 'European breakfast...in the English fashion'.[58] He was now some forty-two or forty-three years of age, 'in the prime of manhood', in Sophia Dobson Collet's admiring description: 'a majestic looking man, nearly six feet in height, and remarkable for his dignity of bearing and grace of manner, as well as for his handsome countenance and sparkling eyes.'[59]

WITH DIGBY'S HELP, Rammohun also began serious study of the English language and of European thought, literature, and culture. This emerges as another vital strand, indeed a profoundly vital strand, in Rammohun's preparation as scholar, reformer, polemicist, and warrior of the mind.

According to different accounts, Rammohun began learning the English language some time between 1794 and 1796. Sophia Dobson Collet placed the date as 1795. The Scottish educationist and missionary Alexander Duff dated the start of Rammohun's English education to 1794.[60] And, according to an account recorded in 1817 by John Digby himself,

> [Rammohun] commenced the study of the English language [in 1796]...which not pursuing with application, he, five years afterwards [1801], when I became acquainted with him, could merely speak it well enough to be understood upon the most common topics of discourse but could not write it with any degree of correctness.[61]

It was only in Digby's employment that (in the Englishman's words),

> pursuing all my public correspondence with diligence and attention, as well as by corresponding and conversing

with European gentlemen, he acquired so correct a knowledge of the English language, as to be enabled to write and speak it with considerable accuracy.[62]

By 1809 Rammohun was fluent in the language, and possessed sufficient self-confidence, to write a letter to none other than Lord Minto (governor-general, 1805–13), lodging a 'Humble Petition' against the 'severe degradation and injury' he had 'unmeritedly experienced' from the district collector of Bhagalpur (in Bihar), one Sir Frederick Hamilton.[63]

The incident occurred when Rammohun, travelling in his palanquin on a visit to Bhagalpur, passed a white man standing by a brick kiln. Not noticing him, Rammohun did not pause to acknowledge him. Unfortunately the man happened to be the collector of the district. As the palanquin passed him, Hamilton 'repeatedly called out' to Rammohun to get out and 'that with an epithet of abuse too gross to admit of being stated here without a departure from the respect due to your Lordship'.[64] One of Rammohun's accompanying servants went up to Hamilton to explain that his master had not observed him.

> ...nevertheless that Gentleman still continued to use the same offensive language, and when the palenqueen had proceeded to the distance about 300 yards from the spot where Sir Frederick Hamilton had stood, that Gentleman overtook it on Horseback.[65]

It was only then that Rammohun realized that the 'Gentleman who was riding alongside...[the] palenqueen' was the collector; and that he, 'your Petitioner', was expected by the man to extend 'a form of external respect'. There ensued an exchange between the two and, despite Rammohun's apology at not having paid the 'act of public respect' the collector had expected, he failed to pacify his temper. Rammohun concluded his letter thus:

> Your petitioner throwing himself, his character and the honour of his family on the impartial Justice, liberality and feeling of your Lordship, entertaining the most confident expectation that your Lordship will be pleased to afford to your Petitioner every just degree of satisfaction for the injury which his Character has sustained from the hasty and indecorous Conduct of Sir Frederick Hamilton, by taking such notice of that Conduct, as it may appear to your Lordship to merit.[66]

Rammohun's 'humble petition' makes fascinating reading. There he was, at once obsequious to the addressee yet the warrior implacably stern in his demand for satisfaction.

The letter caused quite a stir in British official circles. When an Englishwoman fresh from Calcutta complained to a friend that 'the natives would no longer get out of their palanquins and bow', perhaps she was alluding to the Rammohun–Hamilton incident.[67] And, judging from the correspondence on the ensuing inquiry which Rammohun's 'petition' provoked, his honour was indeed given satisfaction. Hamilton was reprimanded under direct orders from Lord Minto, and cautioned 'against having any similar altercations with any of the Natives in future'.[68]

There is another more interesting aspect of Rammohun's letter to Lord Minto. The 'petition' appears to be Rammohun's earliest known piece of writing in English and gives some sense of his fluency in the language, circa 1809. In fact, by 1818 he had apparently so mastered the language that an English journalist freshly arrived in Calcutta, James Silk Buckingham, editor of a periodical called *Calcutta Journal* from 1818 to 1823, would remark that prior to meeting Rammohun he had 'never heard any foreigner of Asiatic birth speak [English] so well'; that Rammohun's 'fine choice of words [were] as worthy the imitation even of Englishmen'.[69] Rammohun's mastery of English would also draw the praise of the British philosopher Jeremy Bentham.[70]

CROSSING BORDERS, BREAKING barriers: we have already seen these happen in this story. Sir William Jones and the Orientalists transgressed a boundary when they learnt Sanskrit and other Indian languages and penetrated deep into Indian antiquity. William Carey and the Serampore missionaries crossed a border when they dared create a prose in a language that was not theirs, in a language that had not known prose before. By doing so, they created for themselves a kind of cross-cultural mentality.

As we shall see, 'crossing borders, breaking barriers' forms an abiding theme of the Bengal Renaissance. When, in one of his most well-known poems, Rabindranath Tagore composed lines which he translated in the English *Gitanjali*[71] as 'When the world has not been broken up into/fragments by narrow domestic walls,' he was giving poetic voice to this very idea.

When Rammohun Roy wrote his 'petition' *in English* to Lord Minto in 1809, he too stepped across a line. In writing to the governor-general in the language, style, and manner he did, Rammohun was announcing to the British ruling class in India that he possessed command of the very language that was *their* language of command.[72] Without setting foot on English soil he *was* on English soil. English was not just a language of command. It was the language of English literature, of British political and philosophical thought, of British science. On more distant shores it was the language of the American Founding Fathers. It was the language of the King James Bible.

When seven years after the letter to Lord Minto, Rammohun published his first major English work, *Abridgement of the Vedant* (1816), he unwittingly transgressed yet another boundary; in effect he launched a new literary genre: 'Indian writing in English'.[73] With Rammohun, English was not just the language of English (and American) literature; or of English (and American) thought. It became a language—yet another language—of Indian literature, of Indian thought.

Rammohun did not, of course, forsake his mother tongue for English. If he initiated a new literary genre, 'Indian writing in English', he was also, in the wake of William Carey, Ramram Basu, and Mrtyunjay Vidyalankar, an experimenter in Bengali prose.[74] A cross-cultural mentality enables one to cross between two worlds back and forth at will. Rammohun's cross-culturalism began in his bilingualism; he crossed the cultural barrier by first breaking the linguistic barrier, using the English and Bengali languages in any which way he could to serve his ends.

Between 1815 and 1819 Rammohun translated the *Vedanta* and several of the Upanishads from Sanskrit into Bengali. In

1815–16 he also translated an abridgement of the *Vedanta* and two of the Upanishads into English.[75] His goal in producing these translations was very different from Carey's. He wanted to convert his own countrymen to a more rational and truthful understanding of their own scriptures and ultimately to defend himself against their charge of his apparent apostasy. It was for this reason that he rendered the *Vedanta* into Bengali and into 'Hindoostani' and distributed them at his own cost. As for translating the *Vedanta* into English, he wanted to strip the Englishman's misapprehension of Hinduism; to persuade them to cast a kindlier gaze on his religion. His English *Vedanta* was 'an endeavour...to prove to my European friends that the superstitious practices which deform the Hindoo religion have nothing to do with the pure spirit of its dictates'.[76]

Most of his countrymen, whether in Bengal or in more distant places, remained deeply hostile to his ideas. Rammohun, however, remained the warrior. When, in reaction to some of his translations and introductions, a gentleman in Madras wrote a letter to a Madras newspaper in defence of idol worship, Rammohun responded with an essay in English titled 'A Defence of Hindoo Theism' (1817)[77]—meaning monotheism.

In Calcutta, a 'learned Brahmin' wrote in both Bengali and English defending idol worship. The writer was none other than Mrtyunjay Vidyalankar, one of William Carey's pandits in the College of Fort William. Mrtyunjay's Bengali work was purposely written in Sanskritized Bengali, in which he used Sanskrit words liberally because he felt they 'lent dignity' to learned prose.[78] The English work was a translation bearing the title 'An Apology for the Present State of Hindoo Worship'.[79] Rammohun replied, characteristically, in both languages, the English response bearing the title 'A Second Defence of the Monotheistic System of the Veds' (1817).[80] His modus operandi in both 'defences' was the same: quoting his opponents' assertions, excerpting passages from his scriptural sources to refute the oppositions' charges, and then amplifying the refutations in his own words.

These were not just intellectual battles. They had political, indeed legal, consequences for the man himself. When the notice in the Baptist Missionary Society's periodical reported that Rammohun 'is pronounced to be a most wicked man by the strict Hindoos',[81] this was no exaggeration; indeed, it was perhaps a wry understatement.

In 1817, Rammohun's nephew—his deceased elder brother's son—filed a lawsuit in the Supreme Court to disinherit Rammohun from the ancestral property. The formal complaint brought against him was complex and tedious but in essence the suit was instigated by Rammohun's mother, Tarini Devi, as a furious reaction to her son's campaign against idol worship.[82] The measure of her fury towards her son was vividly recorded in the text of the written questions that were to be put to her by Rammohun's lawyer. It makes fascinating reading.

> Have you not had serious disputes and differences with your son the Defendant Rammohun Roy on account of his religious opinions and have you not instigated and prevailed on your Grandson the Complainant to institute the present suit…as a measure of *revenge* because the said Defendant hath refused to practise the rites and ceremonies of the Hindu religion in the manner in which you wish the same to be practised or performed?[83]

Thus the interrogation began. And it continued: 'Have you not repeatedly declared that you desire the *ruin* of the Defendant and there will not only be no sin but that *it will be meritorious* to effect the temporal ruin of the Defendant provided he shall not resume or follow the religious uses and worship of his Forefathers?'[84] Desire of a son's ruin was apparently not enough for the mother, the interrogation insisted: 'Have you not publicly declared that *it will not be sinful to take away the life* of a Hindoo who forsakes the idolatry and ceremony of worship, usually practised by persons of that Religion?'[85]

A NEW WAR on another front commenced in 1818 when Rammohun launched his campaign against sati—a word, anglicized in the nineteenth century to 'suttee', and actually meaning a chaste and faithful wife, that had come to designate the practice of widows being burnt on the funeral pyres of their husbands.

First idolatry then sati. Both recall the Orientalist Henry Thomas Colebrooke who wrote an essay in 1795 in *Asiatick Researches*, 'On the Duties of a Faithful Hindoo Widow', and another article in the same journal in 1805, 'On the *Vedas* or *Sacred Writings* of the Hindoos'.[86] In the latter he concluded that the Hinduism of the *Vedas* was monotheistic; in the former, he demonstrated that according to the Hindu scriptures the Hindu widow does not *have* to commit sati.

How influenced was Rammohun by Colebrooke's work? After all, he had 'European' friends in Calcutta; and some of the city's European intellectual community would have been associated with either the Asiatic Society or the College of Fort William. He also knew Horace Hayman Wilson, surgeon, chemist, preeminent Sanskritist, later the first Boden professor of Sanskrit in Oxford, and an influential figure in the educational controversy that would play a vital role in the unfolding of the Bengal Renaissance.[87] Wilson was intimately involved with both Fort William College and the Asiatic Society (of which he was a secretary, 1815–32),[88] and Rammohun corresponded with him in 1819 on the Vedanta and related scholarly matters.[89]

Rammohun also knew the Serampore missionaries and had even visited them.[90] The Serampore trio shared his repugnance of idolatry (though for different reasons) and like him campaigned passionately for the abolition of sati.[91] (However, Rammohun and the Serampore trio fell out with each other over their vigorous disagreement over Christianity—but *that* is another story to be told, another war to be waged!) Finally, John Digby had been a student in the College of Fort William, in 1801–3, when Colebrooke was one of its professors.[92]

So quite possibly, Rammohun had encountered Colebrooke's essays in *Asiatick Researches*. On the other hand, people quite independently often converge on the same 'discovery' simply because they have thought long and hard about the same subject or because certain ideas are 'in the air' at a certain time. It could well be that Rammohun's rationality led him to reject idolatry (after all, as we have seen, he was writing a treatise against idolatry at age sixteen), and that his personal morality produced in him his detestation of sati; these in turn may have led him to examine the Hindu sacred texts for what they had to say on these matters.

Rammohun was a scholar so that he could be an activist, just as William Carey was a scholar so that he could be an evangelist. He wrote not so much *on* monotheism as *for* it and *against* sati, not *about* it. On the other hand, Colebrooke's tracts on sati and on monotheism remained in the pages of a learned journal for the eyes of fellow scholars. This was their key difference.

THE OFFICIAL BRITISH attitude towards social reform in India had always been cautious. Apprehensive of violating the teachings of the Hindu scriptures on sati, the government had attempted, from 1813, to merely 'regulate' the practice: 'to allow the practice in those cases in which it is countenanced by the Hindoo religion and law' but prevent its enforcement by any other means or under circumstances not prescribed by the scriptures.[93] The effect of these regulations, legalizing sati with governmental blessings, actually led to an increase in the number of sati incidents recorded.

Disturbed by the great increase in sati in 1817 and 1818, Governor-General, the Marquess of Hastings issued orders in 1818 against the practice altogether; in effect the earlier regulations were withdrawn. Certain citizens of Calcutta promptly submitted a petition to the Marquess protesting the order.[94] In response, another group of Calcuttans wrote a 'counter-petition'.[95] This petition, signed by 'a great number of the most respectable inhabitants of Calcutta' was printed, curiously enough, in the *Asiatic Journal* of July 1819,[96] and is believed to have been authored by Rammohun.[97] And it laid out in no uncertain terms the horrors that actually attend the practices of sati.

...[women] have been forced upon the pile, and there bound down with ropes and pressed by green bamboos consumed by the flames.[98]

...some, after flying from the flames, have been carried back by their relations and burnt to death.[99]

...women have been permitted to burn themselves on the funeral piles of men who were not their husbands...[100]

...girls of tender years, pregnant women, and women who have been unfaithful to their husbands have burnt on their funeral piles...[101]

...mothers of infant children, have, contrary to the dictates of nature and morality, as well as of law, abandoned their helpless and innocent offspring, to burn themselves with their deceased husbands...[102]

Rammohun, inevitably, was not satisfied with petition alone. A polemic soon followed, and it took the venerable form of the dialogue beloved of philosophers of old, though he himself preferred to call it a 'conference'. It was between an 'advocate' of sati and its 'opponent'.[103] Characteristically, he wrote it first in Bengali, in which it was 'for several weeks past in extensive circulation' and then translated the Bengali tract into English, hoping that it 'might tend to alter the notions that some European gentlemen entertain on this subject'.[104]

Initially, both advocate and opponent—the latter, of course, Rammohun's alter ego—appealed to the scriptures as grounds for their respective arguments. But ultimately, Rammohun-as-opponent set aside the religious texts and drew on his moral code. He first pointed out the reality of sati as actually enforced by men; and, as in the 'counter-petition', he did not mince words.

> [*advocate*]: Though tying down in this manner be not authorized by Shastrus [*shastras*] yet we practice it as being a custom that has been observed throughout Hindoosthan.[105]

Not so, the opponent retorted:

> [*opponent*] : ...it never was the case that the practice of fastening down widows on the pile was prevalent throughout Hindoosthan: for it is but of late years that this mode has been followed, and that only in Bengal...[106]

Rammohun had done his homework here. According to official statistics for 1815–18, the actual number of sati incidents not only varied among different locations, but also the number was startlingly higher for the Calcutta region compared to other localities: for those four years, sati incidents in the Calcutta 'division' numbered 1,528; the total for the divisions of Dacca (now Dhaka), Murshidabad, Patna, Benares (now Varanasi), and Bareilly taken together was 837.[107] And, in any case, the opponent scoffed:

> [*opponent*]: No one...who has the fear of God and man before him, will assert that male or female murder, theft, &c, from having been long practised, cease to be vice.[108]

The advocate was stung by the opponent's charge that 'from want of feeling we promote female destruction'. He protested that according to the teachings of the Vedas and Manu, 'mercy is the root of virtue and from our practice of hospitality, &c, our compassionate dispositions are well known'.[109] The opponent's response was to appeal to a regrettable facet of human psychology: the effect of habit and over-exposure on one's sensibilities:

> [*opponent*]: ...by witnessing from your youth the voluntary burning of women amongst your elder relatives, your neighbours, and the inhabitants of the surrounding villages, and by observing the indifference manifested at the time when the women are writhing under the torture of the flames, habits of insensibilities are produced.[110]

The fictive advocate promised to reconsider his position. Rammohun thus ended the 'conference' on an optimistic note.

The supporters of sati in the real world were not as malleable as their fictive counterpart. Rammohun continued to agitate against sati by way of both petition and polemic: a letter to an English language newspaper in 1819, using a pseudonym;[111] a second, long 'conference' in 1820, once more between an advocate of sati and an opponent[112]—and always with an eye to gaining the attention of people in high places, he dedicated this tract to the Marchioness of Hastings: 'as an appeal to reason in behalf of humanity, I take the liberty to dedicate to your Ladyship...'[113]

Rammohun was not alone in his campaign against sati.[114] There were those 'respectable inhabitants of Calcutta' who had signed the 'counter-petition' sent to the Marquess of Hastings. The Serampore trio too campaigned vigorously for abolishing it and, in this respect, they were at one with Rammohun,[115] as was Dwarakanath Tagore.[116]

It turned out to be a long, protracted war. Alas, neither the Marchioness of Hastings nor her husband did anything about sati. Like their predecessors in power they were apprehensive of making waves on Hindu waters. The Marquess's governor-generalship ended in 1823. His successor Lord Amherst came, stayed for five years, and departed with no further changes regarding sati. It was not till Lord William Bentinck's arrival in 1828 that, finally, sati was abolished in 1829.[117] This prompted Rammohun to write, on behalf of some three hundred Calcutta citizens, a grateful address to the governor-general.[118]

The supporters of sati still would not yield: they submitted a 'memorial' to the government requesting repeal of the abolition law; this in turn provoked a 'counter-petition' composed by Rammohun which he took with him to England when he finally made the journey he had long desired to embark upon. The counter-petition was submitted to the House of Commons. The memorial from the advocates of sati was dismissed by Parliament in 1832.[119]

THE FIGHT AGAINST sati was not Rammohun's only campaign for women's rights. He also wrote a pamphlet on their rights of inheritance.[120]

If the war against sati was for the Hindu widow's right to live rather than die—or, rather, her right to choose between dying under duress and dying in the natural course of things—his advocacy for women's inheritance rights was an argument for the Hindu female's right to live as well as the Hindu male. As in the case of sati, here too Rammohun argued by appealing to the ancients. He saw a 'state of civilization' in the ancient days and its 'subsequent gradual degradation': [121] 'I am induced to give as an instance the interest and care which our ancient legislators took in the promotion of the comfort of the female part of the community...'[122]

When one compared the laws of female inheritance pronounced by these 'ancient legislators' with those which the 'moderns and our contemporaries' have established, the contrast was stark: the laws of the ancients 'afforded that sex the opportunity of enjoyment of life', while the laws established by the moderns have led '...to their complete privation, directly or indirectly, of most of those objects that render life agreeable.'[123] Thus, he proceeded to argue that all 'our ancient legislators' unanimously award to the mother an equal share with the sons of the property left by the deceased father. The supporting evidence followed, with quotes from the ancient law givers. Rammohun contrasted these pronouncements with those of the 'moderns'—and the moderns included the author of *Dayabhaga*, which was the standard code of law of property division in Bengal. The moderns limited the rights of women—once again, widows—to inherit their dead husbands' properties. Mothers whose husbands have passed away could be rendered destitute by their sons if the sons so chose; a widow with no issue was, of course, beyond the pale. 'The consequence is, that a woman who is looked up to as the sole mistress by the rest of the family one day, on the next, becomes dependent on her son, and subject to the slights of her daughter-in-law.'[124]

Polygamy, still legal amongst kulin Brahmins, created its own horrors: on the death of the father, there may be stepmothers who 'are still more shamefully neglected in general by their stepsons'; if they were without sons they could be treated 'sometimes dreadfully' by their co-wives—'sisters-in-law'—who happened to have sons by their late common husband.[125]

Under such circumstances one can understand why widows may choose sati. The alternatives were too awful to contemplate. And, Rammohun noted, if one notices the staggeringly higher rates of 'female suicide' in Bengal compared to other regions of India—a ratio of 'almost ten to one'—one may 'safely attribute' this disproportion to the prevalence of 'a plurality of wives' in Bengal. It was this that caused Rammohun to speak, expressively, of '[t]his horrible polygamy'—which, he emphasized, was not countenanced by the ancient law givers.[126]

RAMMOHUN'S RELATIONSHIP WITH the women in his family appears in curious contrast to these battles he fought on women's rights. He was polygamous (which though, as we have seen, was a fait accompli, a 'done deal' before he had any say in the matter, having been married off by his father when he was still a child); his relationship with his two wives was strained; and, most of all, there was his troubled, tortuous relationship with his mother, Tarini Devi. While Rammohun admired his mother's strength and independence he was quite willing to publicly humiliate her. There was also the fact that Rammohun could only make the case for women by appealing to the shastras, rather than on strictly secular grounds;[127]

that, in particular, he fought his war against sati on scriptural grounds.[128]

Yet the fact remains that his war against sati was a war on behalf of women's rights. His impassioned argument for women's inheritance rights to property was a campaign on behalf of women. Despite his contradictory personal traits, when all is said and done, Rammohun *was* a feminist amongst men.

SOME TIME IN 1816 or 1817 (the date is unclear), Rammohun wrote to John Digby, his erstwhile employer, now back in England, a 'summary account' of his doings since the Englishman left India in 1814. The same intellectual curiosity that had led him to inquire into Islam and Buddhism had drawn him to the New Testament:

> The consequences of my long and uninterrupted researches into religious truth has been that I have found the doctrines of Christ more conducive to moral principles and better adapted for the use of rational beings than by others which have come to my knowledge.[129]

This would have pleased the Serampore missionaries. They would have been happier still—and the Hindu orthodoxy as enraged—to read that: '[I] have also found Hindoos in general more superstitious and miserable both in performance of their religious rites and in their domestic concerns than the rest of the known nations of the earth...'[130]

Alas, any bonhomie the Baptists and other denominations of the Christian faith (with one exception) may have felt towards Rammohun rapidly evaporated. Rammohun was attracted to Christ's teachings but he could not accept the idea of the Trinity nor the divinity of Christ. Thus commenced another war, this time with Christian orthodoxy. If the Hindu orthodoxy branded him a heretic for his rejection of polytheism and idol worship, so too would the Christian orthodoxy brand him a heretic for questioning Christ's divinity. A monotheist in the Hindu faith, Rammohun became a Unitarian in the Christian faith.

Indeed, writing in 1823, in the wake of earlier tracts addressing Christianity (and using as was his occasional whim another name, in this case the name of one of his friends), Rammohun embraced all faiths that believed in one God, including the faith of 'foreigners': '…those Europeans who believe God is in every sense one and worship him alone in spirit…should be regarded by us with affection on the ground of the object of their worship being the same as ours.'[131] As for those Christians 'who believe Jesus Christ to be God himself and conceive him to be possessed of a particular form, and maintain Father, Son and Holy Ghost to be one God',[132] they should not be cast out as enemies. 'On the contrary we should act towards them in the same manner as we act towards those of our countrymen who, without forming any external image meditate upon Ram and other supposed incarnations and believe in their unity.'[133]

For Trinitarians—those who believe in the Holy Trinity of Father, Son, and the Holy Spirit, which would encompass most denominations of the Christian faith—this identification with Hindu polytheism must have been an unkind cut; yet unkinder was Rammohun's suggestion that towards such

Christians 'we' should not show hostility but 'compassion on account of their blindness to the errors into which they themselves have fallen'.[134]

The unkindest cut, though, must have been the conversion, in 1821, of a Baptist minister, William Adam of the Serampore Mission, to Unitarianism. Adam and another Baptist minister, William Yates, collaborated with Rammohun in translating the Gospels into Bengali. The outcome of this intercourse was dramatic: Yates parted ways with Rammohun while Adam began to 'entertain some doubts' about the divinity of Christ,[135] and was himself, converter by vocation, converted. He renounced the doctrine of the Trinity and became a Unitarian.

Other objects of Rammohun's 'compassion' reacted in different ways. Thomas Middleton, Bishop of Calcutta, reading some of Rammohun's writings on Christianity, read him wrongly and attempted to convert Rammohun to Christianity—not so much for the 'true light' but for the 'honour and the glory and fame it [would] bring him', according to an account by William Adam.[136] Rammohun indignantly rejected such an overture. From Serampore, Joshua Marshman, one of the original Serampore trio, issued a lengthy refutation of Rammohun's arguments in his own periodical, *Friend of India*,[137] and the Baptist Mission Press in Calcutta, which had previously printed Rammohun's writings on Christianity, would have no more to do with him.[138]

Arguably, the most heated and protracted reaction to Rammohun's polemic against the doctrine of the Trinity came from Robert Tytler, a 'certain fiery doctor of medicine'.[139] Tytler was himself something of a polymath: a surgeon, member of the Asiatic Society, learned in Arabic and Persian, and even some Sanskrit, and sometime lecturer in English and mathematics in Hindu College,[140] where (as the story will tell) he would play a small, unexpected, but constructive role in the unfolding of the Bengal Renaissance.

The 'Tytler controversy' took the form of a passionate exchange of letters in the summer of 1823 in the periodicals the *Bengal Hurkaru* and *India Gazette*. Tytler, who initiated the exchange, saw Rammohun's writings as a throwing down of the gauntlet which 'has been accordingly taken up by me'.[141] He offered to meet Rammohun 'in either Public or Private disputation' on the subject, an offer that Rammohun, 'notwithstanding he is so great an advocate for free discussion' refused to accept unless Tytler's arguments were vetted by a 'Missionary Gentleman'.[142] Tytler then asked his readers to form their own opinion about Rammohun's 'line of conduct'.[143]

A gauntlet for a gauntlet! Rammohun, predictably, rose to the bait. Thus followed the volley of letters, first to the *Bengal Hurkaru*, by Tytler, by Rammohun (in his own name and under a nom de plume he commonly used in his Bengali works),[144] by a writer who signed-off as 'Orthodox', and by another writer who signed off as 'A Christian'. The controversy carried over into the pages of the *India Gazette*. And, like many intellectual controversies, this had no victor.

RAMMOHUN HAD ANTAGONIZED the Hindu community, and enraged the Christians. As ever, he resided in his own particular no-man's land. And his most significantly original idea entailed the blending of Hinduism and Christianity:

the creation in 1828 of the monotheistic Brahmo Samaj, a Unitarian form of Hinduism.

There were precurors to the Samaj. In 1815, soon after Rammohun settled in Calcutta, he started a small society called Atmiya Sabha (Society of Friends) that met weekly at his residence to recite from the scriptures and sing hymns composed by Rammohun and others. Amidst all his other preoccupations and interests, Rammohun also found time to compose devotional songs about his monotheistic beliefs. These songs are today called Brahmo-sangeet. One of his famous compositions, 'Mon eki bhranti tomar', asks 'How can you blunder, my heart, by welcoming or wishing goodbye to God who is everywhere and ever present?' Another, 'Ki swadeshi, ki bideshi', says 'Either at home or abroad I live here and there, and I see you everywhere in the middle of your own creation. / As each moment declares your glory through endless space and time, I see you everywhere.'[145]

Amongst the regular attendees at these gatherings was the young Dwarakanath Tagore who had come to know Rammohun about this time and was immediately attracted to the much senior man (Dwarakanath was twenty-two years younger) and his ideas, despite the fact that Dwarakanath was, at the time, a far more orthodox Hindu than Rammohun.[146] The Atmiya Sabha soon died. However, in 1823—the year of the Rammohun–Tytler controversy, and William Adam's conversion to Unitarianism—Rammohun, Adam, and Dwarakanath Tagore established the Calcutta Unitarian Committee and the Unitarian Press.[147]

To the English (and later, American) Unitarians Rammohun was one of them though he never converted to the Christian faith. As William Adam put it to a correspondent in response to a question, 'Does Rammohun profess to be a Christian?': '…the nearest approach to the truth, although…it is not the truth itself, would perhaps be to say that he is…Christian with Christians, and a Hindu with Hindus.'[148] Adam continued that Rammohun's one 'absolute, total, public, uncompromising' stance was rejection of idolatry; yet he did not relinquish his 'Brahminical rights' since otherwise he would incur 'loss of caste, loss of property, loss of influence, loss of everything but a name'.[149]

English Unitarianism was yet another step in Rammohun's preparation for what followed in August 1828: the establishment of the Brahmo Samaj.

The Trust Deed of the Samaj's 'church' states that the premise would be used 'for the worship and adoration of the Eternal Unsearchable and Immutable being who is the Author and Preserver of the Universe'.[150] Moreover, the church would not be used to worship 'any particular Being or Beings', nor would it admit any 'graven image stature or sculpture painting picture portrait or the likeness of anything'.[151] In these few words the goals and purpose of the Brahmo Samaj were encapsulated. It was a community and a church dedicated to anti-idolatry, monotheism, and the worship of Brahman, the Supreme Being.

The Brahmo Samaj and its creed were an invention. And like any other act of creation, Brahmoism did not arise de novo. It came out of Rammohun's reading of the Hindu shastras and it found confirmation in Christian Unitarianism. Its sole object of worship was Brahman, the Supreme Being, and no other—not the Hindu Trinity of Brahma, Vishnu, Maheswara, not the Mother-Goddess Devi in the incarnations of Durga or Kali, nor any of the numerous associated gods and goddesses of the Hindu pantheon.

As an act of creation it was as if Brahmoism began with what might be called the basic pattern of Hinduism, from which were weeded out undesirable or unwanted aspects (idolatry, multiple gods, the many Hindu customs and rituals); some elements were then replaced with new ones (the Christianized Brahmo marriage service for example); and finally, entirely new elements were added, some of which were possibly borrowed from other religions (such as the congregational mode of worship). The outcome was a new form of Hinduism, for the rational, modern Indian.[152]

Almost two years after the formation of the Brahmo Samaj, its Trust Deed was executed in the presence of eight other trustees that included Dwarakanath Tagore. At about the same time a place on Chitpore Road was opened and consecrated as the Samaj's church.[153]

The Brahmo Samaj would have its own internal strifes and controversies in the course of the nineteenth century.[154] There was a time in the years following Rammohun's death in 1833 when the Samaj had scarcely any congregation at all, as Dwarakanath's son Debendranath Tagore would recall.[155] Still, by 1872, despite the different factions within the Samaj, there were over a hundred Brahmo Samaj organizations in Bengal, Bombay, Oudh (Awadh), Orissa, the Central Provinces, Assam, Bihar, and even Burma.[156]

Insofar as Hinduism in India, or even in Bengal, was concerned, Brahmoism would remain a minority faith in terms of the numbers of its believers. In its appeal to monotheism, its rejection of idolatry, and its Christian influences, it was a religion for the intellectual elite rather than the masses.[157] Yet, because of its espousal of liberal ideas that spanned science, literature, nationalist consciousness, education, social reform, and women's rights, the influence of Brahmoism in Bengal through the nineteenth and into the twentieth centuries, and its place in the awakening of the Indian mind was far in excess of its size.[158] Many of the key players in this story, as we shall see, were Brahmos and the rational, puritan Brahmo ethos permeated Bengali society.

That Rammohun marched to his own drumbeat is as much evident in the manner of dress he adopted as a Brahmo. Some sixty years after his death, Debendranath Tagore, Rabindranath's father, would reminisce that when attending service at the Samaj, Rammohun would never wear the usual attire of the Bengali bhadralok—the dhoti and chaddar—but rather the court dress of Muslims:

> The Raja had a great regard for the externals of Moslem civilization. His idea...was that God being man's King and Master, in going to His court, one must dress oneself properly, and must appear before Him as one fit to be present at the Court of the Prince of Princes. He had imbibed this idea... from the Mahommedans.[159]

Debendranath recalled that Rammohun expected his friends to attend the Samaj similarly attired and was disappointed that Dwarakanath, Debendranath's father, could not be bothered to follow this custom.[160]

As far back as 1816 or 1817 Rammohun had hoped to visit England.[161] That wish was finally realized in 1830 when, as he wrote to Lord William Bentinck, then governor-general: 'Having at length surmounted all the obstacles of a domestic nature that have hitherto opposed my long cherished intention of visiting England, I am now resolved to proceed to the land of liberty...'[162]

And proceed he did, in November 1830. He set sail for England as a private individual but also as unofficial emissary for Akbar II, the Mughal king of Delhi who had been seeking from King George IV an increase of his pension. Rammohun, in fact, drafted Akbar's petition, both the Persian original and its English translation.[163]

When Rammohun left India he did so bearing the grand title of 'Raja', conferred upon him by Akbar II, a title that no doubt served him very well, as Sophia Dobson Collet breathlessly described, in the

> court of the King, in the halls of the legislature, in the select coteries of fashion, in the society of philosophers and men of letters, in Anglican church and Nonconformist meeting house, in the privacy of many a house, and before the wondering crowds of Lancashire operatives.[164]

Rammohun may not have been the first Indian to cross the 'black water', but he was almost certainly the first Indian to set foot on Western shores who placed a substantial imprint on the Western mind. Here was an encounter of truly strange proportions. We have seen how the British Orientalists had their own consciousness reshaped by their discovery of the

Indian past.¹⁶⁵ The British of 1830s England would have their understanding of the Indian present altered by their encounter with Rammohun.

The English Unitarians of course adopted Rammohun as one of their own.¹⁶⁶ Indeed, some of them may have taken him to *be* a 'proper' Unitarian. Thus William Roscoe, lawyer, parliamentarian, abolitionist (of slavery, a major issue of the time in England), and poet, while praising Rammohun as one who had understood the 'true and genuine nature of Christianity',¹⁶⁷ also mistook him for an 'illustrious convert from Hindooism to Christianity'.¹⁶⁸ The Unitarians in England also revered Rammohun for his role in the abolition of sati. In London, they welcomed their 'illustrious oriental friend' with an address in which the speaker recollected that some writers '…had endeavoured to imagine what would be their sensations if a Plato or a Socrates, a Milton or a Newton were unexpectedly to honour them with their presence'.¹⁶⁹ The speaker identified with them, for he too had the same feeling when he 'stretched out…the hand of welcome to the Rajah…'¹⁷⁰ The same speaker later reminded his audience: 'If at this moment Hindoo piles are not burning for the reception of widows, it is owing to his interference, to his exhortations, to his arguments.'¹⁷¹

EVEN MORE UNEXPECTED than the English encounter was Rammohun's effect on America, even though he never set foot on that land. There was a period when Rammohun became something of a household name in New England.¹⁷² And, apparently, his work and ideas were known to the leading spirit of American Transcendentalism, Ralph Waldo

Emerson[173]—but then, Emerson's Transcendentalism had one of its tendrils rooted in Unitarianism and he was, after all, the son of a Unitarian minister.

In his time, Rammohun was known mainly to the American reading public through their periodicals, most notably the *Christian Register*, published from Boston.[174] And through these publications, two views of Rammohun were presented to the American public. First, that he was a Hindu man of letters and a philosopher; and second, that he was a man of religion and a Unitarian Christian.[175]

The literary/philosophical perception—which emanated from articles explaining the *Vedas* as literature and philosophical doctrine, and Rammohun's attempts to 'restore the pure doctrines of the Vedas'[176]—was that even though Rammohun was not a Christian his basic religious philosophy was very similar to the Christian doctrine about the nature of the Deity.[177] The religious perception, as we might expect, provoked considerable heat, and led to debates on whether Rammohun was or not a Christian. A Baptist publication, the *Christian Watchman*, locked horns with the Unitarian *Christian Register*, while an article in the *Watchman* castigated Rammohun for having 'no more faith in the gospel than Mahommet had', and for not believing in the Bible as God's revelation.[178]

The *Register*, responding to this 'harsh and virulent attack' on Rammohun, retorted: 'Those who allow no man the name of Christian…who does not admit into his creed the whole circle of Trinitarianism and Calvinistic jargon may well call such a man…no Christian.'[179] In this attempt to denigrate Rammohun, the *Christian Register* continued, 'is evident with how much dread his influence is regarded as an opposer of Trinitarian and Calvinist dogmas'.[180]

Thus the battles Rammohun fought with the Trinitarians—Anglican and Nonconformist alike—in Calcutta seemed to be replicated, though without his physical presence, in America. The Raja was as much the warrior in the New World as in his own world.

RAMMOHUN FELL SERIOUSLY ill while in England, and lived his final days there amidst his Unitarian friends.[181] The precise nature of his illness remains unknown. However, his last days were accompanied by fever, spasms, and 'convulsive twitchings of the mouth',[182] and a postmortem revealed inflammation of the brain.[183] Upon his death in October 1833, a death mask was cast. Ever the man who marched to his own tune, the founder of Brahmoism had expressed a wish to preserve his caste even in death, and not be buried near Christians. He was buried in a private garden belonging to one of his friends 'in a shrubbery…and under some fine elms' in a place called Stapleton Grove, and mourned there by his Unitarian friends.[184] A decade later, Rammohun's coffin was removed to Arno's Vale Cemetery near Bristol, and 'a handsome monument' was erected to mark the grave by his old friend and fellow Brahmo Dwarakanath Tagore.[185]

And so, in this cemetery lay the remains of a man who conformed to no stereotype: a follower of Christ's doctrines but who reacted sharply to an Anglican bishop's suggestion that he might convert to Christianity; a Hindu who knew Arabic and Persian well, had studied the Koran, had written a theological tract in Persian and dressed like a Muslim;

a battler for women's rights who had an uneasy relation to the women in his own life; a Brahmin who abhorred the rituals of Hindu orthodoxy and founded a reformed Hindu faith in response—and yet would not part with his sacred thread for fear of losing caste and, indeed, even in death insisted on preserving his caste. All this would have served as a fitting epitaph on his monument in Arno's Vale.

Notes

1. Collet [1900] 1988, pp. 122–3. Quoted from *Periodical Accounts Relative to the Baptist Missionary Society*, Vol. VI (Bristol 1817), No. 31 (from June 1815 to Jan 1816), pp. 106–7.
2. Collet [1900] 1988, pp. 122–3.
3. Ibid.
4. Ibid.
5. In English, the first name is also sometimes spelt as 'Rammohan'.
6. Das 1966, p. 127.
7. Joshi 1975.
8. Collet [1900] 1988, p. 1; Biswas and Ganguli 1988a, pp. 9–11.
9. See Ghose 1885b, pp. xv–xvi.
10. Roy 1833.
11. See Chapter one.
12. Home 1933b, p. 28.
13. Roy 1833, p. 23.
14. Collet [1900] 1988, pp. 3, 21–2.
15. Ibid., p. 5.

16. Ibid., p. 3, fn 6.
17. According to Geraldine Forbes, Rammohun's third marriage took place when he was twenty-one. She does not, however, cite her source for this information. See Forbes 1996, p. 10. A quite recent book-length study of Rammohun by Bruce Robertson agrees with Sophie Dobson Collet and her later editors, Dilip Kumar Biswas and P.C. Ganguli, on this matter. See Robertson 1995, p. 14.
18. N.N. Chatterjee to S.D. Collet, January 2, 1883. Quoted in Collet [1900] 1988, p. 196.
19. Roy 1822, p. 365.
20. Roy 1833, p. 23.
21. Collet [1900] 1988, p. 4; Sastri [1911] 1933, p. 9.
22. Roy 1833, p. 23.
23. Collet [1900] 1988, p. 6.
24. Roy 1833, p. 23.
25. Sastri [1911] 1933, p. 9; Das 1974, p. 18; Collet [1900] 1988, p. 4; Raychaudhuri 1999, pp. 99–100.
26. Roy 1833, p. 24.
27. Biswas and Ganguli 1988d.
28. Home 1933b, pp. 29–30.
29. Collet [1900] 1988, pp. 7–8.
30. Biswas and Ganguli 1988c.
31. Biswas and Ganguli 1988e.
32. See Chapter two.
33. Biswas and Ganguli 1988e, p. 24; Robertson 1995, p. 19.
34. Robertson 1995, p. 19.
35. Biswas and Ganguli 1988b.
36. Ibid., p. 24.
37. Ibid., pp. 25–6.

38. Ibid., p. 25.
39. Ibid., p. 25.
40. Ibid., p. 27.
41. Ibid., p. 24.
42. Roy 1833, p. 24.
43. Ibid.
44. Ibid.
45. Biswas and Ganguli 1988e, p. 27.
46. Collet [1900] 1988, p. 8; Biswas and Ganguli 1988f.
47. Roy 1833, p. 24.
48. Ibid., pp. 24–5.
49. See footnote by D.K. Biswas and P.C. Ganguli, in Collet [1900] 1988, pp. 28–9.
50. Robertson 1995, pp. 24–9.
51. Ibid., pp. 25–6.
52. Home 1933c.
53. Biswas and Ganguli, 1988g.
54. Ibid.
55. As it turned out, probably out of political spite, because of a confrontation between Rammohun and a district collector, the Company refused to approve Rammohun's appointment as a dewan. See Biswas and Ganguli 1988g, pp. 46–8.
56. Biswas and Ganguli 1988g, p. 48.
57. Collet [1900] 1988, p. 69.
58. See discussion in this chapter.
59. Collet [1900] 1988, p. 69.
60. Collet [1900] 1988, p. 8; Robertson 1995, p. 23, note.
61. This passage is excerpted from a preface by John Digby to his edited reprint of two of Rammohun's English works. The preface is quoted in full in Biswas 1992, pp. 21–3.

62. Biswas 1992, pp. 21–3.
63. 'Rammohun's letter addressed to Lord Minto, Governor-General of India, April 1809, in Biswas 1992, pp. 1–5.
64. Biswas 1992, p. 2.
65. Ibid., p. 3.
66. Ibid., p. 6.
67. Quoted in Johnson 1991, p. 794.
68. G. Dowderwell, secretary to government in the judicial department in Fort William, to the magistrate of Bhaugulpore [Bhagalpur], June 12, 1809, in Biswas 1992, pp. 10–11.
69. Home 1933b, p. 33.
70. Ibid., p. 33.
71. See Prologue.
72. Cohn 1996, pp. 16–56.
73. Das 1991, pp. 78–9; Robertson 2003.
74. Das 1966, pp. 126–60.
75. Home 1933c, pp. 133–46.
76. Roy 1833, p. 4.
77. Ghose 1885a, pp. 103–18.
78. Das 1966, p. 123.
79. Collet [1900] 1988, p. 80.
80. Ghose 1885a, pp. 119–48.
81. See this chapter.
82. Biswas and Ganguli 1988i, pp. 57–9.
83. Ibid., pp. 58–9. Emphasis added.
84. Ibid., pp. 58–9. Emphasis added.
85. Ibid.
86. See Chapter one.
87. See Chapter five.
88. Anon [1885] 1986, pp. 85–6.

89. R. Roy to H.H. Wilson, August 9, 1819; September 29, 1819, in Biswas 1992, pp. 44–5, 46–7.
90. Elliott 2007, pp. 6–7.
91. Ibid., pp. 70–2.
92. Kopf 1969, p. 197.
93. Collet [1900] 1988, p. 85.
94. Ibid., p. 90.
95. 'Counter-Petition of Some Hindu Inhabitants of Calcutta to the Marquess of Hastings, re, Suttee order of Government,' pp. 27–32 in Biswas 1992.
96. 'Notes and Comments' to 'Counter-Petition', pp. 32–7 in Biswas 1992, pp. 32–3.
97. Biswas 1992, pp. 33–7.
98. Ibid., p. 28.
99. Ibid., pp. 28–9.
100. Ibid., p. 29.
101. Ibid.
102. Ibid.
103. Roy 1818.
104. Ibid., p. 296.
105. Ibid., p. 307.
106. Ibid.
107. Collet [1900] 1988, p. 89.
108. Roy 1818, p. 307.
109. Ibid., p. 308.
110. Ibid., p. 309.
111. 'Rammohun Roy's letter to the "India Gazette" on the Suttee question in the name of Hariharananda Tirthaswami, March 27, 1819,' in Biswas 1992, pp. 38–40.
112. Roy 1820.

113. 'Rammohun's letter to Lady Hastings,' February 16, 1820, in Biswas 1992, pp. 58–9.
114. For accounts and reports on the nineteenth century debate on sati see, in particular, Chapters 5–8 in Major 2007.
115. Elliott 2007, p. 72; also, Major 2007, pp. 78–96.
116. Kripalani 1981, p. 40.
117. Bentinck 1829.
118. Roy 1830. According to J.C. Ghose, based on both language and substance, it seemed most probable that the address was written by Rammohun. See Ghose 1885a, p. 483.
119. Anon n.d., pp. 19–20.
120. Roy 1822.
121. Ibid., p. 359.
122. Ibid., pp. 359–60.
123. Ibid.
124. Ibid., p. 363.
125. Ibid., pp. 363–4.
126. Ibid., p. 265.
127. Bagchi 1995b, p. 3.
128. Mani 1990, p. 91.
129. 'Extract from Rammohun Roy's letter to John Digby written some time in 1816 or 1817,' in Biswas 1992, pp. 19–20.
130. Biswas 1992, pp. 19–20.
131. Roy [P.K. Thakoor] 1823, p. 246.
132. Ibid.
133. Ibid.
134. Ibid.
135. William Adam to N. Wright, May 7, 1821. Quoted in Collet [1900] 1988, p. 131.
136. Quoted in Collet [1900] 1988, pp. 132–3.

137. Collet [1900] 1988, p. 140.
138. Ibid., p. 141.
139. Ibid., p. 143.
140. Biswas 1992, p. 143.
141. 'Robert Tytler's letter to the Bengal Hurkaru of April 30, 1823,' pp. 87–9 in Biswas 1992, p. 88.
142. Biswas 1992, p. 88.
143. Ibid., p. 89.
144. Ibid., p. 147.
145. Translation by Deben Bhattacharya, 1995. Liner notes, *Two Centuries of Bengal Songs*, compact disc 5503. Vista India.
146. Kripalani 1981, pp. 33–6.
147. Kopf 1979, pp. xxi, 12.
148. Quoted in Collet [1900] 1988, p. 211.
149. Ibid.
150. Ghose 1885a, pp. 489–95.
151. Ibid.
152. Dasgupta 2007, pp. 47–8.
153. Collet [1900] 1988, p. 265.
154. Kopf 1979; Das 1974, pp. 62–100.
155. Tagore 1896.
156. Kopf 1979, pp. 325–7.
157. Raychaudhuri 1999, p. 100.
158. Kopf 1979, pp. 313–34.
159. Tagore 1896, p. 175.
160. Ibid.
161. Biswas 1992, p. 20.
162. R. Roy to Lord William Bentinck, September 29, 1830, pp. 489–90 in Biswas 1992, p. 489.

144 • Awakening

163. 'English translation of the original Persian petition of the Mughal King Akbar II of Delhi to King George V of England,' in Biswas 1992, pp. 419–34.
164. Collet [1900] 1988, pp. 290–1.
165. See Chapter one.
166. Carpenter [1866] 1915.
167. Ibid., p. 81.
168. Quoted in Carpenter [1866] 1915, pp. 84–5.
169. Ibid., p. 93.
170. Ibid.
171. Ibid., p. 95.
172. Moore 1947, pp. 2–3.
173. Ibid., p. 3.
174. Ibid., pp. 125–41.
175. Ibid., p. 154.
176. Ibid., p. 155.
177. Ibid.
178. Ibid., p. 157.
179. Ibid.
180. Ibid.
181. Carpenter [1866] 1915, pp. 158–67.
182. Ibid., pp. 164–5.
183. Ibid., p. 168.
184. Ibid., p. 169.
185. Ibid., p. 206.

Five

Bhadralok in Class, English in Taste

RAMMOHUN ROY DOES not quite fade from this story yet. Indeed, his presence hovers like a luminous ghost throughout this narrative. Let us return to 1815 and the Atmiya Sabha, the informal association Rammohun established that year.[1] This society was the antecedent of the Brahmo Samaj—and that is, perhaps, its main claim to fame.

As the story is told by Peary Chand Mittra (who wrote the Bengali proto-novel, *Alaler Gharer Dulal*, published in book form in 1858), Rammohun, entertaining some friends at his house, suggested the formation of an 'Atmiya Sabha' for 'improving the moral condition of our countrymen'. By 'moral condition' he was referring to the 'swamp of idolatry and superstition' which he desired to eliminate.[2] Present at the gathering was a Scot named David Hare who, according to Peary Chand Mittra, proposed, instead, the establishment of a college. 'It was Hare's considered opinion that education of native youth in Western literature and science would be a far more effective means of enlightening their understanding and of purging their minds of pernicious cants.'[3]

The consequences of this proposal—which, as Mittra tells us, Rammohun and his friends liked—are crucial to our story;

for David Hare's suggestion became the seed for the formation of Hindu College.

DAVID HARE (1775–1842) was one of three Scots who informed and enriched the Bengal Renaissance, the others being David Drummond and Alexander Duff. Hare was born in 1775, making him a few years Rammohun's junior. David Hume, the Scottish philosopher and one of the leading figures of the Scottish Enlightenment, died the year after. The Scottish Enlightenment embodied tinkers as well as thinkers: thus there was James Watt, developer of the steam engine, who began life as an instrument maker. David Hare who, we might say, carried the spirit of the Scottish Enlightenment into Bengal where he arrived in 1800, was also a craftsman. He came to India and set up a shop in Calcutta as a watchmaker. And just as Watt became much more than instrument maker so also Hare evolved into much more than a watchmaker. The Scottish Enlightenment made something special even out of its craftsmen.

The watchmaking business was a livelihood—evidently a livelihood that brought Hare some prosperity. But this was not what drove the man. His avocation was the 'study of the native society of Calcutta'.[4] The Scottish Enlightenment embodied not only rationalism but also a solid dose of Scottish practicality. Hare was no mere passive observer of Calcutta's social culture; he translated his observations into action. He became in the course of his long life in Calcutta—he died in the city in 1842—a philanthropist, a social reformer, and, above all, an educationist.

THE IDEA OF Hindu College was, by all evidence, David Hare's brainchild. Had Hare done nothing else, this idea alone assures him a place in the annals of the Bengal Renaissance, and of Indian intellectual history.

He took it upon himself, following the meeting in Rammohun's home, to write up a proposal for the establishment of a college. Another person present at the gathering, Baidyanath Mukherjee, delivered the proposal to Sir Edward Hyde East, chief justice of the Supreme Court. East responded positively. He called a meeting at his house of some of the 'distinguished native gentlemen and pundits' to whom the proposal was put forth. They too responded enthusiastically, and it was resolved that a college would be established 'for the education of native youths'.[5] Donations were promised.

On January 20, 1817, Hindu College—such was the name chosen—came into being. Its fundamental objective was '... the tuition of the sons of respectable Hindoos in the English and Indian language [sic] and in the literature and science of Europe and Asia.[6]

Peary Chand Mittra tells us that when Hare mooted the idea it was 'enthusiastically accepted' by Rammohun.[7] Yet controversy of one sort or another was never too far from Rammohun's presence. In the case of the origins of Hindu College, it was a case of the dog that did not bark in the night. For after that first meeting in his house Rammohun's absence in the formation of Hindu College was palpable.

In polite, orthodox Bengali Hindu society Rammohun was persona non grata; his very name caused displeasure, and had he been associated with the project, the 'distinguished native gentlemen' who had assembled in Sir Edward Hyde East's home to hear Hare's proposal would have withdrawn their support. East says as much in a letter he wrote to a friend. Speaking to this company of 'distinguished native gentlemen',

> I found that one of them in particular...was mostly set against Rammohun... He expressed a hope that no subscription would be received from Rammohun... I asked why not? 'Because he had chosen to separate himself from us... Rammohun Roy...is a Hindu, and yet has publicly reviled us and has written against us and our religion...'[8]

In the interest of the cause, Rammohun was persuaded, apparently by David Hare, to not express any interest in the matter, to which he willingly agreed.[9]

Hare was not, of course, persona non grata amidst the eminent Bengali Hindus of the Black Town. Yet there were some who wished to deny his place as the originator of the idea. They would claim that the credit lay with Sir Edward Hyde East, as was stated emphatically by an unnamed 'Director of the Hindoo College' in two successive letters to the editor of the *Government Gazette*, years later, in June 1830.[10]

Perhaps these very letters and the general denial of Hare's place in the founding of Hindu College prompted some 565 'young native gentlemen' to present an address of welcome to Hare in February 1831, in which they pointedly noted that

> It has been the misfortune and reproach of many an age to permit its best benefactors to go to the grave without one token of its respect and gratitude for their endeavours... it is our desire to avoid it, and to let it be known that, however

your eminent services to this country may be overlooked by others, they are appreciated by those who have experienced their advantages...[11]

The aim of the newly formed Hindu College, as stated in its 'Rules', was to educate 'sons of respectable Hindoos'. Sons, not daughters—only Hindu sons; and only Hindu sons who were 'respectable' in lineage. Sons of the bhadralok class, in other words.

AS THIS STORY has already described, the nineteenth-century Bengali bhadralok was a social class by virtue of a shared economic status, lifestyle, and similar levels of education.[12] This might explain why two men so far apart in their religious outlook and mentality as Radhakanto Deb and Rammohun Roy could both enthusiastically support the idea of a college that would impart Western education.

Radhakanto Deb, scion of the Deb family of Sobhabazar, was 'in religion...a bigoted Hindu—a strong supporter of the many prejudices and superstitions of his country';[13] a member of the ultra-right Dharma Sabha, founded in 1830 to defend such Hindu social practices such as sati and, indeed, to protect perceived Hindu order against all that Rammohun Roy and the Brahmo Samaj represented.[14] Yet the same Radhakanto Deb became a director of Hindu College, created to educate sons of the bhadralok class along Western lines. He was also a leading light in the formation and management of the Calcutta School Book Society, founded in 1818 to facilitate the production of adequate textbooks for schools; and he took up the cause of female education.[15]

150 • Awakening

On the one hand Radhakanto and Rammohun epitomized the ideological split of the bhadralok into 'conservatives' and 'liberals'.[16] Yet there were bhadralok liberals whose actions would have gained the approval of bhadralok conservatives and vice versa. Nor could bhadralok liberals find fault with the bhadralok conservatives who controlled the management of Hindu College and forbade religious instruction of any kind in the college.[17] In all this, the bhadralok were indeed a motley crew.

THE EDUCATION OF the 'native' youths in Western literature and science. This was David Hare's proposal and it became the prime mandate of Hindu College. The introduction of what historians of modern India call 'Western education', or more specifically 'English education', began properly and in a concerted manner with these events of 1815–17.

By 1828 some four hundred students were receiving English education in Hindu College alone, and a thousand or so in other institutions; by 1835 there were some twenty-four schools imparting English education in Calcutta and many others in the smaller towns of Bengal. And, according to one report, by 1836 there were about six thousand students (all boys) studying English.[18]

In 1823, the General Committee for Public Instruction was established by the government to set up what came to be called the Sanskrit College. But the vision for this new college was in complete opposition to that of Hindu College. Here is Rammohun (never far from a fight) in 1823 writing to Lord Amherst, freshly arrived earlier that year as the new governor-general.

> When this Seminary of learning was proposed we understood that the Government in England, had ordered a considerable sum of money to be devoted to the instruction of its Indian subjects...

> ... We were filled with sanguine hopes that this sum would be laid out in employing European Gentlemen of talents and education, to instruct the Natives of India, in Mathematics, Natural Philosophy, Chemistry, Anatomy and other useful Sciences which the nations of Europe have carried to a degree of perfection, that have raised them above the inhabitants of the other parts of the world.[19]

Rammohun's 'sanguine hopes' were not ill-founded, for the Act of 1813 had indeed promised to allot money (Rs 100,000) not only for the 'revival and improvement of literature' but also 'the introduction and promotion of a knowledge of the sciences'.[20]

Yet ten years after the passing of the Act the government had reneged on that promise. Rammohun, the consummate scholar of Sanskrit, Persian, Arabic, and Hebrew, and the scriptures of at least two major world religions, harboured no illusion of what this new proposal to establish a Sanskrit institution in Calcutta promised: 'This Seminary...can only expect to load the minds of youth with grammatical niceties and metaphysical distinctions of little or no practical use, to the possessors or to Society...'[21]

He likened it to the institutions of medieval Europe when scholasticism reigned 'before the time of Lord Bacon', and gave a litany of examples of the kind of 'metaphysical speculation' and 'grammatical niceties' the proposed Sanskrit College would promote amongst its students. He pleaded that since the 'improvement of the native population' was the proper aim of the government it must promote 'a more liberal and enlightened system of education' involving the sciences and that the promotion of Sanskrit education would keep the country in 'darkness'.[22]

Rammohun's passionate eloquence was to no avail. The memorial (as the letter was called) evoked no response from the governor-general's office; it was simply passed on to the General Committee for Public Instruction with an accompanying letter bearing the laconic comment that '... defects and demerits of Sanscrit literature and philosophy are therein represented in an exaggerated light and...the argument in favour of encouraging native learning...have been wholly overlooked by the writer'.[23]

Nor did the General Committee see fit to reply. However, J.H. Harrington, president of that body, recorded in the latter's *Minutes and Proceedings* that Rammohun's letter

> ...bears the signature of one individual alone, whose opinions are well known to be hostile to those entertained by all his countrymen. The letter...does not therefore express the opinion of any portion of the natives of India, and its assertion to that effect is a dereliction of truth which cancels the claim of its author to respectful consideration.[24]

Rammohun's memorial, however, reveals the split regarding official British educational policy in India. This debate would come to be known as the 'Anglicist-Orientalist controversy'.

Rammohun's was the epitome of the Anglicist position which advocated Western learning, especially Western literature and science. The Orientalist position which, in 1823, was the position taken by the General Committee for Public Instruction was to introduce Western learning in a manner that would not offend conservative or orthodox Hindu sensibility; such learning must be coated with Sanskritic sugar. At the same time, it was to encourage indigenous knowledge systems.

We find the Orientalist argument in a memorandum dated August 1824, written by the General Committee for Public Instruction to the governor-general, in which it was argued: 'In proposing the improvement of men's mind [*sic*] it is first necessary to secure their convictions that such improvement is desirable.'[25] However, the memorandum continued, the experience of all those British who have communicated with the 'natives' 'both the learned and unlearned classes' was that in general they 'hold European literature in very slight estimation'.[26] Thus, as long as such prejudice against Western learning prevailed, any attempt to impress upon Indians the 'superiority of intellectual produce...of the West' would only foster discontent. The Committee admitted that the 'prejudices of natives against European interference' in their education had declined—this, after all, was seven years after the foundation of Hindu College—but it feared that native hostility could easily be 'roused by any abrupt and injudicious attempts at innovation'.[27] They must, therefore, be won over by more conciliatory means.

Rammohun would not live to see the resolution of the Anglicist–Orientalist controversy (which, strictly speaking, surfaced in its full glory in 1834–5) but he would have rejoiced had he lived.

For over a decade after his memorial to Amherst, the debate over the appropriate British educational policy continued. Amherst's tenure as governor-general ended in 1828. His successor was Lord William Bentinck, and it was near the end of *his* long tenure (1828–35) that the controversy was finally laid to rest. And no one was more influential in this resolution than Thomas Babington Macaulay. But we cannot speak of Macaulay without ushering James Mill into our story. In Macaulay (as we shall see) we find a profound, even violent, *contempt* for all things and persons (Indian) much like James Mill's. This contempt, incidentally (as the story will relate), plays its own strange role amongst Indians in the unfolding of the Bengal Renaissance.

Let us reverse the historical tape, and rewind it back to 1817, the year in which Hindu College was founded. James Mill's *History of British India* appeared in the same year.

JAMES MILL (1773–1836) WAS almost exactly Rammohun's contemporary. We might well speculate on how they would have reacted to each other had they met. They did have a common acquaintance, in the philosopher Jeremy Bentham. Bentham was a founding father of utilitarianism, the political/social/economic/moral doctrine which (in its simplest terms) proclaimed that the 'rightness' (or 'utility') of an action is in direct proportion to its promotion of happiness or pleasure and in inverse proportion to its production of unhappiness or pain.

Long before the *History of British India* was published (it was a project that occupied its author for a decade) Mill fell under the spell of Bentham's doctrine. He became not just a 'Benthamite' but Bentham's interpreter. 'Bentham gave Mill a doctrine, and Mill gave Bentham a school.'[28] Mill's *History* transformed utilitarianism into a 'militant faith'.[29]

Bentham, it turns out, happened to admire Rammohun's English writing style. In a letter to the Indian he praised Mill on his *History* but went on: 'though as to style I wish I could with truth and sincerity pronounce it equal to yours.'[30]

Mill's *History* would go into three editions in his own lifetime. A fourth edition appeared in 1840, edited by the eminent Orientalist and a leading spirit in the Asiatic Society, Horace Hayman Wilson (another acquaintance of Rammohun's who also, as it turned out, was in the 'Orientalist' camp in the Anglicist–Orientalist controversy).

The book became required reading for a generation of British officials and administrators in India; and we can well imagine how its opinions (and prejudices) must have shaped the minds of those who ruled India. The *History* would also secure Mill an important position in the East India Company's London headquarters. Mill never set foot on India but from his vantage point in the Company from 1818 to his death sixteen years later, he would cast another kind of influence on British policy in India.

What interests us here, though, is Mill's judgement of Indian culture and history.

Mill chose literature as his paradigm, since literature was a realm from which, he argued, 'the surest inferences' may be drawn about the state of a civilization.[31] And he considered, in particular, poetry. It was through poetry, he said, that men recorded their ideas, their histories, their religious precepts, their rules of law, before writing was invented. Through 'versification' the 'minds of rude men' were stimulated.[32] And even after the advent of writing, the 'habit of consigning' ideas to verse prevailed. Eventually, though, this 'habit' of versifying everything must stop. People must move on to the next stage in the advancement of a culture. This was where the Hindus failed, according to Mill; they never moved to the next stage. The habit of versification remained. All their literatures—history, law, scientific works, sacred books, even dictionaries—were in the form of verse.[33]

The *Ramayana* and the *Mahabharata* were, Mill conceded, two 'great poems'; yet their admirers wonder whether they are histories or epic poems. Indians regard them as 'books of religion', as 'books of law', even as 'books of philosophy'. Mill, referring to Charles Wilkins's translation of the *Bhagavada Gita*,[34] said it had been presented by the translator as if it were an example of Indian philosophy.[35] The withering tone is unmistakeable.

Mill was openly disdainful of the British Orientalists of the Asiatic Society. No Orientalist evoked his wrath more than William Jones. And no literary work evoked his disdain more than *Sakuntala*.[36] He conceded that the poem had some 'beautiful passages'. But this was damning with faint praise, for these passages were precisely the sort of 'ideas and affections' that may be found in a rude society.[37]

Mill took issue with Sir William Jones's paean to the civilization that produced a Kalidasa and a language of the sophistication of Sanskrit. He was especially affronted by

Jones's remark that Kalidasa lived in a time when—he quoted Jones—Britons were 'as unlettered and unpolished as the army of Hanumat'.[38]

Ultimately, for James Mill, a culture might well possess a rich dramatic tradition and yet have little to show in terms of progress in knowledge creation and knowledge acquisition. Such, he believed, was the case with India.

When it came to science—astronomy and mathematics, especially—Mill refused to believe that Indians of antiquity were at all *capable* of creating the knowledge the Orientalists had claimed for them. He suggested that it may have been 'derived' from other more 'advanced' nations.[39] Likewise, the ancient Hindus must have gained their mathematical knowledge from a culture more advanced and more inventive than their own:[40] from the Persians, perhaps, who learned from the 'Greeks of Constantinople'.[41]

THIS BRINGS US back to Thomas Babington Macaulay, later Lord Macaulay (1800–59): historian, parliamentarian, poet, and essayist. Born in 1800, he was a mere seventeen-year-old when Mill's *History of British India* was first published. In 1833 he called the *History* 'on the whole the greatest historical work which has appeared in our language since that of Gibbon'.[42] Mill, in turn, recommended to the directors of the East India Company that Macaulay be appointed as legal member of the governor-general's supreme council in India.[43] It was in this capacity that Macaulay arrived in Calcutta in 1834.

His tenure in India was brief: from 1834 to 1838. And it was an uncomfortable sojourn to say the least. Macaulay detested Indian food, disliked the Indian people, and, above all, hated the Indian climate. He was homesick for England.[44] But he stayed long enough to cut, almost single-handedly, the Gordian knot that had entangled the 'Anglicists' and 'Orientalists' in their controversy.

In England, Macaulay's reputation would rest on his historical writings and parliamentary speeches but in India it was his 'Minute on Education', dated February 2, 1835, that placed him permanently in the annals of modern Indian history. The 'Minute' was not his only writing on India but it was arguably the work for which he is best known amongst Indians—and for which he is most reviled. It was written in extravagant but memorable prose and laid to rest the Anglicist–Orientalist controversy once and for all, laying the foundation on which the revolution, the awakening that was the Bengal Renaissance, would evolve to its fullest form.

The language, contents, and tone of the 'Minute' sound offensive today. Yet what Macaulay said in the 'Minute'—once we have waded through, and shrugged off, its purple prose—was remarkably in harmony with what Rammohun Roy wrote in his memorial to Lord Amherst in 1823.[45] If Macaulay is deemed 'Anglicist' (as he undoubtedly was) then so was Rammohun. And so were David Hare in 1817 and all those who founded Hindu College.

Macaulay began where Rammohun had begun: in the Act of 1813 and the promise of the government to allocate an annual sum of money for the education of the Indians: 'We now come to the gist of the matter. We had a fund to be employed as Government shall direct for the intellectual improvement of the people of this country. The simple question is, what is the most useful way of employing it?'[46]

It cannot be in any of the vernaculars, for they had no capacity, Macaulay insisted, to transmit 'literary or scientific information'; indeed, they were 'so poor and rude' that unless they were 'enriched' by some means one could not translate into them 'any valuable work'. In other words, the vernacular languages—Bengali, Hindi, Urdu, Marathi, Punjabi, and so on—did not have it in them the necessary vocabulary to cope with Western literature and ideas. As for Arabic and Sanskrit, Macaulay admitted he knew neither; but he had read translations of Arabic and Sanskrit works, he had conversed with those adept in 'Eastern tongues', and he had 'never found one among them who would deny that a single shelf of a good European library was worth the whole native literature of India and Arabia'.[47]

Like Mill, he pointed to poetry since the common view was that in the realm of literature 'Eastern writers stand highest in poetry'. Mill, at least, seemed to have read *Sakuntala*. Macaulay was content to learn *about* Indian poetry from others: 'I certainly never met with any Orientalist who ventured to maintain that the Arabic and Sanscrit poetry could be compared to that of the greatest European nations.'[48] (We wonder, had he lived to read Goethe on *Sakuntala*, what he would have made of the German poet's quatrain?)[49]

The situation was this, Macaulay said. A people need to be educated, but not in their mother tongue if that was not up to it. A foreign tongue was needed. The choice was obvious: it had to be English which 'stands preeminent even among the languages of the west'. There was also the practical advantage that it was the language of the 'ruling class', the tongue known to the 'higher classes of natives', and likely to be the 'language of commerce' in Asia.[50]

The alternative, for Macaulay, was laughable. It was to teach in languages in which there were not only no books on any subject that 'deserve to be compared to our own' but also—and here followed a diatribe that Mill would have delighted in—to teach

> ...medical doctrines which would disgrace an English farrier,—Astronomy, which would move laughter in girls at an English boarding school,—History, abounding with kings, thirty feet high, and reigns thirty thousand years long,—and Geography made up of seas of treacle and seas of butter.[51]

Macaulay pointed out that the 'natives' themselves wished to be taught in English; that they did not wish to be taught in Sanskrit or Arabic. But he also agreed with the Orientalist faction, whose opinions he otherwise opposed, that it would be impossible to educate 'the body of the people'. Rather, a new class had to be created who would serve as intermediaries and interpreters between the rulers and the 'millions whom we govern'. This new class would be, he said in the most infamous passage in the 'Minute': '...a class of persons, Indian in blood and colour, but English in taste, in opinions, in morals, and in intellect.'[52] It would be this class's task to refine the vernacular languages, introduce new terms of science taken from Western vocabulary, and eventually make these tongues 'fit vehicles' for carrying the knowledge of the West to the 'great mass of the population.'[53]

This new class was already in place in Bengal: they were the bhadralok.

Matters moved swiftly thereafter. Lord William Bentinck resolved that the government would promote Western science and literature in India; that funds for higher education would be deployed for such purposes alone.[54] The Orientalist faction protested. In 1836, Bentinck's successor Lord Auckland, newly arrived, tempered his predecessor's rather extreme resolution and restored some amount of Indian learning.[55] But the Anglicists were the undoubted victors.

INDIAN IN BLOOD and colour, bhadralok in class, but English in taste and in opinions. Perhaps Macaulay did not know this (or perhaps he did), but there were already, even before his time, some young men in Calcutta who answered to these traits. And they had caused, and continued to cause, great consternation amongst the bhadralok who had so enthusiastically sent their sons to Hindu College. The bhadralok orthodoxy wanted to have their cake and eat it too: they desired their Hindu sons to imbibe Western ways in the classroom but not to bring those ways into their baithak khana, their living room. What they did not understand was that the Pandora's box once opened could not be shut. They could not have imagined that when Hindu College opened its doors in 1817 it also paved the way for the onset of a paradigm shift: the displacement of one intellectual tradition by another, one collective identity by another—the kind of paradigm shift that becomes the agent of intellectual revolutions.[56]

And these 'respectable Hindu gentlemen' of Calcutta certainly could not have anticipated the tempestuous arrival in their midst of a young man by the name of Henry Louis Vivian Derozio.

Notes

1. See Chapter four. Also Collet [1900] 1980, p. 76.
2. Mittra 1877, p. xii. 'Mittra' is the spelling of the author's name on the title page of the book. The usual spelling is 'Mitra'.
3. Mittra 1877, p. xii.
4. Ibid., p. vii.
5. Ibid., pp. xii–xiii.
6. Ibid., Appendix A ('Rules of the Hindu College').
7. Ibid., p. xii.
8. Quoted in Biswas and Ganguli 1988j, p. 103.
9. Mittra 1877, p. 6.
10. Biswas and Ganguli 1988j, pp. 108–9.
11. Mittra 1877, p. xv.
12. See Chapter two.
13. Lethbridge 1907, p. 162.
14. Sinha 1978, p. 93.
15. Lethbridge 1907, p. 162.
16. Mukherjee 1970.
17. Ibid., pp. 67–8.
18. Majumdar 1960, pp. 128–9.
19. Ibid.
20. Quoted in Biswas 1992, p. 206.
21. Ibid., p. 192.
22. Ibid.
23. Quoted in Biswas 1992, pp. 198–9.
24. Ibid., pp. 200–1.
25. Ibid., pp. 202–4.
26. Ibid.
27. Ibid.

28. Halevy [1928] 1955.
29. Majeed 1992, p. 123.
30. Quoted in Home 1933b, p. 37. Reprinted in S.C. Chakravarty 1935.
31. Mill [1817] 1975, p. 190.
32. Ibid., pp. 190–1.
33. Ibid., p. 191.
34. See Chapter one.
35. Mill [1817] 1975, p. 192.
36. See Chapter one, for more on *Sakuntala*.
37. Mill [1817] 1975, p. 197.
38. Quoted in Kopf 1969, pp. 115-6.
39. Mill [1817] 1975, p. 217.
40. Ibid., pp. 218–9.
41. Ibid., p. 219.
42. Quoted in Clive, 1975, p. viii.
43. Majeed 1992, p. 192.
44. Dasgupta 2004, p. 84.
45. This point is made in Dasgupta 1995a, pp. 156–7.
46. Macaulay 1835.
47. Ibid.
48. Ibid.
49. See Chapter one.
50. Macaulay 1835.
51. Ibid.
52. Ibid.
53. Ibid.
54. Majumdar 1965, p. 47.
55. Ibid., p. 48.
56. Kuhn 1970.

Six

Enfant Terrible

'WHOM THE GODS love die young,' said the Greek dramatist Menander. What is certain is that Henry Derozio (1809–31) was adored by his pupils and abhorred by their parents. The young poet and his disciples came to be called Young Bengal, intellectual, social, cultural trouble makers. Les enfants terrible. And the most 'terrible' of these infants was Derozio himself.

Derozio has been described as an Eurasian, a rather nineteenth-century term for one of 'mixed European and Asiatic parentage',[1] or even, more particularly, as an offspring of a native mother by a European father.[2] His grandfather was described in a local directory of his time as a 'Portuguese Merchant and Agent in Calcutta';[3] his father Francis married twice, both his wives being English. Henry's mother Sophia, who died in 1815, was Francis's first wife.[4] Derozio no doubt had Indian blood for the only portrait known of him, a lithograph miniature, suggests a darker-than-European complexion—'as dark as that of the darkest native', in the words of his biographer.[5] We must assume then that Derozio's Indian blood either came from his grandmother's side or that his grandfather had Indian ancestry tucked away somewhere.[6]

Enfant Terrible • 165

At any rate, Derozio was born into prosperous circumstances. The family abode was a substantial one. The Derozio family home was situated on what was then called Circular Road in the Grey Zone, at a location that seems appropriate for both his ethnicity and the kind of person Derozio would become, where the White Town and the Black Town came together.[7]

There was an interesting link between the Derozio family and some of the characters already encountered in this story, a link established even before Derozio's birth: his grandfather Michael was closely associated with the Serampore trio, Ward, Marshman, and Carey.[8] Michael, a Protestant, an apostate (so to speak) amidst the overwhelmingly Catholic Portuguese, may have converted under the Serampore Baptists' influence.[9]

The man most influential in Derozio's childhood was a Scot, the second Scot to have a part in this story: David Drummond, in whose school, Dhurromtollah Academy, located not too far from Circular Road in what is now called Dharmatala, Derozio studied from age six to fourteen. Born circa 1785,[10] Drummond was some ten years younger than his compatriot David Hare. Like Hare, perhaps more than him, he was a legatee of the Scottish Enlightenment for, as Thomas Edwards tells us, the 'orthodox inhabitants of Calcutta' looked askance at him as being 'if not an open disciple of David Hume', still a 'very doubtful person'.[11]

Drummond left Scotland in his late twenties, probably because of 'theological differences' with his family.[12] He arrived in Calcutta in 1813. Like David Hare, he never returned to his native land; like Hare he too would be buried in a Calcutta cemetery (in 1843).

In Calcutta he taught for a few years in the school of which he ultimately became the proprietor. Dhurromtollah Academy was designed to educate both English children whose parents could not afford (or perhaps did not wish) to ship them off to boarding schools in England, as well as Eurasians and Indians. It was a school that was apparently free of class and race consciousness—where 'European, Eurasian and native lads conned the same lessons, and mingled together in the same school sports'.[13]

Drummond personified the rationalist, sceptical spirit of the Scottish Enlightenment. Take his attack on phrenology which Derozio's biographer describes at length. Phrenology, founded by the Viennese anatomists Franz Joseph Gall and Johann Kasper Spurzheim, was the doctrine that each particular quality of an individual's mind such as pride, courage, kindness, poetic sense, intelligence, memory was located in its own distinct 'organ' in the brain; thus, an examination of the skull (the 'bumps') would help one understand the individual's personality and their strengths or weaknesses.[14] Phrenology as a scientific doctrine would eventually be discredited by the neurological community, but in early nineteenth-century Europe it was much in vogue. A 'Phrenological Society' was established in Calcutta in 1825 by some British enthusiasts, and Drummond attended its meetings for two years as a 'silent listener' before publishing a two-hundred-page book *Objections to Phrenology* where he called the science a gross deception. The title page bore the uncompromising epigram: 'He, who will not reason, is a bigot; he who cannot, is a fool; and he who dares not, is a slave.'[15]

Drummond argued that phrenology's notion of physically separate organs corresponding to distinct mental traits went against a person's subjective sense of unity and selfhood.

> If the human mind consists of thirty five organs, each of which is unconnected with, ask no advice from, and is ignorant of the 'sayings and doings' of its neighbours as if they were all inhabitants of different skulls, how has the foolish pronoun I so cunningly, and yet so unnecessarily obtruded itself into every human language since the thirty five different organs are exactly so many…different beings…[16]

HE CHALLENGED THE phrenologists to 'reconcile the possibility of his own personal identity' with their 'hypothesis' of this 'thirty five existences, each independently possessing the faculties of perception, volition and memory'.[17]

Interestingly, this same question, though in more sophisticated form, of how the various mental facilities distributed across the brain join in endowing a person with a sense of self or identity continues to plague modern-day cognitive and brain scientists and philosophers.[18]

Drummond disdained tradition and authority and believed only that which was founded on reason and evidence.[19] And though he was no atheist—the city's orthodox could never accuse him of 'open atheism'[20]—his scepticism apparently shaped his religious outlook.[21]

This, then, was the manner of man in whose school Henry Derozio studied for eight years; where he imbibed his mentor's critical, sceptical, independent mode of thinking. There were other good 'English medium' schools in Calcutta, including

Sherbourne School where Rammohun's friend and fellow Brahmo Samajist Dwarakanath Tagore studied.[22] But it was, Thomas Edwards writes, Dhurromtollah Academy where parents sent their sons if they believed that the 'true aim of education' was to inculcate amongst students 'thought and the power of thinking'.[23]

DEROZIO'S GREAT PLEASURES as a student, besides cricket and amateur theatricals—both of which he enjoyed with his 'boy-companions' in the school—were the 'literature and thought of England'.[24] Literature and the power of ideas would become the twin pillars of his tempestuous, creative, critical, radicalizing, and appallingly brief life. All these adjectives seem necessary when speaking of Derozio. His was a creative life in the very literal sense for he was a poet; his was a critical life for it would be the great ideas of the times as they were emerging in the West that he would proselytize in the classrooms of Hindu College, in his prose, and in the discussion society he would found; his was a radicalizing life for he was the begetter of a spirit that went exuberantly and excessively against the grain of Bengali bhadralok society: those who embraced this spirit would come to be called 'Derozians' or 'Young Bengal'.[25] And because of all this he raised a tempest that would agitate both his own life and the Bengali society in which he lived and worked.

LEAVING SCHOOL AT fourteen Derozio found work for a while in the firm his father had been long employed in, chafed at the drudgery of the clerical life, left two years later, and found a more congenial milieu in his uncle's indigo plantation in

Bhaugulpore (Bhagalpur). It was a countryside along the Ganga whose sights and sounds appealed to him, and it was from this time that Derozio's literary career took proper shape. (Even while at school, not yet thirteen, his first published poem had appeared in the *India Gazette* in 1822.)[26]

From Bhaugulpore, under the nom de plume of 'Juvenis', Derozio's poems began to appear regularly in the pages of the *India Gazette*.[27] It was at Bhaugulpore that he witnessed a sight on the river, a location called Jungheera, that later inspired him to write his longest poem, *The Fakir of Jungheera*. And it was at Bhaugulpore where, Thomas Edwards discreetly and tantalizingly briefly, informs us, 'Derozio realized what it is to love and be loved':[28] 'Here he saw that light which never shone on land or sea and which only beams from the eyes of those whose lives are entwined in the bonds which love alone can weave.'[29]

Edwards confessed that

> ... what the circumstances were which parted their lives will probably never now be known; but it is very evident that this episode, in his life made a lasting impression on him, and he steadily refused to marry, though frequently solicited to do so by his mother and sister.[30]

A slightly melodramatic statement: it was not as if Derozio lived to an old age in memoriam to a lost or unrequited love; after all, he died at twenty-two! Indeed, there seems to be no evidence of any romantic episode in Derozio's brief life.[31]

Derozio's two volumes of poetry, *Poems* (1827) and *Fakeer of Jungharee, A Metrical Tale, and Other Poems* (1828) established his reputation as a poet and, at least in Bengal, he 'immediately found himself famous'.[32] Fame, of course, is a very relative term. To achieve literary fame as a poet in the English language far away from the centre of English literary activity, fame that might find its way to that very centre, was no easy task.

In Derozio's case, his literary fame was in essence local. What is noteworthy, though, is that it caught the attention of the Scottish poet Thomas Campbell who published a short review in a periodical called the *New Monthly Magazine* in March 1828: '...it is not in the nature of things that [the 'Colonies of Great Britain']...should add much to her literary stores in the way of direct contribution', the review began. But the 'little volume of poems before us' was an exception, and not only because 'it comes from a British settlement', but 'by the further circumstance that the author is a youth of eighteen, born and educated in India'. The author's 'cleverness', Campbell went on to say, was such that the book deserved serious and 'favourable' consideration. The language was 'elevated and poetical'; thoughts were expressed with 'grace, elegance and spirit'; the verses were 'flowing' and 'polished'.[33] (Notwithstanding Campbell's favourable notice, Derozio's reputation in the West as a poet in the English language evidently did not make much headway over the long term. The *Cambridge Guide to Literature in English* [1988], which includes English writing from India, could not find a place for Derozio.)[34]

At any rate it was time to abandon his life as an indigo planter and assume the role his past years had consciously and unconsciously prepared him for. In 1828 Derozio returned to Calcutta and joined Hindu College as a teacher of English literature and history, and coupled his teaching with writing: some essays but mostly poetry. He became a poet, philosopher, and free thinker. A lithograph miniature of him, done perhaps at about this age, shows something of a foppish young man, his hair parted down the middle, and dressed elegantly in a high-collared coat and a cravat swathed high round his neck.[35] His biographer tells us that he was 'rather below' middle height.[36]

POETRY—SACRED OR secular, recited, performed or sung—had been the métier of Indian imaginative literature through history. (Even James Mill sourly acknowledged this before embarking on his diatribe against Indian culture in *The History of British India*.)[37] It was not that literary prose did not exist before. But, till the nineteenth century, the quality and quantity of prose literature in India compared unfavourably with those of poetry;[38] this, incidentally, was as true for women writers as for men.[39]

As we have already seen, Bengali literary history was no different from the larger Indian scene: poetry dominated till the emergence of prose in the early years of the nineteenth century.[40] What then was the significance, if any, of Henry Derozio as poet in this vast, rich Indian literary landscape?

The answer is that Derozio was a pioneer of what is now called 'Indian literature in English', where 'literature' embraces poetry, drama, fiction, essays, and autobiography.[41] It might be wrong to say that he founded a new literary *tradition*—for a tradition implies a sense of continuity,[42] and in the remainder of the nineteenth century only a few Indian poets and writers are known to have written anything significant in English. (Amongst them, most notably in this story, as we will see, were Madhusudan Datta, Toru Dutt and others of her family, and Bankimchandra Chattopadhyay.)[43] The tradition of Indian literature in English would properly take shape in the twentieth century.

Thus, it would be incorrect to claim that Derozio's poetry shaped in any significant way the Indian poetry in English that came later. Still, at least one of Derozio's students, Kashiprasad Ghosh, 'the first Bengali poet to write in English', *was* apparently stimulated by Derozio's poetry:[44] his *Shair and Other Poems* (1830) was published in Calcutta in Derozio's lifetime.[45] Most strikingly, the eighteen-year-old Toru Dutt would publish a critical essay on Derozio in 1874[46]—one of her first publications.[47] Derozio's poems in English, on Indian themes along European lines, must have struck a chord in the future poet-writer in English and French.[48]

Thus, Derozio was a somewhat lonely *pioneer* of Indian writing in English. He planted a literary seed where no such seed existed. If the Bengal Renaissance was marked by the awakening of the Indian mind to new intellectual, creative, social, and political possibilities, Derozio's poetry was the harbinger of such an awakening in the Indian literary scene—firmly recognized by later historians of Indian literature.[49]

For his *was* an *Indian* literature. Derozio, though born and bred in Bengal, did not know the Bengali language. But he was a native of India and he had never stepped out of Bengal; thus it was as an Indian that he wrote his poetry, often describing Indian scenes and people in his writings. Speaking of himself in the third person, he said simply, in a preface to his *Poems*: 'Born and educated in India, and at the age of eighteen, he ventures to present himself as a candidate for poetic fame.'[50] Elsewhere, in one of his essays, he again boldly announced his Indianness: 'I was born in India and have been bred here; I am proud to acknowledge my country, and to do my best in her service…'[51]

Most of all, though, Derozio let his poetry do the talking, and so we turn to two of his most well-known poems to get a sense of both his own Indianness and the Indian content of his poetry. Thus, *Poems* begins with a sonnet, 'The Harp of India,' a lament for a civilization that was no more. He imagined India as a harp:

> The music once was sweet—who hears it now?
> …
> Neglected, mute, and desolate art thou,
> Like ruined monument on desert plain!
> O! many a hand more worthy far than mine
> Once thy harmonious chords to sweetness gave,

Derozio also prefaced his second volume, *The Fakeer of Jungeera, A Metrical Tale and Other Poems*, with a similar poem that, initially untitled, would come to be named by a much later compiler of Derozio's poems as 'To India–My Native Land':[52]

> My country! In thy day of glory past
> A beauteous halo circled round thy brow,
> And worshipped as a deity thou wast—
> Where is that glory, where that reverence now?

Once more, the poet was painfully and acutely aware of the 'glory past' that was no more. Indeed, more than loss of glory, there was humiliation:

And groveling in the lowly dust art thou:
Thy minstrel hath no wreath to weave for thee
Save the sad story of thy misery!

Perhaps *he* could be the new minstrel:

Well—let me dive into the depths of time,
And bring out the ages that have rolled
A few small fragments of those wrecks sublime,
Which humble eye may never more behold;
My fallen country! One kind wish for thee!

WHAT DEROZIO BROUGHT to Indian poetry was something relatively new to the Indian literary tradition: a cross-cultural mentality. ('Relatively new', for we have already seen this mentality in the writings of Rammohun Roy).[53]

More particularly, it was an Indo-Western mind. Derozio was rooted in Indian culture and history, addressing Indian issues and themes, yet drew upon ideas and style strongly influenced by the Western intellectual tradition. His patriotic poems were about India, but their lush, emotional style and the idea of tyranny and freedom that we find in them came from the Romantic poets such as Shelley and Byron; similarly his long picaresque poem, *Don Juanics* (1825–6) was modelled after Byron's *Don Juan* but was set in Calcutta.[54] The Indo-Western mind *conciliates* between what it values in its Indian sources and what it wishes to absorb from its Western sources. It is an act of creation in its own right—a form of self-invention. And as such it represents the highest and most distinctive level of the awakening we call the Bengal Renaissance.

For Derozio the world was Calcutta. But then, in his time, Calcutta was after all the 'second city of the British Empire', where books and ideas (even on phrenology!) poured in from the world beyond the 'black water', the city where even in the early 1790s one admiring English observer would exclaim that if the number of publications was an index of a city's 'learning and refinement', then Calcutta outranked Vienna, Copenhagen, St Petersberg, Madrid, Venice, Turin, Naples, even Rome.[55]

By the time Derozio left school, printing presses had proliferated across the city, owned and operated by both Europeans and Indians, busily producing not only books in English and the vernaculars but also newspapers and periodicals.[56] It was the literature and philosophy not only of Britain but of Continental Europe that Derozio would have imbibed in his preparatory years in David Drummond's school. From Scotland came David Hume; there were also the poets, Robert Burns and Thomas Campbell; from England the Romantic poets, all of whom were still living in his time, though some would die about the time Derozio left school: Keats, Wordsworth and, of course Byron and Shelley. From Ireland there was the poet Thomas Moore. From England, via the Continent, via America there was Thomas Paine.

Regardless of their literary merits or their place in Indian literary history, Derozio's poems interest us for what they reveal of his ideas and ideals, for he would transmit these to his Hindu College students and profoundly shape their minds. The ideas that fuelled the American and French Revolutions, and, more generally, the Romantic poets' passion for liberty and protest against oppression and injustice, the rights of human beings, anti-slavery, and women's rights were the intellectual ingredients that found their way into Derozio's poems.[57]

DEROZIO'S REPUTATION AS an enfant terrible rested not on his poetry but on his role as a teacher in Hindu College and the ideas he passed on to his students. In 1828, age eighteen, he was appointed a master of English literature and history[58]—an appointment which the bhadralok guardians of the students of Hindu College would rapidly rue.

In 1828, the year of his appointment, Hindu College was just over a decade old. Originally, it was divided into junior or school (pathsala) and senior or college (mahapathsala) sections. The former gave instructions in English, Bengali, grammar, and arithmetic; the latter taught languages, history, geography, 'chronology', astronomy, mathematics, chemistry, and other sciences.[59] The senior section was known by various names including 'Anglo-Indian College', perhaps because it taught courses in English, Bengali, and Persian.[60]

Within the first three months of its opening, Hindu College had almost seventy students. Over the decade, till Derozio's time, it would suffer considerable financial difficulties to the point of having to apply to the government for aid. By 1824 the college was financially and administratively under joint, private, and public control with the Orientalist Horace Hayward Wilson, representing the government, appointed to the college's managing committee as 'visitor'.[61]

An important milestone in the early life of Hindu College was its move, in 1826, from a location in Bowbazar, in the heart of the Black Town, to a new building nearby, in College Square, which it would share with Sanskrit College.[62] The latter was housed in the central block and the two sections of Hindu College were located in the two wings. An 1825 painting of the building housing Sanskrit and Hindu Colleges gives an impression of space and elegance: an environment fit to educate the sons of the bhadralok elite.[63]

Academically, the college flourished in those early years with student enrolment increasing annually and with expansion of the curriculum. Even a 'drawing class' was added in 1827, and classes in law and political economy were introduced in 1831.

Derozio's mind and personality dominated the 'spirit of the age' of Hindu College in its early life—a fact all the more remarkable since his career in the college spanned only three years.

The same year Derozio was appointed, a boy by the name of Ramtanu Lahiri, born 1813, four years younger than Derozio, was admitted to the College, and became one of his pupils. Ramtanu was just one of several young men, scarcely younger than Derozio, who became for all intents and purposes, disciples of Derozio—the 'Derozians'—though of them all, Ramtanu was not the enfant terrible some of the others would become. Soon after his education was completed, in 1833, Ramtanu joined the teaching staff of the College, and then of the newly formed Krishnagar College; he became in his time a distinguished educationist and supporter of women's causes[64]— this, despite Peary Chand Mittra's rather odd remark that Ramtanu was known more as a '*moral* than an *intellectual* man'.[65]

Peary Chand Mittra (whom we have already encountered as David Hare's biographer),[66] was himself another Derozian. A year younger than Ramtanu, he would later become a librarian, businessman, and literary man-at-large, but most famously, under the nom de plume of Tekchand Thakur, the author of *Alaler Gharer Dulal* (The Spoilt Pet of a Rich Family, 1858), regarded generally as the first novel in Bengali. This was also a work which pioneered the use of the colloquial language (chalit bhasha) in Bengali prose.[67]

There was Krishna Mohun Banerji, Ramtanu's exact contemporary. He too belonged to Derozio's first batch of students. He converted to Christianity in 1832 (thus invoking the wrath of his countrymen)[68] and became the Rev. K.M. Banerji, a pastor, teacher, journalist, polyglot, man of learning, and prolific author of academic works in English and Bengali on philosophy, education, and other related topics.[69] In later life he was appointed a professor in Bishop's College, an Anglican seminary (where Michael Madhusudan Datta would study for a while),[70] awarded the title of doctor of laws by the future University of Calcutta, and served as a commissioner of Calcutta Corporation.[71] An enfant terrible in youth, openly ridiculing Hindu prejudices, raising the ire of the Hindu orthodoxy by 'eating and drinking what was abomination to them',[72] cast out from his own home, ejected by a friend's father (the friend having given him shelter) who would have nothing to do with him and, thus, homeless for a while,[73] Krishna Mohun would die, in 1885, a much respected man.

Another Derozian was Ram Gopal Ghosh who, like the reverend, went against the Hindu religion—though without converting—and later distinguished himself in business, social reform, politics, and oratory. Indeed, such was his oratorical prowess that a leading periodical of the day called him the 'Indian Demosthenes'.[74] Whether it was Derozio's unwitting influence or not, we cannot say, but Ram Gopal's

Indo-Western mind took an unusual turn: he was at once a committed patriot *and* a committed Anglophile.[75] Yet another of Derozio's students was Rasik Krishna Mullick, who opposed idolatry and Hinduism, and became a deputy collector in the vast bureaucracy of the Raj.

A Derozian who stood out from the others was Peary Chand Mittra's close friend Radhanath Sikdar. Radhanath was an enthusiastic and avowed partaker of beef—his 'hobby was beef'[76]—for he believed that Indians would only improve physically and mentally if they became beef eaters.[77] Along with Peary Chand Mittra he established a monthly Bengali magazine which ran for three years.[78] But these are not his main claims to being remembered. He stood out from his fellow Derozians because he forged a very distinctive and distinguished life in science. In Hindu College, Radhanath learnt his science as a student of Robert Tytler—the same Robert Tytler, Christian Trinitarian, who had waged a battle in words with Rammohun over Christianity and the divinity of Christ.[79] Tytler introduced Radhanath (and others) to Isaac Newton's *Principia*[80] and, indeed, in Hindu College Radhanath was considered 'the best mathematician in the group of Derozio's friends'.[81] Later, as an applied mathematician in the grandiosely named Great Trigonometrical Survey of India, Radhanath would contribute seriously to geodesy, the science of measuring the earth's three-dimensional surface and projecting it onto the plane of two-dimensional maps.[82] He stands out because he was almost certainly the first Indian in modern science to rise above the ranks of the anonymous.[83]

These were just some of the youths whom Derozio taught, who 'constantly sought' his company[84] both in and outside the classroom, during 'tiffin time',[85] and beyond the time spent within the Hindu College precincts. His spell on his pupils seemed total: they visited him in his house and so his home became an extension of the classroom.[86] Peary Chand Mittra tells us of his 'affable manners'.[87] He dared them to speak out and freely, to think for themselves; to not be swayed by 'idols', intellectual or otherwise; 'to live and die for truth'.[88] He encouraged them to read books that went beyond the curriculum. 'These books were chiefly political, metaphysical, and religious.'[89] The official curriculum (an 'Anglicist' curriculum) entrusted to him by the college's management committee (which included David Hare and Horace Hayward Wilson) had 'Goldsmith's History of Greece, Rome and England, Russell's Modern Europe, Robertson's Charles the Fifth, Gay's Fables, Pope's Homer's Iliad and Odyssey, Dryden's Virgil, Milton's Paradise Lost, Shakespeare, one of the Tragedies'.[90]

Unknown to the authorities, Derozio's own readings and intellectual taste became those of his students:[91] Kant, Voltaire, Hume, and Thomas Paine,[92] the Romantic poets of England and Scotland; Thomas Moore from Ireland; 'in fact the whole fraternity of the most subtle and philosophical of the modern free-thinkers', as the *Calcutta Courier* would report almost a decade after his death.[93] And especially, Shelley. A writer in the *Calcutta Literary Gazette*, reminiscing in 1834 about Hindu College and Derozio, remembered the latter's 'partiality' for Shelley and his tendency to pour the English poet's 'sentiments' into his pupils' minds.[94]

Derozio founded a discussion group, the 'Academic Association' which met on evenings at a private house, and these meetings were attended not only by his students but also others, including David Hare.[95] Indeed, after Derozio's death, the group remained active under Hare's leadership.[96] At the meetings of the Academic Association, the 'lads' of Hindu College read papers to one another, argued, and debated, mainly poetry and philosophy. Ethical, moral, and social questions were discussed.[97] Rebelliousness, another Shelleyan characteristic, found its way, through Derozio, to his students.

The prime target of the Derozians was Hindu orthodoxy: to question, debate, attack, and reject the rites of Hinduism. It was in this realm that some of Derozio's disciples became themselves enfants terrible, and they included, in particular, Krishna Mohun Banerji, Rasik Krishna Mullick, and Ram Gopal Ghosh. As Peary Chand Mittra remembered, the 'uppermost thought' in the minds of these youths was to 'expose' and 'renounce' Hinduism.[98] 'Down with Hinduism! Down with orthodoxy! Was the rallying cry everywhere.'[99] ' "Down with idolatry, down with superstition," became the general cry of young Bengalis.'[100]

A clerk of Hindu College of the time, one Hara Mohan Chatterjee, would recollect: 'The principles and practices of Hindu religion were openly ridiculed and condemned and angry disputes were held on moral subjects... the Hindu religion was denounced as vile and corrupt, and unworthy[sic] the regard of rational beings.'[101] Peary Chand Mittra, a participant in these events, recalled: 'The junior students caught from the senior students the infection of ridiculing the Hindu religion, and where they were required to utter *mantras* as prayers, they repeated lines from the Iliad [sic]. There were some who flung the Brahminical thread instead of putting it on.'[102]

For these youths there was no better way to taunt the Hindu conservatives, to flaunt their own unorthodoxy, than by violating taboos. Thus there were those like Radhanath Sikdar who ate beef; and those who imbibed wine. Inevitably there were excesses; most of these young men were after all adolescents. On one occasion several of the enfants terrible met in Krishna Mohun's house, ate bread bought from a Muslim bakery and roast beef from a butcher, and threw the remains into the courtyard of a neighbouring house, shouting 'this is beef, nothing but beef'. As it happened, Krishna Mohun was not among the culprits but because the incident originated from his house he was expelled from the parental home by his grandfather who was threatened with excommunication from Hindu society by outraged neighbours.[103]

There are other stories of conflicts between the Derozians and their elders. Summoned as a witness in the law courts, and required by custom to swear on a copper vessel containing tulsi leaves dipped in holy water ('ganga jal'), Rasim Krishna Mullick, repulsed by any sort of idolatry, declared that as he was not a Hindu he would not take the oath. The Hindus present 'hissed in scorn'.[104] The Derozian youths refused to accept the Brahminical thread ('paita').[105] And instead of chanting mantras to their Hindu gods they would orate passages from the *Iliad*.[106]

Some parents, in desperation, were no less given to extremes than their offspring. Rasik Krishna's mother, in an attempt to prevent him from joining a social and religious reform group, and believing him to be 'possessed' by some evil spirit, fed him a powder to drive away the spirit; the powder proved to be a poison. Rasik Krishna fell unconscious and, in this state, he was put on a boat to take him to Benares. Fortunately he regained consciousness and managed to escape. Needless to say, he did not return to his parental home.[107]

Yet, by all accounts the integrity of these reckless young men was admired by many outside Hindu College: 'they were all considered men of truth,' so much so that being a 'Hindu College boy' was regarded by some as identical to being 'incapable of falsehood.'[108]

They looked after one another, these Derozians, both in their youth and afterwards. When Krishna Mohun Banerji was ejected from his home his friend Dakhinaranjan Mukherji gave him shelter (till *his* father forced the guest to leave, as alluded to earlier); when another (much older) Derozian, Tarachand Chakravarti, was in financial difficulties, Dakhinaranjan made him an anonymous gift of a thousand rupees, to Tarachand's mystification.[109] When Ramtanu Lahiri was in need of money, Ramgopal Ghosh secured him a job as a munshi to a local merchant.[110] When Rasik Krishna Mullick fell seriously ill Ramgopal made 'lavish arrangements for his treatment and comfort'.[111]

If the Hindu religion and its practices were objects of the Derozians' wrath, the status of women, women's rights, and women's education were yet other issues that attracted their passionate attention. Hara Mohan Chatterjee, again: 'The degradation of the female mind was viewed with indignation. The resolution, at a very large meeting, was carried unanimously that Hindu women should be taught...'[112]

Derozio expressed his own tender regard for his disciples in verse, his 'Sonnet to My Pupils' (1829):

> Expanding, like the petals of young flowers,
> I watch the opening of your infant minds,
> And the sweet loosening of the spell that binds
> Your intellectual energies and powers,
> That stretch like young birds in soft summer hours,
> Their wings to try their strength. O! how the winds
> Of circumstance and gentle April showers
> Of early knowledge, and unnumbered kinds
> Of new perceptions shed their influence;
> And how you worship truth's omnipotence!
> What gladness rains upon me, when I see
> Fame, in the mirror of Futurity,
> Weaving the chaplets you are doomed to gain—
> And then I feel I have not lived in vain.[113]

INEVITABLY, THE 'WINDS of circumstance' would blow against the man who was causing all this furore in bhadralok Calcutta. 'The convulsions caused by Derozio was great,' as Peary Chand Mittra would recall. 'It pervaded the house of almost every advanced student.'[114] Grandmothers listened in shock to their grandsons taunting their gods; fathers watched in dismay their sons refusing to perform hallowed rituals.[115]

Rumours spread through the bhadralok community. We hear of a Brahmin who would daily do the rounds of houses reporting on the students' open contempt of Hinduism, their avowal of atheism, their disrespect of parents, and their tendency to commit 'the most heinous sins'. The man insinuated that they even condoned incestuous marriage between brother and sister; and that Derozian Dakhinaranjan's sister was being given in marriage to 'his

Eurasian *Guru*'. Derozio was, of course, accused as the root of all such evil.[116] Such rumours naturally created 'immense excitement' within the city.[117] To add fire to the fury of the Hindu orthodoxy, this was the time when (in December 1829) Lord William Bentinck issued his order of banning sati.

The managers of Hindu College commanded their headmaster—no friend of Derozio—to 'check as far as possible all disquisitions tending to unsettle the beliefs of the boys in the greater principle of national religion'.[118] Horrified parents withdrew their sons from the college. The managing committee passed a resolution that forbade teachers of the college from teaching anything that subverted the Hindu religion or 'Hindu notions of propriety'.[119] Any teacher who violated this injunction would be dismissed. Interestingly, this resolution apparently prompted some of the city's newspapers and periodicals to protest against what they perceived as violation of the 'right of public discussion' and of 'the right of private judgement' in politics and religion.[120] The *India Gazette* maintained that the authorities of Hindu College had no right to decide what students could say or how they should behave in such matters outside the college.[121]

The Christian missionaries and clergymen, notably Rev. Alexander Duff (the third Scot of prominence in this story), tried to seize the moment. Perceiving anti-Hinduism amongst the students of the college, they offered a course of lectures 'to educated Bengalees' on 'Natural and Revealed Religion' in Duff's house on College Square, almost cheek by jowl with Hindu College.[122] The choice of subject matter was interesting, for they seemed to want to hedge their bets: 'natural religion' would (presumably) embrace what Reverend William Paley had famously called 'natural theology'—deism, the 'argument for God by design'; 'revealed religion', on the other hand, would address the theism of the Bible. The managers were even more alarmed. They also heard that the students of the college attended meetings of societies where political and religious issues were debated; thus they announced that any student found attending such meetings would 'incur their serious displeasure'.[123]

Derozio was, of course, the prime object of their 'displeasure'. In April 1831, led by Ram Comul Sen, eminent bhadralok citizen, philanthropist, lexicographer, 'firm friend of orthodox Hindus',[124] and opponent of the abolition of sati—and, ironically, the grandfather of Keshab Chandra Sen, later a pre-eminent 'alternative' Brahmo Samaj leader[125]—the managers of the college pondered whether Derozio, the 'root of all the evils and cause of public alarm' should be removed from Hindu College.[126] They debated whether there was sufficient evidence that Derozio's 'morals and tenets' had rendered him 'an improper person to be entrusted with the education of youth'.[127]

David Hare and the distinguished Orientalist Horace Hayman Wilson, both members of the managing committee, believed otherwise; in fact the majority of the managers were in favour of Derozio on this count. However, when the motion was considered that Derozio was dismissible on the strength of public feelings, several of the committee members felt it either 'necessary' or 'expedient' that he be dismissed.[128] Hare and Wilson declined to vote on a decision that relied on the 'state of native feelings alone'.[129]

Thus, the majority voted to dismiss Derozio. Horace Hayman Wilson communicated this decision to him.

There followed an exchange of letters between Derozio and Wilson.

On April 25, 1831, as his first response, Derozio submitted his letter of resignation with an accompanying letter to Wilson in which he denied any admission of guilt. To Wilson, he wrote:

> The accompanying is my resignation; but you will observe that I have taken the liberty of departing from your suggestion of making it appear a merit on my part. If I had grounds to believe that my continued connection with the College could be really and permanently prejudicial to that institution, the spirit to leave it without any suggestion but that of my own mind would not be wanting.[130]

He did not believe, though, that the circumstances demanded such a 'sacrifice' from him. And so this resignation was nothing but 'compulsory'. His letter of resignation to the managing committee reiterated this point: 'I am induced to place my resignation in your hands, in order to save myself from the mortification of receiving formal notice of my dismissal.'[131]

Characteristically, he did not end there. He pointed out 'certain facts': that no charge was brought against him; that if there were any accusations, he was not informed of them; that he was not given the chance to face his accusers; that no witnesses were summoned; that he was given no opportunity of defending himself against 'scrutiny' of his 'conduct and character'; that a verdict to dismiss him was decided 'without even the mockery of a trial'.[132]

Horace Hayman Wilson's reply, dated the same day, is fascinating for two reasons. First, he pointed out that whatever 'proof' Derozio produced in his own defence would not have changed his accusers' minds. And, second, he identified three charges brought against Derozio and he asked, 'speaking confidentially', how Derozio would answer them: 'Do you believe in God? Do you think respect and obedience to parents no part of moral duty? Do you think the intermarriage of brothers and sisters innocent and allowable?'[133] He went on: 'Have you ever maintained these doctrines by argument in the hearing of our scholars?'[134]

Derozio replied the next day: 'I have never denied the existence of a God in the hearing of any human being.'[135] However: 'If it be wrong to speak at all upon such a subject, I am guilty, but I am neither afraid nor ashamed to confess having stated the doubts of philosophers upon this head because I have also stated the solution of these doubts.'[136]

As to the other charges, he dismissed them scornfully. On the question of respect and obedience to parents: 'For the first time did I learn from your letter that I am charged with inculcating so hideous, so unnatural, so abominable a principle.'[137] As regards the marriages of brothers and sisters: ' "No" is my distinct reply; and I never taught such an absurdity.'[138]

At the end of the letter 'of inordinate length', for which he apologized, Derozio had this to say about the 'Native Managers' of the college: 'Excuse my saying it, but I believe that there was a determination on their part to get rid of me not to satisfy popular clamour but their own bigotry.'[139] They could not have found any proper grounds to dismiss him, he wrote, based on his 'religion and morals'; and so they dispensed with any proper inquiry and chose to remove him in any case: 'The slovenly manner in which they have done so is a sufficient indication of the spirit by which they were moved; for in their rage they have forgotten what was due even to common decency.'[140]

AFTER LEAVING HINDU College, Derozio became more the journalist and less the poet. He founded and edited a newspaper, the *East Indian*, which became a voice for the Eurasian community and their rights as Christians, residents of British India, and subjects of the Crown.

His journalistic career was appallingly short-lived: less than eight months after he resigned from Hindu College, on December 17, 1831, Derozio was infected with cholera, and passed away six days later. He was buried in Park Street Cemetery where Sir William Jones had been lain a long time before, leaving behind his stepmother, younger sister Amelia, and a host of friends and former students. He was still only twenty-two years old.

WHAT HENRY DEROZIO created was two-fold. As a poet he planted one of the first seeds of a new literary genre, Indian writing in English; and as a teacher and intellectual he influenced a generation of Bengalis. 'Young Bengal' was the name used to describe these youths who were taught by Derozio and who grew into men after his death. (The term 'Young Bengal' to describe the Derozians was probably coined sometime in the 1830s or 1840s (it appeared in the Calcutta newspapers of the time), perhaps inspired by the Italian organization called Young Italy, founded by Giuseppe Mazzini in 1831.)[141]

Theirs were minds shaped by Western ideas of justice and liberty, including the liberty of thought itself. They were contemptuous of superstition and dogma; they opposed authoritarianism; they hated oppression, including the oppression of women. They had absorbed these ideas from Derozio and the philosophical and literary writings of Europe he introduced them to. But they were all Bengalis, all Indians. They looked to Europe for inspiration but only that they could apply what they learnt to their lives and, later, livelihood as Indians. It was Derozio who had bequeathed them this Indo-Western mind, this ability to move between two worlds.

Long after Derozio was gone and the Anglicist–Orientalist debate (that was contemporaneous with their student days) was finally laid to rest thanks to Macaulay's 'Minute' and William Bentinck's decision to promote Western-style education—after both these men left India and Bentinck's successor, Lord Auckland arrived[142]—the Derozians started another association, in 1838. They called it the Society for the Acquisition of General Knowledge. We have a sense of the tone of this society from the topics lectured upon and discussed at its meetings. 'Reform, civil and social, among educated natives,' 'Topographical and statistical survey of Bankura,' Condition of Hindu women,' 'Brief outline of the history of Hindustan,' 'Descriptive notices of Chittagong,' 'State of Hindustan under the Hindus,' 'Descriptive notices of Tipperah [Tripura],' 'The physiology of dissection.'[143] Indian matters—matters to do with Bengal, touching history, geography, and social reform—dominate. They took up, in particular, the cause of women's rights: female education and the subjugation of women.[144] They founded and edited for a time a periodical named *The Bengal Spectator*,[145] and in its pages they espoused the remarriage of Hindu widows[146] even before Ishwar Chandra Vidyasagar made it a major reform issue and cause célèbre.[147]

We notice too, the presence of science amongst the topics discussed at meetings of the Society for the Acquisition of General Knowledge: the physiology of dissection. This was, no doubt, due to the fact that somewhere between the deaths of Derozio and Rammohun and the formation of this society, another remarkable institution had come into being in Calcutta: a Western-style medical college. But that is a tale to be told later.

The Indo-Western mind was also manifested among Derozians in the realms of creative science and literature. Radhanath Sikdar established a successful career as an applied mathematician in the Great Trigonometrical Survey of India.[148] And as we have seen, his friend Peary Chand Mittra, using the nom de plume Tekchand Thakur, wrote what is considered one of the first novels in the Bengali language, *Alaler Gharer Dulal*.[149] Like Derozio's English poetry this work did not initiate a *tradition* of the Bengali novel but, again, like Derozio's work, planted the first seeds of a literary genre, and thus belongs really to the prehistory of the modern Indian novel.[150]

SOME CONSERVATIVES COULD not forget or forgive Derozio even after his death. Almost a decade after his death, in August 1840, the *Calcutta Courier* (which up till 1831 had been the *Calcutta Government Gazette* and, thus, somewhat of a government mouthpiece)[151] carried an article on the 'late Mr. D'Rozio' in which he was once more accused of spreading the 'leaven of atheism' and the 'pestilent doctrine of infidelity' in the minds of his students.[152] Derozio's one-time teacher David Drummond rushed to his defence, and a fierce exchange of letters erupted in the pages of *The Weekly Examiner*, founded by Drummond, and the *Calcutta Courier*.[153]

But if his detractors could not forget him, nor could his friends and pupils. John Grant, editor of the *Indian Gazette* in which so many of Derozio's poems had appeared, wrote a long obituary notice soon after Derozio's death.[154] A proposal to put up a stone monument in his memory was announced in the *India Gazette*, sponsored by several citizens of Calcutta, including David Hare and Krishna Mohun Banerji;[155] the monument was never erected because the funds raised for the project was embezzled. The *East Indian* published its own obituary. In 1833, John Grant wrote a memoir of Derozio in the *Calcutta Literary Gazette*.[156] As noted before, a 'reminiscence' of the man appeared in the same periodical signed by 'J' who was evidently a Derozian.[157] And forty-six years after Derozio's death, his student Peary Chand Mittra, then into mature years—librarian and curator of the Calcutta Library, successful businessman, public servant, writer, and distinguished citizen of Calcutta—would remember vividly his former teacher.

> He used to impress upon his pupils the sacred duty of thinking for themselves...to live and die for truth... He often read examples from ancient history of the love of justice, patriotism,

philanthropy and self-abnegation, and the way in which he set forth the points stirred up the minds of his pupils. Some were impressed with the excellence of justice, some with the paramount importance of truth, some with patriotism, some with philanthropy.[158]

It may have been a brief life, but Derozio's shadow stretched long.

Notes

1. Lal [1917] 2001, p. 109.
2. Edwards [1884] 1980, p. ii.
3. Cited in Chaudhuri 2008b, p. xlviii.
4. Chaudhuri 2008b, pp. xlviii–xlix.
5. Edwards [1884] 1980, p. 185.
6. Rosinka Chaudhuri, personal communication, email, March 6, 2009.
7. Chaudhuri, 2008b, p. xlvii.
8. See Chapter three.
9. Chaudhuri, 2008b, p. xlviii.
10. Edwards [1884] 1980, p. 10.
11. Ibid., p. 5.
12. Ibid., p. 11.
13. Ibid., p. 12.
14. Clarke and Jacyna, pp. 220–5.
15. Drummond 1829.
16. Ibid.
17. Ibid.

18. Dennett 1991, pp. 253 ff.
19. Edwards [1884] 1980, p. 19.
20. Ibid., p. 5.
21. Ibid., p. 19.
22. Lethbridge 1907, p. 163.
23. Edwards [1884] 1980, p. 6.
24. Ibid., p. 7.
25. Chaudhuri 2008b, p. lix.
26. 'Sonnet to Night,' reprinted in Chaudhuri 2008a, p. 5.
27. Chaudhuri 2008a, pp. 3 ff.
28. Edwards [1884] 1980, p. 26.
29. Ibid., pp. 26–7.
30. Ibid., p. 27.
31. Rosinka Chaudhuri, personal communication, email, March 6, 2009.
32. Edwards [1884] 1980, p. 28.
33. The review is reprinted in Chaudhuri 2008a, pp. 394–5.
34. Ousby 1988.
35. Chaudhuri 2008b, p. xx.
36. Edwards [1884] 1980, p. 185.
37. See Chapter five.
38. Das 1991, p. 70.
39. Tharu and Lalita 1991.
40. See Chapter three. See also De 1961, p. 413; Das 1966; Sen 1979.
41. Mehrotra 2003; Mukherjee 2000.
42. Hobsbawm, 1983, p. 1.
43. Elsewhere in India, there were, notably, Pandita Ramabai Saraswati, Krupa Sattianadhan, and Govardhanran Tripathi. See Tharu and Lalitha 1991, pp. 243–55, 275–80; Chandra 2003; Mukherjee 2000, pp. 68–88.

44. Murshid 2003, p. 184.
45. Kashiprasad's poetry has been described by later commentators as 'derivative and imitative', 'made up mainly conventional descriptions and tedious moralizing', 'prosaic and inane'. Das 1991, p. 79.
46. Mukherjee 2000, p. 94.
47. Lokugé 2006c, p. xxiv.
48. See Chapter nine.
49. Das 1991, pp. 79–80; Chaudhuri 2008a; Mukherjee 2003; Mehrotra 1990.
50. Chaudhuri 2008a, p. 96.
51. R. Chaudhuri 2008a, p. 89.
52. Ibid., p. 173.
53. See Chapter four.
54. Chaudhuri 2008a, pp. 33–48.
55. Sarkar 1990, p. 128.
56. Ibid., pp. 132 ff.
57. Chaudhuri 2008b, pp. xxxi ff.
58. Edwards [1884] 1980, p. 30.
59. Mittra 1877, Appendix A ('Rules of the Hindu College').
60. Sengupta 1955, p. 3.
61. Anon 1955, p. 293.
62. See Chapter nine, for more on Sanskrit College.
63. Anon 1955, Plate I.
64. Sastri [1907] 2002.
65. Mittra 1877, p. 35.
66. See Chapter five.
67. Ghose 1948, pp. 127–9.
68. Sastri [1907] 2002, p. 67.
69. Ibid., p. 167.

70. See Chapter eight.
71. Sastri [1907] 2002, p. 167.
72. Ibid., p. 166.
73. Ibid., p. 167.
74. Poddar 1970, p. 129.
75. Ibid., pp. 129–30.
76. Mittra 1877, p. 36.
77. Edwards [1884] 1980, pp. 131–2.
78. Mittra 1877, p. 36.
79. See Chapter four.
80. Poddar 1970, pp. 139–40.
81. Edwards [1884] 1980, p. 31.
82. Chakravarty 1995.
83. Kochhar 1991.
84. Mittra 1877, p. 31.
85. Ibid., p. 16.
86. Ibid., p. 31.
87. Ibid., p. 16.
88. Ibid., p. 31.
89. Ibid., p. 17.
90. Edwards [1884] 1980, p. 66.
91. Ibid., p. 67.
92. Ibid., p. 40.
93. Quoted in Chaudhuri 2008a, p. 446.
94. 'J' 1834. Quoted in Chaudhuri 2008a, pp. xxxvi–xxxvii.
95. Edwards [1884] 1980, pp. 31–2.
96. Sastri [1907] 2002, p. 96.
97. Ibid., p. 86.
98. Mittra 1877, p. 32.
99. Ibid., p. 17.

100. Sastri [1907] 2002, p. 90.
101. Quoted in Sastri [1907] 2002, p. 86.
102. Mittra 1877, p. 18.
103. Sastri [1907] 2002, p. 90.
104. Ibid., p. 171.
105. Edwards [1884] 1980, p. 69.
106. Ibid., p. 69; Mittra 1877, p. 18.
107. Sastri [1907] 2002, p. 171.
108. Ibid., p. 85; Edwards [1884] 1980, pp. 67–8.
109. Sastri [1907] 2002, p. 177.
110. Ibid., p. 169.
111. Ibid.
112. Quoted in Sastri [1907] 2002, p. 86.
113. Edwards [1884] 1980, p. 121.
114. Mittra 1877, p. 18.
115. Sastri [1907] 2002, p. 87.
116. Ibid., p. 87.
117. Ibid.
118. Quoted in Mittra 1877, p. 17.
119. Mittra 1877, p. 18.
120. Edwards [1884] 1980, p. 71.
121. Ibid., pp. 71–2.
122. Ibid., p. 70; Mittra 1877, p. 18.
123. Ibid., p. 70.
124. Ibid., pp. 72–3.
125. Kopf 1979, pp. 249 ff.
126. Edwards [1884] 1980, p. 75.
127. Ibid., p. 76.
128. Ibid.
129. Mittra 1877, p. 19.

130. H.L.V. Derozio to H.H. Wilson, April 25, 1831, in Edwards [1884] 1980, pp. 77–9.
131. H.L.V. Derozio to the Managing Committee of Hindu College, April 25, 1831, in Edwards [1884] 1980, pp. 79–80.
132. Ibid.
133. H.H. Wilson to H.L.V. Derozio, April 25, 1831, in Edwards [1884] 1980, pp. 80–1.
134. Ibid.
135. H.L.V. Derozio to H.H. Wilson, April 26, 1831, in Edwards [1884] 1980, pp. 82–9.
136. Ibid.
137. Ibid.
138. Ibid.
139. Ibid.
140. Ibid.
141. Chaudhuri 2008b, pp. lix–x.
142. See Chapter five.
143. Sastri [1907] 2002, pp. 96–7.
144. Edwards [1884] 1980, p. 68.
145. Sastri [1907] 2002, p. 96.
146. Ibid., p. 111.
147. See Chapter seven.
148. See Chapter twelve.
149. Sen 1979, pp. 208–10.
150. Das 1991, pp. 114, 197.
151. Chaudhuri 2008a, p. 442.
152. Ibid., p. 443.
153. Ibid., pp. 441–58.
154. Ibid., pp. 426–30.

155. Ibid., p. 431.
156. Ibid., pp. 436–40.
157. Ibid., pp. xxxvi–xxxvii.
158. Mittra 1877, p. 31.

Seven

Humanist by Creed, Humanist in Deed

THE YEAR WAS 1829. Derozio was mesmerizing his students in the classrooms of Hindu College with talk of Shelley and Hume and Thomas Paine. In another wing of the same building but carefully separated from it, a boy of nine was admitted into an institution called Sanskrit College.

The boy's name was Ishwar Chandra Bandyopadhyay (1820–91). He would be far better known in India as Vidyasagar (ocean of learning). And though that day in June 1829 he began a long apprenticeship within shouting distance of the students of Hindu College, he might as well have been a continent away, so vastly different was his milieu from that of the wealthy sophisticates of Hindu College.

Sanskrit College, opened in 1824, was one of the sources of Rammohun's ire when he wrote his 'memorial' to Lord Amherst in 1823.[1] It was the 'seminary of learning' he referred and objected to in his letter,[2] and it occupied a central place in the Anglicist–Orientalist battle which would be ultimately won by the Anglicists in 1835. The college opened for business on New Year's Day, 1824.[3] Like Hindu College, it too was meant for the bhadralok: essentially, Brahmins, Vaidyas, and Kayasthas.[4] Three years earlier, the Marquess of Hastings, then governor-general, had stated that: '...the immediate object of the institution is the cultivation of Hindu literature. Yet it is...a purpose of much deeper interest to seek every practicable means of effecting the gradual diffusion of European knowledge.'[5] Thus, the 'higher and educated class among the Hindus', the governor-general suggested, may be induced to savour 'a taste for the European literature and science' by way of their 'sacred language'. This might be as effective as more 'direct instruction'.[6] This was, of course, the 'Orientalist' agenda in the educational debate.

Sanskrit College acquired its own building in 1826. In fact, by design, the building was separated into two sections, one for Sanskrit College itself, the other given over to Hindu College, though the two institutions were separated by 'a strong railing' (to keep the pandits of one and the baboos of the other apart).[7]

ISHWAR CHANDRA VIDYASAGAR'S PLACE in the tale of the Bengal Renaissance is manifold: as educationist, as writer, as feminist, and as social reformer. Yet hovering over all of these was his compelling need to put humanism into action in the real world.

'Man,' said the fifth century BCE Greek philosopher Protagoras, 'is the measure of all things.' A famous dictum that captures the core of the humanist creed. Presumably, Protagoras meant that human needs, concerns, values, and interests are what matters. As to the gods, Protagoras was said to have said, 'I have no means of knowing either they exist or do not exist.' Humanism as a worldview has travelled far since Protagoras, but its concern with 'the full whole nature of man' has remained.[8] In modern times the humanist creed has been linked to the idea that man is part of nature; to human development; to democracy and egalitarianism.[9] It is in this light that we see Vidyasagar as a humanist.

It is tempting to compare Vidyasagar to Rammohun Roy, for Rammohun too was a feminist and a social reformer. He too wrote extensively and argued eloquently for a different kind of education for Indians. But Rammohun's worldview was always theocentric. The Hindu religion and, later, Christianity dominated his thoughts. One of his two main social concerns was to reform Hinduism, and he devoted much time to the nature of Christianity. Even his long-waged war against sati was grounded in large part by appeals to the shastras. His argument on behalf of female inheritance rights drew on ancient Hindu laws. He returned again and again to the Vedantic texts. Rammohun's humanism lay buried deep beneath his theocentric and monotheistic worldview. And at best his humanism was of a cerebral or theoretical kind.

Vidyasagar's humanism was anything but theoretical. It was anything but theocentric. If Vidyasagar had any religious beliefs these did not surface in his life's work. (Some thought he was an agnostic.)[10] In contrast to Rammohun, his religion, if any, lay buried deep beneath his concern for the human condition. As a writer, feminist, educationist, and social reformer he revealed a manifestly secular worldview. Man *was*, for him, the measure of all things. Nor was his commitment to egalitarianism, to the improvability of his countrymen, to philanthropy, just ideas. Vidyasagar was, as we shall see, the paradigm of the practical humanist. This practical humanism was, ultimately, *his* contribution to the Bengal Renaissance.

It would be wrong to claim that modern humanism is solely a product of the West[11] as some thinkers believe.[12] Thus, to speak of Vidyasagar as a humanist is not to mean that his creed came only from his encounter with Western thought. What then were the roots of his humanism? A large part no doubt came from his personal experience, especially in childhood, boyhood, and youth. The rest, surely, came from his learning. By training he was a Sanskritist; but as a product of his time he was also taught European Enlightenment thought: rationalism, secularism, agnosticism, religious tolerance, egalitarianism, liberty. Vidyasagar's humanism was very much his own, but it lay in a symbosis of these ingredients.

VIDYASAGAR WROTE MUCH but (like Rammohun Roy) not much about himself. All we have as autobiography is a brief memoir of his immediate ancestry and childhood, published posthumously.[13] It is a memoir of contrasts; of deprivation, desperation, and hardship (but never, it seems, of despair or hopelessness); and as much of compassion, love, and kindness.

It is a tale of the paternal grandfather who abruptly left his wife, six children, and domestic responsibilities (sansar) and disappeared for seven or eight years; of an abandoned grandmother, forced to return to the paternal home but then, shunned by a brother and sister-in-law who did not care for the burden of feeding seven more mouths, having to fend for her children by taking up spinning yarn. It is a story of the maternal grandfather who went mad; and his wife, also forced to return to the parental home with children and a mad husband—but in her case, to a family of four brothers who lived in harmony, the ideal joint family, headed by the eldest brother who made no distinction between his own children and the children of his siblings. A man of saintly disposition.

It is about travel, between villages. From ancestral village to the village that became home, Birsingha; from village to the big city, Calcutta; but always, it seems, movement by foot, walking long distances on mud paths and paved roads, marked by milestones, and through fields.

There was the mother, Bhagabati, raised in her maternal uncle's home, her mamabari, the recipient of unending care and love from her uncle and his family. And, in contrast, there was the father, Thakurdas, the eldest son of the delinquent grandfather, who left home at the age of fourteen or fifteen and went to Calcutta in search of work. The memoir is as much a remembrance of Thakurdas's youth—reconstructed from stories told to Ishwar Chandra by his parents and grandmother—as of Ishwar Chandra's own childhood.

We hear that Thakurdas had aspirations to become a Sanskrit scholar and teacher. But circumstances bade otherwise. He badly needed a job; and at a time when a smattering of English could land a person a job in a merchant's shop or office, he decided to study English in Calcutta. He was fortunate to be given shelter by a kindly distant relative, and through this relative he also acquired an English teacher. But he could only study evenings, for the teacher had a day job. The outcome was that by the time Thakurdas returned to his abode at night after his tutorial, dinnertime was long past in the relative's establishment, and he had to go without food.

There is an element of black humour in all this and what followed. For lack of food Thakurdas became emaciated;

noticing this, his teacher wanted to know why. Thakurdas explained. Another person who happened to be present took pity on him and suggested that the youth move in with him. Thakurdas agreed. Unfortunately, his new benefactor's income did not match his good intentions, and the result was that neither had enough to eat.

One day Thakurdas was wandering the streets exhausted and dizzy with hunger. A middle-aged widow, a seller of sweetened puffed rice (muri murki) in a nearby shop, noticed the boy's condition. Hearing that he had not eaten that day she took pity on him and gave him food from her shop and yogurt from a nearby seller; and told him that if he was in this condition again he should come to her shop. Vidyasagar wrote: 'Had the person been a man he would never have shown this kind of compassion for Thakurdas.'[14]

With his host's help Thakurdas got a job that paid two rupees a month. He was a good worker; in two or three years time he was earning five rupees per month, thus helping ease his mother's financial burden back home.

One day the prodigal grandfather returned. The family, a forgiving one it seems, rejoiced. The grandfather, named Tarkabhushan, came to Calcutta to see his son. There was a positive outcome here, for he had a friend in Calcutta called Bhagabatcharan Sinha, a kind, compassionate person apparently, for he invited Thakurdas to stay in his house. For the first time since coming to the big city Thakurdas was free of hunger. Moreover, Bhagabatcharan found him another job, one that paid eight rupees a month. Came the time for marriage. Thakurdas's bride was Bhagabati, whose father (as we have seen) had gone mad.

Vidyasagar's remembrance of his own childhood is peppered by episodes of kindness shown to him by those who need not have done so. There was Radhamohan, his mother Bhagabati's maternal uncle, under whose benign roof she had spent her life before marriage. Hearing that the six-year-old Ishwar Chandra was ill, he took him back to his home, tended to him, had local vaidya doctors treat him to recovery. 'During that time I was under the care and kindness of Radhamohan Vidyabhusan and his family.' [15]

Taken to Calcutta at age eight by his father Thakurdas, he took lodging in the house where Thakurdas had once lived with the benevolent Bhagabatcharan Sinha. Bhagabatcharan had long passed away and the head of the household was now his only son Jagatdurlabh, then some twenty-five years of age. The household was full: in addition to Jagatdurlabh and his wife, there was an elder sister and her husband with two sons, and a younger widowed sister and her son. Here too, Ishwar Chandra found only kindness and he was treated as one of the family, a younger brother to Jagatdurlabh. Most of all, the widowed sister Raimoni was fondest of Ishwar Chandra; she treated him as she did her own son. 'She became a *debi* in my eyes.'[16] Any homesickness the boy may have felt was greatly alleviated because of her affection. Vidyasagar wrote later of Raimoni:

> It has been said by many that I am a supporter of women. This is not untrue. But for one who has received the love, kindness and care of Raimoni, it is hardly surprising that he would be a supporter of women. Otherwise there would not be any one as ungrateful as such a person.[17]

Humanity alone does not make a humanist. But without humanity one can be a humanist in theory only. The stories of generosity young Ishwar Chandra heard from his parents and grandmother, and that he personally experienced—from men certainly but most of all from women—must have implanted the first seeds of the practical humanism that became his later creed.

The many acts of kindness, large and small, to others in adulthood now belong to the lore surrounding the man. Perhaps the most well-known of his beneficiaries was (as we shall see) the poet Michael Madhusudan Datta who appealed to him again and again, often in desperation, for help, and who was never disappointed by Vidyasagar.[18] Indeed, had it not been for Vidyasagar's help in securing monies owed to him and in repaying debts, Madhusudan's later life might have taken a very different turn.

Another instance, though on a much smaller scale and less known, was the Derozian Ramtanu Lahiri. In keeping with his professed anti-Hinduism, Ramtanu renounced his Brahminical thread (paita). Predictably, he was persecuted by other Hindus and became a virtual outcast in the community. Vidyasagar, in the words of Sivanath Sastri, 'sent him servant after servant' to help him in these difficult times.[19] Another time, when Ramtanu was in financial difficulties and hard-pressed to support his family, Vidyasagar appointed one of his sons as a librarian in a school with which he was associated.[20]

Most importantly, people trusted Vidyasagar completely. He was never known to go back on his word, and he bore his responsibilities seriously. As he once wrote to Madhusudan Datta, 'Many believe that if I give my word I will most certainly keep it…for this reason they act in good faith without ever questioning what I say.'²¹

As for academic matters, Vidyasagar was relatively diffident about himself in this respect, and we hear only in passing of his passage through this pathsala and that. The one tale he tells with evident pleasure is of how he learnt the English numerals. This happened at the time he and his father first set out for Calcutta. He was about eight years old then. It was, of course, a journey by foot—in fact, there would not have been a story to tell otherwise. They were walking to Calcutta and Ishwar Chandra noticed implanted on the roadside a stone slab that looked like the slabs used in Indian kitchens for grinding spices (sil). Curious, he wanted to know what it was. Thakurdas told him that it was a milestone and that this was an English word. He explained that after every mile there was such a stone and that on them were inscribed '1', '2', '3', etc. On the milestone before them was written '19', so that travellers would know that Calcutta was 19 miles away.

> I knew that 'one followed by nine is nineteen'. Seeing this milestone, putting my hand first on the '1' then on the '9' I said that this is the English 'one' and this the English 'nine'. And then I said to my father that the next milestone must show 'eighteen', the one after that 'seventeen' and so on. I then told him that on this road I will learn the English numerals.²²

The boy learnt the English numerals following the succession of milestones down to the tenth one. But Thakurdas was sceptical.

My father tested me with the ninth, eighth, seventh milestones. I told him what they were...he did not allow me to see the sixth milestone. Showing me the fifth one he asked what this was. I replied that the milestone had been wrongly inscribed. It should be '6' instead of '5'.²³

An elated Thakurdas related this episode to friends and relatives whose advice he sought concerning Ishwar Chandra's future education. They thought he should study English and suggested David Hare's school where he would be taught for free. If he did well he could go on to that citadel of 'English' education, Hindu College.

But Thakurdas, who could not pursue his dream of becoming a Sanskrit scholar and teacher, decided to realize his thwarted ambition through the son. Ishwar Chandra must study Sanskrit and become a teacher in a Sanskrit school. The implication seems clear enough: to a person of Thakurdas's class, caste, and social background, David Hare's school and Hindu College may have appeared too anglicized and not 'respectable' enough for the making of a serious Sanskrit scholar/teacher.

A relative happened to teach in Sanskrit College. He advised Thakurdas to place his son there. Moreover, there were practical possibilities for useful employment: those who studied at Sanskrit College and went on to study for the law committee examination and pass, could find jobs as judge-pandits in the law courts. Eventually, a decision was made and in 1829, the nine-year-old Ishwar Chandra entered Sanskrit College. Though he would not know it then, he had entered the realm of an Orientalist vision of education for Indians.

ISHWAR CHANDRA REMAINED A student in Sanskrit College for twelve years, the first of three periods in his life in which he would be associated with the college.

These student years were a time of academic accomplishments. He won prizes and scholarships.[24] As relatives and well-wishers had hoped, he passed the Hindu Law Committee examination in 1839, well before he obtained his college leaving certificate in December 1841. His law examination certificate honoured him with the title of 'Vidyasagar' which became his de facto name thereafter.[25]

But his was never a life confined simply to the groves of academe. The learning life was interwoven with other concerns: marriage, for one, at the age of fourteen; and domestic life, including cooking, marketing, and other household chores.

Compassion—the core of his humanity, an essence of his humanism—was already an aspect of his character: he tended to the sick, including those stricken with the much-dreaded cholera; he helped indigents.[26] And all the time he was reading and learning.[27] This was a life far removed from those of the Derozians in the other wing of the building. It was also a life far removed from that of a young Rammohun Roy a generation ago.

Ishwar Chandra became a master of Sanskrit in all its manifestations: poetry, logic, and grammar. But the curriculum at Sanskrit College had more to offer. There were English classes and some science, even anatomy. Robert Tytler, Rammohun's foe, and teacher of the likes of Radhanath Sikdar in Hindu College even introduced anatomical dissection.

Despite his law certificate Ishwar Chandra disdained a career as judge-pandit. Instead as soon as he graduated from

Sanskrit College he was appointed a sheristadar (head pandit) in the Bengali Department in Fort William College (though, in the aftermath of the Anglicists' triumph, the college was in its waning years).[28] The secretary of the college was George T. Marshall, himself an alumnus of the college, and he became a mentor and patron to the scholarly young man.[29]

When Vidyasagar joined Fort William College his knowledge of English was quite limited. But by 1846, as Marshall, now secretary to the General Committee on Public Instruction, noted (in an echo of Digby about Rammohun), he had acquired a 'very considerable degree of knowledge of the English language'.[30] That same year Vidyasagar returned as assistant secretary to his alma mater which, he found, had declined in both academic and disciplinary aspects. Vidyasagar began a serious revision of the institution.

Very soon, however, there were differences with his boss, the college secretary Russomoy Dutt, a judge by day and only with half an eye on college matters. He had little time for Vidyasagar's plans; besides, Vidyasagar's outspokenness did not sit well with him as his superior. Vidyasagar who did not suffer the incompetent or the inefficient, gladly resigned in 1847.

There followed a brief interlude in—almost incongruously it might appear—business where he established, with a partner, a printing press. He succeeded, quite quickly, in obtaining contracts from Fort William College for producing reliable editions of two Bengali texts.[31] Eventually, George Marshall, still his mentor, secured him a job as 'head writer' and treasurer in Fort William College, which he took up in 1849.[32]

When the professorship of literature in Sanskrit College became vacant, Vidyasagar was offered the chair by the

Bengal Council of Education. He agreed to take it up only if he was given the authority of a principal. Given verbal assurance of this he accepted and returned to Sanskrit College in December 1850. His appointment as principal was formalized in the New Year.[33] Thus began his career proper in the college. He had just entered his thirties. Portraits of Vidyasagar—and there are several done at different stages of his life—show him wearing a dhoti and chaddar. With his grave, aloof, ascetic face, a high forehead and a well-receded hairline, he projects a formidable demeanour.

THE ONE HALLMARK of the unordinary creative mind is that it is guided by some all-encompassing, often compulsive drive.[34] Perhaps some such drives are innate—biologically 'hardwired' into the genetic code—needing only the right stimulus; perhaps others are culturally acquired; or perhaps (as most traits seem to be) they are a symbiosis of nature and culture. As we have already hinted, in Vidyasagar's case his need was to put humanism into action.

In the course of his mature life—say from 1850 when he became principal of Sanskrit College (he resigned in 1858) till near his last days (he died in 1891)—we see three clear strands that entwine and inform his humanism: the teacher, the man of letters, and the social activist. But they were just that—strands, not distinct phases—for they fused with one another and they overlapped in time.

NOT ALL TEACHERS are in the business of preaching humanism. Nor are they all in the business of practising it. But if we accept that the modern humanist creed is committed to (among other things) egalitarianism, the development of human potential, and the progress of *all* human beings, then Vidyasagar-as-teacher was profoundly in the business of not just preaching but practising humanism.

His wish was to 'extend the benefit of education to the mass of people', he wrote to the Council of Education in 1853. This was the 'darling object' of his wishes.[35] No anglicist elitism here. Vidyasagar was not the first to express a desire to educate the rural masses. Almost a decade earlier, the Bengal government had decided to establish over a hundred vernacular schools in rural Bengal. The project had come to naught. The numbers in the late 1840s make for dismal reading: according to one estimate only eight percent of boys in Bengal and Bihar had any schooling; only six percent of adults were known to be literate.[36]

Nor was Vidyasagar's a voice in the Anglicist wilderness: the first lieutenant-governor of Bengal, F.J. Halliday, a supporter and, in a sense, a follower of Vidyasagar as it happened, brought forth a minute of the Council of Education in March 1854. In this he expressed his desire to establish a system of model schools throughout the region along the lines pioneered in the North-Western Frontier Provinces by their lieutenant-governor James Thomason.[37] This would entail a scheme of regular visitations by inspectors of schools. He was also prepared to give financial support to missionary and other vernacular schools on the condition that they would open themselves up to visitation by government inspectors.

Shades of Vidyasagar were present in this proposal, for earlier that year Vidyasagar had written a memorandum to the Council of Education in which he argued for education through the vernacular and stated his willingness to serve (in addition to his duties as principal of Sanskrit College) as the chief inspector of a system of model schools. Halliday's minute drew upon this memorandum; and the lieutenant-governor was quite happy to accept Vidyasagar's offer of serving as chief inspector of these model schools.[38]

Indeed, 1854 was a seminal year in the annals of Indian education, for this was the year in which Sir Charles Wood's celebrated and hugely influential Education Despatch arrived in India from London. Amongst much else, Wood, then president of the Board of Control in Britain, dismissed the Anglicist idea of educating only the elite and hoped that its effect would trickle down to the masses. All must be given the opportunity to obtain practical knowledge so that they could be useful members of society. Moreover,

> ...while the English language continues to be made use of as by far the most perfect medium for the education of those persons who have acquired a sufficient knowledge of it to receive general instruction through it, the vernacular language must be employed to teach the far larger classes who are ignorant of, or imperfectly acquainted with English.[39]

Thus, Vidyasagar's vision found official resonance.

Not withstanding petty bureaucracy and prejudice against a 'native' given responsibility for the supervision of this scheme, and thanks to Halliday's persistence, Vidyasagar was appointed a salaried assistant inspector of schools. With characteristic efficiency he set about his task. Sub-inspectors were appointed; sites for the model schools were selected. Between late August 1855 and mid January 1856, twenty schools were founded across four major districts. Even the villagers contributed to the cost of erecting school buildings. The government ensured free tuition for the first six months, and gave operating funds for each school.[40] Student numbers increased. Their elders were so enthused that, according to Vidyasagar's first quarterly report to the government, they would visit the schools and 'sit for hours' watching and listening to the boys at their lessons.[41]

In 1860, Vidyasagar became associated with yet another educational venture: he was appointed to the managing committee of the Metropolitan Institution, a private school founded (as the Metropolitan Training School) in 1859 in the heart of the Black Town. Within four years he was given total responsibility for its administration, and he renamed it the Metropolitan Institution. Under his stewardship it made impressive progress: it became affiliated with the University of Calcutta in 1872 and started offering the 'First Arts' (FA) course; two years later, of some twenty-one candidates who appeared for the FA examination, a higher proportion passed than the candidates of the elite Presidency College (the former Hindu College, renamed and a government institution in 1855). 'The Pundit [Vidyasagar] has done wonders,' according to the university's registrar.[42] Later, when permitted to offer BA courses, its first batch of BA candidates achieved a pass rate comparable to Presidency College.[43]

To OPEN UP teaching in Bengal one had to teach in Bengali. Yet, 'if one does not know Sanskrit well, one cannot become adept in Bengali, Hindi, etc.'[44] So, education for all; education in Bengali, but a Bengali language that was founded on a sound knowledge of Sanskrit. But *what* should be taught in Bengali? Vidyasagar's answer lay not just in policy statements—though he made such statements in his correspondence with the provincial government on his vision for Sanskrit College.[45] We find his answer more directly in what he wrote *for* the students themselves.

There was, arguably his most familiar work for most Bengalis *to this day*, his 'primer' on written Bengali—*Barnaparichay* (literally, 'knowledge of the alphabet')—which introduced systematically, first the letters of the alphabet, then simple words, then compound words, progressing to simple sentences, then more complex sentences, to paragraphs, to short narratives.[46] There were no prescribed rules for the learner to learn; they were introduced to the signs for the basic sound patterns (phonemes) and to the basic meaningful units of sounds (morphemes) directly, through examples. *Barnaparichay* was a 'how-to' primer: the reader learnt by way of examples, by 'doing' and thus practising reading.

There were also Vidyasagar's expository essays which discussed people, ethics, history, culture, and society. These included both translations of English works and original compositions. Thus, a small collection of biographical pieces on such figures as Copernicus, Galileo, Newton, William Herschel, Linnaeus were translations of the Scottish brothers Robert and William Chambers' biographical articles. Even William Jones found a place in these biographies.[47]

In a preface Vidyasagar explicated the purpose of writing life-stories: first they showed how some overcame immense obstacles to achieve great things; and second, they illuminated the cultural, social, and historical backdrops against which such persons played out their lives.[48] In fact, his own memoir was a small case study of this same determination, his father's and his own, to succeed against all odds.

Amongst his original expository essays, an especially arresting example was 'Bodhodaya' (literally, 'enlightenment'). In plain Bengali, Vidyasagar presented to his reader essays on aspects of what might be called the Enlightenment view of the world: natural and human. Short sections were given to such topics as matter and materialism, God, consciousness, humanity, the senses, language, time, arithmetic, shape-size-form, diversity and variety, metals, non-metals, rudimentary economics, water, rivers and seas, the earth, and the ethics of property rights.[49]

Woven into this material were snippets of what might represent Vidyasagar's own worldview.

On God:

He is the Supreme Creator; and though invisible he is omniscient and omnipresent. He sees everything, he knows all that we think. He is ever merciful, ever compassionate. He is the savior and preserver of all.[50]

On effigies and idol worship:

An effigy has eyes but it cannot see; it has a mouth but it cannot eat; it has a nose but it cannot smell; it has hands but it cannot do any work; it has ears but it cannot hear; it has legs but it cannot walk. And the reason is that an effigy is inanimate, it has no consciousness. God has given consciousness only to animals. ... You will see humans make an effigy with mouth, eyes, ears, nose, arms and legs, and they may dress it in any way they fancy, but they cannot endow it with consciousness. It remains inanimate.[51]

And then there was a passing nod to egalitarianism:

There is no hierarchy in the animal world. Humans call the lion the king of beasts. But that is not God's intention. Compared to other animals the lion seems stronger and braver. For this reason humans call it the king of animals, but otherwise the lion is no better than any other beast.[52]

On the sources of knowledge and judgement:

The five senses are the sources of our knowledge. Without the senses we would be unconscious of everything. Through our senses we gain experience. And it is by way of experience that we make judgements of what is good, what is bad, what is beneficial and what is harmful.[53]

VIDYASAGAR-AS-TEACHER and Vidyasagar-as-man of letters came together in his narrative writings. If popular education was to happen through the medium of the vernacular then students in Bengal must be exposed not only to exemplary Bengali expository prose but also to exemplary Bengali literary prose. Characteristically, Vidyasagar demonstrated what such literary prose should be like by way of his own narrative writings, and it was as an innovator of Bengali prose that he has a place in the annals of Bengali literature and, by extension, Indian literature as a whole.[54]

Vidyasagar was, thus, the final link in the chain of pioneers of Bengali prose, a chain that began with William Carey.[55] He created a literary prose in Bengali believing that the language could yield a rhythm and musicality comparable to that found in good verse. To that end he used Sanskrit-based words provided that they made harmonious sense in the context of the sentences in which they appeared.[56] He sometimes wrote in a colloquial style, but more often opted for a literary style because of its greater 'musical potentialities'.[57]

Thus, he preferred the word rajasva rather than khajna, both meaning 'taxes' in the context of the sentence

tapasvira rajasva denna
[ascetics do not pay taxes]

perhaps because rajasva is more pleasing and, in this sentence, coheres more musically with the preceding word than the more colloquial but jarring khajna.[58]

He often used compound words that were clearly chosen for their musicality:[59]

ghana ghata [multitude of clouds]
manab samagan sunya [devoid of human habitation]
nabamalika kusuma komola [newly blossomed soft jasmine]

In the opening paragraph of what is often thought as Vidyasagar's most widely read literary work, *Sitar Banabas* (Sita's Banishment to the Forest), we find the sentence:

tahar sasanguné swalpa samaye smasta kosalrajya sarbatra
sarbaprakar sukhasamridhité paripurna hayie uthila[60]

[Through the beneficence of his rule, within a short time the entire kingdom became prosperous]

The great man of letters Bankimchandra Chattopadhyay would later remark: 'Neither before nor after did anyone write Bengali prose of such sweetness as did Vidyasagar.'[61]

But this 'sweetness' alone would not have distinguished Vidyasagar's prose were it not conjoined with clarity and fluency. His was the middle ground between the pedantic and the colloquial, and nowhere was this better illustrated than in his autobiography which eschewed literary flourishes in favour of a matter-of-fact narrative tone marked by short sentences.

VIDYASAGAR'S PURELY NARRATIVE writings included both translations and originals. A selection of Aesop's Fables were translated from the English.[62] His first book was a translation from the Hindi of a Sanskrit original which he produced while at the College of Fort William in reaction to (in his opinion) the unsatisfactory Bengali literary text then available to students of the college.

In 1854, he published a translation of Kalidasa's *Abhijnana Sakuntalam* from the Sanskrit[63] and he also translated into prose Shakespeare's *Comedy of Errors*.[64] While he took care in preserving the meanings of the original words, he would go beyond the literal to the spirit and deeper meaning of the original text.[65]

Vidyasagar's original literary writings included, in addition to his autobiographical fragment,[66] *Sitar Banabas*[67] which, though its plot was known to every reader of the *Ramayana*, became in Vidyasagar's hands 'a good and gripping story'.[68]

To this extent the book has a place in the early history of the Bengal novel.[69]

WE RECALL VIDYASAGAR'S confession in his childhood memoir of his attitude towards women. Recounting how a complete stranger, a woman who ran a roadside food-stall, had taken pity on his starving father and had fed him, he would write: 'After I heard this story of the woman's kindness from my father I developed a deep sense of reverence for the female sex.'[70] And later, he himself, a small boy alone in Calcutta, living in the home of a family friend, would be adopted as virtually a second son by the widow Raimoni. 'She became a *debi* in my eyes.'[71]

He was not just a 'supporter of women' but a passionate advocate of women's rights, an activist especially in the cause of female education, opposition to child marriage, and kulin polygamy and, most of all, on behalf of widow remarriage.

Kulin polygamy had once drawn Rammohun Roy's attention. In the 1850s it drew the protest of such Derozians as Kishorichand Mitra, a prominent social reform activist, writer, and public servant.[72] Vidyasagar wrote several lengthy tracts on and against polygamy (bahu-bibaha).[73] He noted that there was a common view that widespread practice of kulin polygamy was a thing of the past; that in modern times it was relatively scarce, and would die out soon. Thus, any legislation against it was unnecessary.

Vidyasagar disagreed. But rather than argue the point he presented the results of a massive survey he had undertaken to ascertain the actual number of kulin Brahmins in just one district, Hooghly, who had more than four surviving wives.

He gave a list of men, by name, age, village, and the numbers of their wives. The list had more than one hundred and thirty names; these were Brahmins with five or more wives. At the top of the list was a fifty-five-year-old with eighty wives, followed by a sixty-four-year-old man with seventy-two wives, then another fifty-five-year-old with sixty-two wives. Twenty Brahmins had between forty and sixty wives. And a total of eighty men had ten or more wives.[74] This was not polygamy but 'hypergamy'.

Arguing against the inhumanity of kulinism, in 1855, Vidyasagar presented to the government a petition signed by 2,500 persons requesting legislation against the practice. Nothing happened. The year after he presented yet another petition carrying, this time, 21,000 signatures.[75] Still no action was taken and despite his continuing campaign against the tradition, the government, wary of upsetting religious sensibilities in the aftermath of the Indian mutiny of 1857, chose not to proceed against it. Eventually, the reform movement died away. And though kulinism was never made illegal, the tradition gradually faded away by the end of the nineteenth century largely due to the growth of women's education, and reform movements which enlarged social consciousness of women's conditions.[76] So perhaps Vidyasagar's endeavours against polygamy did pay off in the long run.

VIDYASAGAR WAS BY no means the first to advocate widow remarriage. In the 1840s, the Derozians, through their publication *The Bengal Spectator*, had taken up this cause. Sivanath Sastri, in his biography of the Derozian Ramtanu Lahiri, tells us that 'Raja Sirish Chandra [of Nadia, a patron of the Derozians and of Krishnagar College] entered into a discussion on it with the pandits of Nadia.'[77] Unfortunately, the liberal, reform-minded Raja would retreat because of a campaign against the Derozians by the local Hindu orthodoxy—a campaign that threatened to do much harm to Krishnagar College 'but for the protecting hand of the Raja'.[78] The fight for widow remarriage was not politically expedient for that time, so far as the Raja was concerned.

Vidyasagar may not have been the first to advocate widow remarriage but, as in the case of vernacular schools for the rural districts, he was arguably the most effective. In 1855 he wrote two pamphlets on the subject.[79] Like Rammohun Roy writing on sati almost a generation earlier, Vidyasagar's polemic for widow remarriage was a melding of the humanist's indignation over the plight of young widows with a cool appeal to the shastras. Like Rammohun—though Vidyasagar was far more the atheist than Rammohun—he recognized that appealing to humanity only would not do. In a basically fundamentalist Hindu world the argument must be supported by scriptural sources to carry any weight.

It is a fact, he wrote, that widow remarriage was not the custom in his country, which meant that if widows were allowed to marry a new custom, a new tradition must be created. If people did not believe that allowing widows to remarry was a matter of duty, an obligation, then it should never be introduced—for which pious person (Vidyasagar asked, dryly) would want to initiate a tradition that was deemed undutiful? And so (he continued) whether or not enabling widow remarriage *was* a matter of social obligation was something that must first be decided.

(A caveat. When Vidyasagar admitted that remarriage was not the custom of the country, he was speaking of the 'respectable' classes—in Bengal, the bhadralok class. Amongst the lower-caste and lower-class Hindus, remarriage or, at least co-habitation (sanga) of widows with men was often socially acceptable in their communities.)[80]

The problem was (Vidyasagar went on), if someone used strictly rational arguments to show that widow remarriage should be allowed, the people of this country would not accept it. However, if the shastras told us that this was the case people would then admit that it was their duty and they should follow it.[81]

And so Vidyasagar combed the shastras. And he found relevant passages in the *Parasara Samhita*. One sloka said that in the case the husband was absent, or if he died, or was impotent, or abandoned his domestic responsibilities (sansar), or had been cast out, then the wife could marry again. As for the widow, the *Parasara Samhita* saw only three paths for her to follow: asceticism (brahmacharya), remarriage, or sati. The last was illegal. In the present age (Kaliyuga) being an ascetic was scarcely possible, and that was why the shastras gave primacy to remarriage, he argued.[82] At any rate, he continued, there were those five situations in which *Parasara* allowed the wife to marry again, hence in similar situations allowing widow remarriage was a matter of duty.

Thus it was established that in this Kaliyuga widow remarriage *is* a matter of duty. What of the offspring born of such a marriage? *Parasara* had something to say on this also. Vidyasagar quoted a relevant sloka.[83] Such a child can never be considered either adopted or illegitimate (kritrim), for that child was born of the widow-mother herself. The child bore the mark of legitimacy, the *Parasara Samhita* clearly stated.[84]

Ultimately, after all the long, dispassionate, logical, scholarly argument, commonsense morality must out. Those whose daughters, sisters, daughters-in-law, and other close relatives had had the misfortune of becoming widows at an early age would know how such unfortunate women suffer, what they have to go through for the rest of their lives. Uncountable widows, unable to maintain their state of asceticism, succumb to unlawful, adulterous, or incestuous relationships, or are forced to undergo abortion. They bring shame upon their mothers and fathers. All this could be prevented.

Vidyasagar appealed to his readers to take all that he had written into consideration; to discuss, debate it all, and then to decide whether the custom of widow remarriage should be established or not.[85]

BY HIS OWN account, Vidyasagar's first pamphlet on widow remarriage evoked enormous interest: it sold out within a week.[86] Three more printings followed in quick succession. Inevitably, the pamphlet provoked much wrath amongst the Hindu orthodoxy. The usual suspects were seen: we hear of the presence, once more, of the indefatigable Radhakanta Deb who had fought battles against Rammohun over sati.[87] And there was Vidyasagar's namesake, Ishwar Chandra Gupta,[88] a few years Vidyasagar's senior, a journalist by trade, a poet by avocation and, indeed, the foremost Bengali poet of the era—an avowed conservative in mentality and a traditionalist in poetic taste and style.[89]

Orthodox anger against Vidyasagar spread to the streets of Calcutta where he was insulted, abused, and even had his life threatened.[90] But he was no less a warrior than was Rammohun before him. He organized a signature campaign and forwarded the petition to the government.[91] The orthodox fought back: led by Radhakanta Deb they too submitted their counter-petition, bearing a much larger number of signatures. If democracy is the enforcement of the will of the majority then what ensued was undemocratic! Vidyasagar won the day: the Hindu Widow Remarriage Act was passed in July 1856.

Despite the passing of the law, there was no rush to take advantage of it: no one wanted to marry widows. Kaliprassana Sinha, one of the city's abhijhat bhadralok, social reformer, and, a few years later, author of the Dickensian *Hutom Pachar Naksa* (Sketches by a Watching Owl, 1862) even offered a cash reward of one thousand rupees but there were no takers.[92]

Eventually, through Vidyasagar's active support the first widow remarriage amongst upper-caste Hindus took place in December 1856.[93] The groom was Srischandra Vidyaratna, Vidyasagar's colleague at Sanskrit College. His incentive was a cash award; his more substantial reward was a deputy magistrateship a few years later.[94] Predictably, a massive uproar ensued throughout Bengal, the likes of which, according to Sivanath Sastri, had never been witnessed before.[95] Another such marriage followed soon after. Several years later, in 1870, Vidyasagar delighted in his own son Narayan marrying a widow.[96] But, as might be expected, he paid a price: he was socially ostracized in some circles, and his own wife was angered by Narayan's marriage—not unlike Rammohun's situation.

As history tells us often enough, tradition is indifferent to—in fact, quite contemptuous of—law. Never mind that widow remarriage was legalized; men could marry widows and widows remarry at their own peril, under threat of complete excommunication by their communities, or worse. We can only imagine and admire the (no doubt apprehensive) courage of those few who took the marriage vow under the new law. And we can only imagine the excitement, the prurient curiosity, and furore that such events must have aroused.

Vidyasagar's son Narayan's decision in 1870 was, in fact, far more the exception than the rule. The Widow Remarriage Act of 1856 did little de facto to change the status (or plight) of Hindu widows.[97] Even as late as 1891, the *Hindu Patriot*, an English weekly read widely by the bhadralok, though devoted to Indian causes proclaimed its opposition to widow remarriage. Lauding Vidyasagar for the 'noblest feelings for the suffering widows', it nevertheless believed that 'Hindu society had been rightly deaf to his arguments'.[98] Still later, in 1895, another English periodical declared that the widow remarriage movement had been a failure. It wrote that Vidyasagar's project to show that the shastras supported such marriage was fruitless. The logic of his argument was impeccable but it was irrelevant since 'Such [re]marriages had fallen into disuse for several centuries.' Almost forty years after the passing of the Widow Remarriage Act very few such marriages had taken place. 'Hindu society had not recognized them.'[99]

One contemporary historian has even claimed that Vidyasagar was a 'failed' reformer.[100] An unduly harsh verdict, perhaps; after all, Vidyasagar was instrumental in bringing a *new law* into effect, despite the will of a far larger majority.

REVOLUTIONS IN THE realm of the mind are initially revolutions of a few, even sometimes of a single person. Its consequences may take years, decades, even a generation or two to mature. Vidyasagar's revolution, ultimately, lay not in his teaching alone, or in his educational reforms, or in his activism on behalf of women, or in his contributions to Bengali prose, or in his extensive literary, pedagogic, and expository writings. Like Derozio, but in a far more enlarged sense, his place in the awakening we call the Bengal Renaissance was much more subtle, almost elusive. It lay in the planting of his own, very distinctive mentality amidst the cultural, social, and intellectual milieu of his age: the mentality of a practical, secular humanist committed to the progress of the human condition, to the principle and practice of egalitarianism, to an integrity that others could rely upon absolutely. A mentality that was not content with preaching but demanded action. Vidyasagar wrote much, but for him it was the deed that mattered.

Perhaps because of this the Word of God was not of much importance to him. His view of God was an abstract one: God was invisible, omniscient, omnipresent, as he wrote in one of his essays. In this he was at one with Rammohun Roy, but there the similarity ended. Vidyasagar's view of God was perfunctory. He had no *use* for God.

He was a secular humanist in a way Rammohun could never be. Yet, his secularism or agnosticism was never strident. When the mystic Ramakrishna (of whom more later in this story) visited Vidyasagar in the latter's home in 1882, he was received with much respect. Vidyasagar listened patiently and courteously to Ramakrishna.[101] But the mystic's words did not move him. Afterwards, Ramakrishna's disciple, 'M', a student in Vidyasagar's Metropolitan Institution recorded: '...when I talked with him [Vidyasagar] I found that he didn't much care for what the Vaishavas call emotion or ecstasy.'[102] Elsewhere, 'M' remarked that, apropos all the suffering in the world, Vidyasagar once said, 'What is the use of calling on God? ... I don't need God, whether He exists or not. I don't derive any good from Him.'[103]

Perhaps it was this indifference to God and religion that made him the effective humanist man of action that he was. Ramakrishna recognized this, though not approvingly, when he said: Vidyasagar has both scholarship and charity but he lacks inner vision. God lies hidden within him. Had he but found it...his activities would have reduced; finally they would have stopped altogether.[104]

If this was the case, God's loss was man's gain.

Notes

1. See Chapter five.
2. 'Rammohun Roy's letter to Lord Amherst on Western Education, December 11, 1823,' pp. 190–5 in Biswas 1992, p. 191.
3. Tripathi 2004, p. 28.
4. Mukherjee 1970, pp. 55–6.
5. Quoted in Tripathi 2004, p. 25.
6. Tripathi 2004, p. 25.
7. Sengupta 1955.
8. Burkhardt [1829] 1975, p. 303.
9. See, for example, Huxley 1964.

10. Tripathi 2004, p. 119.
11. Sen 2005, pp. 3–33.
12. Bullock 1985.
13. Vidyasagar 1891.
14. Ibid., p. 460. Freely translated from the Bengali.
15. Ibid., p. 466. Freely translated from the Bengali.
16. Ibid., p. 470. Freely translated from the Bengali.
17. Ibid. Freely translated from the Bengali.
18. Murshid 2004, Chapters four and five. See also Chapter eight.
19. Sastri [1907] 2002, p. 118.
20. Ibid., p. 139.
21. Vidyasagar to Madhusudan Datta, July/Aug 1867. Quoted in Murshid 2003, pp. 190–1.
22. Vidyasagar 1891, pp. 473–4. Freely translated from the Bengali.
23. Ibid.
24. Tripathi 2004, p. 29.
25. Ibid., p. 30.
26. Ibid.
27. Ibid., p. 29.
28. Kopf 1969, pp. 236 ff.
29. Ibid., pp. 234–5.
30. Quoted in Tripathi 2004, p. 31.
31. Tripathi 2004, p. 36.
32. Ibid., p. 49.
33. Ibid., p. 131.
34. Dasgupta 2007, p. 15.
35. Quoted in Tripathi 2004, p. 49.
36. Tripathi 2004, p. 57.

37. Majumdar 1965, p. 75.
38. Tripathi 2004, pp. 58–9; also pp. 134–5, note 16.
39. Quoted in Tripathi 2004, p. 60.
40. Tripathi 2004, p. 62.
41. Ibid.
42. Quoted in Acharya 1990, p. 94.
43. Acharya 1990, p. 94.
44. Vidyasagar 1889, p. 168.
45. Tripathi 2004, pp. 44–45.
46. Vidyasagar 1855.
47. Vidyasagar 1876.
48. Ibid., p. 91.
49. Vidyasagar 1889.
50. Ibid., p. 157. Freely translated from the Bengali.
51. Ibid., p. 158. Freely translated from the Bengali.
52. Ibid., p. 160. Freely translated from the Bengali.
53. Ibid., p. 166. Freely translated from the Bengali.
54. See, for example, Ghose 1948, pp. 123–7; De 1962, pp. 627–8; Sen 1979, pp. 171–4; Das 1991, p. 106.
55. Das 1966.
56. De 1962, pp. 627–8.
57. Das 1966, p. 229.
58. Ibid.
59. Ibid., p. 231.
60. Vidyasagar 1860, p. 310.
61. Chattopadhyay 1892, p. 862.
62. Chattopadhaya, Bandyopadhay, and Das 1939, pp. 303–55.
63. Vidyasagar 1854.
64. Vidyasagar 1869.
65. Das 1966, p. 221.

232 • Awakening

66. See this chapter.
67. Vidyasagar 1860.
68. Das 1966, p. 222.
69. Ibid.
70. See this chapter.
71. See this chapter.
72. Sinha 1965, p. 77.
73. Vidyasagar 1855a.
74. Vidyasagar 1855a, Part I, pp. 232–7.
75. Forbes 1996, pp. 22–3.
76. Karlekar 1995.
77. Sastri [1907] 2002, p. 111.
78. Ibid.
79. Vidyasagar 1855b.
80. Banerjee 1990, p. 146.
81. Vidyasagar 1855b, pp. 13–14.
82. Ibid., pp. 28–9.
83. Ibid., p. 29.
84. Ibid., p. 30.
85. Ibid., p. 36.
86. Ibid., pp. 39–40.
87. Tripathi 2004, p. 82.
88. Ibid.
89. De 1962, pp. 568–74.
90. Sen 1977, p. 60.
91. Forbes 1996, pp. 21–2.
92. Murshid 2003, p. 113.
93. Tripathi 2004, p. 94.
94. Murshid 2003, p. 113.

95. Sastri 1904. *Ramtanu Lahiri o Tatkalin Bangasamaj* [Ramtanu Lahiri and the Bengali Society of His Time]. Quoted in 'Preface', pp. i–xii in Chattopadhyay, Bandyopadhyay, and Das 1938, p. v.
96. Tripathi 2004, p. 86.
97. Forbes 1996, p. 22.
98. Quoted in Sinha 1965, pp. 127–8.
99. Ibid., p. 127.
100. Sarkar 1997, p. 236.
101. Nikhilanand (Swami) n.d., pp. 98–110.
102. Ibid., p. 888.
103. Ibid., pp. 160–1.
104. Ibid., p. 267.

Eight

A 'Jolly Christian Rhymer' of 'Exquisite Graces'

SOMETIME OVER THE summer and early autumn of 1864, Ishwar Chandra Vidyasagar received a barrage of letters from Versailles in France. They spoke of despair, desperation, and even a tinge of terror: 'I am going to a French jail and my poor wife must seek shelter in a charitable institution.' This, dated June 2. 'You are the only friend who can rescue me…'[1] The writer signed off as 'Michael M. Dutt'—though two years later he would write to Vidyasagar as 'Datta', saying 'You might drop the vulgar form "Dutt".'[2]

We will know him in this story as Michael Madhusudan Datta (or simply as either 'Madhusudan' or 'Michael', 1824–73): revolutionary poet, playwright, a Derozian long after Derozio was dead, an enfant terrible who Peter Pan-like remained both enfant and terrible into middle age, who suffered from alcoholism, poverty, and an untimely death at age forty-nine.

Fortunately, he was saved from the fate of a French jail 'by a young, beautiful and gracious French lady who has…consoled us in our misfortune & assisted us with her purse'.[3] This was merely a temporary respite: 'God alone knows how we shall continue to live' if help does not come soon.[4] To exacerbate matters a child was on the way, he told Vidyasagar in that same letter. And a few days later: 'I have been obliged to appeal to the generosity of the English Clergyman here to save us from starvation.'[5] 'My heart is full of bitterness, rage and despair.'[6] Even in early September, matters looked miserable: the children wanted to go to a local fair but his wife had only three francs.[7] Later that month, at last, relief was at hand. Vidyasagar had done the needful: money from Calcutta had reached the local bank. 'I scarcely know how to thank you for your kindness in the undertaking to look after my affairs...'[8]

Vidyasagar, who helped Madhusudan in his most desperate hour of need, would eventually abandon him in despair at his errant, profligate, spendthrift ways. Yet, despite their profound outward differences—one spare, ascetic looking, enrobed in dhoti and chaddar, the other extravagantly moustachioed, in coat-tails and waistcoat—there was a delicate strand that entwined them together. For, Madhusudan was a humanist who expressed his creed in poetry just as Vidyasagar manifested his humanism in teaching, polemics, and social activism. They were 'the twin offspring of Bengal's New Age';[9] their objectives were alike though their spheres were different.

Madhusudan's sorry financial state in Versailles where he lived en famille for two-and-a-half years was not from inherent want. It was because the remittances he was supposed to receive from Calcutta would arrive irregularly; indeed, in that time we find him appealing to Vidyasagar for help, it had stopped altogether, because of the negligence of the friend whom he had entrusted with the responsibility of sending him the money.

But then, it seemed Madhusudan's destiny was to place himself in one predicament after another. Fortunately for Bengal's (and India's) literary history it was also his destiny to forge new forms of Bengali poetry. The West gave him his models: he imported and adopted the blank verse to the cause of Bengali poetry; and introduced the sonnet into Bengali poetry. For these creative endeavours alone he has a place in the awakening of nineteenth century Bengal. But there was a deeper aspect to his poetry, especially the great narrative epic poem that critics and scholars deem his masterpiece, the work he is most identified with. For this too he becomes one of the protagonists of our story.

MICHAEL MADHUSUDAN WAS not Michael at birth in the sense that Henry Derozio was Henry from birth. Born in January 1824 into a Kayastha family in a village in the district of Jessore (now in Bangladesh) he was named Madhusudan. He was born into affluent if not overly wealthy circumstances. The affluence, however, was of a relatively recent pedigree, a matter of a single generation. The grandfather was not particularly well-off, but Rajnarayan Datta, Madhusudan's father, became a lawyer who made good, and Rajnarayan's brothers were also successful in their chosen careers. The Datta family was thus very much of the nouveau riche.[10]

Madhusudan was the oldest offspring of his parents and, as it turned out, the only surviving offspring, for his two younger brothers died at ages one and five; he was nine when the youngest died.[11] As an only child in a well-to-do family, we can well imagine that he must have been a spoilt child. Madhusudan's well-documented arrogance in later life, his petulance and extravagance that would later cause him so much grief, can probably be traced back to the privileges of his childhood; his was probably a case of what Peary Chand Mittra would call, in his satirical novel, 'alaler gharer dulal', the pampered son of a rich family.

Michael Madhusudan's biographer points out that the mother, Jahnabi Debi, possessed two noticeable qualities: a penchant for bestowing great affection—more than the usual affection a Bengali mother was known to shower—not just upon her child but also on the children of others; and the fact that she was literate in an age (she was born about 1807–8) when women's education was decidedly frowned upon from the fearful belief that educated women would turn into widows.[12] She also apparently had a remarkable memory: she could memorize large chunks of verse—from the *Ramayana* and *Mahabharata*, of course—and would recite them to her son. Thus, it was through Jahnabi Debi that the boy was introduced to the world of poetry.

When Madhusudan was about five or six, his father moved to Calcutta, leaving his family in their village, and set up practice as a lawyer. He was quickly successful, and bought a house in the Kidderpore area. Jahnabi Debi and Madhusudan—he was by then the only child, the youngest brother having died—joined him sometime around 1833–4.[13] In his village school Madhusudan had been a good student, and had learnt Persian, as all ambitious fathers would want their sons to learn. But, apparently, no English.[14] Nothing seems to be known about Madhusudan's first school in Calcutta. It seems that his father sent him to one that had British or Eurasian teachers.[15] This was the era of Macaulay's famous 'Minute'. One had to learn English to be anything. The rumour goes that in whichever school the boy first went to in Calcutta, he learnt not only English but also Latin, Greek, and Hebrew.[16]

What *is* certain is that Madhusudan joined Hindu College in 1837. He was then thirteen. Thus began his serious apprenticeship in English literature: his preparation for the life of a poet.

Derozio had been dead for six years but his spirit and influence still prevailed. David Hare was still active. The post-Derozio Derozians, we know,[17] formed in 1838 a Society for the Acquisition of General Knowledge, where young men such as Peary Chand Mittra and Krishna Mohun Banerji delivered lectures on social, historical, and scientific themes. The least tempestuous of the Derozians, Ramtanu Lahiri, was a teacher in Hindu College.[18] Across the railings, on the other side of the same building, Vidyasagar was still learning his trade in Sanskrit College.

THEN THERE WAS Captain David Lester Richardson, former army officer in service with the East India Company: educationist, poet, journalist, literary editor, anthologist, and, above all, teacher.

We have noticed this aspect of the Bengal Renaissance: the importance of teachers and their role in its unfolding. The earliest teachers were the munshis to William Jones and the Orientalists, then there was Carey and the Fort William project. But there are other kinds of teachers in our story as well. Teachers who inspire, who fire the imagination of their students. For Henry Derozio there was David Drummond; for the students of Hindu College between 1828 and 1831 there was Derozio himself; and for Madhusudan there was David Lester Richardson. Derozio would not have been what he was without Drummond; the Derozians would not have been what they were without Derozio; and Madhusudan would probably have been a very different being without Richardson.

The teacher is, thus, as much a creator as is the poet or the artist or the inventor of a new religious belief system—for by way of his teaching he can alter the very identity of his students.

At the time Madhusudan entered Hindu College, Richardson was its professor of English, quite recently appointed. Soon after, he became its principal.[19] Later, in 1846, he would move to Krishnagar College as its first principal.[20]

Poetry was Richardson's avocation. Early in his career, well before he joined Hindu College, two volumes of his poems were published in quick succession in London.[21] Other poetry followed and he also edited several Calcutta periodicals. In 1840, he edited an anthology of poems, *Selections from the British Poets from the Time of Chaucer to the Present day with Biographical and Critical Notes*. The usual English suspects were all there, of course. Several of Shakespeare's plays were included, in full. Richardson also included translations of the European classics: from ancient Greece, Homer; from ancient Rome, Virgil; from Italy, Dante and Tasso; from Germany, Goethe.[22] With a nod to India he even included Derozio, and—a touch of conceit here—himself. There were also short lives of the poets and analysis of their styles. Madhusudan imbibed deeply the founts of English and Continental poetry from Richardson's *Selections*.

Richardson was more than a published poet and assiduous anthologist. He was a brilliant teacher of literature. As the story goes, the formidable Thomas Babington Macaulay was once held spellbound listening to Richardson reading Shakespeare in class, and would write to him later saying, 'I may forget everything about India but your reading of Shakespeare, *never*.'[23] As for Madhusudan, attending college made sense only if Richardson was present. He once told his closest and lifelong friend Gourdas Basak that he would keep away from the college when Richardson was absent on leave, no matter how long that was.[24]

Sivanath Sastri, narrating the life of the eminent Derozian Ramtanu Lahiri, tells us that Derozio alone should not be blamed for the Hindu students' contempt for Hindu conservatism or their passion for all things Western: vices as well as virtues. There was also Richardson. 'He took his pupils through the works of Shakespeare in a way to enrapture them. They admired the Captain and the race to which he belonged, and tried to imitate him.'[25]

There is a distinct touch of irony in the later Derozians (or perhaps they should be called simply 'Young Bengal' as they often are by historians) using Richardson as their role model as the earlier Derozians had used Derozio as *their* role model, for the two mentors could not have differed more, despite their shared passion for English literature and a desire to move their students. Derozio was the radical and the iconoclast while Richardson was a political conservative, 'a Tory to the backbone' and utterly loyal to the government. When one of the students was delivering a talk at a meeting of the Society for the Acquisition of General Knowledge on the courts and police in Bengal, Richardson, in attendance, attempted to silence the speaker—an incident reported in a Calcutta periodical.[26]

Richardson clearly respected Derozio as a poet and writer; he not only included the latter in his *Selections* but published two of his prose pieces posthumously in the *India Gazette*.[27] But we can only wonder how they would have fared as Hindu College colleagues.

The two men would influence their students in ways that mirrored their predilections. Derozio, like his hero Shelley, was passionate about philosophical and social issues; Richardson was quite indifferent to such matters. Thus Derozio's students mostly turned to social reform when they entered the 'real world'. Ramtanu Lahiri was perhaps the archetype here. Richardson's students showed a decided preference for literature. Madhusudan was the exemplar. He showed no interest in social or philosophical topics.[28]

AFTER ITS PUBLICATION, Richardson's *Selections from the British Poets* was added to the Hindu College syllabus, which also included courses in mathematics, English grammar, history and, in the final two years, specific British luminaries: Bacon, Milton, Shakespeare, Thomas Gray, Gibbon, Pope, and others.[29] Science was conspicuously absent from Madhusudan's syllabus. Bengali was present in the syllabus but—notwithstanding that one of its teachers was Ramtanu Lahiri—the students evinced little interest in it. Macaulay's dream had materialized. None was more 'English in taste' than Madhusudan.

He was especially attracted to the Romantic poets—the Scots Thomas Campbell and Robert Burns,[30] but Byron was his favourite. While reading Thomas Moore's biography of the poet, he fantasized that one day, if he himself became a 'great poet'—'which I am almost sure I shall be'—his friend Gourdas would write his 'Life'.[31] He was now signing off as 'M.S. Dutt'.

Thus, by 1842—he was about eighteen—Madhusudan knew what he wanted to be: a poet. His earliest known English poems date from 1841, and by 1842 his works were gracing the pages of various Calcutta periodicals.[32] Encouraged by his success in Calcutta, he sent poems to *Blackwood's Magazine* and *Bentley's Miscellany*, two of Britain's most prominent literary periodicals. With characteristic bravura he even dedicated some of them to Wordsworth.[33] Neither periodical accepted his poems. But already, he was looking longingly at imagined English shores.[34]

Madhusudan may have wished to be a poet but his father had other ambitions for his only son and heir. Perhaps Rajnarayan Datta was alarmed that Madhusudan was keeping the wrong sort of company in Calcutta, that he was frittering away his time in useless pursuits. At one point he ordered Madhusudan to leave Calcutta and return to their village home. Madhusudan, who revelled in his Calcutta life, was distraught at being sent away from what he considered his 'home'.[35] During the Durga Puja season, the youth was packed-off to Tamluk, some distance from Calcutta. He chafed at being away from the big city in 'this nasty place',[36] though while there he had 'a little love affair', an experience which, he claimed archly, changed him from 'an anchorite and a monk' to 'a decided Rake'.[37]

Then, in November 1842, all hell broke loose. He learnt that a marriage had been arranged for him by his father to take place in three months' time.[38] He took matters into his own hands, in about as drastic a way as can be imagined. On February 9, 1843—before the ominous three months had elapsed—he converted to Christianity in a ceremony in the Old Church on Mission Row, with armed guards in attendance (in case his father attempted to forcibly remove him).[39]

In his biographer's opinion there were two reasons for this precipitous—and for the parents, calamitous—action. One was to avoid the forthcoming marriage which, of course, would be immediately aborted; the other was Madhusudan's hope that once converted, the Christian community in Calcutta would help him in what he desired most: a passage to England.[40]

As for abandoning the religion of his birth and espousing Christianity, Madhusudan would, some years later, say that 'the Mission of the Anglo-Saxon' was 'to renovate, to regenerate, to Christianize the Hindu'.[41] Even later, he would remark, albeit airily, that '...as a jolly Christian youth'—though he was well past youth by then—'I don't care a pin's head for Hinduism.'[42] His passion for English and European poetry, and his respect for Richardson may have led him to look favourably towards the religion of all his heroes, dead or alive, distant or near. Still, his decision to convert appears to have been a severely pragmatic one—even though, for the occasion of his conversion he composed a hymn. Sung during the ceremony, the hymn began with the verse

Long sunk in superstition's night
By sin and Satan driven—
I saw not,—cared not for the light
That leads the blind to Heaven

and ended with

> I've broken Affection's tenderest ties
> For my blest Saviour's sake;—
> All, all I love beneath the skies
> Lord! I for Thee forsake![43]

Madhusudan was not the first upper-caste Hindu nor the first Hindu College student to convert. Prominent amongst his immediate predecessors (as we have seen) was Krishna Mohun Banerji, later a highly respected Anglican priest, who had been a student of both David Hare and Derozio. Krishna Mohun had known the bitter consequences of his conversion in the Bengali community,[44] but had survived and emerged in considerable triumph as an eminent scholar and educationist.

Perhaps Madhusudan, his much younger contemporary, did not anticipate the social consequences of his decision. His beloved teacher David Lester Richardson left Calcutta to retire in England (though he would later return) and his successor as principal of Hindu College was James Kerr whom Madhusudan loathed. Madhusudan was isolated, but there was worse news to come. Hindu College would no longer have him since the college was open only to high-caste Hindu boys. In fact, the college authorities, fearful of further conversions, forbade its students from seeing any Christians without the principal's permission. Even Madhusudan's closest friend and confidante, Gourdas Basak, was annoyed with him, and Madhusudan found himself deserted by friends, perhaps because of the principal's injunction.

CHRISTIAN THOUGH HE now was, he was still 'Madhusudan'; the name 'Michael' would come later.[45]

A new life began. His parents, infuriated and devastated though they must have been, could not forsake their only child. Rajnarayan provided for him. 'I have plenty of money,' Madhusudan bragged to his friend Gourdas.[46] But there were limits to which Rajnarayan was willing to relent. Madhusudan wrote to Gourdas: 'I am now about to come to live with or rather near to my father.'[47] Not live with but only be near to his parents! There were strong prejudices still extant in upper-caste Hindu Bengal. As for his dream of going to England—that too was put on hold for the present, though he remained optimistic: 'I won't go to England till December next…my father won't allow that,' he wrote to Gourdas.[48] His optimism was misplaced. England, as it turned out, was quite a while away.

Spurned by Hindu College, Madhusudan's formal education was abruptly disrupted. At this time, he met Thomas Smith, a priest associated with the local Scottish church who offered him the hospitality of his home. This was a fortuitous meeting, for Smith had serious literary interests and, about the time Madhusudan moved in with him, was appointed editor of the literary periodical *Calcutta Review*. Under Smith's influence over a stay of about a year, Madhusudan's literary taste changed; his allegiance shifted from the Romantic poets to Shakespeare, Milton, the classical works—and Christianity.[49]

Madhusudan's conversion had initially been a pragmatic, even cynical, act. But now, cut-off from his familiar social and intellectual moorings—no Hindu College, no Richardson, friends keeping away—he was facing, as his biographer puts it, a possible identity crisis; and so he turned to his new religion. He toyed with the idea of becoming a missionary.[50]

Late in 1844, Madhusudan crossed the Hooghly to the suburb of Sibpur and entered Bishop's College, lying cheek by jowl with the luxuriant Indian Botanical Gardens where Sir William Jones and his lady used to take the evening air.[51] Bishop's College—which another celebrated Hindu College alumnus convert, the Rev. Krishna Mohun Banerji, would one day join as professor[52]—educated and trained students to become Anglican missionaries. All its students received scholarships.

However, Rajnarayan Datta, already horrified and now even more fearful that his Christian son would become a Christian missionary, insisted on paying Madhusudan's college fees and for upkeep. This meant that the youth was not bound to become a missionary as he would be if he accepted a college scholarship. Thus, Madhusudan was accepted by Bishop's College as a lay student.[53]

He resumed formal studies after a hiatus of almost two years. In the somewhat Gothic environment of the college precincts, his European learning was resumed. There were courses on Greek and Latin literature; he learnt Italian and was able to read Tasso in the original; he also learnt Sanskrit and Bengali. He became a scholar of classical literature. The Romantic poets—even Byron—receded from the forefront of his literary consciousness. 'Byron, Scott and Moore, very nice poets in their way, no doubt,' he would write condescendingly years later to his friend Rajnarayan Bose, 'but by no means of the highest school of poets, except perhaps Byron, now and then. I like Wordsworth better.'[54] It was Homer and Virgil,

Milton, Dante, and Tasso who beckoned him now rather than his former Romantic heroes. He was not to know then, but in historical hindsight *we* can say that Madhusudan, the future poet of an epic masterpiece, was significantly shaped by his time in Bishop's College.

Here was a kind of serendipity in evidence: had Rajnarayan Datta not arranged Madhusudan's marriage, no conversion to Christianity; no conversion, no rejection by Hindu College, and thus no Bishop's College; and with no Bishop's College, no grounding in classical literature, in Greek or Latin, in Biblical themes.

In May 1847, he found himself 'half-dead with all manners of troubles'.[55] The 'troubles' no doubt had to do with family matters. By December that year, three years after he resumed studies in Bishop's College, he left the college because his father had stopped paying his fees.[56] Perhaps Rajnarayan's patience had been exhausted; perhaps any hopes he had harboured that his son would revert to Hinduism had finally dissolved; perhaps it was because Rajnarayan lost the position he had held in the civil court in Calcutta and so his income had diminished.[57]

The relationship between father and son, always strained since the conversion, could not have improved by the fact that Rajnarayan married again while Jahnabi Debi was still alive and, when the second wife died, yet a third time. Polygamy still remained a reality in an era in which people from Rammohun Roy to Vidyasagar were railing against it.[58]

Any intention Madhusudan still had of becoming a missionary—more to be financially independent of his father than from a genuine calling to spread the Word[59]—collapsed when he withdrew from Bishop's College before taking his final exams, a necessary condition to qualify as an Anglican missionary. He was in need of a job. The Muse of poetry retreated while he ruminated on ways and means to survive. Finally he decided to leave Calcutta. Without telling his parents or his once-dearest friends from Hindu College, he set sail for Madras at the end of 1847 and reached his destination on a 'slow boat' on January 18, 1848, just short of his twenty-fourth birthday. Only his two closest friends in Bishop's College, Charles Eggbert Kenner and Robert Walker, and possibly two of his college professors knew of his departure.[60]

THUS BEGAN A third phase in his already tempestuous life. He could not have had an easy time in his first days in Madras. 'Since my arrival here, I have had much to do in the way of procuring a standing place for myself,' he wrote to Gourdas over a year later.[61] But then, 'my trials are, in a certain measure at an end'. For one thing, he had a job, though an ill-paying one: he was an assistant teacher in the school attached to the Madras Male and Female Orphan Asylum; for another, he had fallen quickly in love and found himself a bride. 'Mrs. Dutt is of English parentage,' he told Gourdas who in distant Calcutta had apparently already heard of his 'matrimonial doings'.[62]

'Mrs Dutt', Rebecca Thompson McTavish, aged seventeen at the time of her marriage was, in fact, in the phrase of a literary scholar 'three-quarters white'.[63] Her late father, a gunner in the East India Company's army, was British while her late Indian-born mother was an 'Indo-Briton'.[64] She herself, a denizen of the Female Orphan Asylum, was a student in the school. Madhusudan was never ever far from making waves, raising hackles wherever he was: first converting to Christianity in Calcutta; then, in Madras, marrying an English girl. We are not surprised that he 'had great troubles in getting her'.[65]

The Muse returned. In November 1848 he began and completed within the month a narrative poem in the Byronic style—Madhusudan was evidently still not free from his old hero's influence—*The Captive Ladie (An Indian Tale) in Two Cantos*, which was published in a Madras periodical.[66] The poem 'has excited great attention here, and many persons of superior judgement and acquirements have induced me to republish it in a *bookish* form'.[67] And, indeed, this was what he decided to do. 'I am republishing my book by subscription,'[68] he wrote to Gourdas and he asked his old friend to help raise subscriptions in Calcutta.

In fact, many of his old Hindu College and Bishop's College friends rallied to his cause. He was delighted to hear from Bhudeb Mukherji (who along with Gourdas was his closest friend from those halcyon, pre-conversion days) and others.[69] Subscriptions were raised and *The Captive Ladie* appeared as a slim volume in April 1849. Madhusudan was now a card-carrying member of the poetic fraternity—if not an English poet, the next best thing, a poet in the English language. Like Derozio some two decades earlier, he had reached out to seek a niche for himself in what would one day be called 'Indian literature in English'.[70]

Yet he emphasized that *The Captive Ladie* was 'a *thorough* Indian work, full of Rishis—Calis [Kalis]—Lutchmee [Lakshmi]—Camas [Kamas]—Rudras and all the Deities incarnate whom our orthodox fathers worshipped'.[71]

He now attired regularly in European clothes—'both on account of my good lady and the situation I hold'—though he would make sardonic digs at himself. 'I make a passable "Tash feringhee",'[72] he wrote to Gourdas, both 'feringi' and 'tash' being derogatory terms for those of mixed Indo-European or Anglo-Indian blood. He was also by now, for the first time, 'Michael Madhusudan Dutt': 'Michael' appeared in the marriage registry in Madras,[73] while the author's name on the title page of *The Captive Ladie* was 'M.M.S. Dutt'.

Nor had his Anglophilia subsided. In 1854 he gave a lecture, published as a booklet, titled *The Anglo-Saxon and the Hindu*, a paean in extravagant prose to the literary West, Christianity, the civilizing mission of the West but, above all, to English language and literature. The 'Mission of the Anglo-Saxon,' he wrote, is 'to renovate, to regenerate, to Christianize the Hindu.' His love for the 'language of the Anglo-Saxon' burst forth: 'I acknowledge to you and I need not blush to do so—that I love the language of the Anglo-Saxon. Yes—*love* the language—the glorious language of the Anglo-Saxon.'[74]

Much name-dropping followed. He had read the Greeks and the Romans, Homer, Virgil, Lucretius, Ovid, Herodotus, Livy, Demosthenes, Cicero, Thycydides. He had read the Indian classics:

> I have heard the melodious voice of him [Valmiki] who from the green tree of Poesy sang of Rama like a Kokila; I have wept over the fatal war of the implacable Courava [Kaurava] and the heroic Pandava. I have grieved over the sufferings of he who lost the fatal ring...[75]

All those, yes, and also the Italians Tasso and Dante and Petrarch, the Frenchman Molière. But none could compare with 'the literature, the language of the Anglo-Saxon!'[76]

Madhusudan's purple prose may lead us to think that here was a case of the young poet protesting too much. Indeed, there was a certain contrariness to his position. *The Captive Ladie*, was, as he insisted, 'a *thorough* Indian work'. His subsequent writings while he was in Madras, though still in English, explored Indian, including Muslim, themes.

More significantly, his mind was turning to his native language (though signs of this would appear only after he left Madras). Perhaps the much-venerated educationist John Drinkwater Bethune—to whom, under Michael's instruction, Gourdas Basak sent a copy of *The Captive Ladie*[77]—had something to do with this, for Bethune had trashed *The Captive Ladie*, saying that Indians should write in their mother tongue.[78] Perhaps Madhusudan himself was not sanguine about the literary merits of *The Captive Ladie*. However, he was satisfied with its favourable reception in Madras and that its publication 'has opened the most splendid prospects for me, and has procured me the friendship some of whom it is an honour to know'.[79] He reiterated this point to Gourdas: 'Remember my friend, that I published it for the sake of attracting some notice in order to better my prospects and not exactly for Fame. However what is done is done.'[80]

Madhusudan lived in Madras till January 1856. Much happened in this time. While still teaching at the Madras Asylum School, he entered journalism, following in the footsteps of his mentor David Lester Richardson. He was appointed editor of a magazine called *Eurasian* and, by all accounts, did his job competently. Later, the owner of the *Eurasian* launched another journal called the *Madras Hindu Chronicle* and Madhusudan was asked to edit this as well.[81] In 1852, he quit the Asylum School to join the Madras High School. His financial situation, always strained, was eased somewhat.[82]

During this time his writing, all in English, continued though rather sparingly: he published his first play, *Rizia: Empress of Inde*. He published poems. Then there was the booklet *The Anglo-Saxon and the Hindu*.

He fathered four children: two daughters and two sons. And he fell in love and began a relationship with Henrietta White, the teenaged daughter of an English friend and colleague.

The centre never ever quite held for Madhusudan. In December 1855, he would write to Gourdas saying, 'I have a fine English wife and four children.'[83] Scarcely a month later, in late January 1856, almost exactly eight years after landing in Madras, he would leave for Calcutta, never to return, never to meet his 'fine English wife and four children' again. Two and a half years later, Henrietta, then about twenty-two, joined him, and while they would never marry (for, so far as is known, Madhusudan and Rebecca never reached a divorce), they would live together in common law bondage (and Michael would refer to her as his wife, as he did in his letter to Vidyasagar)[84] for the rest of their lives.

Madhusudan's mother Jahnabi Debi had passed away in 1851, at which time he had briefly visited Calcutta. Rajnarayan died in December 1856. His father's death raised all kinds of problems about the disposition of his property; his relatives, including his stepmother (Rajnarayan's third wife) were already fighting over the inheritance. Madhusudan himself would have some claims of inheritance, and it was no doubt the thought of sorting out this problem that prompted him to leave Madras for good and return to Calcutta. However, his affair with Henrietta, and the fact that he abandoned Rebecca and the children would suggest that this was yet another reason.

IF FOR ANY reason Michael Madhusudan had stopped writing at this point in his life, he would not have a place in this story. For, in hindsight we realize that what has transpired thus far, despite all its sound and fury, was but the preamble for what followed. And what followed in this, the fourth phase in his restless life, was a level of creative output that he may well have dreamt of but could never have imagined its direction or shape. A creativity by way of which he carved for himself a massive niche in the story of the Bengal Renaissance, in the literary part of this awakening.

This fourth phase of his life, his anni mirabilis, occupied the larger part of the six years or so, from his return to Calcutta from Madras in February 1856 to when he set sail—finally—for England in June 1862.

For the moment let us ignore the upheavals in his personal life—that was an ongoing aspect of his entire life—and turn our gaze to his creative life. In this period, Madhusudan wrote three substantial plays and two short ones; he composed three long narrative poems, tried his hand at a sonnet, wrote a collection of odes, and a collection of verse-letters or 'heroic epistles'.

But there was more: he invented a form of the blank verse—verse without rhyme—for his own purposes; and that purpose was *Bengali literature*. Here was the ardent, defiant

Anglophile, the poet who above all loved the 'language of the Anglo-Saxon', whose literary endeavours till then were entirely in English, the poet whose heroes belonged to the pantheon of Anglo-European literature, who disdained literary India, performing an about-face.

Madhusudan also translated three Bengali plays (including one of his own) into English; and the first translation was significant, for the reinvention of his literary identity began when, in 1858, he was commissioned by two noblemen-brothers and patrons of the Bengali theatre, Pratapchandra Singha and Ishwar Chandra Singha of Paikpara, to translate a Bengali play called *Ratnabali* (written by a leading playwright of the time) into English so that their British guests could watch its staging.[85] He was in his 'Anglo-Saxon' element in this, his first literary endeavour since returning to Calcutta: 'I flatter myself you will at once see how I have tried in pure Saxon English, the language of the best Dramatists,' he wrote to Gourdas, sending him a part of the translation.[86] At the same time he was too much the creative being to not impose his own imprint in the process: '...I have tried to impart an air of originality to the affair, careless where the ideas are inextricably damnably Bengali.'[87]

He found the original play 'a very commonplace affair'.[88] Realizing that the standard of Bengali drama of the time was so much inferior to 'the Dramatic portion of English literature',[89] he decided with characteristic bravura to write a play in Bengali, to prove that he could do a better job than what was at hand.[90] The outcome, produced within a few weeks and completed in July 1858, was his first original composition in Bengali and his first original work since leaving

Madras. He called the play *Sermistha*, and it was based on the story from the *Mahabharata* about the king Jayati, his wife Debjani, and her maid Sarmistha: a story of the 'eternal triangle'. Madhusudan's biographer makes the plausible point that Madhusudan was attracted to this story because of his own situation: the clear similarity between the story and his own relationship with Rebecca and Henrietta (who joined him in Calcutta at the end of the year).[91]

For Madhusudan, here was the opportunity of melding West with East; of writing a Bengali play not in the Sanskritic mould along received wisdom but on Western lines. 'I am aware, my dear fellow, that there will, in all likelihood, be something of a foreign air about my drama.'[92] But that does not matter. 'Do you dislike [Thomas] Moore's poetry because it is full of orientalism? Byron's poetry for its Asiatic air? [Thomas] Carlyle's prose for its Germanism?'[93]

His play would not only reflect his own cross-cultural, Anglo-Indian worldview but was also meant for a like-minded audience: 'I am writing for that portion of my countrymen who think as I think, whose minds have been more or less imbued with Western ideas and *modes of thinking*...'[94]

And so, perhaps unwittingly, he announced his future approach: to summon Western literary ideas to the Bengali (or Indian) cause. And just as he was contemptuous of a 'servile admiration of everything Sanskrit',[95] he would not merely imitate the 'Anglo-Saxon' whom he so adored. The product would be original and resoundingly his own. 'In matters literary, old boy, I am too proud to stand before the world in borrowed clothes. I may borrow a necktie, or even a waistcoat, but not the whole suit.'[96]

The floodgates had opened. 'Now that I have got the taste of blood, I am at it again. I am now writing another play.'[97] This would be *Padmavati*. The 'necktie' he borrowed was the story of the golden apple of Greek mythology, but Madhusudan melded it with Indian classical sources, and preened with the artist's satisfaction for a work well done: '...there are fewer prettier plots in any Drama that you have read! I invented it one blessed Sunday.'[98]

He was now very much in an experimental mode—but with something more substantial than a mere necktie. He was working with the poetic form called blank verse—unrhymed verse. 'I need scarcely tell you that the Blank form of verse is the *best* suited for Poetry in every language. A true poet will always succeed best in Blank verse as a bad one in Rhyme.'[99]

He explained to the actor Keshabchandra Ganguli what he was attempting to do with the blank verse in Bengali, and admitted he had at first to struggle. 'When I first began to write my ear used to rebel'; but then, gradually, 'I have grown completely reconciled to Bengali Blank verse and its melody and power astonish me.'[100]

Madhusudan was now ensconced in a house on Chitpore Road in the heart of Black Town Calcutta, symbolic perhaps of his new literary leanings.[101] In April 1860, we find him writing to Rajnarayan Bose, a close contemporary in Hindu College, whose literary judgement he apparently trusted. He confided in Rajnarayan about his literary volte-face:

> I do not know what European told you that I had a great contempt for Bengali but that was a fact. But now—I even go the length of believing that our Blank Verse 'thrashes the

Englishers' as an American would say. But joking apart, is not Blank verse in our language quite as grand as any other?'[102]

And then, almost off-handedly, he adds: 'I enclose the opening invocation of my...[*Meghnadabadh*]—you must tell me what you think of it. A friend here, a good judge of poetry, has pronounced it magnificent.'[103]

MADHUSUDAN HAD, THEN, just begun composing what is universally acknowledged by scholars and critics of Bengali literature as his masterpiece, the epic poem *Meghnadabadh Kabya* (The Slaying of Meghnada).[104]

In *Meghnadabadh* we find the realization of his remark to Gourdas Basak all those years ago, from Madras, 'Am I not preparing for the great object of embellishing the tongue of my fathers?'[105] That embellishment came by way of a fusion of all that Madhusudan revered in Western literature with his Indian source material. But not his original heroes—not Byron and the other Romantics. 'I never read any poetry except that of Valmiki, Virgil, Kalidas, Dante...Tasso...and Milton.'[106]

Meghnadabadh would realize his 'ambition to engraft the exquisite graces of the Greek mythology to our own'.[107] By this he did not mean to borrow Greek *stories*. The poem would remain Indian. 'You shan't have to complain...of the un-Hindu character of the Poem. I shall...try to write as a Greek would have done.'[108]

The poem was based on an episode from the *Ramayana*. It told the story of the third and final battle between Meghnada (also called Indrajit in the original epic), the eldest son of Ravana, the king of the 'rakshasas' (the demons), and his slaying by Lakshmana, Rama's brother, and the funeral rites that follow.

As every Indian knows, the *Ramayana*, one of the two great epics of Hindu mythology, tells the story of the prince Rama, in self-imposed exile from the kingdom of Ayodhya, accompanied in his exile by his wife Sita and brother Lakshmana. In the course of their wanderings, the demon king Ravana, lusting for Sita, abducts her and takes her to his island kingdom of Lanka. This act brings about a war on Lanka between Ravana and his kin and Rama, Lakshmana, and their allies, a tribe of monkey-like beings, led by Hanuman. A section of this war was the subject of the poem.

The *Ramayana,* is a sacred text for the Hindus.[109] Rama is not only a Hindu hero but one of the incarnations of the god Vishnu, which makes him a god as well. Madhusudan was not interested in what the *Ramayana* meant to traditional Hindus. It was the human aspect of the epic that interested him.

> I must tell you, my dear fellow, that though as a jolly Christian youth I don't care a pin's head for Hinduism, I love the grand mythology of our ancestors. It is full of poetry. A fellow with an inventive head can manufacture the most beautiful things out of it.[110]

It was as if he had discovered for the first time 'what a vast field our country now presents for literary enterprise'.[111]

And so he invented and manufactured. He turned the *Ramayana* on its head: for him Meghnada was not a demonic villain, nor was Ravana's younger brother Bibhisan a righteous rakshasa who condemned Ravana for going to war with Rama, who advised his brother to restore Sita to her husband—and got ejected from the rakshasa clan for his pains. Rather, Meghnada became 'the glorious son of Ravana…a noble fellow'; and Bibhisan was but a 'scoundrel'.[112] Ravana was 'a grand fellow', one who 'elevates and kindles my imagination'.[113] As for Rama, he would write, 'I despise Ram and his rabble.'[114] Madhusudan's heart—'the heart of the Poet'—was 'with the Rakshasas', the readers of *Meghnadabadh* grumbled.[115] (This grumbling has persisted even 120 years after.)[116]

Even in his own time *Meghnadabadh* was quickly appreciated. 'The poem is rising into splendid popularity,'[117] the poet wrote to Rajnarayan Bose—this on January 15, 1861, just two weeks after the first part of the poem has been published.[118] He added coyly: 'Some say it is better than Milton—but that is all bosh—nothing can be better than Milton.'[119]

It was Milton who provided him his model for blank verse. 'Good Blank Verse should be sonorous and the best writer of Blank Verse in English is the *toughest* of poets—I mean old John Milton.'[120] When 'many [said] it licks Kalidasa', Madhusudan with no false modesty could live with that.[121] Nor did he think it 'impossible' to match Virgil or Tasso. They were 'glorious' but mortal. But Milton was 'divine'.[122]

Still, he was flattered to be compared to both Milton and Kalidasa.[123] He related to Rajnarayan Bose 'a jolly little anecdote' of coming across a stranger in a Calcutta bookshop 'deeply poring over' *Meghnadabadh* who, not knowing his identity, assured him that 'here is poetry that would make any nation proud'.[124]

Here was a case of vox populi. Madhusudan had every reason to be happy. 'I have not yet heard a single line in

Meghnada's disfavour.'¹²⁵ Within a year of its completion, a thousand copies of the work had been sold; the poem was to appear in a second edition with annotations. Moreover, 'a real BA'—one of the first graduates of the recently formed University of Calcutta¹²⁶—'has written a long critical preface'.¹²⁷ *Meghnadabadh* was even achieving academic respectability!

DISSATISFACTION WITH THE way things are is undoubtedly a prime fount of creativity.¹²⁸ But it is not the only such fount. There is also curiosity: to see if one can do something one has never done before.¹²⁹ And there is also, perhaps most compelling of all, the desire or need to break away from the past, to do what *no one* has done before; to deviate from history itself and thereby make history.¹³⁰

In Madhusudan, we find manifestations of all these qualities. It was dissatisfaction with (his perception) of the moribund state of the Bengali theatre that led him to write *Sermistha*. It was curiosity and the attendant desire to be original that goaded him to accept a friend Jatindramohun Tagore's challenge that Bengali poetry did not lend itself to blank verse and compose the narrative poem *Tilottamasambhab Kabya* (1860).¹³¹

Still, some sceptics were not convinced: 'I have heard that V[idyasagar] has been speaking of it with contempt.'¹³² But then he won over his critics, including the 'renowned Vidyasagar' who 'has at last condescended to see "Great merit" in it…'¹³³

It was a confluence of curiosity and the desire to make history that led him from *Tilottoma* to the effort of composing not just a poem in blank verse but a veritable epic, *Meghnadabadh*. This same desire to deviate from the norm also led him to invent his own Meghnada, his own Rama, his own Ravana.

It was this same fusion of dissatisfaction with existing poetic form, curiosity, and the desire for originality that prompted him to experiment with the first Bengali sonnet. 'I want to introduce the sonnet into our language,' he wrote to Rajnarayan Bose, and so he did with the poem *Kabi-Matribhasa* (The Poet's Mother-Tongue, 1860).[134] A few years later, in another place and very different circumstances, he would write over a hundred sonnets, in some of which he paid homage to many other poets, Western and Indian.[135]

Curiosity and the quest for new poetic forms led him to experiment with yet another poetic genre, inspired by the Roman poet Ovid:[136] verse-letters. 'I have been scribbling a new thing...[*Birnangana*] ... Heroic Epistles from the most noted Puranic women to their lovers or lords.'[137]

BUT DISSATISFACTION HAS its dark, destructive side—in Madhusudan's case, self-destructive. If in the years between 1856 and 1862 we find him the creator, in the years that followed he became the self-destroyer.

But first, what of his personal life during his creative period? Henrietta was with him, and though not married, he referred to her as 'Mrs. Dutt'.[138] By his account, she even learnt Bengali, at least enough that she was the 'first lady-reader' of *Tilottama*.[139] (Rajnarayan Bose's wife was the second.) They named their first child, a daughter, born 1859, Sarmistha. There would be another child born in this Calcutta period.

There seemed to have been a measure of stability on the domestic front.

The property and inheritance matters that had drawn Madhusudan to Calcutta from Madras were gradually resolved. Court cases were won. He was by no means wealthy but there was some measure of financial stability. 'I am prosperous, thank God!'[140]

Yet there was—there must have been—the shadow of his act of abandonment of Rebecca and four children in Madras. The letters of this, Madhusudan's most brilliantly fertile, period say nothing of that past, that appallingly shameful act. There was, however, a short poem he wrote titled 'Atma-bilap' (Self-lament, 1861). It was a poem of self-searching, melancholic anguish in which the poet spoke of the years spent in search of fame and wealth and love, and wondered what fruits he had gained by this search.[141]

As a poet, Madhusudan had achieved the kind of fame he had perhaps dreamt of when as a Hindu College student he wrote to Gourdas Basak of becoming a 'great poet' (though then it was the larger world, across the oceans, he had fantasized about: the world of London, of *Blackwood's Magazine*, his mentor David Lester Richardson's 'other' world). Yet, despite his fame in Bengal, he was dissatisfied with his lot. Being a brilliant, successful Bengali poet did not suffice; fame he had gained, and love, but not wealth, not the status that only came from wealth—the kind of status his Hindu College friends, few of whom were as gifted as he was, were enjoying. Those of comparable intellectual ability, Rajnarayan Bose and Bhudeb Mukherji, not to speak of Gourdas Basak, were also earning more than him.[142] At the very least, 'I sigh for some

A 'Jolly Christian Rhymer' of 'Exquisite Graces' • 263

independent position, so that I might devote myself wholly and solely to my favourite studies.'[143]

Law—his father's profession—beckoned. We find him writing to Gourdas Basak that he was 'dreadfully busy reading up for the Law Examination that was coming up'.[144] He was studying for the 'Sudder Law Examination' which would qualify him as a lawyer for the Sudder Court, the civil court. 'Law and Poetry!' he exclaimed, dryly.[145] Strange bedfellows they may seem, though perhaps not so strange in a Calcutta where the gifted were so often polymathic.

He was thwarted in this ambition, however. The examination, for whatever reason, kept being cancelled. 'It seems to be the decree of fate that I should write idle verses and make no money,' he laments.[146] Eventually, with characteristic bravura, he decided that if he could not become a lawyer of the sort Indians mostly were at the time, he would join the ranks of the Englishmen and become more than a mere lawyer; he would become a barrister. This way he could kill two birds with one stone; for not only did barristers earn more than lawyers, he would also, finally, realize his early dream of going to England which he would have to do to qualify for the Bar. 'I am making arrangements to go to England to study for the Bar.'[147] 'Arrangements' meant a great deal of money, for reading for the Bar in England was an expensive affair. 'The thing will cost me about Rs. 20,000 and I can spare that.'[148]

However, there were still complications concerning ownership of his assets. No less a person than 'the great Vidyasagar'—a 'convert to the new poetical creed'—helped him by arranging a mortgage on his property.[149]

'I must bid adieu to the Muse... No more Modhu the ... [poet], old fellow, but Michael M.S. Dutt, Esquire of the Inner Temple, Barrister-at-Law! Ha! Ha! Isn't that grand?'[150] He was finally away, in June 1862, to his longed-for England. Henrietta and the two children stayed behind in Calcutta, with the arrangement that she would receive a regular monthly remittance, as would he.[151]

In London, he was admitted not to the Inner Temple as he had hoped but to Gray's Inn. And though he delighted in some of the 'wonders' of England—Hampton Court, especially—he was soon homesick, 'dull and melancholy'.[152] The climate depressed him as it would countless visitors from the subcontinent. 'What a brutal country is this, by Jove,'[153] he would write to Manomohun Ghose.

Things went terribly wrong. Henrietta did not receive her remittances, nor was he sent the funds he was supposed to receive.[154] And when Henrietta did manage to recover some of the money due to her, she fled from Calcutta with the children for England. In May 1863, less than a year after Madhusudan arrived in London, she and the children joined him.[155]

London was expensive; so was studying for the Bar. The available money was simply not enough for his legal studies and to maintain his family. He decided to leave London—and his studies—temporarily for Versailles in France. Madhusudan's biographer suggests that the real reason for leaving England was the racism in England against Indians and other Asians.[156] Indeed, Madhusudan found Versailles agreeably different.

> I wish I could live here all the days of my life with means to take occasional runs to India to see my friends... This is

unquestionably the best quarter of the globe...the...[heaven] of our ancestral creed. Come here and you will soon forget that you spring from a degraded and subject race. Everyone, whether high or low, will treat you as a man, not a 'damned nigger.'[157]

This letter to Gourdas Basak had an altogether pleasant, relaxed tone that contrasted starkly with the series of despairing, anguished letters to Vidyasagar over the preceding months,[158] in which Madhusudan desperately appealed to Vidyasagar for help in resolving his financial predicament—a crisis brought about (as we have seen) by the irresponsible behaviour of a friend he had entrusted with the task of sending his remittances.

Fortunately, through Vidyasagar's efforts, monetary troubles were resolved, at least for a while. Madhusudan could now write to Gourdas not only of the pleasure of living in France but of his children. Sarmistha, he wrote, 'is already quite French'. Their second child, a son, Milton 'is also getting on well'. Their third child, born in Versailles, did not, however, live long.[159] Madhusudan was even planning to resume his legal studies in London, though he planned to leave Henrietta and his family in Versailles.[160]

The Muse had, for the moment, deserted him. 'I have not been doing much in the poetical line of late, beyond imitating a few Italian and French things...'[161] But he had not been entirely idle. 'I have nearly mastered French and Italian and am going on swimmingly with German.'[162]

Financial worries, however, intruded unendingly. Once more, Vidyasagar, infinitely compassionate, helped. 'My distinguished friend Ishwar Chandra Vidyasagar has taken me by the hand...'[163]

Despite his disclaimer to Gourdas, Madhusudan had been doing something 'in the poetical line' while in Versailles. He returned to the sonnet form which he had once wished to introduce into Bengali poetry. 'I have been lately reading Petrarch—the Italian poet and scribbling some "sonnets" after his manner.'[164] In fact 'some' sonnets turned out to be over a hundred,[165] including one in tribute to Dante on the occasion of the Italian poet's 600th birth anniversary. He sent this sonnet to the king of Italy with a covering letter:

Sir,
A poor rhymer who does not give himself the name of a poet, born on the shores of the Ganges, and a passionate admirer of the father of Italian poetry, takes the liberty of presenting at the feet of your Majesty, along with this letter, a Bengali sonnet, a little oriental flower, which he wishes to join the garland to be wreathed in Italy for decorating the tomb of the illustrious Dante.[166]

The letter was signed 'Michael Madhusudan Datta'—not 'Dutt'. The Bengali poet was emphasizing his Bengali-ness.

Amidst all his financial problems, Madhusudan returned to London and resumed his studies. His doggedness finally paid off, and he was able to write triumphantly to Vidyasagar from London, on November 19, 1866, that '...you will be highly delighted to hear that I was called to the Bar last night by the Society of Gray's Inn and that I am at last a Barrister-at-Law'.[167] He did not forget his debt to Vidyasagar. 'All this I owe to God and to you under God, and I assure you I shall ever think of you as my greatest benefactor and truest friend. But for you what might have become of me!'[168]

Now that he had his 'name down in the list of English Barristers', he changed the spelling of his name and gave it 'the true Sanscrit form'. He was 'Michael Madhusudan Datta'. The 'vulgar form "Dutt"', he told Vidyasagar, could now be dropped.[169]

THE SIXTH AND final phase. The barrister—he was, in fact, the third Bengali to be called to the Bar—returned to Calcutta in February 1867. Once again, typically bizarrely, he left Henrietta, the two children and one more on the way, in Versailles. Once again she was strapped for money. Ultimately, Henrietta, with Sarmistha, Milton, and the new baby, named Napoleon, rejoined him in Calcutta in May 1867.[170]

The two would live for another six years. But not the poet. There was only the ambitious barrister whose dream of wealth and status by way of his legal practice was bitterly shattered over the next few remaining years.

Thus began the steady decline: the all-too-familiar pattern of flamboyant living beyond one's means; debts; abandoning a home in White Town's Loudon Street for Black Town Entally and then Uttarpara; alcoholism; utter poverty; and ill-health. Henrietta's health also declined. On June 26, 1873, Madhusudan, himself in a Calcutta hospital, learnt that Henrietta had died. Three days later, Michael Madhusudan Datta, rebellious, revolutionary 'rhymer' passed away.

Notes

1. Michael Madhusudan Datta to Vidyasagar, June 2, 1864, pp. 199–201 in Murshid 2004, p. 200.
2. Madhusudan to Vidyasagar, November 19, 1866, pp. 270–1 in Murshid 2004, p. 271.
3. Madhusudan to Vidyasagar, June 9, 1864, pp. 202–5 in Murshid 2004, p. 203.
4. Ibid.
5. Madhusudan to Vidyasagar, June 18, 1864, pp. 206–8 in Murshid 2004, p. 206.
6. Madhusudan to Vidyasagar, June 18, 1864, pp. 206–8 in Murshid 2004, p. 207.
7. Madhusudan to Vidyasagar, September 2, 1864, pp. 215–16 in Murshid 2004.
8. Madhusudan to Vidyasagar, September 18, 1864, pp. 217–20 in Murshid 2004, p. 217.
9. Dasgupta [1956] 1999, p. 173.
10. Murshid 2003, pp. 7–8.
11. Ibid., p. 12.
12. Ibid. See also Chapter nine.
13. Ibid., p. 13.
14. Ibid., p. 16.
15. Ibid., p. 17.
16. Ibid., pp. 17–18.
17. See Chapter six.
18. Sastri [1907] 2002, pp. 92 ff.
19. Murshid 2004, pp. xxxviii–ix.
20. Sastri [1907] 2002, p. 108.
21. Murshid 2004, pp. xxxviii–ix; Murshid 2003, pp. 20–1.

22. Murshid 2003, p. 23.
23. Quoted in Sengupta 1955, p. 4.
24. Madhusudan to Gourdas Basak, November 25, 1842, pp. 28–9 in Murshid 2004.
25. Sastri [1907] 2002, p. 106.
26. Ibid., p. 97.
27. Chaudhuri 2008b, p. xliv.
28. Murshid 2003, pp. 21–2.
29. Ibid., pp. 23–4.
30. Madhusudan to Gourdas, October 18, 1842, pp. 24–5 in Murshid 2004.
31. Madhusudan to Gourdas, November 25, 1842, pp. 28–9 in Murshid 2004, p. 29.
32. Murshid 2003, p. 35.
33. Madhusudan to Gourdas, October 7, 1842, pp. 22–3 in Murshid 2004.
34. Madhusudan to Gourdas, November 25, 1842, pp. 28–9 in Murshid 2004.
35. Madhusudan to Gourdas, August 7, 1842, pp. 20–1 in Murshid 2004.
36. Madhusudan to Gourdas, October 21, 1842, p. 25 in Murshid 2004.
37. Madhusudan to Gourdas, October 18, 1842, pp. 24–5 in Murshid 2004.
38. Madhusudan to Gourdas, November 27, 1842, pp. 32–3 in Murshid 2004.
39. Murshid 2003, p. 49.
40. Murshid 2003, pp. 45–6.
41. Datta 1854.
42. Madhusudan to Rajnarayan Bose, May 15, 1860, pp. 121–3 in Murshid 2004, p. 122.

43. Quoted in Murshid 2003, p. 49.
44. Sastri [1907] 2002, p. 167.
45. Seely 2004, pp. 20–1.
46. Madhusudan to Gourdas, May 1843, pp. 38–9 in Murshid 2004.
47. Madhusudan to Gourdas, April 1843, p. 37 in Murshid 2004.
48. Ibid.
49. Murshid 2003, p. 56.
50. Ibid.
51. See Chapter one.
52. Sastri 1907, p. 167.
53. Murshid 2003, p. 58.
54. Madhusudan to Rajnarayan Bose, September 1860, pp. 152–3 in Murshid 2004, p. 153.
55. Madhusudan to Gourdas, May 19, 1847, p. 47 in Murshid 2004.
56. Murshid 2003, p. 63.
57. Ibid., p. 66.
58. See Chapter four.
59. Murshid 2003, pp. 64–5.
60. Murshid 2004, p. 63, note 2.
61. Madhusudan to Gourdas, February 14, 1849, pp. 61–6 in Murshid 2004.
62. Ibid.
63. Dyson 2004.
64. Murshid 2004, p. 63, note 5.
65. Madhusudan to Gourdas, February 14, 1849, pp. 61–3 in Murshid 2004, p. 62.
66. Murshid 2003, p. 79.
67. Madhusudan to Gourdas, February 14, 1849, pp. 61–3 in Murshid 2004, p. 62.

68. Ibid.
69. Madhusudan to Gourdas, March 19, 1849, pp. 65–7 in Murshid 2004.
70. Mehrotra 2003.
71. Madhusudan to Gourdas, March 19, 1849, pp. 65–7 in Murshid 2004.
72. Ibid.
73. Seely 2004, p. 21.
74. See excerpt from *The Anglo-Saxon and the Hindu*, in A Chaudhuri 2001, p. 6.
75. Ibid.
76. Ibid.
77. Madhusudan to Bhubeb Mukherji, March 27, 1849, pp. 7–71 in Murshid 2004.
78. Murshid 2003, p. 89.
79. Madhusudan to Gourdas, July 6, 1849, pp. 74–6 in Murshid 2004.
80. Ibid.
81. Murshid 2003, p. 97.
82. Ibid., p. 100.
83. Madhusudan to Gourdas, December 20, 1855, pp. 79–80 in Murshid 2004.
84. See this chapter.
85. Murshid 2004, p. 84.
86. Madhusudan to Gourdas, circa June 1858, pp. 104–5 in Murshid 2004, p. 105.
87. Madhusudan to Gourdas, circa June 1858, pp. 104–5 in Murshid 2004, p. 105.
88. Madhusudan to Gourdas, circa mid June 1858, pp. 105–6 in Murshid 2004, p. 106.

272 • Awakening

89. Ibid., p. 105.
90. Murshid 2004, p. 84.
91. Murshid 2003, pp. 118–19.
92. Madhusudan to Gourdas, mid July, 1858, pp. 106–7 in Murshid 2004.
93. Ibid.
94. Ibid. Emphasis in original.
95. Madhusudan to Gourdas, mid July, 1858, pp. 106–7 in Murshid 2004.
96. Ibid.
97. Madhusudan to Gourdas, March 19, 1859, pp. 110–11 in Murshid 2004.
98. Madhusudan to Gourdas, May 3, 1859, pp. 112–13 in Murshid 2004.
99. Madhusudan to Keshabchandra Ganguli, circa April 1860, pp. 114–15 in Murshid 2004.
100. Ibid.
101. See Chapter two, for more on the Chitpore area of Calcutta.
102. Madhusudan to Rajnarayan Bose, April 24, 1860, pp. 117–19 in Murshid 2004, p. 118.
103. Ibid.
104. Seely and Datta 2004.
105. Madhusudan to Gourdas, August 18, 1849, pp. 77–8 in Murshid 2004.
106. Madhusudan to Rajnarayan, July 1, 1860, pp. 127–9 in Murshid 2004, p. 129.
107. Madhusudan to Rajnarayan, end June 1860, pp. 124–7 in Murshid 2004.
108. Ibid.
109. Seely and Datta 2004, p. 42.

110. Madhusudan to Rajnarayan, May 15, 1860, pp. 121–3 in Murshid 2004, p. 122.
111. Ibid.
112. Madhusudan to Rajnarayan, July 14, 1860, pp. 130–1 in Murshid 2004, p. 131.
113. Madhusudan to Rajnarayan, late June 1861, pp. 168–9 in Murshid 2004, p. 169.
114. Ibid.
115. Ibid.
116. Nandy 1983, p. 19.
117. Madhusudan to Rajnarayan, January 15, 1861, pp. 156–7 in Murshid 2004, p. 157.
118. Ibid., note 2.
119. Ibid., p. 157.
120. Madhusudan to Rajnarayan, April 24, 1860, pp. 117–19 in Murshid 2004, p. 117.
121. Madhusudan to Rajnarayan, January 15, 1861, pp. 156–7 in Murshid 2004, p. 157.
122. Madhusudan to Rajnarayan, January 15, 1861, pp. 156–7 in Murshid 2004, p. 157.
123. Madhusudan to Rajnarayan, end May 1861, pp. 165–7 in Murshid 2004, p. 166.
124. Madhusudan to Rajnarayan, end June/early July 1861, pp. 171–2 in Murshid 2004, p. 172.
125. Madhusudan to Rajnarayan, August 29, 1861, pp. 175–6 in Murshid 2004, p. 176.
126. See Interlude.
127. Madhusudan to Rajnarayan, June 4, 1862, pp. 180–2 in Murshid 2004, p. 180.
128. Dasgupta 1996, pp. 23–4.

129. Ibid., pp. 24–5.
130. Gruber 1989, p. 8.
131. Murshid 2004, p. 86.
132. Madhusudan to Rajnarayan, end June 1860, pp. 124–6 in Murshid 2004, p. 126.
133. Madhusudan to Rajnarayan, end September 1860, pp. 152–3 in Murshid 2004, p. 153.
134. Madhusudan to Rajnarayan, end September 1860, pp. 152–3 in Murshid 2004, p. 152.
135. Murshid 2004, p. 193.
136. Ibid., p. 92.
137. Madhusudan to Rajnarayan, early February 1862, pp. 177–8 in Murshid 2004, p. 177.
138. Madhusudan to Gourdas, January 1859, pp. 108–9 in Murshid 2004.
139. Madhusudan to Rajnarayan, May 15, 1860, pp. 121–3 in Murshid 2004, p. 123.
140. Madhusudan to Rajnarayan, April 1861, pp. 164–5 in Murshid 2004, p. 164.
141. Murshid 2004, p. 93.
142. Ibid., p. 102, note 44.
143. Madhusudan to Rajnarayan, April 1861, pp. 164–5 in Murshid 2004, p. 164.
144. Madhusudan to Gourdas, January 1859, pp. 108–9 in Murshid 2004, p. 108.
145. Madhusudan to Rajnarayan, April 24, 1860, pp. 117–19 in Murshid 2004, p. 118.
146. Madhusudan to Rajnarayan, July 1860, pp. 133–4 in Murshid 2004, p. 133.

A 'Jolly Christian Rhymer' of 'Exquisite Graces' • 275

147. Madhusudan to Rajnarayan, February 1862, pp. 177–8 in Murshid 2004, p. 178.
148. Ibid.
149. Ibid.
150. Ibid.
151. Madhusudan to Vidyasagar, June 2, 1864, pp. 199–201 in Murshid 2004, p. 200.
152. Madhusudan to Manomohun Ghose, September (?) 16, 1862, p. 187 in Murshid 2004.
153. Madhusudan to Manomohun Ghose, January 8, 1863, p. 199 in Murshid 2004.
154. Murshid 2003, p. 160.
155. Ibid., p. 161.
156. Ibid., p. 162.
157. Madhusudan to Gourdas, October 26, 1864, pp. 222–5 in Murshid 2004, p. 223.
158. See this chapter.
159. Madhusudan to Gourdas, October 26, 1864, pp. 222–5 in Murshid 2004, p. 224.
160. Ibid.
161. Ibid.
162. Madhusudan to Vidyasagar, November 3, 1864, pp. 228–30 in Murshid 2004, pp. 229–30.
163. Madhusudan to Gourdas, January 26, 1865, pp. 240–3 in Murshid 2004, p. 241.
164. Ibid.
165. Murshid 2003, p. 174.
166. Madhusudan to the king of Italy, May 5, 1865, p. 248 in Murshid 2004.

276 • Awakening

167. Madhusudan to Vidyasagar, November 19, 1866, pp. 270–1 in Murshid 2004, p. 270.
168. Madhusudan to Vidyasagar, November 19, 1866, pp. 270–1 in Murshid 2004, p. 271.
169. Ibid.
170. Murshid 2004, p. 279.

Nine

Voices of Their Own

SOME TIME BETWEEN 1821 and 1823—the precise year is uncertain—a girl of twelve woke up in the morning to find herself on a boat amongst strangers. She started to cry. Her companions tried to console her, but the more she heard their kind, well-meant words the more the tears flowed. All she could think of were her mother, her brothers, other relatives, playmates, neighbours, none of whom were present. To make matters worse, the boat ride was making her sick. Terrified, she thought of God and spoke His name as her mother had told her to do whenever she was afraid.

The girl was probably bedecked in wedding finery, for she had got married the evening before. The boat was bringing her from her parental home, her baperbari, in a village called Potajia, to another village called Ramdia, in the East Bengal district of Faridpur—to her brand new sasurbari, the home of her new in-laws and of her new husband. Her companions on the boat belonged to the groom's wedding party.

A commonplace story in nineteenth century Bengal, of ancient vintage, no doubt: the story of a pre-pubescent girl being married off and whisked away from the familiarity of a childhood environment to an alien, hostile world. This was the social institution of child marriage that Ishwar Chandra Vidyasagar would rail against.[1] But this particular story we are listening to here was not one narrated as a cautionary tale by Vidyasagar or any other reformist writer. Nor was it a story narrated by a socially conscious novelist of that time or after.

It was, rather, a fragment of a tale told by the girl herself—or rather, by the woman who had been the girl. Her name was Rassundari Debi (1810–?). This was what made this particular story unique: that it was a tale told by Rassundari of her own life. We are hearing her own voice. We are listening to Rassundari telling us *what it was like to be* a traditional Bengali Hindu female in the nineteenth century.

RASSUNDARI DEBI'S *AMAR JIBAN* (My Life) was published in two parts: the first, consisting of sixteen 'compositions' in 1876, the second comprising of fifteen 'compositions' in 1906.[2] What she could not have known when she wrote the book was that she was making literary history. *Amar Jiban* was probably the first autobiography of any kind, authored by male or female, in the Bengali language.[3] It was almost certainly the first autobiography by an Indian woman.[4]

In fact, Rassundari made more than literary history. As the story will relate, she was acutely conscious of her womanhood and of what being a woman meant in the world she inhabited. If feminism arises out of one's awareness of—and discontent with—the disempowerment of women in a society, then Rassundari must count as a feminist—moreover, as a *female* feminist in a milieu which nurtured eminent male feminists such as Rammohun Roy, Derozio and the Derozians, and Vidyasagar.[5] Thus, quite unselfconsciously, Rassundari was a revolutionary thrice over: as an *autobiographer* when autobiography was virtually unknown in Bengal; as a *woman* autobiographer when women reading and writing was a rarity in India; and as a woman who espoused what in a later time would be called a feminist consciousness.

Most strikingly, in writing *Amar Jiban*, Rassundari quite unwittingly melded into the cross-cultural mentality of the Bengal Renaissance. For, if we are to believe autobiographical scholars, the autobiography was a peculiarly Western literary genre,[6] reaching back to St Augustine's *Confessions* (late fourth century CE).[7] Indeed, the autobiography entered the Indian literary scene only in the nineteenth century;[8] Rammohun Roy's *Autobiographical Letter* (1832/1833) was a pioneering example of the genre in Indian literature. In *Amar Jiban* Rassundari had consciously or unconsciously transposed a very Western literary genre into a very Indian setting. This act, as the story has elaborated so far, was a prime feature of the Bengal Renaissance.

HOW DID THIS happen? How did this woman who was, well into her mid twenties, *illiterate*, become the most improbable participant of the Bengal Renaissance? And in what way was she formed by the Renaissance?

To answer this question we must first ask another question: why did Rassundari Debi, an utterly unknown Indian, wish to write the story of her utterly anonymous life?

The answer to this perhaps lies in that an autobiography is a *story* and the autobiographer is a story teller. The narrative is a powerful way of making meaning out of our experiences.[9] It is the means by which the autobiographer understands and expresses her own identity.[10]

Uncountable, unnameable, faceless women all over India suffered as she suffered, experienced as she experienced, thought as she thought. But she took it upon herself to turn all of that into literature. In doing so she became a representative voice of her sex; and also the voice of her own self. When we read *Amar Jiban* we are hearing at once the voice of every woman of her time, space, and circumstance who had no voice, as well as the voice of one particular woman in desperate search of identity. The distinguished scholar Dinesh Chandra Sen, a contemporary of Rabindranath Tagore, recognized this when he wrote that *Amar Jiban* 'is...not merely the account of Rassundari but a story of all Hindu women of her time'.[11]

SHE WAS NOTHING without God, she recognized and said again and again throughout her story. Rassundari's quest for identity was inextricably entwined with her faith. Lest we forget this she prefaced each composition with an invocation, a kind of one-voice chorus that set the theme of that composition. She began the whole story with an invocation to Saraswati, goddess of learning and wisdom, in the hope that the goddess would 'dwell' in her voice.[12] Her personal relationship with God, her closeness to Him was, perhaps, yet another reason why she wrote her autobiography, as has been suggested by one historian: she wished to record this closeness.[13]

As a little girl, she was in a perpetual state of apprehension, indeed, fright, of one thing or another. Being timid, she was an easy victim of teasing and bullying, even physical abuse, by both boys and girls. She was more naïve and credulous than her playmates and, thus, more vulnerable, more susceptible to their often cruel pranks. They told her improbable tales which she believed, stole from her, and made her obey their commands. They made her cry. She cried all too easily and so, inevitably, she was known as a crybaby, an object of some ridicule both at home and outside.[14]

Rassundari had no memory of her father who died when she was four years old.[15] Since by her own admission she had no memory of her own self for the first four or five years of her existence,[16] she had no idea that she had had a father. Indeed, she had no inkling of the idea of fatherhood. She thought she was her mother's daughter,[17] and when one day she overheard her uncle tell someone that she was the daughter of one 'Padmalochan Rai', she was profoundly upset.

She brooded over this intelligence, and asked her father's sister (pishi) where this Padmalochan Rai had gone. Thus she learnt that she had had a father and that he was dead.[18] She also learnt that her father had married her mother, and that was how she came into the world.[19] Perhaps this was her first intimation of the mystery of sex—and entwined with it, her first acquaintance with the mystery of death. More fear. Her mother had told her that whenever afraid she should pray to the family deity, Dayamadhav. And so whenever she saw a dead person she called to their god.

At first she personified Dayamadhav. Once, fleeing from their house which had caught fire, Rassundari stood by the river bank with her two brothers and stared at the fiery spectacle. Fearful for their lives the siblings called out to Dayamadhav. Some neighbours seeing them alone took them home, and later one of them delivered the children to their grateful family. Rassundari thought that the man who brought them home *was* Dayamadhav. Even her younger brother was more savvy than her: he scoffed at her and told her that their benefactor was no god but a human being.[20] Her mother explained that Dayamadhav, though their family deity, was God; that God was omnipresent and omniscient; that there was only one God who was everyone's God.[21]

When she was eight, she was permitted to attend—just attend, nothing more—a boys' school, located in the outer house of their family home. The teacher was an Englishwoman.[22] (Who was this Englishwoman, we wonder, teaching in a Bengali school in some obscure village? Was she a missionary? Where did she live?) Rassundari observed the boys write the letters of the Bengali alphabet on the schoolroom floor and heard them read out the letters. In the course of the two years she kept the English lady company, she secretly taught herself the Bengali alphabet.[23]

She was a girl. She was not allowed or encouraged to learn to read or write. Her furtive 'education' abruptly came to a halt when their home, including the outer house, caught fire.[24]

On the other hand, as a girl, no one objected to her developing domestic skills. A distantly related aunt at whose home she spent entire days, taught her household chores and cooking. Again, no one in her own home knew this. It seems that Rassundari delighted in learning by stealth. When eventually they came to know of her newly acquired domestic skills the family was naturally delighted.[25]

Thus passed the first twelve years of her life. Despite her fears and anxieties, they were 'happy and carefree' years.[26] Then came talk of marriage. Her emotions at the prospect were mixed. On the one hand, she understood the inevitability of this; every girl gets married. Moreover, there was the prospect of the joyous sounds and sights that one associated with a wedding: wedding music, the peculiar, celebratory yet poignant sound made with the mouth by Bengali women known in English as 'ululating', jewellery, the red wedding sari. On the other hand, marriage meant venturing into, being hurled into the unknown, and the thought made her miserable.[27]

The wedding ceremony was over; came the dreaded day after when she must leave. She entreated her mother not to send her away but to no avail. She was a girl, and every girl must go to her in-laws' house, her mother told her.[28] And so, amidst all the tears—her own, her mother's, her brothers', aunts' and uncles'—she departed in a palanquin. Emotionally spent, she fell asleep. When she awoke it was the next morning and she was in a boat, being escorted by a sea of strangers, the grooms' folks, to her sasurbari: the home of her in-laws (and, of course, of her husband).

As it turned out, Rassundari was extremely fortunate for she found herself in a loving sasurbari. Homesick and miserable in the beginning, she was embraced by a mother-in-law who comforted her as she would her own daughter.[29] Indeed, she was treated lovingly by all around her in her new environment. They took more care of her, she admitted, than had her own people in her parental home. Her mother-in-law showered the new child-bride with all sorts of toys; the neighbourhood girls were invited to play with her and keep her company.

The elderly Rassundari, looking back, had nothing but affectionate things to say not only about her immediate sasurbari family but even the servants and neighbours. They were always kind to her. 'It is as though God had asked them to be particularly nice to me.'[30] She remembered her three sisters-in-law, her husband's sisters ('nanads'). All three were widowed and had returned to live in their baperbari. They too loved Rassundari. She admitted, dryly, that the love they bore for their brother's wife was 'something of a rarity' in Bengali circles.[31] She reciprocated their affection. Even when she became mistress of the house and, as their elder brother's wife—their boudi—their senior in the hierarchy, she consulted them on domestic matters.[32]

Thus, as was the case with other young brides in countless families in countless villages, towns, and cities all over India, Rassundari's identity evolved. What had been her home—her parental home, baperbari—was no longer that; her sasurbari became home. It was her sasurbari she identified with. Her baperbari receded from the forefront of her consciousness. Except for her mother, we hear no more about her parental family, not even of her two brothers.

There was nothing uncommon about this transformation. What *was* uncommon was her recording of it. And if any one of the millions of anonymous Indian women of nineteenth century (or even of the early twentieth century) were to have read this account, she would no doubt murmur to herself, 'This is me—this is my story.'

THE TRANSFORMATION OF child-bride to mistress of the house—karta-thakurani, as everyone called her[33]—entailed certain obligations. And it had its pains. The mother-in-law was struck with typhoid which left her blind and helpless. It was Rassundari's task to care for her, and to assume her mantle.[34] She had to run the household—and it was no small household to run. The family deity must be appeased with daily offerings; guests must be given hospitality; everyone must be fed.

Rassundari's sasurbari was affluent, and there was no dearth of domestic help—some twenty-five all told at one time, including eight or nine maidservants[35]—but only one worked inside the house. And they too, all of them, had to be fed. Her husband had no brothers, hence she had not even a sister-in-law ('ja') to share the load with. In effect, she was on her own. She was cook and housemaid—and nursemaid to her mother-in-law—rolled into one. Her daily grind began early morning and ended well past midnight.

Then there was the pain of childbirth. Unending childbearing. In a span of twenty-three years from the age of eighteen, she was pregnant twelve times. She miscarried once and gave birth to nine sons and two daughters. She delivered her last child, a son, when she was forty-one, a year after her eldest son married and her first daughter-in-law entered the home.[36] 'God only knows what I had to go through during those twenty three years.'[37]

She suffered the pain, as did many women of the period, of outliving five of her sons and one daughter. One son died at the time of his annoprasan, the ceremony at which a child is fed its first rice; another at age three; a third when he was four; another at thirteen; the fifth when he was twenty-one. A daughter died at seventeen soon after giving birth.[38] She also lost two grandchildren. Yet, as she was fortunate in her sasurbari people so also in her children, for they—both those who survived and those who did not—never troubled her. 'I never had to suffer on account of their character.'[39]

Still, they all needed to be fed and bathed and clothed and tended to. There were days when she had no time to eat at all, for by the time the chores were done and the children put to bed, she must still wait for her husband to return and serve him his food, only then could she eat; there were days when by this time one or another child would wake up and had to be tended to again, and after that she could hardly be bothered to dole out rice for herself.[40]

The husband! As a good Hindu wife she could not take his name, so he remained anonymous. With all her frankness about all else, Rassundari scarcely mentioned him in her story. He was a shadow whose presence was implicit by way of his manifold fatherhood. A few times he appeared in the narrative as the 'master'. On one rare occasion she mentioned him as working in his office located in the outer house.[41] Her husband possessed and rode a horse. Since the horse belonged to him she even felt 'bashful' of appearing before it. 'Suppose the horse saw me—that would be a matter of great shame.'[42] Another time she waited for his return from work so that she could serve him food. Elsewhere, she admitted that 'the man who was my master happened to be a likeable person'.[43]

Only near the end of the first part of the book, almost as an apologetic afterthought, she gave her husband narrative space. By then he had passed away. It was a brief but unexpected reference to his physical appearance: he was 'flabby'.[44] He was very much the master of the house, we learn, but he was a kind, generous, and good man; a solicitous host to guests and visitors. And 'competent in administration'.[45] A man of influence apparently, and much given to lawsuits with zamindars[46]—and always successful in such legal battles. Precisely what his occupation was she did not say, but he was most likely a zamindar himself. At any rate he was 'a great man' who did 'many good deeds'.[47]

EVEN AS A child, well before marriage, Rassundari was aware of what her gender entailed: girls did not go to school.[48] She had the unusual experience of witnessing close at hand the privilege of being a boy when, sitting alongside the English schoolteacher, she observed the boys learning the alphabet.[49] The first embers of her recalcitrant mind were fanned: she was not willing to accept the dictates of her era. And, as we have seen, in the two years spent in the schoolroom, from age eight to ten, she taught herself the Bengali alphabet.

We are reminded of the boy Ishwar Chandra Vidyasagar learning the English numerals from milestones encountered on the road to Calcutta.[50] The difference was that while the boy Ishwar Chandra could demonstrate his newfound knowledge to his father who then publicly bragged about his son's prowess, Rassundari, a girl, had to keep her learning a secret. No one must know. One wonders how her mother, her uncle, her brothers would have reacted had they known. Would they too have boasted about her prowess to others? Or would they have shushed her not to tell others?

The prospect and then the experience of her marriage reinforced her self-awareness of femalehood: girls were married *off* young and then given away; girls had no say in the matter. She compared herself to the goat dragged to the sacrificial altar in the ceremony known as pathabali. It was 'the same hopeless situation, the same agonized screams',[51] she would write.

She would describe her marriage with yet another animal metaphor, one that Maya Angelou would also use a century later: she was the 'caged bird'. Despite the kindness and lovingness of her sasurbari folks, she felt trapped. 'People put birds in cages for their own amusement. Well, I was like a caged bird. And I would have to remain in the cage for life. I would never be free.[52] Reflecting back on those early days of her married life, she acknowledges, ruefully, that very soon the bird was tamed.[53]

Or was it? Unlike a tamed cage bird, she chafed at the emptiness of her first years when she was still a child-bride, when she was not allowed to work; for there were the maidservants and, of course, her mother-in-law. She tried to occupy her time by designing stone moulds to make sweets; she shaped clay into images of various sorts.[54] Did her new husband help alleviate her ennui in these first few years? Was he sufficiently near her age that he could empathize with her, or was he so much older as to rule out the possibility of teenage conjugal romance? There is no word on her husband's place in her early marriage—but then, perhaps she was reluctant to talk of such matters. Eventually, her apprenticeship as the future mistress—karta-thakurani—began.

She was then fourteen years old. A thought crept into her head: 'the idea that I should learn how to read books.'[55] She was aware that this smacked of heresy. She was a girl, and girls were not supposed to read! The elderly narrator Rassundari remarked that things were very different 'now': 'These days women are becoming famous and men seem good for nothing.' Indeed, there was 'even a woman ruler on the throne'.[56]

The young Rassundari was petrified by her realization of her desire to read. As she had never told anyone she had learnt the alphabet all those years ago, so also now she could not divulge this desire to anyone. She felt so guilty she did not even dare to glance at a written page lest this betrayed her secret desire.[57]

The need to read emanated from her piety. She wanted to read religious books, and naturally, she prayed that God might help her. Ultimately, the only one she could confide her desire to was God.

The desire became overwhelming. It 'grew very strong in me.'[58] It became an all-encompassing need. And this fact—the fact that she *had* this need—made her angry with herself. 'What a peculiar situation I had placed myself in. What was I to do?'[59] She remembered the time spent in the boys' schoolroom when she secretly learnt the alphabet. Perhaps she could dredge up that knowledge. She realized that she really needed a teacher, but that was out of the question. Her desire infiltrated her sleep: she dreamt one night of reading a holy book, the *Chaitanya Bhagavata*. Waking up, 'enthralled' with the experience, she tried to relive that dream.[60]

The *Chaitanya Bhagavata* was one of several religious books in her home which her husband read, and one day, by chance, he left the book—which was in the form of a sheaf of sheets held between wooden frames—in the kitchen where she was working. She took her chance. She removed a page and hid it in a storage place in the kitchen where no one but herself was likely to go.[61]

Now what? She had an idea. She stole one of the palm leaves on which her then eight-year-old eldest son practised his handwriting. (She was twenty-six at this time, which meant that she had nursed her secret desire for a dozen years!) 'One look at the leaf, another at the sheet, a comparison with the letters I already knew, and, finally, a verification with the speech of others—this was the process I adopted for some time.'[62] She was like the decipherer of some forgotten script. Her son's palm leaf and the fragmentary remembrance were her precious Rosetta Stone. This was her modus operandi.

But all done furtively, even though her husband—her 'master' and a 'likeable person'[63]—would probably not object. She was palpably aware of the power of custom and tradition, by which women were not meant to read. The elderly narrator mused over the customs and prejudices that governed womanhood of her younger days: the prejudice against women being educated; or, for that matter, the heavy dresses and jewellery women were expected to wear, the conch-shell bangles, the 'large vermillion dots'. The elderly autobiographer, no longer frustrated, could afford to be phlegmatic: 'it is no use crying over spilt milk.'[64]

And so slowly, painfully, methodically, constantly comparing the letters of her memory and those scratched by her son on the palm leaf with the contents of the precious page from the holy book, she unravelled the secret of the written word. Eventually she was able to 'stumble through' the *Chaitanya Bhagavata*.[65] In time she would read all the other books, all scriptural texts, available in the house.

She was not yet able to write, and would not do so for a long time. That was another endeavour altogether, for it needed material resources, 'paper, pen, ink, ink pot and so on'.[66] One could hardly embark on that project in secret.

The first ones to know of her new skill were the maidservants and some of the village neighbours. Eventually, she plucked up courage to confide in her three widowed sisters-in-law, the nanads. They were delighted, and two of them even started taking reading lessons from her, for a while.[67] Now that the secret was out she could read aloud the scriptures to them.

For a very long time, till her sons were old enough to go to Calcutta to study, she did not learn to write. But not knowing writing was as much her secret as had been her knowing reading, for her seventh son, studying in Calcutta, one day complained that she never replied to his letters. She confessed that she did not know how to write. He was adamant; she must reply to his and his brothers' letters, and left her with paper, pen, and, ink in inkpot. The assumptions and expectations of her sons' generation—these were the 1860s—were already different from those of her own: this son was *surprised* that she could not write; would her husband have expected her to know how to write? Surely not.

Thus she was forced to teach herself to write. She was in her mid fifties. It was a laborious task, and housework did not give her much spare time to practise. Came a time when she accompanied her husband to Krishnagar for treatment of his eyes, damaged by an attack of typhoid, and there, living with one of her sons, with much lighter housework, she found more time. It was then that she finally learnt to write.[68] The caged bird could now properly sing.

RASSUNDARI'S FEAR OF revealing even her desire to read was not some unfounded paranoia. There was an extraordinary belief held by Hindus, including their women, that a girl who learns to read and write may become a widow soon after marriage.[69] Were Rassundari to express her desire aloud or, worse still, if she were to reveal her secret efforts to learn to read, she may well have been accused of wishing her husband's death. There was also a fear, shared by Hindus and Muslims, that literacy fostered intrigue amongst women.[70]

There were, of course, some women from the privileged classes who were literate even in the first decades of the nineteenth century. We know that Madhusudan Datta's mother, roughly Rassundari's contemporary, was not only literate, she could recite chunks of poetry from memory.[71] Some of the women from such notable Calcutta families as the Tagores and the Debs were known to be literate.[72] But they were a miniscule minority.

The elderly Rassundari somewhat wistfully recognized that by the time she was writing her autobiography in the last quarter of the century, things had changed. 'These days, women are becoming famous…'[73]

Things were indeed very different by this time (the mid 1870s). Rassundari must have been aware of the progress made in women's education. Perhaps this awareness added to her compulsion to write her life story: it was not only a means to establishing her identity; it was also a way of announcing her identity to the world beyond her home; and so a way of partaking in the movement for women's emancipation. Perhaps her awareness of this movement gave her the courage to write. If she was indeed so motivated then in this sense the awakening marking the Bengal Renaissance made her as much as she in turn was a maker of the awakening.

THE PROGRESS IN women's lives and the battles that were fought—from Rammohun through to Vidyasagar and the Derozians—on their behalf was one of the strands of the Bengal Renaissance. From the abolishment of sati to the need for widow remarriage and the arguments against kulin polygamy, many of the issues the reformers of the nineteenth century fought for were women's issues.

Female education was very much in the forefront of many minds also, particularly from the mid nineteenth century onwards. It was a central issue for the post-Derozio Derozians and the later Brahmos. In 1841, Krishna Mohun Banerji—still a Hindu—wrote an essay on *Native Female Education*.[74] The year after, Madhusudan Datta—still a Hindu and still in favour with the authorities of Hindu College—also wrote an essay on women's education for a prize competition, for which he won a gold medal (his friend Bhudeb Mukherji winning the silver medal).[75]

But for Madhusudan, then only eighteen, it seemed that women's education was a means to an end—the end being the gratification of the intellectual male ego. With characteristic hauteur, he wrote that it was the educated woman who 'first gives ideas to the future philosopher and would-be poet'.[76] The 'future philosopher' and 'would-be poet' were, by implication, men; the educated woman was, so to speak, a superior kind of handmaid for the male intellectual. She was also, Madhusudan insisted, necessary for domestic bliss.

Madhusudan was not the only man with such an attitude. One of the early arguments given for female education in Bengal was that schooling was necessary not for women in their own right but that they could become 'better' *wives*, that they could become equal partners and helpmates to their educated husbands.[77] Indeed, how to educate women, what to teach them and to what end would remain burning issues through the century because of this.[78]

Just about the time Rassundari was secretly absorbing the Bengali alphabet in the boys' schoolroom, there was a movement afoot in Calcutta to provide and encourage female education. This movement would advance in fits and starts over the next few decades. Women's schooling began in Bengal in the 1820s clearly in response to the developments in England where, by the period, it was not uncommon for girls to be sent to school.[79] Jane Austen's novel *Emma* (1816) has (Mrs) Goddard run a boarding school for girls, and another eminent woman novelist Elizabeth Gaskell attended a boarding school in Cheshire in the 1820s.

The missionaries, as we might expect knowing what we know of their place in this story,[80] had a prominent place in this movement. In fact, they began it, more or less, though as we shall see, they also created impediments. In 1818, a missionary named Robert May established a girls' school in Chinsurah, a place not far from Calcutta. This may have been the first institution of the kind in India.[81] The same year in which May founded his school in Chinsurah, a gathering of Calcutta notables, all men, led by the then Chief Justice J.H. Harrington, and including the indefatigable William Carey and the equally energetic David Hare, founded the Calcutta School Society. Its fundamental aim was to 'assist and improve existing schools and to establish and support any further schools and seminaries'.[82]

Three years later, female education entered the society's agenda: the chief justice recorded that 'some natives of the highest respectability' were giving attention to 'the subject' of education for women.[83] One of these 'respectable natives' was Raja Radhakanta Deb of the Deb family of Sobhabazar, a perplexingly Janus-faced individual, implacable foe to both Rammohun in the fight over sati and Vidyasagar in the debate over widow remarriage,[84] and yet one who patronized all sorts of educational reform, including the cause of female education.

By then, in 1819 in fact, the wives of some Baptist missionaries had formed the 'Female Juvenile Society for the Establishment and Support of Bengali Female Schools', which had established a link with the Calcutta School Society by way of its president, the Reverend W.H. Pierce, who was also the secretary of the latter society.[85] The Juvenile Society, with characteristic missionary zeal, wasted no time: it established its first girls' school in that same year—no caste taboos were observed in its admission policy—and by the end of 1821, it had an enrolment of thirty-two pupils.[86] When the School Society held its annual examination (in Radhakanta Deb's house) of students from some of the boys' schools and Hindu College, the girls of the Juvenile Society's school were also awarded 'presents'.[87]

By 1823 (about a year into Rassundari' marriage), the Juvenile Society was operating eight girls' schools in and around Calcutta.[88] Some 140 Hindu and Muslim girls were examined that year before such luminaries as William Carey and Horace Hayman Wilson in spelling, reading, geography, and 'elementary ethics'.[89] Predictably, the instinct to proselytize overcame the missionaries, and the Juvenile Society introduced

Christian tracts into the curriculum. Inevitably there was a reaction: the society's schools shrunk from twenty in 1829 to only three in 1834.[90]

Indeed, the desire to evangelize kept intruding and proved to be the chief barrier to the growth of women's education in Bengal. Owing to a munificent gift of Rs 20,000 from Raja Baidyanath Ray, a 'central' girls school was founded in 1827. It achieved rapid success, with enrolment rising to 320 by 1834. But with some conversions to Christianity, the upper-class Hindus who had begun to send their daughters to the school rapidly withdrew their patronage.[91]

All this changed with John Elliot Drinkwater Bethune, an Englishman trained in law and the son of a distinguished historian. His school named, at first, Hindu Balika Vidyalaya (Hindu Girls' School) was inaugurated in May 1849 as a secular, vernacular institution in which religious instruction of any sort was taboo. However, like Hindu College, only daughters from 'respectable' Hindu families were admitted.[92] Ishwar Chandra Vidyasagar was appointed the school's secretary.

With Bethune's passing in 1851, the school, renamed Bethune School, went through rough times—this despite the school's conservative curriculum that was geared to train its students to become 'better wives'.[93] Such was the prevalent general hostility amongst upper-class Hindus against female education that by 1863 the school had ninety-three students of which three-quarters came from the 'lowest classes'.[94] But the school survived—and thereby hangs another tale, in which the Brahmo Samaj and two Englishwomen played profound roles.

ONE OF THE women was Mary Carpenter (chronicler of Rammohun Roy's last days in England):[95] Unitarian, humanitarian, a worker on behalf of the industrial proletariat, reformist, and feminist activist in England who visited India several times.[96] In England, Carpenter had come to know and befriend one of Madhusudan Datta's friends, Manomohun Ghose, a progressive Brahmo and (unlike Madhusudan) a successful barrister. Thus, in Calcutta, with Manomohun Ghose's support, Carpenter came to be closely associated with the 'progressive' or 'liberal' faction of the Brahmo Samaj.[97] She proposed the creation of a Brahmo 'normal' school to train teachers for girls' schools. The Brahmo leader Keshub Chandra Sen and other fellow Brahmos began such a normal school.[98]

The other Englishwoman who enters this tale is Annette Akroyd, also a Unitarian, whose father, a liberal industrialist from the English Midlands, had helped establish, in 1849, Bedford College, the first degree-awarding women's college in England. Annette Akroyd was a graduate of this college, receiving her degree in 1863.[99] She too came to know and befriend Manomohun Ghose. She also attended one of Keshub Chandra Sen's lectures while he was in England in 1870.[100]

Influenced by her Brahmo acquaintances, Akroyd arrived in Calcutta in 1872. More radical in her views on women's emancipation, and soon impatient with what she perceived as Keshub's pusillanimity on the 'women question', she decided, that same year, to begin a new girls' school based on her own ideas. Keshub, for instance, did not wish women to study certain subjects he felt were the preserve of men, such as geometry, logic, science, and history. Moreover, he selected teachers who were educated along traditional Hindu rather than Western lines.[101] Akroyd invited Keshub to join in her effort, but he backed away, arguing for a more 'gradualistic' policy. He was also wary of Akroyd's Anglicized curriculum and, indeed, contemptuous of her proposals on Anglicizing habits, clothing, and customs for Bengali girls.[102]

Annette Akroyd's school, named Hindu Mahila Vidyalaya (Hindu Women's School) opened in 1873, without Keshub Sen's 'blessing'. The school was supported by the Brahmo 'progressives' or 'liberals' who by now were completely associated with the cause of female education. Amongst her supporters, which included Manomohun Ghose of course, was the much-respected Ramtanu Lahiri.[103] Another was the wealthy liberal Dwarkanath Ganguli, who served as its headmaster.[104] Dwarakanath would marry Kadambini Bose; she and Chandramukhi Basu became, in 1883, the first two women university graduates in India—indeed, in the British Empire.[105] It is worth noting that in England, Oxford awarded its first degrees to women in 1878/9,[106] about the time the University of Calcutta first admitted women as candidates for the Bachelor of Arts examination.[107] The development of university education for women in India was, then, roughly synchronous to its British counterpart. (Kadambini would also be the first woman to be admitted, in 1884, to Calcutta Medical College, though two other women, Bidhumukhi Bose and Virginia Mary Mitter, completed their degrees before her.)[108]

In 1875, Annette Akroyd married the civil servant Lord Beveridge, and in her new capacity had to give up the school. Her husband suggested that she reconcile her differences with Keshub Sen and temper her identification with the excessively

Anglicized Bengalis (which included Manomohun Ghose and his wife).[109] The same year Mary Carpenter arrived in Calcutta on her third (and last) visit. For Ackroyd this was a fortuitous event, for Carpenter took over her school.[110] And in 1876, Carpenter and Akroyd collaborated to establish the first women's college in India, named the Banga Mahila Vidyalaya (Bengali Women's College). Two years later, in August 1878, this institution merged with Bethune School to become Bethune College—and thereby win governmental recognition and backing as an affiliated college of the University of Calcutta.[111] Kadambini Bose graduated from Calcutta University as a student of Bethune College.

TORU DUTT (1856–77) could never have felt the particular angst of social censure experienced by Rassundari and other like-minded women who yearned to be educated. Nor would she suffer the slings and arrows suffered by those young women who ventured out of the security of their homes to make their public way to public schools. For one thing she was educated in the privacy of her home, first by her father and then by a tutor;[112] she would never fear what her father would say, for he was her friend, philosopher, and guide. For another, she with her father, brother, and sister converted to Christianity when she was six years old[113]—her mother converted some years later—and so she could afford to ignore the censure with which bhadralok Hindu society looked upon those who flaunted its customs and beliefs. As a Christian convert she was already beyond the Hindu pale.

Indeed, through her brutally short life (she died at the age of twenty-one) Toru was an outsider—as was her whole family, as were so many other Hindus who converted. She was an outsider because, in an age when Indian women were still struggling to win the right to be educated, when to be just literate was to be *something*, she was ultra-literate: she became a poet, novelist, and woman of letters. She was an outsider because she was an Indian woman writer who eschewed her native language as her literary métier and espoused instead English and French. She was an outsider because in an age when even men hesitated to cross the 'black water' for fear of losing caste and excommunication, she and her sister Aru not only crossed the seas—they were almost certainly the first Bengali women and among the first Indian women to do so[114]—but lived for four years in France and England. She was an outsider by the fact that she experienced an intellectual environment beyond the comprehension of almost any other Indian woman of her time, as a student at a French school in Nice, and as an attendee of the 'Higher Lectures for Women' at Cambridge University.[115]

Toru Dutt enters our story partly because of these curiosities; she also does so because she was the first Indian woman writer in the English language. She was the female counterpart to Henry Derozio.

Toru Dutt—'Dutt' an Anglicization of the Kayastha surname 'Datta'—was born in 1856 into privilege and distinction. Her paternal grandfather Rassamay Dutt, of one of the 'great houses' of Calcutta in Rambagan, was a younger contemporary of Rammohun Roy: a lawyer, co-founder of Hindu College,[116] and a member of the managing committee of the Calcutta School Society.[117] Toru's father, Govindchandra Dutt—Madhusudan Datta's classmate at Hindu College[118]—

inherited Rassmay's penchant for all things British and went one step farther. He, along with his children, son Abju and daughters Aru and Toru, converted to Christianity in 1862. Abju was then eleven, Aru eight, and Toru six. Govindchandra's wife Kshetramoni, who learnt English after her marriage (itself a notable achievement for an Indian woman of her generation) was baptized along with her family but became a practising Christian later.[119] Abju died in 1865 aged fourteen, Aru in 1874 when twenty, and Toru in 1877.

As noted, conversion to Christianity almost inevitably made the convert an alien in Hindu society. Some converts became anti-Indian, more at home in not just the religion but the culture of Christian Europe than in their original milieu. And some were disowned by their families. We get a vivid sense of how isolated some Indian converts felt from a poem called 'The Hindu Convert to His Wife', written by one of Toru's uncles. The poet-convert mournfully tells his wife:

> Nay, part not so—one moment stay,
> Repel me not with scorn.
> Like others, wilt thou turn away,
> And leave me quite forlorn?
> Wilt thou too join the scoffing crowd,
> The cold, the heartless, and the proud,
> Who curse the hallowed morn,
> When daring idols to disown,
> I knelt before the Saviour's throne?[120]

Ostracization by the Hindus was, then, the norm rather than the exception. Moreover, despite all the missionary activities, conversion to Christianity was still a relatively rare event, at least among the bhadralok. Missionary influence was more pervasive within the poorer realm of Hindu society.[121]

When those of the bhadralok did convert it was cause for much commotion as when, in 1845, the wife of one Umesh Chandra Sarkar was converted with her husband by the indefatigable Scot Reverend Alexander Duff. In his *Autobiography*, Rabindranath Tagore's father Debendranath remembered the occasion and his sense of outrage that even women of 'our Zenana' were being made Christians.[122]

TORU WAS BORN not only into the privilege of affluence but also into a richly intellectual, creative, and liberal milieu. Her uncles, Govind's brothers and cousins, wrote poetry and essays—in English—that were published in both Calcutta and London.[123] This was indeed a 'joint family' of poets: in 1870 they published en famille, in London, without bylines of individual authorship, *The Dutt Family Album*, which began with a preface asserting that

> They [the authors] are foreigners, natives of India, of different ages and in different walks of life, yet of one family, in whom the ties of blood relationship have been drawn closer by the holy bond of Christian brotherhood. As foreigners educated out of England, they solicit the indulgence of British critics to poems which on these grounds alone may, it is hoped, have some title to their attention.[124]

The *Album* reveals something of the intellectual and literary environment in which Toru and her sister Aru were raised.

Unmistakably Anglicized in their literary taste we find poems dedicated to Wordsworth, for instance, while another paid explicit homage to Shakespeare, Milton, Spenser, and Scott; some were profoundly and avowedly Christian and several sonnets were hymnal in their themes; and yet they were unmistakeably Indian, with poems addressing episodes from Indian history. ('The Hindu Convert to His Wife' appeared in the *Album*.)

For Toru, the seminal event was the four-year period spent in France and England. Govindchandra Dutt, wife Kshetramoni, and the two girls arrived in France in 1869. Toru was then fourteen. The sisters attended a school in Nice and Toru's passion for French literature must have begun there. A year later they moved to England and the *Dutt Family Album* was published at the time. In 1871 they moved to Cambridge where the sisters extended their study of French and attended the 'Higher lectures for Women' at the university. Here Toru met Mary Martin, a vicar's daughter,[125] and later herself an Anglican missionary who would visit Calcutta twice in the early twentieth century. Martin became Toru's one serious friend outside the Dutt family circle, and she would carry on an extensive correspondence with Martin to the end of her life.

In 1872, the Dutts moved to a seaside town, and the year after they returned to Calcutta. Aru died a year later at the age of twenty. Toru would divide the remaining few years of her own life between their Calcutta house in Rambagan and the family's garden home in Baugmaree, the days devoted to intensive reading and writing, and a very modest amount of socializing, mostly within family circles.[126] Her life after returning to India was ultimately an intensely secluded and lonely one, almost entirely confined to the Rambagan family home in Calcutta and the garden home in Baugmaree. There were visits to church, of course, and occasional outings to 'take the air' as on the Calcutta maidan. Her social life was defined by visits from and visits to sundry relatives.

Toru's literary activities occurred in these last three years of her life, 1874–7.[127] She contributed essays to the *Bengal Magazine* and *Calcutta Review*, and published (as her letters reveal) a labour of love, *A Sheaf Gleaned in French Fields* (1876), a collection of English translations of French poetry. In fact, this was her only book published during her life. According to one commentator, *A Sheaf* 'still remains a marvel of translation...and made some of our poets interested in French poetry'.[128] A year after her death, Govindchandra Dutt—one can only wonder how he and his wife coped with the death of all three of their offspring—published Toru's unfinished novel, *Bianca, or the Young Spanish Maiden* serially in the *Bengal Magazine*.[129] He also brought out a second edition of *A Sheaf* that same year, adding a 'prefatory memoir' of his daughter. A novel in French, *Le Journal de Madamoiselle d'Arvers*, was published in Paris in 1879.[130] A third edition of *A Sheaf* was published in London in 1880. Finally, a collection of Toru's original poems, *Ancient Ballads and Legends of Hindustan*, was published in London in 1882.[131]

Rassundari Debi and Toru Dutt were worlds apart but both shared a certain kind of loneliness: Toru was as isolated in giving expression to her voice as was Rassundari in claiming hers. And if Rassundari's desire to learn to read and write, if penning her autobiography was her road to giving voice to her identity, so also Toru's writings—what she wrote as well as her very act of writing—gave expression to her identity.

LET US TAKE a look at her, the young woman that she was. In a photograph, she stands alone, poised, hand resting on the back of a chair. She is attired, as a well-bred Victorian-age European woman would be, in an elaborate dress, covered up to her chin and down to the floor so that even her toes do not show, nor her arms; the sleeves, ending in white cuffs, show only the hands. Her hair is drawn back tightly. She would look a prim Victorian maiden but for her face which is anything but prim. She cannot be said to be beautiful but it is a face that compels the onlooker's attention.

Here is another photograph, this time with sister Aru. Aru is sitting while Toru stands by her side slightly behind, her hands resting lightly, affectionately, protectively on Aru's shoulders. This time her hair is loose, cascading down to her breasts and back. The loose hair gives her a faintly provocative air. The faces of the two sisters are in marked contrast. Perhaps Aru is already very sick, for her face looks wan. Toru's hair frames her face and, if anything, enhances the firmness of her features.

Gazing at Toru in these photographs we are reminded irresistibly (yet again) of Macaulay's dictum on persons Indian in blood and colour but English in taste. In her defiantly Western dress out of which a dark face emerges, she seems to personify this Macaulayan ideal.

NOT ENGLISH ONLY however, but rather Anglo-French in taste, unmistakeably, aggressively so. Back in Calcutta from their sojourn in France and England, she makes us almost forget that she was a Bengali. She was, rather, the cultivated Francophile Anglo-Indian who suffered Calcutta because she had to, much as the wives and daughters of resident Europeans would. Her body was in Calcutta, her mind and soul in France and England. She was forever reading French authors: a history of the French Revolution and Molière, for instance;[132] French books were ordered from England and their arrivals were occasions worth reporting to Mary Martin: '*Les Châtiment* by Victor Hugo'—one of Toru's favourite poets—'a book which I have been longing to see; the poems therein are very beautiful;[133] so much so, she copied one of Hugo's originals and her translation of the poem for her friend. 'The last batch of French books arrived by last mail,' she reported happily.[134] When she had nothing of her daily life to write about, she would copy out for Martin her 'latest translations' of French poetry which would make up her first book.[135]

In the manner of many Englishwomen in India, she pined to be back in England almost from the time the Dutt family returned to Calcutta. 'We hope…to return to England and settle there for good; wouldn't that be jolly?'[136] This hope seemed to sustain her in the weeks and months that follow. 'We hope to go to England…this time Papa says we will sell all we have and go to England and settle there for good.'[137] 'We all want so much to return to England. We miss the free life we led there.'[138] It was as if Calcutta constrained her: 'The free air of Europe, and the free life there are things not to be had here.'[139] She dreamt of settling 'in some quiet country place. The English villages are so pretty.'[140] At every moment, it seems, England and the Continent beckoned. As Christmas approached: 'there were no hot Christmas puddings as in England, but there were Christmas cakes full of plums.'[141] Even the local jail became her 'Calcutta Newgate'.[142]

Toru's Christian faith sustained her as strongly as did Rassundari's Hindu faith. 'The Lord has taken dear Aru from us,' she wrote a few months after her sister's passing. 'It is a sore trial for us, but His will be done. We know He doeth all things for our own good.'[143] Of her grandmother: 'She is, I am sad to say, still a Hindu.'[144] In properly seasoned Anglo-Indian fashion, she observed and reported on the Durga Puja season: 'Calcutta has been very noisy and gay… The streets were blocked up by devotees going to throw their idols in the river Ganges; our ears are deafened by the continual din of drums, fifes, flutes, violins, &c., all imaginable instruments of music, playing together in exquisite discordance.'[145]

She addressed Indians as 'natives': 'a native' was discovered hanging on a tree in the grounds of their garden house.[146] In 1875, 'three or four natives' sat for the Indian Civil Service examination but none succeeded.[147] She was suitably ashamed when Mary Martin chastised her for calling her countrymen 'natives'. '…the reproof is just, and I stand corrected. I shall take care and not call them natives again. It is indeed a term only used by prejudiced Anglo-Indians, and I am really ashamed to have used it.'[148]

So far, Toru Dutt appears to be an Anglo-French woman trapped in an Indian body situated in a foreign India-land. This seems to be her identity and the only way she could give voice to it was through her writings. Thus, *A Sheaf*.

Thus she wrote a French novel, *Le Journal*, and an English one, *Bianca*.

But then there was an unexpected turn: 'Papa and I are going to begin Sanskrit in December… I am glad of this. I should so like to read the glorious epics, the Ramayana and the Mahabharata in the original.'[149]

Once more we are witnessing a recurring feature of the Bengal Renaissance: the Indo-Western mind, the fusion of two cultures, two traditions, even two religions. The switching from one to the other and back. 'I am busy with my Sanskrit. The grammar is awfully difficult, though in reading and understanding we get on pretty swimmingly.'[150] Almost in the same breath: 'I have not read *Middlemarch*…you should read *Wives and Daughters* by Mrs. Gaskell.'[151]

As with Madhusudan Datta,[152] Toru owed her acquaintance with the Indian epics to her mother who told Toru and her siblings tales from the epics when they were small.[153] And—hauntingly reminiscent of Madhusudan's rapture over the 'grand' Hindu mythologies, despite his disdain for Hinduism itself—Toru, realized 'how grand, how sublime, how pathetic our legends are. The wifely devotion that an Indian wife pays her husband, her submission to him even when he is capricious or exacting, her worship of him…'[154]

Inspired by her readings, she wrote a collection of nine poems which, along with additional 'miscellaneous' ones, were published posthumously as *Ancient Ballads and Legends of Hindustan* (1882) by the London publisher Kegan Paul, with an introduction by the English critic Edmund Gosse, an admirer of Toru's work.[155] By far the longest of the collection, 'Savitri', was inspired by an episode from the *Mahabharata*.

Two others, 'Lakshman' and 'Sita', drew on 'the grand legend of Ram and Sita' from the *Ramayana*.[156] Some literary scholars believe that she created a new poetry; the language was English, the 'sensibility Indian'.[157]

Toru did not live the two years she needed to read the Hindu epics in the Sanskrit. The letters to Mary Martin were sprinkled with mention of her poor health. '[M]y cough troubles me.'[158] And, ominously, 'I have been ill with a very bad cough accompanied with a good deal of blood-spitting and fever.'[159] By June 1877 she was 'very ill.'[160] A month later, she was so weak that 'I have to be taken downstairs in a chair when I go out for a drive.'[161] On July 30, 1877, she was still confined to bed. 'Your letters are a great comfort, dear. I feel sometimes very tired and weary and lonely, and this illness has made me suffer very much.'[162] The illness was, of course, consumption.

These were her last letters. On August 30, 1877, she passed away, aged twenty-one.

THE SEARCH FOR identity and selfhood takes many forms. Both Toru and Rassundari Debi found theirs against the backdrop of the female education movement, yet both remained outside it. Rassundari came a generation too early, Toru was from a family so Anglicized that she was a step ahead. In Haimabati we see a woman who was undoubtedly a product of her times.

Vidyasagar had written passionately against child marriage.[163] Others had also protested against this practice. In 1860 an Act was passed which mandated that sexual intercourse with a girl under the age of ten (with one's wife or otherwise) was rape.[164] (This 'age of consent' would be raised to twelve in 1891.)[165] Notwithstanding the Act of 1860, its flaunting was alive and well in 1875 when a nine-and-a-half-year-old girl called Haimabati was married off to a forty-five-year-old man.

We know this because Haimabati told a tale of this experience and what happened to her after.[166] It is a tale as extraordinary as Rassundari's, though in a very different way, for Haimabati's life was vastly different from Rassundari's. She, at least, had a secure life; her home was her life. Haimabati's life was far from secure, for it mirrored the sordid plight of widowhood and, especially, child widowhood which Vidyasagar had railed against. And, born half a century after Rassundari, Haimabati's story, as she told it in her mature years, is also a story of the making of the New Indian Woman, the woman who ventured well beyond the home and into the world in search of independence and identity.

HAIMABATI SEN (1866–1933) was born into a once prosperous family in the Khulna district of East Bengal. Her birth caused much consternation amongst certain family members, including her mother, because she was not a boy. Indeed, her mother would have little to do with her in her first few years.[167] Her father, however, reacted in an unexpected way: he decided to bring her up as if she was a son. Her daknam—nickname— was 'Chuni', a boy's name. In the first few years of her life she was even dressed as a boy.

Like Rassundari, Haimabati was allowed to sit in on school lessons given to the boys in the outer quarters of their house. Yet, though born over fifty years after Rassundari, the basic prejudice against female literacy had not disappeared: she could only listen and memorize what the teacher taught the boys but she could not be taught herself.[168] It was only when she so impressed a school inspector by answering questions the boys could not that her father allowed her to be taught along with them—without the women of the family being told, for fear they would object.[169]

So here she parted company with Rassundari. She learnt to read; and she learnt fast. When the women of the household finally came to know that she could read—she read from the *Ramayana* to them, to their astonishment, and then outrage—they accused her of becoming a 'masculine woman'.[170] When she won school prizes they lamented that nobody would marry her.

On the matter of marriage the women—especially Haimabati's 'two grandmothers'—evidently ruled the roost. When she was nine a marriage was arranged, on their insistence, sweeping over her father's objection, to a deputy magistrate, forty-five years old, twice widower, with two daughters by his first marriage.[171] The daughters were scarcely younger than their new 'mother'. If her father had qualms about the age of the groom, her mother had none.

Haimabati remembered being 'asleep at the time of the wedding' and waking up to find, in place of her grandmother, 'a strange man' beside her on the bed.[172] Later, in her husband's and in-laws' home, her sasurbari, 'My elder sister-in-law used to escort me to the bridegroom's room. I would lie silently, stiff like a piece of wood. When I fell asleep, someone removed my clothes. I woke up, felt scared, and again wrapped my clothes round my body.'[173]

She was fortunate that, like Rassundari, her mother-in-law treated her well. But while the girl-bride Rassundari had neighbourhood girls as her playmates, Haimabati inherited two stepdaughters only slightly younger than herself.[174]

Her husband, 'the babu', she discovered somewhat confusedly, was a lecher and a drunkard who entertained prostitutes in their bedroom in her presence. One night, waking up to go to the toilet she witnessed 'the babu and a woman clasping each other and thrashing around'.[175] Another night, pretending to be asleep, Haimabati heard her husband tell another female visitor that he has to 'keep hatching the egg', meaning Haimabati. Later that night, observing them on a mat on the floor, she was so terrified that she lost consciousness.[176]

Within the first year of the marriage the husband died, apparently of liver disease and pneumonia.[177] Inevitably, both in her sasurbari and back at her parental home she was blamed for the death. 'My widowhood was entirely my own fault. My first fault was acquiring an education, my second was that I had jumped out of the bridal chamber and run away...'[178]

HAIMABATI'S STORY BEGAN at this point. Her awakening, her search for identity, her self-creation as an independent woman began when she realized that now that she was a widow, education could no longer hurt her. She could not be widowed again. She resumed her studies at her parental home with her brothers' books and her brothers as teachers.[179] She would ignore all criticism from now on. Forced to return to her sasurbari—as much by her grandmothers who thought this would put an end to her studies as by her mother-in-law's insistence—she took her books with her and studied on her own, aided by a dictionary. She learnt Bengali 'quite well' but her great desire was to learn to read English and Sanskrit.[180]

For a time life in her sasurbari, a large joint family, was tolerable enough, though there were the inevitable unpleasant episodes and family squabbles. She could at least continue with her studies. Haimabati's *Memoirs*, written some time in the last decade of her life (1923–33), are full of details of the minutae of this life and of the time when she would visit her parental home. By and large her sasurbari existence was pleasanter than life in the parental home.

When her father, her main ally in the parental home, died, matters became progressively complicated; her mother had never been accepting of her and her brother was greedy and scheming. Haimabati was left penniless, deprived of the inheritance promised by her father. Then when her mother-in-law died her chief protector in her sasurbari was gone. Neither her brother nor brother-in-law was willing to support her or give her shelter.

Thus began a journey. First, armed with her brother-in-law's promise of a monthly stipend of ten rupees from her share of the sasurbari property, she went to Benares (Varanasi), the Hindu holy city and supposedly a haven for Hindu widows. When the promised remittance stopped after the first two or three months she was offered by a well-wisher a job as a teacher in a girls' school which she accepted. She would write, 'great was my joy the day I received my pay from the school. I wept for sheer joy.'[181]

After teaching for eight months she desired more education and, thereby, a better job. 'This desire for higher education had persisted throughout my life.' She wanted to 'pass some examinations'.[182]

Having resigned her job, and fortified with two letters of introduction to prominent members of the Brahmo Samaj, Durgamohan Das and Sivanath Sastri (who was later a biographer of Ramtanu Lahiri), she came to Calcutta. Unfortunately both these Samajists were about to leave for England; Sivanath Sastri, whom she met, could not help her till his return some six months later. In the meantime she was entrusted to a Brahmo in Dacca (now Dhaka, capital of Bangladesh).

Thus began the next part of her wanderings, an extraordinary journey of a young widowed woman, in her twenties, through East Bengal amongst total strangers. It is a tale that tells of seduction of women in widows' shelters, of Haimabati being physically beaten, of her attempt to escape, of living amongst unknown people, of occasional and intermittent encounters with kindness and compassion, of encounters with both Brahmos and the aristocracy, neither of whom come out entirely well, of a job as a private tutor to a rani, of sexual overtures to be rebuffed, of proposals to be refused.

Eventually, she returned to Calcutta, wanting to continue her studies. Her milieu was the Brahmo community.

She was introduced to a young Brahmo named Kunjabehari Sen, who was 'deeply religious' and lived 'like an ascetic'. He wished to marry her[183] and she agreed. For a time leading up to the wedding, she lived in the house of Bipin Chandra Pal (1858–1932), a Brahmo and, later, a distinguished teacher, journalist, and nationalist.[184] The wedding, held in 1890, was celebrated 'with due pomp and ceremony' with nearly two hundred people in attendance.[185] A widow remarriage, no less.

A new phase. The marriage was 'a powerful bond' in her life.[186] Yet, like so much in her life, this wedding too was attended by a bizarre twist: her husband told her on the night of the wedding that he had taken a vow of celibacy for six months.[187] She agreed to honour his vow, and continued to live in Bipin Chandra Pal's house for a while longer.

The first few years after the marriage were not with travails: a stillborn child; income so meagre that husband and wife 'were overwhelmed with poverty'.[188] Haimabati made socks and other items of clothing to earn some money while Kunjabehari was without work; she also taught girls in the neighbourhood to sew, wove carpets and did embroidery with beads, made baskets. There was a modicum of financial relief; then, a long pilgrimage with her husband.

And then, returned to Calcutta, began the culminating phase of her younger life; a new idea: 'Many girls had joined medical schools at that time and I decided I would do the same.'[189]

With the help of a Brahmo acquaintance, she prepared for the admission test for Campbell Medical School, established in the 1870s, to which women were first admitted in 1888.[190] She was coached in grammar, mathematics, and English. The emancipated Brahmo milieu notwithstanding, her husband's friends 'tried to stop me in so many ways'.[191] Fortunately, Kunjabehari paid no attention to them.

Indeed, he escorted her to the admission examination which was taken by seventeen women. Haimabati stood second. She entered Campbell Medical School in 1891, aged twenty-six. Three years later, along with motherhood, household work, and financial support through scholarships, she completed her course of study with the highest marks amongst both men and women.

She should have received the gold medal. The year was 1894, but male hubris flourished as never before: the male students were enraged and went on a strike—indeed, on a rampage—in protest. Ultimately she was awarded two silver medals and a scholarship to continue her studies at Calcutta Medical College.[192] There 'I stood first this time as well by the grace of God.'[193]

Haimabati's *Memoirs* did not end here, of course. The professional workplace then as now was a man's world and medicine was no exception. Sexual discrimination certainly, and the fact that her qualifications were inferior to a university medical degree would play their parts in raising obstacles to her medical career. So would sexual harassment. She would have four sons and a daughter, all of whom were well educated and she would share a medical practice with her second son, a member of the Indian Medical Service, who served in the Army Medical Corps. She became a widow a second time and eventually died of breast cancer in 1933.

HAIMABATI SEN'S *MEMOIRS* is almost picaresque. Innumerable characters float in and out of the story, many of whom are distinctly roguish—including her first husband, one of her brothers, her grandmothers, and her mother. As such it is a compelling story.

More compellingly, the *Memoirs* is a travelogue: in the obvious sense that she travels across geographic space, from Khulna to Benares to Calcutta to Dacca and other East Bengal parts, back to Calcutta, then a pilgrimage, and finally back to Calcutta. But it is also the story of a long psychological journey in which she evolved through several selves that were the outcomes of her vastly contrasting situations at different stages of her life. Along this journey we see the formation of the identity of an emancipated, fiercely independent *woman of science*, at the core of which was an inexorable desire to learn, be educated, and work. As in the case of Rassundari, though in a very different way, her autobiography is a witness to her self-creation.

THREE WOMEN, THREE stories. Each tells of an awakening underpinned by a particular brand of *loneliness*.

Rassundari's loneliness lay in her intense desire to learn to read so that she could read religious books; a desire she could not divulge to anyone. Toru's loneliness lay in her situation as an ultra-literate, multi-lingual, Christian, well-travelled Indian woman, a circumstance that would scarcely make sense to any other woman (except her own sister) in her Bengali milieu. Haimabati's loneliness lay in her status not just as a Hindu widow but one who harboured an intense need to learn and achieve in a formidably man's world.

Each made her loneliness work for her by revolting against it. Rassundari not only satiated her desire to learn to read, so that she could know first hand the contents of her precious holy books, she went one step farther; she learnt to write and, then, the ultimate awakening: she told the story of her *self*. Her autobiography was both the medium whereby she expressed, and the message of her personal identity, her selfhood. Toru sublimated her loneliness in probably the only way she knew how: as a writer; a translator, critic, poet, novelist, and letter writer; with a sensibility that fused the European with the Indian.[194] Haimabati reacted against her loneliness at the first opportunity she had: when she became a widow. She had to do battle against forces that neither of the other two had to fight for she had to create for herself a space in a patriarchal world. But unlike Rassundari she could at least take advantage of the movement for women's education. She worked that to her advantage.

The awakening we call the Bengal Renaissance, as we have seen so far, took many forms. For these three women, it was ultimately the awakening of their own distinctive voices. Yet their awakening was resonant with the social milieu of their times—in the context of the women's emancipation movement, the progress made in women's education, and the Western influences that shaped the renaissance. The voices were their own, but they were not voices in a wilderness.

Notes

1. Vidyasagar 1850.
2. Rassundari Debi [1906] 1999. There seems to be some inconsistency concerning the publication dates (as there is about Rassundari's life span). Rassundari herself tells us that the book was 'first published' in 1868 (the Bengali year 1275) when she was fifty-nine, and the later version in 1901 (Bengali year 1308) when she was eighty-eight [*Amar Jiban*, p. 74]. Authoritative literary scholars, however, attribute the earlier and later publications to 1876 and 1908, respectively. See Tharu and Lalita 1991, p. 191.
3. Tharu and Lalita 1991, p. 190.
4. Das 1991, p. 177.
5. See Chapters four, five, and six.
6. Gusdorf 1980, p. 28.

7. Anderson 2001; Olney 1988.
8. Das 1991, p. 177.
9. Bruner 1990.
10. Eakin 1999, p. 100.
11. Sen n.d., p. 11.
12. Rassundari [1906] 1999, p. 19.
13. Sarkar 2003, pp. 98–101.
14. Rassundari [1906] 1999, pp. 21–5.
15. Ibid., p. 26.
16. Ibid., p. 21.
17. Ibid., p. 26.
18. Ibid., p. 27.
19. Ibid., p. 26.
20. Ibid., p. 30.
21. Ibid.
22. Ibid., p. 24.
23. Ibid.
24. Ibid., p. 31.
25. Ibid., p. 32.
26. Ibid.
27. Ibid., p. 33.
28. Ibid., p. 34.
29. Ibid., pp. 38–9.
30. Rassundari [1906] 1999, p. 45.
31. Ibid., p. 57.
32. Ibid.
33. Ibid.
34. Ibid., p. 41.
35. Ibid., pp. 40, 41, 46.
36. Ibid., p. 62.

37. Ibid., p. 66.
38. Ibid., p. 65.
39. Ibid., p. 60.
40. Ibid., p. 48.
41. Ibid., p. 47.
42. Ibid., p. 58.
43. Ibid., p. 54.
44. Ibid., p. 89.
45. Ibid.
46. Ibid.
47. Ibid., p. 91.
48. Ibid., p. 23.
49. Ibid., p. 24.
50. See Chapter seven.
51. Rassundari [1906] 1999, p. 35.
52. Ibid., p. 37.
53. Ibid., p. 39.
54. Ibid., pp. 40–1.
55. Ibid., p. 44.
56. Ibid.
57. Ibid.
58. Rassundari [1906] 1999, p. 51.
59. Ibid., p. 51.
60. Ibid.
61. Ibid., pp. 52–3.
62. Ibid., p. 54.
63. Ibid.
64. Ibid.
65. Ibid., p. 55.
66. Ibid.

67. Rassundari [1906] 1999, pp. 64–5.
68. Ibid., p. 71.
69. Forbes 1996, p. 33.
70. Ibid.
71. Murshid 2003, p. 12. See also, Chapter eight.
72. Tripathi 2004, p. 65.
73. Rassundari [1906] 1999, p. 44.
74. Tripathi 2004, p. 67.
75. Murshid 2003, pp. 31–2.
76. Quoted in Murshid 2003, p. 31.
77. Forbes 1996, p. 41; Kopf 1979, p. 34.
78. Kopf 1979, pp. 36–41.
79. Johnson 1991, p. 733.
80. See Chapter three.
81. Tripathi 2004, p. 65.
82. Quoted in Mittra 1877, p. 52.
83. Mittra 1877, p. 58.
84. See Chapters four and seven.
85. Tripathi 2004, p. 65.
86. Ibid.
87. Mittra 1877, p. 59.
88. Ibid., pp. 61–3; Tripathi 2004, p. 65.
89. Tripathi 2004, p. 65.
90. Ibid., p. 66.
91. Ibid.
92. Ibid., p. 68.
93. Kopf 1979, p. 34.
94. Forbes 1996, p. 39.
95. See Chapter four.

96. For an account of Mary Carpenter's activism on behalf of the poor and the disenfranchised (including women) in England, see Kopf 1979, pp. 32–3.
97. Kopf 1979, p. 34.
98. Ibid.
99. Ibid., p. 35.
100. Ibid.
101. Ibid., p. 36.
102. Kopf 1979, p. 37.
103. Sastri 1907, p. 131.
104. Kopf 1979, p. 38.
105. Forbes 1996, 122.
106. Kopf 1979, p. 40.
107. Ray and Gupta 1957, p. 122.
108. Forbes and Raychaudhuri 2000, p. 21.
109. Kopf 1979, p. 38.
110. Ibid.
111. Kopf 1979, p. 39; Forbes 1996, p. 43.
112. Lokugé 2006c, p. xx.
113. Ibid., p. xvi.
114. Ibid., p. xvii.
115. Ibid., p. xvii.
116. Mittra 1877, p. 45.
117. Ibid., p. 56.
118. Chaudhuri 2003, p. 58.
119. Lokugé 2006c, p. viii.
120. Anon 1870, p. 28.
121. Das 1974, p. 60.
122. Tagore [n.d.] 2002, p. 40.
123. Chaudhuri 2003, pp. 55–6.

124. Anon 1870.
125. Lokugé 2006a, p. 376, note 1.
126. For a chronological outline of Toru's life, see Lokugé 2006b.
127. Lokugé 2006c, p. xxiv.
128. Das 1991, p. 181.
129. Reprinted in Lokugé 2006a, pp. 89–126.
130. For an English translation by Prithwindranath Mukherjee, see Lokugé 2006a, pp. 1–88.
131. Reprinted in Lokugé 2006a, pp. 127–212.
132. Toru Dutt to Mary Martin, May 8, 1874, pp. 226–8 in Lokugé 2006a.
133. Toru Dutt to Mary Martin, April 23, 1875, pp. 238–41 in Lokugé 2006a.
134. Toru Dutt to Mary Martin, October 12, 1875, pp. 246–50 in Lokugé 2006a.
135. Ibid.
136. Toru Dutt to Mary Martin, December 19, 1873, pp. 222–4 in Lokugé 2006a.
137. Toru Dutt to Mary Martin, March 10, 1874, pp. 225–6 in Lokugé 2006a.
138. Toru Dutt to Mary Martin, May 9, 1874, pp. 226–8 in Lokugé 2006a.
139. Toru Dutt to Mary Martin, September 19, 1874, pp. 229–31 in Lokugé 2006a.
140. Toru Dutt to Mary Martin, May 9, 1874, pp. 226–8 in Lokugé 2006a.
141. Toru Dutt to Mary Martin, December 15, 1874, pp. 234–5 in Lokugé 2006a.
142. Toru Dutt to Mary Martin, January 11, 1875, pp. 235–7 in Lokugé 2006a.
143. Toru Dutt to Mary Martin, September 19, 1874, pp. 229–1 in Lokugé 2006a.

144. Toru Dutt to Mary Martin, May 9, 1874, pp. 226–8 in Lokugé 2006a.
145. Toru Dutt to Mary Martin, October 12, 1875, pp. 246–50 in Lokugé 2006a.
146. Toru Dutt to Mary Martin, September 19, 1874, pp. 229–31 in Lokugé 2006a.
147. Toru Dutt to Mary Martin, June 6, 1875, p. 242 in Lokugé 2006a.
148. Toru Dutt to Mary Martin, March 13, 1876, pp. 262–8 in Lokugé 2006a.
149. Toru Dutt to Mary Martin, November 23, 1875, pp. 254–6 in Lokugé 2006a.
150. Toru Dutt to Mary Martin, December 1875, pp. 256–8 in Lokugé 2006a.
151. Toru Dutt to Mary Martin, December 1875, pp. 256–8 in Lokugé 2006a.
152. See Chapter eight.
153. Lokugé 2006c, p. xvi.
154. Toru Dutt to Mary Martin, April 24, 1876, pp. 271–5 in Lokugé 2006a.
155. Lokugé 2006a, p. 363.
156. Toru Dutt to Mary Martin, April 24, 1876, p. 273 in Lokugé 2006a.
157. Das 1991, p. 164.
158. Toru Dutt to Mary Martin, December 18, 1874, pp. 234–5 in Lokugé 2006a.
159. Toru Dutt to Mary Martin, January 11, 1875, pp. 235–7 in Lokugé 2006a.
160. Toru Dutt to Mary Martin, June 18, 1877, p. 343 in Lokugé 2006a.

161. Toru Dutt to Mary Martin, July 17, 1877, p. 343 in Lokugé 2006a.
162. Toru Dutt to Mary Martin, July 30, 1877, p. 344 in Lokugé 2006a.
163. Vidyasagar 1850
164. Tripathi 2004, p. 91.
165. Forbes 1996, p. 85.
166. Forbes and Raychaudhuri 2000.
167. Ibid., p. 57.
168. Ibid., p. 64.
169. Ibid., p. 65.
170. Ibid., p. 67.
171. Ibid., pp. 69–70.
172. Ibid., p. 70.
173. Ibid., p. 81.
174. Ibid., pp. 82–4.
175. Ibid., p. 84.
176. Ibid., p. 85.
177. Ibid., p. 93.
178. Ibid., p. 100.
179. Ibid., p. 101.
180. Ibid., p. 103.
181. Ibid., p. 139.
182. Ibid.
183. Ibid., p. 233.
184. Ibid., p. 236.
185. Ibid., p. 239.
186. Ibid.
187. Ibid.
188. Ibid., p. 250.

189. Ibid., p. 290.
190. Forbes 2000, p. 23.
191. Forbes and Raychaudhuri 2000, p. 291.
192. Ibid., p. 303.
193. Ibid., p. 312.
194. See, for example, Mukherjee 2000, p. 90.

Interlude

'Where the Intellect May Safely Speculate...'

IN THIS STORY, 1857 was not so much the year of the Indian Mutiny as the year of the Indian university. For, in that year the country's first universities were created in Calcutta, Bombay, and Madras. And since the University of Calcutta was established in January 1857, preceding by a few months the birth of its sisters in Bombay (July) and Madras (September), it became India's first ever (Western-style) university.

Perhaps it is fitting that this was so. In the words of Cardinal John Henry Newman, written five years earlier, a university is a place where 'the intellect may safely speculate...where inquiry is pushed forward, and discovery verified and perfected, and rashness rendered innocuous, and error exposed, by the collision of mind with mind, and knowledge with knowledge.'[1] In 1857, the revolutionary awakening in Bengal was still work-in-progress, with new minds colliding with old minds, new knowledge with old. If the eminent cardinal's lofty words are taken as the very ideal of the university, then the University of Calcutta could surely offer an abode, a home for furthering the revolution.

THE NOTION OF establishing a university in Calcutta had been 'in the air' for some years—since 1845 in fact, when the Council of Education in Bengal (which included as a member Toru's grandfather Rassamay Dutt) mooted the idea.[2] Not that *this* idea of a university resonated with Cardinal Newman's, for what the Council of Education had in mind was a centralized body not for teaching, research, and intellectual inquiry but for setting syllabi, administering examinations, and awarding degrees.[3] Candidates for such degrees would be drawn from institutions in and around Calcutta such as Hindu College and the like. The model for the envisioned university was the University of London.

Still, it took a dozen more years for the original idea to reach fruition. Governors-general would come and go, as would members of the Council of Education. Opinions would change. There would be enthusiasts and sceptics. A select committee of the House of Lords was formed to consider the matter in 1853.[4] Old India hands had their say and amongst them were C.H. Cameron, then president of the Council of Education, and the missionary-educationists John Clark Marshman (son of the Serampore trio's John Marshman)[5] and the doughty Scot Alexander Duff (himself founder, in 1830, of a highly successful school, the General Assembly's Institution, and then two decades later, the Free Church Institution). Marshman suggested that not only Bengal but all the presidencies of British India should house universities.[6] As for Cameron, in an address to the British Parliament in 1853, he argued eloquently for universities in Calcutta, Agra, Bombay, Madras, and Colombo (in Ceylon, now Sri Lanka).[7]

The tipping point was the education dispatch of 1854 of the then president of the Board of Council, Sir Charles Wood, to Governor-General Lord Dalhousie. Wood's dispatch, described by some as the 'Magna Carta of English education in India'[8] because of its comprehensive scheme for an educational policy that would extend from primary school to university, laid the foundation for establishing universities in Calcutta, Bombay, and Madras, all modelled, along the lines earlier suggested, on the University of London.

JOHN HENRY NEWMAN'S idea of a university as a place where the intellect may safely range and speculate, where minds and kinds of knowledge may collide, suggests something nobler than a mere organization that administers examinations, sets syllabi, and confers degrees. It suggests rather a grove of academe in the manner of the Lyceum, the Athenian garden where Aristotle walked and his pupils walked with him as he taught. Yet, despite its prosaic objectives, the creation of the University of Calcutta did, in a manner of speaking, give birth to such a grove where none had existed before. For, it almost immediately drew together under its watchful care, like a giant banyan tree, a cluster of existing institutions.

Arguably the most well-known of these, being the oldest, was Hindu College—but no longer so called, for in 1855 it moved from being a private to a public institution and was renamed Presidency College.[9] But Presidency College was (and remains to this day), in modern American jargon, a college of liberal arts devoted to the humanities and the natural sciences (though, as we shall see shortly, it has had its hiccups in that role).

In the early years of the university's life, Presidency College was by no means the only such institution in Bengal. Across the city, in the White Town, there was La Martiniere.[10] Elsewhere in the presidency, there was Hooghly College; Dacca College; and Berhampore College. There was Krishnagar College where Madhusudan's mentor David Lester Richardson had once presided,[11] and the Derozian Ramtanu Lahiri had taught. Then there were the citadels of Christian faith of various persuasions, including Serampore College up the river;[12] Bishop's College across the river, once Madhusudan's safe haven;[13] and Alexander Duff's Free Church Institution.

They all, and others, clamoured for 'affiliation' to the university.[14] In 1860, Vidyasagar's beloved Sanskrit College entered and expanded the grove.[15] And, once more in the White Town, not far from La Martiniere, a new institution called St Xavier's, founded by Belgian Jesuits,[16] also entered the grove in 1862.[17] (Institutions such as La Martiniere and St Xavier's had both school and college sections.) Indeed, this grove of academe spread well beyond Bengal: institutions from as afar as Benares, Agra, and Colombo sought affiliation and were accepted in the early 1860s.[18]

As for the much fought-for higher education for women, this, predictably, would have to wait a while for recognition by the university. Male chauvinism in Victorian India was as alive and well as it was in Victorian Britain, and it would take its own time to soften. In 1882, we find recorded that Bethune College[19] had six students and another women's college, the Free Church Female Normal School, had three—all studying for a university examination.[20] A year later, exactly a quarter century after the University of Calcutta produced its first two male graduates (including a certain Bankimchandra Chattopadhyay),[21] it awarded the Bachelor of Arts degree to Chandramukhi Basu and Kadambini Ganguli, not only the first women graduates of the university[22] but also of the British Empire.[23]

BUT IN 1857 the architects of the University of Calcutta had still larger ambitions. The knowledge it would nurture must go beyond the realm of the liberal arts; it must engender the pursuit of modern (meaning Western) medicine, of engineering, of law—the realms of the professions, in other words.[24]

Here, at least in part, infrastructures were already in place, longest in medicine and more recently in engineering and law.

As far back as 1835, when William Bentinck was governor-general—this, we recall, was the climactic time of the 'Anglicist–Orientalist controversy' and the year of Macaulay's 'Minute' on education—a medical school along Western lines had been founded in the metropolis, called Calcutta Medical College.[25] Amongst the guiding spirits in its formation were its first principal, Mountford Bromley, a surgeon[26] and—predictably, given his liberal, progressive mentality—David Hare who from 1837 to 1841 served as the college's secretary.[27] Thus, when the university elected to establish a faculty of medicine and to establish a degree in medicine and surgery, Calcutta Medical College became a natural 'resource' in affording the requisite medical education.

It was also fortuitous that when the university was inaugurated there was a foundation in place to support a faculty of engineering: a professorship in civil engineering had been created in Hindu College (thus making it that much more than a liberal arts college) in 1843–4,[28] and soon after its renaming as Presidency College, the Calcutta Civil Engineering College was separately established in 1856. Almost a quarter century later, it would take over the lush campus of what had been Bishop's College in Shibpur across the Hooghly next to the Indian Botanical Gardens.

Bengal, however, cannot claim to be the first in engineering education in India. That honour goes to the town of Roorkee in what was then the United Provinces (now Uttar Pradesh). The British historian of science and technology Donald Cardwell has wryly remarked that engineering colleges and technological universities are developed by governments for strategic reasons (but then, so are most professional schools, including those in medicine).[29] In nineteenth century India, the desire of the British to tap the land's vast natural resources for agricultural and other purposes through improved irrigation and canal systems, and for enhancing transportation and communication was compelling. It was thus that the Thomason College of Engineering, named after the lieutenant-governor of the United Provinces, was established in Roorkee in 1847; the objective was to train irrigation engineers for the public works department.[30] Thomason College was thus India's first engineering school. Civil Engineering College in Calcutta, the country's second engineering school, became affiliated in 1857 with the University of Calcutta.[31]

As for law, here too Hindu/Presidency College played its part. In 1843–4, the then advocate-general delivered a course of lectures attended by students of Hindu College and

Hooghly College.³² Then in 1852–3 an 'eminent barrister' was appointed professor of law in Hindu College (thus also enlarging its liberal arts temper) and the law classes were apparently well attended.³³ The formal study of law in academe was then already 'in the air' by way of the law department in Presidency College when the university's faculty of law was established in 1857.

An anomaly in the formation of India's first university was that its constituent faculties had no separate place for the natural sciences. The faculties created were for arts, law, medicine, and civil engineering.³⁴ There was no faculty of (natural) science—despite the fact that amongst the subjects in which a candidate for the BA degree would be examined were mathematics, 'natural philosophy', (meaning physics) and 'physical sciences' (which includes chemistry and physiology).³⁵ Indeed, there would not be a faculty of science for many years. The natural sciences, thus, were folded into the realm of the faculty of arts—meaning, of course, liberal arts in its broadest sense, meaning liberal education. And even as the university matured and evolved over its first quarter century of existence, there were degrees to be won in medicine and surgery, in civil engineering, in law, but in general education there were degrees to be had only in the 'arts'—BA and MA—whether the candidate aspired to specialize in the humanities or the sciences.³⁶

As PARADOXICAL AND ironic was that the 'arts' in the jargon of academe excluded *art*. There was no place in this grove of academe for the visual arts. Clearly, the latter—drawing, painting, sculpting, design—were not deemed by the architects of the university as 'academically respectable'. If art was to have a place in the annals of the Bengal Renaissance we must look elsewhere for its nurture.

That was the Calcutta School of Art (more precisely, the Government School of Art, Calcutta), established through private funding in 1854.[37] This school was designed to provide 'an alternative to a literary, university education' to inculcate the skills and mentality for those of the educated middle class, the bhadralok, who desired to become 'respectable' artists.[38]

The nineteenth century ethos in British India, thus, subscribed to the now jaded distinction between verbal (that is, literary, textual, or logocentric) thinking and non-verbal (specifically, visual) thinking. In Bengal, the former was to be the domain of the University of Calcutta; the latter of the Calcutta School of Art. And so it would remain till Rabindranath Tagore founded his school (in 1901) and university (in 1921) in a place he named Santiniketan, some distance from Calcutta.

FOR THE HISTORIANS of the University of Calcutta, its formation in 1857 was the 'logical culmination' of the awakening that began with Rammohun Roy.[39] If the cultivation of the Indo-Western mind lay at the core of the Bengal Renaissance then most certainly the creation of the university was a facet of this awakening. One might even say that it was a *product* of a collective Indo-Western mind. For, though established by the British, a host of Indians were closely associated with its early development. Its 'founding fellows' included Alexander Duff; but they also included Vidyasagar, Prasunno Coomar Tagore (who would later endow the Tagore chair in law), the

Derozian Ramgopal Ghosh, and Rammohun's son, Ramprasad Roy.[40] Later, the Orientalist and Asiatic Society stalwart Rajendralal Mitra and another Derozian, Peary Chand Mittra, would become associated with the university.[41] Rajendralal and another already familiar figure, the Derozian Krishna Mohun Banerji, were amongst the first batch to be awarded the honorary degree of doctor of law by the university, in March 1876.[42]

Even the British recognized the symbiosis of East and West in the university's early life: in his convocation address in March 1882, Viceroy Lord Ripon would say that on this twenty-fifth year of the university, 'we are meeting together to celebrate the Silver Wedding of Western and Eastern learning'.[43]

More interesting, however, was a (most likely unintended) *effect* of the university's creation. When it was formed its first chancellor, Viceroy Lord Canning, addressing the university senate, spoke of it as a place for the education of 'the nobility and upper classes of India'.[44] It turned out otherwise. Nine years later, the vice-Chancellor, Henry James Maine, in his convocation address, confessed that the idea of 'an *aristocratic* institution' had never materialized: 'in spite of themselves they [the founders] have created a *popular* institution.'[45]

In other words, the university helped extend the intellectual awakening we call the Bengal Renaissance to a larger population. It became an agent for enlarging the scope of Western-style learning. Ripon's 'silver wedding of western and eastern learning' was to be celebrated and enjoyed by more than the elite, more than the 'aristocrats'.

The numbers give us some sense of this. In 1857, 244 students sat for the university entrance examination; in 1862, this had increased to 1,114.⁴⁶ According to one report published in the *Hindu Patriot* in 1882, between 1858 and 1881, 1,726 men were awarded bachelor's degrees in arts and law (BA and BL).⁴⁷

These were, of course, only two of the degrees on offer. By the end of its first quarter century (1882), the University of Calcutta was administering examinations leading to a large variety of degrees and diplomas: these included the 'first examination' in arts and in engineering; licentiate in civil engineering (LCE) and in medicine and surgery (LMS); bachelor and master of civil engineering (BCE and MCE); bachelor and doctor of medicine and surgery (MBBS and MD); bachelor and doctor of law (BL and DL); and bachelor and master of arts (BA and MA).⁴⁸

The university was not just in the business of disseminating knowledge for its own sake. The degrees and licentiates it offered transformed learning into marketable skills. The 1,700 (and more) BAs and BLs produced between 1758 and 1881 (some of whom were also MAs) found occupation mostly in education (as school teachers, lecturers, professors, one a college principal, another a rector); law (as law students, articled clerks of the high court, judges' clerks, munsiffs, pleaders, attorneys, a few barristers, some subjudges, and even a judge); and in the government bureaucracy (as deputy collectors, assistant commissioners, assistant and joint magistrates, assistant comptrollers, municipal inspectors, clerks, translators, and police inspectors). A few found employment as private secretaries and tutors to rajas; some became editors and missionaries.⁴⁹

Last but not least, the university, within its first quarter century, produced young men who were at the forefront of the Indian nationalist movement that took shape in the last quarter of the century.[50] One of the most important early nationalist organizations, founded in 1876, was the Indian Association, a forerunner of the Indian National Congress. This would organize the first India-wide agitations on issues related to the civil service and the press.[51] Amongst its founders were Anandamohun Bose (1847–1906), Sivanath Sastri (1847–1919) and Surendranath Banerjea (1848–1925), all graduates of Calcutta University.

Notes

1. Newman [1852] 1938, p. 38.
2. Ray and Gupta 1957, p. 44.
3. Ibid., pp. 44–5.
4. Ibid., p. 47.
5. See Chapter three.
6. Ibid.
7. Ray and Gupta 1957, p. 49.
8. Majumdar, Majumdar, and Ghose 1965, p. 50.
9. Anon 1955.
10. See Chapter two.
11. See Chapter seven.
12. See Chapter three.
13. See Chapter seven.
14. Ray and Gupta 1957, p. 65.
15. Ibid., p. 82. See also Chapter eight.
16. Namboodiry 1995, p. 46.
17. Ray and Gupta 1957, p. 83.

18. Ibid.
19. See Chapter nine.
20. Ray and Gupta 1957, p. 147.
21. See Chapter ten.
22. Ray and Gupta 1957, pp. 122–3.
23. Forbes 1996, p. 43.
24. For an articulation of such 'professional' knowledge, see, for example, Schön 1983; Simon 1996; Dasgupta 1996.
25. Gorman 1988, pp. 276–98.
26. Ibid., p. 282.
27. Mittra 1877, pp. 50–1.
28. Ray and Gupta 1957, p. 34.
29. Cardwell 1994, p. 185.
30. Headrick 1988, p. 179.
31. Civil engineering will not, of course, remain the college's only provenance; other branches of engineering are added in the twentieth century. In 1920, it is renamed Bengal Engineering College and so it remains till it becomes a university in its own right as the Bengal Engineering and Science University in 2005.
32. Ray and Gupta 1957, p. 39.
33. Ibid.
34. Ibid., pp. 61–2.
35. Ibid., p. 64.
36. Ibid., p. 98.
37. Guha-Thakurta 1992, p. 11.
38. Ibid.
39. Ray and Gupta 1957, p. 25.
40. Ibid., pp. 59–60.
41. Ibid., p. 124.

'Where the Intellect May Safely Speculate...' • 339

42. Ibid., p. 120.
43. Quoted in Ray and Gupta 1957, p. 125.
44. Ibid., p. 127.
45. Ibid. Emphasis in original.
46. Ray and Gupta 1957, p. 75.
47. Sinha 1965, pp. 161–99.
48. Ray and Gupta 1957, p. 98.
49. Sinha 1965, pp. 161–99.
50. Ray and Gupta 1957, p. 127.
51. Sarkar 1983, p. 88.

Ten

Bachelor of Arts, Master of Letters

THE UNIVERSITY OF Calcutta proudly held its first Bachelor of Arts examination in 1858. Ten students took it but none passed in all the six required subjects. However, two of the candidates passed 'credibly in five of the...subjects and... failed by not more than seven marks in the sixth'. They were awarded their degrees 'as a special grace' and placed in the second division. One of these candidates was one 'Judoo Nath Bose'; the other was 'Bankim Chunder Chatterjee'.[1]

Thus did Bankimchandra Chattopadhyay (1838–94) enter the annals of the Bengal Renaissance.[2] He was then about twenty years old.

Bankimchandra was a man of letters—a term now fallen into disuse yet one that fits him perfectly. Essayist, novelist, critic, journalist, polemicist, a worrier over ideas and issues, Bankimchandra wrote himself into the story of the Bengal Renaissance as a creative, consummate, complete man of letters. Shall we say, as a master of letters.

The best-known image of Bankimchandra today is a portrait painted of him in 1890.[3] He is in his early fifties, a portly, broad-faced man. Beneath a headgear, some sort of pugree, we see a wide forehead, thin lips, quizzical eyes. He is wearing what seems like a loose, flowing robe or gown and sits on a chair with his left arm resting on it. In his right hand he holds a sheaf of papers, indeed a manuscript for we can just discern the title in Bengali of one of his novels. There is none of the rakishness of Rammohun's face, nor the asceticism of Vidyasagar, and certainly not Madhusudan's swagger. Rather, we see the face of one who appears to enjoy his creature comforts but not in excess, a face with the calm repose of one who has had success and knows it, but is not yet done with his life's work.

In fact, Bankimchandra was as much a creature of conflicts and contradictions as was Rammohun. In the words of one of his biographers, Bankim could be 'now colossal, now petty, now a defiant genius, now a narrow puritan, now a rational thinker, and now an orthodox Hindu'.[4]

BANKIMCHANDRA, BORN IN 1838 in a small Bengali village called Kanthalpara, was the third son and fourth child of a successful civil servant. His father Jadavchandra was a deputy collector, competent in his work and a man of some culture—learned in Sanskrit, Persian, and English, fond of music and poetry—with a reputation for kind-heartedness and an extravagant lifestyle that went beyond his means.[5]

Bankimchandra's relationship with his father was ambivalent. By and large, we are told, it was a cordial relationship.[6] Yet there were tensions. He navigated between a deep, lifelong sense of filial piety—we hear that he never sat down in his father's presence[7]—and bitter resentment for having to pay-off his father's debts incurred by his life of excess.[8] To complicate matters, though Jadavchandra was apparently much attached to his celebrated offspring,[9] when the time came for the father to disburse his estate amongst his four sons, the eldest, Shyamacharan, and the third, Bankimchandra (perhaps because they were more affluent) were excluded from any share in the family property.[10]

As for Bankimchandra's mother, Durgasundari, all we know is what the son told an admirer: that his mother was old-fashioned and he learnt nothing from her.[11] We must infer that there was no conflict between mother and son here as there was between Rammohun and his mother;[12] nor perhaps did little Bankim learn his Hindu epics on his mother's lap as did Madhusudan.[13]

Bankimchandra's sense of duty was as much fraternal as filial. The eldest of Jadavchandra's sons was a deputy magistrate and thus a man of independent means. The second son Sanjib's potential career as a deputy magistrate was aborted because he crossed swords with his English boss and thereafter made no independent living—though he was a gifted if indisciplined writer of both fiction and travelogue, and served for a while as editor of *Bangadarshan*, the literary magazine Bankimchandra would found.[14] The youngest brother Purnachandra was also a writer—and, incidentally, the author of the first Bengali short story, published in *Bangadarshan* in 1873.[15] Bankimchandra was very fond of both these brothers, and supported them financially.[16] But like their father they too were extravagant in their ways; this, no doubt, was a source of exasperation for him.

While the relationship between the four brothers remained very close throughout their lives,[17] Bankimchandra's greatest solace came from the connubial life, with Rajlakshmi, his second wife. He had been married off the first time at the age of eleven to a pretty five-year-old, Mohini, who died six years later.[18] Six years on—he was then twenty-two—Bankim married Rajlakshmi, who was younger than him by ten years. They lived happily for the remaining thirty-four years of their life.

Bankim once confided to a friend that the greatest blessing in his life was his marriage to Rajlakshmi.[19] Elsewhere, he would remark, 'a biography of mine is not possible without hers'.[20] Yet all that is known of her is that she bore her husband three daughters, outlived him by almost three decades, passing away in 1919, aged seventy-one.

BANKIM'S EDUCATION BEGAN when he was six years old, when his father placed him in a school run by an Englishman in the moffusil town of Midnapore, where Jadavchandra was posted. He studied here for three years and achieved proficiency in English. When Jadavchandra's posting in Midnapore ended and he moved on (in the usual manner in the civil service of the time) so did Bankim, who was returned to Kanthalpara to the (somewhat indifferent) educational care of eldest brother Shyamacharan. There was not much formal education to be had under the brother's watch, but it was a time when young Bankim discovered music. He took lessons from Jadu Bhatto, a well-known musician of the time.[21]

At the age of eleven, he entered Hooghly College, situated across the river; and so, with younger brother Purnachandra, every morning for the next seven years he took the ferry to attend this institution. His education included English and Bengali; literary studies that ranged over the works of Joseph Addison, Alexander Pope, Francis Bacon, John Dryden, Richard Southey, some Shakespeare, and the Romantic poets;

mathematics, geography, and something of political economy.[22] He excelled in his studies. One biographical sketch tells us that he won a variety of scholarships during his tenure there.[23]

In the midst of this 'Anglicist' education, he took time to study Sanskrit in a local village school, and became acquainted with Kalidasa and Sanskrit grammar.[24] The kernel of an Indo-Western, cross-cultural mind was in the making.

His intellectual capability was such that when—having first enrolled in law at Presidency College in 1857—he sat for the entrance examination at the brand new University of Calcutta, he passed and was accepted as a candidate for the Bachelor of Arts degree course. The scope of the examination was formidable: languages, specifically English and one of Greek, Latin, Bengali, Persian, or Sanskrit; history and geography; mathematics and natural philosophy; and natural history.[25]

The subjects for the BA degree course covered languages; history—of England, British India, Ancient Greece, and Rome; mathematics and natural philosophy—including trigonometry, hydraulics, optics, and astronomy; physical science—meaning chemistry, physiology, and geography; and mental and moral science—logic, ethics, and psychology.[26]

And, as we have already noted, Bankimchandra (and Jadunath Bose) passed 'by special grace'. His law studies at Presidency College, however, were interrupted, for his success in the BA examination led to employment as deputy magistrate and deputy collector, positions that bhadralok fathers covet for their sons. He would eventually acquire his law degree in 1869.[27]

Bankim spent his entire adult life in government service in various capacities, till his retirement in 1891.[28] His career as a civil servant is not without interest. There were episodes of humiliation, of friction with British bureaucrats and superior officers as were not uncommon in the Raj. In an episode reminiscent of what Rammohun Roy once experienced,[29] Bankim's palanquin passed through a cricket ground where some British officers were playing a match. One of the officers, furious at the temerity of this Indian, physically assaulted Bankimchandra. Later, the officer had to apologize.[30]

Yet there were some British men and women with whom he had cordial relations and, indeed, he acquired English friends in quite high places.[31] And despite his frequent spats with his superiors, his career as a Bengali civil servant in the service of the Raj was as successful as it could be—success reflected, after retirement, in the award by the Crown of the titles of both Rai Bahadur and the Commander of the Order of the Indian Empire (CIE),[32] honours that doubtless caused more embarrassment than pleasure to one who achieved a reputation for raising a nationalist consciousness amongst his countrymen. And that, of course, is what interests us in this story.

THE NOVEL IS a child of the secular imagination. In the words of Sir Walter Scott, it is 'a fictitious narrative...accommodated to the ordinary train of human events'.[33] Its origins reach back to the novella or short tale of the kind the fourteenth century Italian Giovanni Boccaccio made famous in *The Decameron* or perhaps even further back to the eighth century *Arabian Nights*. The novel 'as we know it' emerged from these misty origins as an invention in eighteenth century Europe. To the nineteenth century English-educated Indian, the novel would be intimately linked to the likes of Daniel Defoe, Jonathan

Swift, Henry Fielding, and, nearer their time, Jane Austen, the Brönte sisters, and of course Walter Scott and Charles Dickens.

In India, the novel took root first in Bengal. Indeed, a Calcutta-born *woman* was one of the pioneers of the Indian novel though there is some controversy whether Hannah Catherine Mullens (1826–61) was in fact a Bengali or not.[34] What is not in doubt is that her *Phulmoni o Karunar Bibaran* (The Story of Phulmoni and Karuna, 1852) was a Bengali work of fiction; and this is seen by some at least as the first Bengali novel.[35]

The common (male) wisdom, however, denies Mullens this honour—is it because she was a woman, and a Christian woman at that?[36]—and ascribes the first Bengali novel to Peary Chand Mittra (whom we have often encountered in this story, as a Derozian and David Hare's biographer) who, under the nom de plume of Tekchand Thakur published *Alaler Gharer Dulal* (The Pampered Son of a Rich Family, 1858).

Bankimchandra, a recent graduate when this work was published, was very much aware of it; indeed, he recognized and lauded it as the first Bengali novel.[37] It contained, he would write, what he desired of the Bengali novel: that it must exclude 'every word or phrase that [has]…a learned appearance'; and that it must draw upon 'nature and life' for its material.[38]

Bankim was less generous about most of Bengali literature. He complained about its effeminacy, arguing that it mirrored the feminine nature of the Bengali (a perception widely held by British observers of Bengalis).[39] He singled out the love poems of Jayadeva, the twelfth century author of *Gita Govinda*.

Despite their lyricism, and the poet's 'exquisite imagery, tender feeling and unrivalled power of expression', he was 'the poet of an effeminate and sensual race'.[40] Scathing words! Had they been written by a foreigner—a Macaulay or a James Mill or a John Ruskin[41]—the wrath of the Bengali literati would have descended upon the author.

Bankim's own wrath with the state of Bengali literature did not end here. Effeminacy was only one source—perhaps a relatively innocuous source—of his dissatisfaction. The Bengali mind was not unproductive, he conceded, but the quality was by and large 'contemptible', often 'positively injurious'. Save for a few, the books published were 'clumsy imitations of good Bengali models' or 'abject copies of the silly stories of the later Sanskrit writers'.[42]

There was also the fact that the 'educated classes' were not inclined to write in their mother tongue. 'It is degrading for the dashing young Bengali who writes and talks like an Englishman to be caught writing a Bengali book' and when one did write in Bengali, one did it 'stealthily'. There were some 'honourable exceptions', and they were those who have done 'immense good' to the cause of Bengali literature. 'It is a fact that the best Bengali books are the productions of Bengalis who are highly cultivated English scholars. The matter for regret is how few these books are and how few the scholars who have written them.'[43] Bankim declined to offer examples of whom he had singled out for praise here.

He was far more forthright about those he despised. There were the 'Nadia poets' for instance, 'those who flourished under the Nuddea Raja, Krishna Chandra', including most famously Bharatchandra Ray. They were 'a very worthless set'.[44] And those who followed the Nadia poets and just preceded Bankim's own generation, produced 'scarcely any readable work'.[45]

There was a strong puritan streak in Bankimchandra which often coloured his literary judgement. He was obsessed about the 'disgusting obscenity' in Bharatchandra's poetry—an obscenity, Bankim wrote, that 'disfigured' the poet's work, and that 'unfits them for republication' in an era in which not all readers belonged to the 'rougher sex'.[46]

The absence of any critical temper was another source of Bankim's discontent with Bengali literature.

> We can hardly hope for a healthy and vigorous Bengali literature in the utter absence of anything like intelligent criticism. The educated Bengali fails in this department almost as much as the antiquated pundit, in consequence no doubt of deficient culture.[47]

Bankim's two English essays, 'Bengali Literature' and 'A Popular Literature for Bengal', partly sought to rectify that 'deficiency'. There he wrote that the Bengali novel should look to nature for its material.[48] 'Nature', of course, meant the world: the human world—human nature—especially. And looking to nature for literary inspiration was the clarion call of the critical mind in English literature, certainly since the seventeenth century but possibly earlier.[49]

This very idea of an 'intelligent criticism', the desire for a critical literary consciousness, may well have been shaped in Bankimchandra's mind by his exposure to the literary and critical essays of Joseph Addison, Richard Steele, John

Dryden, Samuel Johnson, and others of the seventeenth and eighteenth centuries—writers who formed the warp and woof of Bankim's English studies as an undergraduate. He may have even encountered and read Wordsworth's celebrated 'Poetry and Poetic Diction' (1800) and Shelley's 'A Defence of Poetry' (1821). Bankim's consciousness of a 'deficient Bengali culture' in the literary realm and his idea of what the novel should be were certainly the consequences of his English literary studies.

By the time his two essays on Bengali literature appeared he was himself well into the writerly life. Intriguingly, he wrote his first novel *in English*.

RAJMOHAN'S WIFE (1864)—really a novella—was not just Bankim's first novel, it was also the first 'Indian English novel'.[50] In its light, Bankim's remark about the Bengali 'educated class' being reluctant to write in the mother tongue, published six years later, is intriguing. Perhaps the remark was a wry mea culpa as much as a caustic reference to others.

In the total corpus of Bankimchandra's novels—he would write eleven in Bengali, beginning with *Durgeshnandini* (1865) and ending with *Rajsingha* (1893)—*Rajmohan's Wife* stands out as an anomaly. For one thing, it was his only English novel. For another, serialized in a Calcutta weekly magazine, it never appeared in book form in the author's lifetime. And third, it was not very widely known outside a small intimate circle and was soon forgotten.[51] It was 'a text more heard of than read'.[52] (Though according to the great American wit Groucho Marx's measure, that would make it a 'classic'.) Bankim's retreat from writing fiction in English, the fact that it was viewed by some as a 'false step',[53] reminds us also of Michael Madhusudan Datta's initial foray into writing English poetry.[54]

Why did Bankim write his first novel in English at all? Perhaps, as he himself noted six years later, because it was the fashion for English-educated Bengalis of the era to write in English. Perhaps because he was still unsure of his medium.[55] Be that as it may, it still compels our attention because of what it was: Bankimchandra's first novel; and *the first Indian novel in English*. Bankim stands out as the pioneer in a literary genre which, in the hands of later Indian writers of the twentieth century and on, would become integral to the landscape of English language fiction.[56]

There is no evidence whatsoever that *Rajmohan's Wife* (or, for that matter, Toru Dutt's *Bianca*, published in 1878)[57] cast any influence on later writers of Indian novels in English.[58] But in 1864 Bankim faced the same problem that some of the Indian-English novelists a hundred years later would face: how to create a narrative voice, a tongue in which the manners, mores, lives, speech, and ethos prevalent in one culture can be represented in the language of another.

Meenakshi Mukherjee, writing on *Rajmohan's Wife*, points out that Bankimchandra had no 'model' to draw upon.[59] This is precisely why *Rajmohan's Wife* has a place in the story of the Bengal Renaissance. What Bankim must have faced, what he must have struggled with, is the cognitive problem of how he could fuse together the form of the *English* novel—its narrative style, dialogue, and the language—and the world around him. Here was an act of creation in its own right that belonged to the revolutionary ethos of the Bengal Renaissance.

Bankim's solutions were not always successful. We get glimpses of the struggle he had to engage in from a few passages from the novel.

> The other laughed and said, 'Oh, it's Didi. What kindness! *Whose face was it that I first saw on getting up this morning?*'[60]

The italicized sentence here is a direct translation of a common Bengali sentiment that signifies mock-gratitude, as if to say, 'I am so lucky that...' No native English writer would invoke this sentence; it simply does not exist in the English idiom.

> The young woman said angrily, '*Go to Jericho!* How she goes on! I would never have come with you if I had known—.'[61]

'Go to Jericho!' makes no sense in an Indian context. Jericho, a city of great antiquity by the Jordan river is, of course, familiar to the reader of the Old Testament. As the story is told in the Book of Joshua, under the Lord's command the walled city of Jericho is given to the Israelites, the 'chosen people', as their land. But to do so, under the Lord's will, the walls of the city will crumble and the armed Israelites will enter, and all of Jericho's inhabitants will be destroyed and the city burnt to the ground. And woe betide anyone who dares to rebuild it. 'Cursed be the man before the Lord that riseth up and buildeth the city Jericho: he shall lay the foundation thereof in his first born, and in his youngest son shall he set up the gates of it.'[62]

'Go to Jericho!' is thus in the nature of a curse, but one that is utterly foreign to the context: the Bengal setting.

At the sight of her silent suffering the cruel man softened a little. He no longer tried to beat her but continued his abuse. It is unnecessary to try the patience of the reader *by reproducing all his Billingsgate...*[63]

The reference to Billingsgate is quite incongruous unless we assume Bankimchandra's reader was English or intimate with London: Billingsgate is the location of a renowned fish market in London's East End, and as renowned for the colourful language of its fishmongers.

There were also the odd uses of 'thou' and 'thee', 'thy' and 'canst' employed by the brutal husband Rajmohan in addressing his wife.

> 'Woman,' he said fiercely, 'deceive me not. *Canst thou? Thou* little *knowest* how I have watched *thee*; how from the earliest day that *thy* beauty became *thy* curse. I have followed every footstep of *thine*...'[64]

These excerpts illustrate yet another aspect of the problem Bankimchandra grappled with in writing his novel in English: the uncertainty, the ambivalence, the 'anxiety' over his readership. Was he writing for the British in India or the English-educated Bengali? Bankim would very soon resolve this by abandoning English as his language of fiction—just as Madhusudan abandoned English as his language of verse. His first Bengali novel, *Durgeshnandini* (1865), was published the year after the appearance of *Rajmohan's Wife*.

But whether his novel was in English or Bengali, there was still the issue of what kind of novel to write. No work of art is created out of nothing. The artist like the scientist, the inventor, the philosopher builds upon the past, upon existing patterns or models.[65] In the absence of a novelistic tradition in Bengali—or indeed, Indian—literature in Bankimchandra's time, the author had to turn to the West.

In the case of *Rajmohan's Wife* Bankimchandra turned to a genre we can call 'contemporary realism' of the kind present in the Anglo-European fiction of his time—the realism which in Bankimchandra's own words must look to 'nature and life' for material and inspiration,[66] though Bankim's realism in *Rajmohan's Wife* was diluted by a tinge of the Gothic and a dash of melodrama.

As the title reveals, the novel is ultimately about a woman, Matangini: beautiful, passionate, impetuous, spirited, married to a boorish, brutal, villainous man; a woman who transgressed the boundaries of female propriety by admitting to an illicit love for her sister's husband. Around this unusual woman revolves a constellation of less interesting characters; but here also were themes all-too-familiar to the middle-class Bengali milieu in which Matangini was situated: female subjugation, polygamy, legal intrigue, and litigation, dacoity, criminal conspiracy against family members by (own) family members, the intimacy of the domestic space in village homes, zamindari life, bonding between women in a zenana environment, the contrast between urban and rural mentalities, and so on. There are interesting and vivid depictions of everyday life in a Bengali village. At one point, for instance, we are privy to the near-bedlam of a 'busy hour of zenana life', as graphic as a Breughal painting.[67]

In *Bishabriksha* (The Poison Tree, 1873), Bankimchandra revisited the genre but this time in Bengali. This novel is interesting because in essential ways it dipped into social issues that were situated in the Bengal Renaissance itself—issues we have already encountered in our story so far, such as widow remarriage and polygamy. Thus, quite naturally, both the Brahmo Samaj and Ishwar Chandra Vidyasagar were alluded to in the novel. The story's main plot revolves round an 'eternal triangle' involving Nagendra, a zamindar, his wife Surjamukhi, and Kunda, a widow with whom Nagendra falls in love and who reciprocates that love, and whom he marries. The reader, however, is left in the dark about Bankimchandra's own position on widow remarriage and polygamy, since by the time the story ends both problems are dispensed with, for Kunda takes poison and dies.

Bankim, however, began his Bengali writing with another literary model. This was the historical novel/romance which situates the story in a time preceding the author's lifetime, usually with actual historical events as a backdrop. Bankim's first Bengali novel, *Durgeshnandini*, was set against the background of sixteenth century Bengal when the Pathans and the Mughals were in conflict.

The historical novel is, of course, inextricably linked with the name of Sir Walter Scott who popularized the genre with such works as *Waverley* (1814), *Rob Roy* (1818), and *Ivanhoe* (1820). Indeed, soon after the publication of *Durgeshnandini* some people accused Bankimchandra of plagiarizing *Ivanhoe*. Bankimchandra's response was that when he wrote his novel he had not read *Ivanhoe*,[68] though there are striking similarities between Scott's novel and Bankim's. Bankim may or may not have been inspired by the plot of *Ivanhoe*, but he certainly imported from Scott 'a basically Western idea of romance'.[69]

Romantic love. The novel was not only a new literary form in Bengali (and, indeed, all Indian) literature. The novel was the means by which the Western idea of romantic love entered into the ordinary Bengali reader's consciousness. Thus Bankimchandra was not only an innovator of a new Bengali literary genre; he was also the harbinger of a new *emotional* consciousness—of premarital romantic love and all that this entailed.

Bengali readers of English literature, having 'tasted romantic love', desired it in Bengali fiction as well. But in contemporary Bengali society there was scant scope for premarital romantic love, especially amongst the 'higher' castes, where girls were married off in their early teens. The *historical* romance in an Indian setting was thus a way in which the Western idea of romance could be offered to the Bengali reader.[70] This may well have been one reason why Bankim favoured the historical model over realism. Eight of his eleven Bengali novels were historical romances. (He also wrote some shorter fiction.)

Such a romance was *Durgeshnandini*, the title meaning the daughter (nandini) of the lord of a castle (durgesh). It tells of the son of a Mughal general who falls in love with the daughter of a Pathan chieftain. But there is also, as a subplot, a love triangle. The novel is set in the backdrop of a rebellion of a Pathan ruler named Katlu Khan against the Mughal emperor Akbar. It is the late sixteenth century. A Mughal general, Mansingh, sends his son Jagat to quell the uprising. On the journey he meets Tilottama—the durgeshnandini of the title—daughter of Birendra, chieftain of Mandaran castle, and falls immediately in love with her.

In the course of a battle between the Pathan and Mughal armies Jagat is seriously wounded and taken captive by a chivalrous Pathan general, Osman. In the enemy camp Jagat is nursed by Ayesha, daughter of Katlu Khan, and she falls in love with him. Jagat, in love with Tilottama, gently rebuffs her. Osman, who loves Ayesha and jealous of Jagat for inspiring Ayesha's love, challenges his perceived rival to a duel and is defeated. Here, then, is the love triangle.

There is, of course, the ongoing strife between the two armies. And there are other complications: the Pathan ruler Katlu Khan executes Tilottama's father Birendra for not joining the rebellion and, in turn, Birendra's wife Bimala seeks revenge.

The story eventually ends with the reunion between Jagat and Tilottama. Ayesha, thwarted in her love for Jagat, contemplates taking poison but finally decides against it, accepting, phlegmatically, her fate.

It is easy to understand why *Durgeshnandini* appealed to the nineteenth century Bengali reader. Here was a 'rollicking' yarn centred around love, passion, and jealousy, war, revenge, chivalry, and bloodthirst against a historical background. Historical accuracy was not important; it was enough that there was historical plausibility, as well as an atmosphere that reeked of a particular past—in this case, the Mughal era. Those who had read Sir Walter Scott's novels or other Western romances would no doubt welcome the importation of this genre into Bengali literature; those who were not familiar with Scott must have been enchanted with their first encounter with historical romance. This was no tale of Radha or Krishna, or other mythical or mythological characters from some remote, hazy antiquity. The novel had arrived with a bang in Bengal.

Durgeshnandini's appeal to the reader was compelling, as Bankim found even before it went to press. As the story goes, he read out the novel to some friends at his home before sending it to the printer. His listeners were apparently 'spellbound'.[71] One friend predicted that Bankim may well write better novels but none would likely be more popular. The prediction proved correct: according to Bankim's distinguished younger contemporary Romesh Chandra Dutt (1848–1909), economic historian, and translator of the *Ramayana* and the *Mahabharata* into English, it was 'as if a new light flashed all of a sudden across the firmament of Bengali literature'. People were singing 'a paean' to the novel. Here was 'a new era,' a 'new spirit'.[72]

Bankim's reputation was not just confined to Bengal. His novels were read in Assam and Orissa, neighbourings regions where people knew Bengali.[73] *Durgeshnandini* was translated into Urdu in 1876 and Kannada in 1885. The first English translation also appeared in the 1880s. In the 1890s, Marathi, Gujarati, and Telugu translations appeared. By the end of the century Bankimchandra's reputation as a novelist was India-wide.[74]

The historical novel was not the only vehicle Bankim used to speak of romantic love. *Rajmohan's Wife* spoke to *extra*-marital, illicit love in a contemporary setting. *Bishabriksha*, also set in Bankim's own time, had adulterous, bigamous, albeit romantic love.

Bengalis of the nineteenth century, thus, became acquainted with premarital romantic love between 'ordinary' humans through literature, at first English, then their own. As Nirad C. Chaudhuri puts it, Bengalis learnt of love from literature. 'At first it was transferred to Bengali literature from English literature, and then taken over from literature to life.'[75] Bankimchandra had no small role in this curious, very Indian process.

SPEAKING OF THE historical novel brings us to *Anandamath* (1882), translated into English some decades later as *Abbey of Bliss*. This was set in the eighteenth century. Some literary scholars find it a deeply flawed work as a novel.[76] Indeed, to call *Anandamath* a novel is perhaps to do injustice to the art of the novel. It is to be overly generous to the book itself.

But that is almost irrelevant. Its much larger significance lay in the fact that it was a literary means by which Bankimchandra induced another kind of consciousness amongst his readers: of nationalism. It may have been set in historical time but it struck nineteenth century nerves.[77]

And then there was 'Vande Mataram' (Hail to the Mother), at once the great battle cry of the swadeshi movement in the early twentieth century and a hymn, a poetic and musical emblem of Indian nationalism and, after Independence, the country's 'national song' (not to be confused with 'national anthem'). Indians may or may not any longer read Bankimchandra's novels; they may or may not read his essays. But they will know him as the man who wrote 'Vande Mataram' even if they are ignorant of *Anandamath* in which the full hymn first appeared.

The story of *Anandamath* is a tale of a band of passionate young Indian ascetics—sanyasis—who thought of themselves as santans, children of the Mother who was India; and who go into battle with the British in the time of Warren Hastings. It is a tale of a fight for freedom from the British. And as in some other of Bankim's novels, the most interesting character is a woman who joins the santans and fights with them alongside her husband.

The story, then, is about freedom struggle. It is worth remembering that *Anandamath* was written and published in a time when political consciousness was very much in the air. In the 1870s and early 1880s there had been widespread peasant uprisings in parts of Bengal against zamindars' rent demands. Bankim himself had supported the peasants' cause.[78] Elsewhere, in Maharastra in the mid-1870s, peasant protest movements had occurred.[79]

Anti-British sentiments were also very much in the air. By the late nineteenth century, Indians were beginning to demand greater rights for themselves and to participate more fully in their country's administration. It led to the formation of a variety of nationalist organizations in different parts of India, including the Indian Association, founded in Calcutta by Surendranath Banerjea, Anandamohun Bose, and others.[80] Several nationalist newspapers came into existence in about the same period.[81] This India-wide political and nationalist awakening led, in 1885, three years after the publication of *Anandamath*, to the formation of the Indian National Congress.

But nationalism also took shape in this era along religious lines: as Hindu revivalism—especially in Bengal.[82] As one historian put it, 'Defence of Hindu traditions became more respectable,'[83] which he attributed to the writings of such latter-day Indologists as the great German scholar Max Müller (1823–1900).[84]

Bankim (as we see below) pondered much in his essays and articles on the Indian psyche, the Indian sense of a national identity, and Hinduism as an aspect of Indian nationalism. But his essays, learned as they were, would probably not find a popular readership. *Anandamath*, as a novel, was a means of dwelling on political and nationalist consciousness that would almost certainly gain a wide readership.

The most striking feature of the novel lay in Bankim's depiction of India as the Mother and Indians as her children. This idea was reinforced throughout the novel by the frequent cry of 'Vande Mataram' by the santans. It became the santans' duty, their obligation, to fight in the cause of Mother's freedom—to free her from her state of famine, disease, death, humiliation, and destruction the British had reduced her to, and restore her to her former glory and dignity. The words of 'Vande Mataram' and the cry of 'Vande Mataram' were what inspired them in their cause.

Much has been said about the political and communal significance of both the novel and the hymn.[85] But ours here is not to ponder on this; ours is rather to dwell on the song and what it reveals of Bankim's creativity.

Bankim first composed the hymn, comprising the first twelve lines, some time between 1872 and 1875. He then elaborated it into the full version in 1881–2, which is how it appeared in *Anandamath*. The words were later put to music by Rabindranath Tagore, but there is more than one melodic version of the song.

The hymn is in Sanskritized Bengali and has been translated into other Indian languages. *Anandamath* itself went through five editions in Bankim's lifetime, and he also revised the words of the hymn. Perhaps the best-known English translation, done in 1909, is by the scholar-nationalist-mystic Aurobindo Ghose (who, upon founding his ashram in Pondicherry took the name 'Sri Aurobindo') and is based on the version appearing in the fifth edition of the novel.[86]

> I bow to thee, Mother,
> richly-watered, richly-fruited,
> cool with the winds of the south,
> dark with the crops of the harvest,
> the Mother!
> Her nights rejoicing in the glory of the moonlight,
> her lands clothed beautifully with her trees in flowering bloom,
> sweet of laughter, sweet of speech,
> the Mother, giver of boons, giver of bliss!
> Terrible with the clamorous shout of seventy million throats,
> and the sharpness of swords raised in twice seventy million hands,
> Who sayeth to thee, Mother, that thou art weak?
> Holder of multitudinous strength,
> I bow to her who saves,
> to her who drives from her the armies of her foemen,
> the Mother!
> Thou art knowledge, thou art conduct,
> thou art heart, thou art soul,
> for thou art the life in our body.
> In the arm thou art might, O Mother,

in the heart, O Mother, thou art love and faith,
it is thy image we raise in every temple.
For thou art Durga holding her ten weapons of war,
Kamala at play in the lotuses
and Speech, the goddess, giver of all lore,
to thee I bow!
I bow to thee, goddess of wealth,
pure and peerless,
richly-watered, richly-fruited,
the Mother!
I bow to thee, Mother,
dark-hued, candid,
sweetly smiling, jeweled and adorned,
the holder of wealth, the lady of plenty,
the Mother!

Bankim was not the first to symbolize the country as Mother. Michael Madhusudan Datta, in his poem 'To Bengal' (1862) too spoke mournfully of the land he was about to leave for England as the 'Mother'. Bankim's imagery was however richer, more powerful.

The Mother is at once the bountiful land—*richly watered, richly fruited, trees in flowering bloom, dark with the crops of harvest*—and the compassionate being—*giver of boons, giver of bliss*.

She is the very embodiment of thought and emotion: *Thou art knowledge, thou art conduct/ Thou art heart, thou art soul*. Indeed, she wields the wand that gives *the life in our body*.

She is fiery, the *holder of multitudinous strength…Terrible with the clamorous shout of seventy million throats*.[87]

And above all she is a goddess: *For thou art Durga, holding her ten weapons of war*. Motherland fuses into the Mother-Goddess, Viswamayee, the Mother of the Universe.[88]

The historian Sabysachi Bhattacharya draws our attention to a possible source of Bankimchandra's identification of the 'Mother-land' with the 'Mother-Goddess':[89] shortly before Bankim wrote 'Vande Mataram', he composed a small essay 'Amar Durgotsav' (My Durga Puja). Here, the narrator described a dream in which he saw the smiling face of the goddess of autumn, Durga. And he recognized her as Mother, the Motherland.[90]

A nationalist consciousness amongst Indians was one of the outcomes of the Indo-Western mind. Bankim recognized this in his own case: English education was the root of his nationalist thinking; it was the unlikely source of 'Vande Mataram'.

The English drew Indian eyes and minds, Bankim wrote in one of his essays, to many things they had not known, seen, or understood before. For instance, the desire for liberty; the wish for a nationality.[91]

The Indian psyche, he believed, lacked the desire for liberty; it was indifferent to who governed or ruled them.[92] 'Give me liberty or give me death,' cried Patrick Henry, governor of Virginia in 1775 on the doorstep of the American War of Independence. This very idea, Bankim wrote, was alien to the Indian mind.

This was the reason for the centuries of Indian subjugation. And from this realization emerged Bankimchandra's own raised consciousness about freedom, liberty, independence, nationalism.

The effect of subjugation was that it fostered a negative identity within the subjugated. Erik Erikson, the American psychoanalyst, following Freud, first gave a name to the idea of negative identity, a century after Bankim pondered on it. Negative identity is the perception of one's own worthlessness, and it may arise because of one's gender or ethnicity, one's class or religion.[93] To this we may add, in the Indian context, caste; and race; and being colonized.

THERE MUST BE *something* in which India could claim superiority over other civilized nations! Not in science certainly, nor in philosophy.[94] Bankimchandra admired the Baconian ethos of observation and experiment that had guided Western science since the seventeenth century and that had passed India by.[95] The Europeans were even superior in India's own backyard, in the realm of Vedic studies.[96] But then, the *Vedas* did not form a 'living religion' for Indians. 'To the Indian student the Vedas are dead.'[97] And, of that 'living religion', the part that attracted Bankim's attention was its moral code. *Here*, in the Hindu ethical system, a system that strove to regulate both personal and social conduct, was something that could match any other ethical system in the world.

He found in Hinduism the one philosophy that placed moral power over physical power.[98]

We are now entering the portals of a particular chamber of Bankim's mind, a chamber which many might regard with ambivalence. Yet even this orthodox Bankim relied on the rational Bankim, for he wished to *reason* himself into his chamber of orthodoxy.

More interestingly, in beating this retreat he appealed to his favourite European thinker—'the profoundest European thinker'[99]—Auguste Comte, the founder of what is known as the philosophy of positivism, an idea which, in Bankim's age, found an excited footing in Bengal.[100] He detected an analogy between Comte's 'religion of humanity', which was the worship of humanity, and the moral code in Hinduism.

Religion, Bankim believed, was not just a belief in God (or even in many gods) but a belief that offered a basis for human conduct. Only then would it mean something.[101] Religion, then, must be both a philosophy of life and a rule of life; it must encompass certain beliefs *and* rules of conduct grounded in those beliefs.[102]

But such rules of conduct alone do not make a religion. Which was why utilitarianism, the philosophy of Jeremy Bentham and James Mill,[103] could not be called a religion. To worship just the good, as the Utilitarians did, was to indulge in a 'wholly false religion'.[104] Religion must also embrace the worship of 'the Beautiful and the True'; in other words, it must embrace the great triumvirate of art, science, and morality.[105] The 'bottom line' was (and here, Bankim appealed to his British contemporary, the historian Sir John Robert Seely) 'the *substance of religion is culture*'.[106]

Here Bankim departed from Comte's religion of humanity. For though it was a moral religion, an altruistic one, founded on love, it was also an atheistic religion, for it had no place for God's presence. Bankim could not accept this. To him, the worship of a personal God represented the 'highest perfection of religion'; only in a personal God is there a realization of the threesome: beauty, truth, and morality.[107]

All this led Bankimchandra to his inevitable, triumphal conclusion: of all the world religions only Hinduism encompasses all these elements. Neither Christianity nor Islam ('Mohammedanism') would do, for they exclude 'nature-worship'.[108] And so: 'Hinduism alone therefore is a perfect religion.'[109]

Bankim offered this argument and his conclusion in English in his 'Letters on Hinduism'. In *Dharmatattva*, a lengthy Bengali tract on religion, he reiterated this final triumphal conclusion: 'Hindu dharma sakal dharmer madhye sreshta dharma' (The Hindu religion is the foremost of all religions).[110]

And that 'most perfect of religions' was most perfectly embodied, according to Bankim, in Krishna—as he propounded and explained and cajoled his reader into accepting, in his monumental treatise *Krishnacharitra* (The Life of Krishna).[111] He also argued, using textual sources, that Krishna was a historical figure, an actual person—and a perfect human being! Needless to say, *Krishnacharitra* was a hugely controversial work, even for Bankim's admirers.[112]

So here we are, back to Bankim's original, plaintive question: was there any area in which Indians could claim superiority over other nations? And his answer was a resounding, relieved '*Yes!*' India had given the world the most perfect religion, for Hinduism alone embraced both an impersonal God of nature and humanity, and a personal God.

This may have appealed to Hindu nationalists but, obviously, not to Indian Muslims.[113] Indeed, Bankimchandra's reputation, from that time on, as a Hindu nationalist and as anti-Muslim—fuelled as much by certain readings of

Anandamath and interpretation of the words of *Vande Mataram* as by his essays—would prevail through the twentieth and into the twenty-first centuries.[114] In 1937, Bengali Muslims made a bonfire out of *Anandamath*;[115] and in more recent times right-wing Hindu extremists have adopted 'Vande Mataram' as their anthem.[116]

AS WE HAVE seen, Bankimchandra was the novelist, the critic, the composer/poet, the essayist, the interpreter of history, the philosophical thinker, the social observer, the religious tractarian. He was also the literary journalist. In 1872 he launched his own Bengali literary periodical, *Bangadarshan* (The Mirror of Bengal); this became the medium in which many of his novels, poems, and essays would be published. He was also a keen observer of science and wrote several popular essays on science for *Bangadarshan* on such topics as the sun, the moon, and the stars, dust, the antiquity of man, and protoplasm.[117]

By 1894 he was the Grand Old Man of Letters in Bengal (though, at fifty-seven he was not *that* old!). Afflicted by diabetes, his health rapidly failed. On April 8, 1894, he passed away.

Two years later, at the twelfth session of the Indian National Congress, the man who succeeded him as the new star in the cultural firmament of Bengal sang 'Vande Mataram'. This was the first time the hymn was sung in public; it was also the first time the hymn had been put to music. The singer was Rabindranath Tagore, who first met Bankimchandra twenty years earlier as a fifteen-year-old.

368 • Awakening

Notes

1. Quoted in Gupta and Ray 1957, p. 87.
2. 'Chatterjee' and 'Chatterji' are anglicization of the Bengali surnames 'Chattopadhyay'.
3. Guha-Thakurta 1992, p. 76. A very similar but definitely different portrait is reproduced as plate 116 in Ray and Gupta 1957, opp. p. 117.
4. Das 1995, p. 21.
5. Ibid.
6. Ibid.
7. Raychaudhuri 2002, p. 109.
8. Ibid.
9. Ibid., p. 110.
10. Das 1995, p. 126.
11. Raychaudhuri 2002, p. 109.
12. See Chapter four.
13. See Chapter eight.
14. Sen 1979, pp. 216–17.
15. Das 1991, p. 304.
16. Das 1995, p. 126.
17. Raychaudhuri 2002, p. 111.
18. Das 1995, p. 32.
19. Ibid., p. 34.
20. Quoted in Das 1995, p. 34.
21. Ibid., p. 23.
22. Raychaudhuri 2002, p. 125; Das 1995, p. 23.
23. Bagal 1969b, p. ix.
24. Das 1995, p. 23.
25. Ray and Gupta 1957, p. 63.

26. Ray and Gupta 1957, pp. 63–4.
27. Bagal 1969b, p. x.
28. Ibid., p. x.
29. See Chapter four.
30. Raychaudhuri 2002, pp. 115–22.
31. Ibid., p. 120.
32. Ibid., p. 117.
33. Quoted in Drabble 1985, p. 706.
34. Tharu and Lalita 1991, p. 204.
35. Das 1995, p. 114.
36. Tharu and Lalita 1991, p. 204.
37. Chattopadhyay 1871, p. 110.
38. Ibid., p. 108.
39. Metcalfe 1995, pp. 105–7.
40. Chattopadhyay 1870, p. 98.
41. For John Ruskin's opinion about Indian art, see Dasgupta [1945] 2004, pp. 68–72. For Macaulay and James Mill on India, see Chapter five.
42. Chattopadhyay 1870, p. 100.
43. Ibid.
44. Chattopadhyay 1871, pp. 104–5.
45. Ibid.
46. Ibid.
47. Ibid., p. 107.
48. Ibid., p. 108.
49. Humphries 1982, pp. 53–4.
50. Mukherjee 2000, pp. 30–50 ('*Rajmohan's Wife*, The First Indian English Novel').
51. Das 1995, p. 35.
52. Mukherjee 2000, p. 30.

53. Das 1995, p. 35.
54. See Chapter eight.
55. Das 1995, p. 219.
56. For discussions of the Indian novel in English see, for example, the essays by Meenakshi Mukherjee, Leela Gandhi, Pankaj Mishra, Anuradha Dingwaney, and Jon Mee in Mehrotra 2003. See also Mukherjee 2000. For examples of the genre since Independence, see Rushdie and West 1987.
57. See Chapter nine.
58. Mukherjee 2000, pp. 33, 49–50, note 4.
59. Ibid., p. 32.
60. Chattopadhyay 1864, p. 27.
61. Ibid., p. 8.
62. *Joshua*, 6, 26.
63. Chattopadhyay 1864, p. 9.
64. Ibid., p. 41.
65. Gombrich 1969, p. 89; Dasgupta 2004; Dasgupta 2007, pp. 11–13.
66. See this chapter.
67. Chattopadhay 1864, pp. 17–18.
68. Das 1995, p. 41.
69. Ray 2003, p. 80.
70. Ibid., p. 80.
71. Das 1995, p. 38.
72. Quoted in Bhalla 2007, p. 11.
73. Das 1995, pp. 232–3.
74. Ibid.
75. Chaudhuri 1989, p. 116.
76. Das 1995, p. 162; Sen 1979, p. 214.
77. See Anand 1928.

78. Chandra 1989, pp. 54–5.
79. Ibid., pp. 56–7.
80. Ibid., p. 72.
81. Ibid.
82. Sen 1993.
83. Sarkar 1983, p. 72.
84. Max Müller's contribution to Indology is discussed in Dasgupta 2008, pp. 61–81.
85. See, for example, Dasgupta 1983; Bhattacharya 2003, Chapters one and two.
86. Bhattacharya 2003, pp. 100–1.
87. The historian Sabyasachi Bhattacharya notes that the reference to 'seventy million throats' suggests that the original version of 1872–5 comprising the first twelve lines is really referring to Banga Mata, Mother Bengal, rather than Bharat Mata, Mother India. According to the census of 1771, the population of the Bengal Presidency was seventy million. S. Bhattacharya 2003, p. 69.
88. Dasgupta 1998.
89. Bhattacharya 2003, p. 90.
90. Chattopadhyay, 1875.
91. Chattopadhyay, 1879.
92. Ibid., p. 237.
93. Erikson 1975.
94. Chattopadhyay 1873, p. 143.
95. Ibid., p. 146.
96. Chattopadhyay 1882, p. 212.
97. Ibid.
98. Ibid., p. 216.
99. Ibid.

100. Bagchi 1995c. See also Forbes 1975.
101. Chattopadhyay 1940, p. 237.
102. Ibid.
103. See Chapter five.
104. Chattopadhyay 1940, p. 237.
105. Ibid., p. 238.
106. Ibid. Emphasis in the original.
107. Ibid., 238.
108. Ibid., p. 265.
109. Ibid.
110. Chattopadhyay, 1888, p. 676.
111. Chattopadhyay 1892.
112. See Raychaudhuri 2002, pp. 147–9; Das 1995, pp. 179–81.
113. Chandra 1989, p. 410.
114. For a history of this 'reputation' see Dasgupta 1983.
115. Dasgupta 1983, p. 23.
116. Sarkar 2003, p. 164.
117. Bagal 1954, pp. 129–58.

Eleven

The Sound of Monistic Music

SOME SEVEN MONTHS before Bankimchandra died, a thirty-four-year-old monk stood before an audience at the World's Parliament of Religions in Chicago. The date was September 11, 1893, and the monk was Swami Vivekananda (1863–1902).

If we are to believe one of his most distinguished European admirers, the French savant Romain Rolland, he must have cut a striking figure that autumn Midwestern day, in his red robe, 'drawn in at the waist by an orange cord', and yellow turban.[1]

'Sisters and Brothers of America,' he began—and this address must have alerted his listeners to expect the unexpected. Which theologian, bishop, rabbi, priest, imam, or monk at that august gathering in September would have addressed the audience in this manner?

> It fills my heart with joy unspeakable to rise in response to the warm and cordial welcome which you have given us. I thank you in the name of the most ancient order of monks in the world; I thank you in the name of the mother of religions...[2]

In these opening words he laid his first claim, not unlike Bankim, on behalf of Hinduism: that it was the 'mother of religions'. And then he went on to make his second claim. 'We believe not only in universal toleration, but we accept all religions as true.'[3] He offered his audience shards of history to bolster his claim. Of how India gave shelter to Jews after their persecution by the Romans; of offering a home to the Zoroastrians who fled from their homeland after Islam arrived in Iran.

As we read the text of this brief address we can easily believe that he scarcely gave his listeners pause to assimilate his thoughts as he poured into their ears now a quote from the *Bhagavada Gita*—'Whosoever comes to me, through whatever form, I reach him; all men are struggling through paths which in the end lead to me'—now a thundering indictment of sectarianism, bigotry, and their 'horrible descendant', fanaticism all of which have 'drenched' the earth with violent and human blood, have 'destroyed civilizations and sent whole nations to despair'.[4]

He ended on a gentler, more optimistic note.

> I fervently hope that the bell that tolled this morning in honour of this convention may be the death-knell of all fanaticism, of all persecutions with the sword or with the pen, and of all uncharitable feelings between persons winding their way to the same goal.[5]

In all, Vivekananda delivered four addresses to the Parliament over some sixteen days. By the end his listeners, those who persisted, would had their full share—perhaps more than they had bargained for—of something most would have never heard of before: the Vedanta. But the most attentive of his audience would have sifted through all he had to say and gleaned a fundamental idea: the idea of a universal religion. It was this he alluded to when he quoted from the *Bhagavada Gita*, asserting that 'all religions are true', when he spoke of 'all persons wending their way to the same goal'.

Yet to speak of universal religion alone does poor justice to Vivekananda. As we shall see, his very identity was defined by a confluence of beliefs about man, nature, and God, which in Sanskrit is called advaita; in English, monism: the idea that there is only one reality in the world which is Brahman and that all human beings are part of it. Divinity thus lies within every individual and this is the only truth; doctrines, rituals, churches, temples, the rest are secondary. The American philosopher-psychologist William James spoke of the Vedanta as 'monistic music', and of Vivekananda as the 'paragon of Vedantic missionaries'.[6]

Vivekananda became a missionary but not in the Christian sense, for he did not have a church to follow as did the Baptists, Anglicans, or Jesuits in India; nor did he found a church as did the Brahmo Samajists. His mission was to spread the gospel of universal religion as the Vedanta taught and thereby awaken the people of India to its meaning for their everyday lives.

How would this happen? In Vivekananda's scheme of things, each nation has a central theme around which the nation revolves. For some it was political power, as in England. For India it was its religious life. Thus, 'you must make all and everything work through the vitality of your religion'.[7] Any social reform in India must work through its religious life. This demanded that the 'most wonderful truths' spoken in the scriptures '...must be brought out from the books...from the monasteries...from the forests...from the possession of selected bodies of people, and scattered broadcast all over the land...'[8]

From the possession of *selected bodies* of people! It is the masses that must hear the truth. For they have, for centuries, been told that they are scarcely human; that they could not 'hear of the *Atman*'. They should now know that they too, 'the lowest of the lowest' have the Atman within them.[9] For only then will they have faith in themselves. And that, for Vivekananda, was the crux of the matter.

> ...what makes the difference between the Englishman and you? ... The difference is...that the Englishman believes in himself and you do not. He believes in being an Englishman and he can do anything. That brings out the God in him...
> You have been told and taught that you can do nothing.[10]

Through religion will come self-belief. This was a modern, new Hinduism for a country awakening to nationalism.

Thus, Vivekananda's mission: he established a monastic order, the Order of Ramakrishna, an association of monks, sanyasis. They would not only spread the Vedantic gospel among the people, but also meld such teaching with social, educational, and humanitarian service for both 'the material and spiritual welfare of the masses'.[11] By this twin process of spiritual teaching and good works (karma yoga) he and his Order would help the people of India awaken to their self-belief, to their own potential.

This was the awakening Vivekananda dreamed of for his countrymen and women. A mass-based, missionary-style

Hinduism, focusing as much on social work as spiritual upliftment; a modern-day interpretation of the Vedanta for a country that was becoming increasingly nationalistic. This was *his* contribution to the Bengal Renaissance.

LIKE MADHUSUDAN, LIKE Vidyasagar, like Toru Dutt and Bankimchandra, Vivekananda was as much a product of the Bengal Renaissance as he was one of its producers. He was born Narendranath Datta into a prosperous bhadralok family. His father Biswanath belonged to the legal profession and was a cultured man, who read not just the *Gita* but also the Bible and the Koran, who knew in addition to Bengali and English, Hindi, Arabic, Urdu, Persian, and Sanskrit, and who while a practicing Hindu enjoyed the delights of Mughal cuisine.[12]

Young Narendranath studied at the Metropolitan Institution (founded by Vidyasagar), briefly attended Presidency College, and then went to General Assembly's Institution (founded by Alexander Duff)—the kinds of schools and colleges one might expect for a bhadralok youth of his time. His formal education, readings, and intellectual taste were eclectic: philosophy, history, Sanskrit, English literature, economics and sociology, biology, physics and chemistry, mathematics, and astronomy.[13] A characteristic Western education. He read the European philosophers: Hume, Mill, Hegel, Spencer, Schopenhauer, Comte. He corresponded with Herbert Spencer, then at the peak of his intellectual fame.[14] His friend from college, Brajendranath Seal—a formidable man of learning in his own right—persuaded him to read Shelley. The poet's pantheism—the belief that the presence of God is manifest in nature itself—and poem 'Hymn to the Spirit of

Intellectual Beauty' greatly affected him.[15] Not unexpectedly, he read Wordsworth.[16] He was drawn to Charles Darwin and his evolutionary theory, as his speeches and writings suggest.[17] He trained in classical music—vocal and instrumental—and learnt Hindi, Urdu, and Persian songs.[18] He was drawn, briefly, to the Brahmo Samaj and even sang in its choir.[19]

A BA degree from the University of Calcutta was obtained in due course. He was articled to a law firm and at the same time he began studying for a law degree.[20] Young Narendranath had, in fact, prepared himself to become a 'good' Bengali intellectual, perhaps even a man of letters in the Bankim style. Except that he met, at age eighteen, the mystic 'Sri' Ramakrishna Paramhansa.

THE CONTRAST IN backgrounds between Ramakrishna and Vivekananda is stark. Here was Vivekananda, an urban sophisticate, nurtured in an Anglicist education, raised on a diet of reason and logic. And there was Ramakrishna (1836–86), born Gadadhar Chattopadhyay in a small village, with scarcely any formal education—indeed, only just literate. They contrasted physically as well. One photograph of Ramakrishna shows him close-up: close-cropped hair, eyes closed, lips open in a wolfish half smile, half grimace. A slightly unkempt beard covers a large part of his face. He could be in a trance; or he might just be expounding to his devotees, making a point, as the posture of his left hand suggests.[21] Vivekananda, as he was in Chicago, is clothed in his ochre robe, wavy hair immaculately, carefully groomed with the suggestion of a parting in the middle, full-faced, unsmiling, slightly plump. The eyes dominate the face. Yet, he looks somehow vulnerable.[22]

So what drew Narendranath to Ramakrishna? They met in 1881 and Ramakrishna died five years later in 1886. Thus they knew each other for only a handful of years—but time enough to change the worldly, intellectually sophisticated would-be lawyer to the charismatic monk, a Narendranath Datta to a Swami Vivekananda, who seven years after Ramakrishna's passing would stand before the world's religious leaders and followers, call them 'brothers and sisters', and preach to them the gospel of universal religion.

RAMAKRISHNA WAS DRIVEN by one overarching emotion: a love for God. 'The one goal in life is to cultivate love for God'—for Brahman, the Supreme Being—said Ramakrishna.[23] But it cannot be achieved by way of reason but only through intuition. 'To know through jnana [knowledge] and reason is extremely difficult,' he said. It can only come from samadhi, for only in samadhi does one realize Brahman.[24] He said this again and again.

In the language of psychology, samadhi is an 'altered state of consciousness',[25] brought about by concentrated and sustained attention to a single entity.[26] Mahendranath Gupta recorded that Ramakrishna very frequently entered into such trance-like states.

Of course most people cannot attain samadhi. So a disciple asked, how should they realize God? Bhakti, Ramakrishna replied. A devotee is one whose mind dwells on God. But this comes at a price: it is only possible if one can divest oneself of 'egoism and vanity'.[27] Here, then, was the essence of Ramakrishna's belief system. There is a Universal Being, Brahman, who is both formless and with form,[28] with and without attributes.[29] Ramakrishna reminded his listeners of what the medieval mystic Kabir sang: 'The formless Absolute is my Father and God with Form is my Mother.'[30] That 'Mother' is the Divine Mother, Kali or Durga. But they—Brahman and Kali/Durga/Divine Mother—are the one and the same reality, differing only in name.[31]

How is it possible that God is at once formless and with form? Ramakrishna explained this by telling his followers to imagine the Supreme Being as an infinite ocean. And just as in extreme cold water freezes into blocks of ice of various forms that float on the ocean so also one might see God in the 'ocean of the absolute'. Devotees—bhaktas—will see these different forms; but when the 'sun of knowledge' rises the ice melts and becomes water once more. For some bhaktas the forms persist forever, just as in the ocean some blocks may not melt.[32]

This is an example of Ramakrishna's mode of teaching; he was a master at drawing upon stories and parables from everyday life, examples from commonsense experience, of physical reality, and these 'folk' teachings, his simplification of religion, and his charisma as a mystic and storyteller led to his extraordinary popularity as a preacher. This was Hinduism reformed from within: a profound response to Christianity and the highly westernized, elitist Brahmo Samaj.

Ramakrishna insisted that God can be realized through all religions.[33] Vaishnavas (worshippers of Vishnu/Krishna), Saktas (worshippers of Kali), Vedantists, Brahmos, Muslims, Christians—they can all realize God. After all, he said, different people speaking different languages call the same thing by different names: what Hindus call jal, Muslims call pani, and Christians call water; what some call Allah, others call God, still others, Brahma. They all denote the Supreme

Being.[34] He used a building analogy to illustrate this point: if the goal is to 'reach the roof' one can take stone steps, wooden stairs, or even climb up a bamboo pole. Any one of these paths will do the job.[35] Here was a way of thinking that was utterly alien to the Christian missionaries who insisted that theirs was the one true path to God.

IT WAS THIS monism that Narendranath imbibed from Ramakrishna, which, after the latter's death, became the fount of his gospel. Speaking to an audience in California in January 1900 (on his second visit to America) Vivekananda spoke, tongue in cheek, of the lessons he had learnt from his guru, a 'peculiar' 'old man' whom he 'happened to get' to teach him.[36]

But, of course, being the kind of intellectual that he was, he did not rely only on his guru's teachings. Ramakrishna may have had no desire to read the Vedanta or the other scriptures but Vivekananda was no mystic. He went to the Vedantic literature: its primary texts, the 'triple canon' of the Upanishads (composed between 900 to 500 BCE), the *Bhagavada Gita* (circa fifth century BCE), and the *Brahmasutra* (circa 200 BCE). He also drew on the various Vedantic schools that developed between the eighth and fifteenth centuries, that appealed to the primary texts but interpreted them—including, in particular, the advaita school of Sankaracharya (eighth–ninth century CE).

Vivekananda was not just a consumer and regurgitator of his guru's belief system, rather, he took Ramakrishna's teachings and built upon them using his readings of the Vedanta and creating his own monistic music.

What was this music?

We have already encountered his message of a universal religion in his first address to the Parliament of Religions, when he quoted the *Gita*: 'Whosoever comes to me, through whatsoever form, I reach him.' This, of course, is what he learnt from Ramakrishna. But Vivekananda went further. He argued that not only were most religions the same but that '... it is the same unity that animates all life forms from its lowest form to its noblest manifestation in man'.[37]

This is where science entered into his discourse. 'Science is nothing but the finding of unity.'[38] Vivekananda, thus, found common ground between science and his religion: they both sought unity in diversity. In this he parted ways from most religions for they tended to distinguish faith from reason.[39] And since modern science was the fountainhead of modern material progress, in his scheme of things, material progress and spiritual progress were not at odds with each other. Here was an expression of his Indo-Western mind.

VIVEKANANDA CAME INTO his own after Ramakrishna's death in 1886. Till then, he served what might be called an apprenticeship, five years of preparation for what he was to become.

Very early in their encounter, Ramakrishna detected a distinctive quality about him: Narendra (as Ramakrishna called him)[40] was of the sort that remained essentially detached from the world, one who did not really care for earthly matters, one who in maturity would reach for God.[41] Once Ramakrishna told a devotee that even in a room filled with people he would seek out Narendra and talk only to him.[42] Ramakrishna's chronicler, Mahendranath Gupta, recalled how another time, seeing Narendra, Ramakrishna touched the young man's chin 'tenderly' as one would a baby's chin.[43] Ramakrishna confessed that he looked upon Narendra as Atman, the 'Supreme Soul'.[44] The mystic had singled him out to be his apostle.

Indeed, as Mahendranath Gupta tells it, the first time Narendra visited Ramakrishna in Dakshineswar, the mystic took him away from the other disciples and asked him 'Why have you been so unkind as to make me wait all these days?... how I have longed to pour my spirit into the heart of someone fitted to receive my message.'[45]

At the time of Ramakrishna's death in 1886, Narendranath was twenty-three. A 'fellowship of apostles' was established by the principal disciples including Ramakrishna's 'Boswell', Mahendranath Gupta, with Narendranath as their leader. A house in Baranagar, a suburb north of Calcutta, near where Ramakrishna was cremated became their first monastery or 'math'.[46]

In 1888, Narendranath left Calcutta and, in the manner of the wandering monk, embarked on his first journey through India.[47] Other journeys would follow in 1889 and 1890,[48] and then a more extended pilgrimage in 1891–2.[49] He 'discovered' India, from the northern reaches of the Himalayas to the southernmost tip, Cape Comorin (now Kanya Kumari), in all its diversity of peoples, cultures, lifestyles, mores—and states of misery. It was during these travels that he resolved that it was the duty of religion to care for the poor and ameliorate their misery;[50] and to induce in the masses a sense of their self-worth, of human dignity, through education.[51]

Such a project needed money. His thoughts turned to the West, to seek from them 'the means to ameliorate the material condition of India'.[52] In exchange they would hear the message of the Vedanta.

He heard of a Parliament of Religions to be held in Chicago. His friend, the Maharaja of Khetri, provided resources for the trip and fitted him with a red silk robe and ochre turban. Thus he could project the 'exotic East'. The maharaja also suggested that he take the name of 'Vivekananda'.[53]

On May 31, 1893, Vivekananda embarked on his sea voyage. Along the way he encountered Ceylon (Sri Lanka), Singapore, Malaya (Malaysia), Hongkong, China, and Japan before arriving at Vancouver harbour in Canada. And thence the long train journey, in July 1893, to Chicago.

CHICAGO WAS THE beginning of a spectacular sojourn in America that lasted for some three years, with a brief interlude in England. He travelled mostly in the East Coast and the Midwest, attracting large audiences wherever he lectured. By all accounts it was a sensational 'visitation' by an Indian man of God in the New World, the first of its kind. He gave classes on the Vedanta and founded a Vedantic Society in New York.[54] Thus began the Vedantic movement in America. He became a celebrity amongst the rich and famous,[55] but also got to meet intellectuals including such luminaries as the philosopher-psychologist William James, brother of the novelist Henry James, the British physicist Lord Kelvin, and the electrical scientist and inventor Nikola Tesla.[56] He lectured on Indian philosophy at Harvard and was even asked to teach there.[57] As one historian has put it, no non-Western, and certainly no Indian, was accorded as much honour in nineteenth century America as Vivekananda.[58]

He was also subject to racial abuse and discrimination, and to charges of being a charlatan and a debauche.[59] By his own account, his detractors in America were not only Christians—'They blackened my character from city to city, poor and friendless though I was in a foreign country'—but also the Theosophists.[60]

In August 1895, invited by some British enthusiasts, Vivekananda took time off from America to visit England. He stayed there through December. And in London on this visit, he met a woman named Margaret Noble.

MARGARET NOBLE (1867–1911) was born into an Irish Protestant family, the daughter of an ordained minister, and was by training and vocation a schoolteacher. When she first met Vivekananda, she was the head of a school she helped co-found in a London suburb.

She was a woman seriously interested in pedagogy. Before coming to London, she had taught in a variety of institutions, in England and Wales[61]—taking time to fall in love with a young engineer and be affianced to him before he died of a lung disease[62]—and learnt from some experimental educationists in Liverpool new methods of teaching imported from the Continent, which she applied in her own school.[63]

In London, Noble joined a pedagogic association and spoke at its meetings.[64] She was committed to social and political issues and even before her time in London, undertook welfare research, wrote articles in local newspapers, and did some pamphleteering.[65]

Ireland, the country of her origin, was then under British rule. Irish nationalism was very much alive, and the struggle for

Home Rule was one of many nationalist movements amongst the Irish.[66] Noble involved herself in the Irish Home Rule movement and spoke publicly for the cause; she also supported the Boers' cause in South Africa against the British.[67] She joined a salon called the Sesame Club, becoming its secretary, and there she met the likes of the drama and music critic and playwright George Bernard Shaw, the scientist Thomas Henry Huxley, and the Russian geographer, geologist, and revolutionary-in-exile Prince Petr Alekseevich Kropotkin.[68] She became romantically involved once more, prepared for marriage, but was jilted by her lover who preferred another woman.[69] All in all, she was a busy young woman moving in interesting professional, social, and intellectual circles.

And then in the private home of someone from her circle she heard a lecture by Vivekananda.[70]

MARGARET NOBLE WAS also a woman of faith—though a troubled woman of faith.[71] To the profound questions she had asked herself from the time she was a student at Halifax College in Yorkshire—about 'the fundamental 'wherefore' of things'[72]—she had found no adequate answers. She continued to be disturbed by the apparent discordance between the 'law of Jesus' and human laws, between being a good Christian and working for the betterment of people.[73] As a result, a scepticism of sorts had infiltrated her faith.

It was in this frame of mind that she first encountered Vivekananda and heard him speak. She then attended more of his lectures; and in his Hinduism she found a religion that healed the schism between the spiritual and the secular, the sacred and the profane.[74] What she heard is well captured in a series of lectures Vivekananda gave in a later visit to London, en route back to India from America in November 1896. The lectures bore the title 'Practical Vedanta'.[75] The philosophy of the Vedanta, he began without preamble, would be valueless if it was 'absolutely impractical'. As a religion it must be 'intensely practical'.[76]

The Vedanta 'preaches the ideal'; and this ideal was that 'you are divine'. As the Upanishads said, 'Tat Twam Asi' (Thou Art That). This was the essence of the Vedanta.[77]

From this advaita idea emanated the essence of Vivekananda's ethics: if the universe is one there is no distinction between 'I' and 'You'. 'We' are 'Them'. In a later lecture delivered in Lahore, he dwelt on this once more: 'whomsoever you hurt you hurt yourself; they are all you.'

> …you are the king enjoying the palace, you are the beggar leading that miserable existence in the street; you are in the ignorant as well as in the learned, you are in the man who is weak, and you are in the strong; know this and be sympathetic … Herein is morality.[78]

To love oneself is to love all. This was the core of Vivekananda's philosophy.

One scholar has called this Vivekananda's 'Vedantic socialism'.[79] His practical Vedanta, in the same writer's words, was a 'Neo-Vedanta'.[80] This meant that there was no such thing as privilege. A person cannot be both a Vedantist and assume privileges of any kind. Practical Vedanta does not grant superiority of one person over another—or, for that matter, of one nation over another.

In these ideas Noble evidently found the essential contact between the spiritual life and the practical life. Vivekananda's Vedantic socialism would have struck a deep chord in her basic political sympathy with the underdog, the unfree, the oppressed.

When Vivekananda returned to America in December 1895, the magic of his presence did not dim. She continued to study his teachings; and when he returned to England in the spring of 1896 on his way back to India, she resumed contact with him. She called him 'Master'. There is the possibility that she fell in love with Vivekananda and imagined herself as his helpmeet and partner, a kind of missionary wife—till he told her that he had taken monastic vows.[81] Be that as it may, she determined to join him in his work in India.

This resolve took some time to translate to reality. Vivekananda left for India in December 1896. Home after a gap of almost four years, he established the Ramakrishna Mission as the organization overlying the Order of Ramakrishna. Its aim was to combine meditation with humanitarian social service: Hindusim in practice. Towards this end there would be established maths (monasteries) and ashrams (retreats) for the education of the sanyasis and those laypersons who wished to devote their lives to this cause. And, more audaciously, the Mission would send members of the Order of Ramakrishna across the country and outside India to establish centres abroad.

Learning of Noble's resolve, Vivekananda was at first uncertain as to what she could do in India: 'You can do more work for us from England than by coming here.'[82] A few days later he changed his mind and invited her to join him: '…I am now convinced that you have a great future in the work for India. What was wanted was not a man but a woman—a real lioness—to work for the Indians, women specially.'[83]

Yet he was apprehensive about what she would face in India: 'You cannot form an idea of misery [sic], the superstition, and the slavery that are here. You will be in the midst of a mass of half-naked men and women with quaint ideas of caste and isolation, shunning the white skin through fear or hatred...'[84]

She took the plunge anyway. In January 1898 Margaret Noble arrived in India. On March 25, at the age of thirty, she was initiated by Vivekananda into the Order of Ramakrishna—and probably became the first Western woman ever to be accepted into an Indian religious order, a Hindu nun so to speak.[85] It was a landmark in the history of Hinduism. Vivekananda named her Nivedita.

From the time he initiated Nivedita into the Order of Ramakrishna in March 1898, Vivekananda had only four more years to live. In this time, amongst his many activities, the Ramakrishna Mission was moved to Belur on the banks of the River Ganga some miles from Calcutta. Belur Math remains to this day the headquarters of the Ramakrishna Mission.

This was a time in which Nivedita would become an apprentice, so to speak, for the work Vivekananda wanted her to undertake: to be an educator of Hindu women; to work for the poor.[86] The apprenticeship was exacting: to teach Hindu women she must herself become a Hindu woman.

In November 1898, Nivedita opened her school for girls with three small pupils.[87] By the time of its first anniversary, the number of students had grown to thirty.[88] She also resumed an occupation from her England days: journalism, writing for both Indian and English newspapers.[89] Her circle widened: she came to know the Brahmo Samajists, and met and befriended the Tagores of Jorasanko. Through her was established a link between the monotheistic Brahmo Samaj and Vivekananda, who had once flirted with the Samaj.[90]

In 1899 Vivekananda went abroad once more, to Europe, England, and the United States, and delivered several lectures there.[91] Nivedita accompanied him on this voyage, returning to London once more, and thence going to America.[92] In Paris, on the occasion of the Universal Exposition, he attended and spoke at a congress on the history of religions.[93] He also heard in Paris, at a physics congress, a companion event in the Universal Exposition, compatriot and contemporary Jagadish Chandra Bose on whom he waxed passionately and eloquently as one who was there to 'glorify India' and 'add fresh laurels to the crown of Bengal'.[94] In December 1900 he returned to India.

His health had been in decline for some time, even before he left for the West, for he was seriously afflicted by diabetes. After his return, his health gradually worsened. On July 4, 1902, he passed away in Belur. He was thirty-nine years of age.

For Nivedita, her task after Vivekananda's death lay in service to India—and not only humanitarian, social, and educational service for the women of India as had been her prior mission. She became a political activist in the cause of Indian nationalism, and as such evoked alarm amidst the British authorities in India as a possible political subvert.[95] She befriended such leaders of the Indian Congress Party as Gopal Krishna Gokhale and Bal Gangadhar Tilak.[96] Inevitably, she drifted from the Ramakrishna Mission. Yet she would continue to speak publicly about Vivekananda and propagate his teachings.

IN THE COURSE of the twentieth century the Order of Ramakrishna established over 140 branches, including one hundred in India, twelve in the United States, ten in Bangladesh, and one each in Argentina, Brazil, Canada, Fiji, France, Japan, Mauritius, Netherlands, Russia, Singapore, Sri Lanka, Switzerland, and Britain.[97] The historical significance of this movement is worth noting. For centuries, Christian missionaries had ventured into India to proselytize on behalf of their church and their faith, and to convert. Vivekananda initiated a Hindu missionary system of a kind never known before—to spread the gospel of the Vedanta in the West. The awakening called the Bengal Renaissance was turned on its head: here was not a case of India being moulded by Western ideas but the West encountering a new brand of Indian thought.

Notes

1. Rolland [1931] 1979, p. 37, note 4.
2. Vivekananda 1893c, p. 3.
3. Ibid.
4. Ibid., p. 4.
5. Ibid.
6. Quoted in Dasgupta 2004.
7. Vivekananda 1893b, p. 220.

392 • Awakening

8. Ibid., p. 223.
9. Ibid., p. 224.
10. Ibid.
11. Rolland [1931] 1979, p. 120.
12. Raychaudhuri 2002, pp. 221–4.
13. Ibid., pp. 224–7.
14. Rolland [1931] 1979, p. 225.
15. Ibid., p. 225; Raychaudhuri 2002, p. 230.
16. Rolland [1931] 1979, p. 225.
17. See, for example, Vivekananda 1893a, p. 14.
18. Raychaudhuri 2002, p. 228.
19. Nikhilananda n.d., p. 56.
20. Raychaudhuri 2002, p. 228.
21. Rolland [1929] 1986, frontispiece.
22. Ibid.
23. Nikhilananda n.d., p. 94.
24. Ibid., p. 103.
25. Tart 1997.
26. Goleman 1975, p. 211.
27. Nikhilananda n.d., p. 111.
28. Ibid., pp. 80, 127, 135, 150, 171, 191.
29. Ibid., pp. 107, 149, 150, 191.
30. Ibid., p. 150.
31. Ibid., pp. 134–5.
32. Ibid., p. 191.
33. Ibid., pp. 111, 135, 191.
34. Ibid., p. 135.
35. Ibid., p. 111.
36. Vivekananda 1900, pp. 78–9.
37. Ibid.

38. Vivekananda 1893a, p. 14.
39. Rolland [1931] 1979, p. 121.
40. Ibid., p. 8.
41. Nikhilananda n.d., p. 88.
42. Ibid., p. 575.
43. Ibid., p. 937.
44. Ibid., p. 693.
45. Ibid., p. 57.
46. Rolland [1929] 1996, p. 276.
47. Rolland [1931] 1979, p. 15.
48. Ibid., p. 17.
49. Ibid., pp. 21 ff.
50. Ibid., p. 26.
51. Raychaudhuri 2002, p. 251.
52. Quoted in Rolland [1931] 1979, p. 28.
53. Rolland [1931] 1979, p. 8, note 32.
54. Ibid., p. 82; Raychaudhuri 2002, p. 251.
55. Raychaudhuri 2002, pp. 256–61.
56. Rolland [1931] 1979, pp. 87–8.
57. Raychaudhuri 2002, p. 259.
58. Ibid., p. 256.
59. Ibid., p. 262.
60. Vivekananda 1893b, pp. 209–10.
61. Reymond [1953] 1985, pp. 21–22.
62. Ibid., p. 24.
63. Ibid., pp. 25–6.
64. Ibid., p. 27.
65. Ibid.
66. Fitzpatrick 1999, pp. 505–7.
67. Reymond [1953] 1985, p. 28.

68. Ibid., pp. 28–9.
69. Ibid., p. 30.
70. Ibid., p. 33.
71. Ibid., p. 31.
72. Ibid., pp. 17, 31.
73. Reymond [1953] 1985, pp. 17, 31.
74. Ibid., p. 38.
75. Vivekananda 1896a.
76. Ibid., p. 291.
77. Ibid., pp. 293, 294.
78. Vivekananda 1897, p. 425.
79. Dasgupta 1995b.
80. Dasgupta 1999.
81. Reymond [1953] 1985, p. 49.
82. Vivekananda to Margaret Noble, Almira, July 23, 1897, pp. 509–10 in Vivekananda 2001e, p. 510.
83. Vivekananda to Margaret Noble, Almira, July 29, 1897, pp. 511–13 in Vivekananda 2001e, p. 511.
84. Vivekananda to Margaret Noble, Almira, July 29, 1897, pp. 511–13 in Vivekananda 2001e, p. 511.
85. Rolland [1931] 1979, p. 97.
86. Reymond [1953] 1985, p. 78.
87. Ibid., p. 162.
88. Ibid., p. 167.
89. Ibid., p. 171.
90. Ibid., p. 173.
91. Rolland [1931] 1979, pp. 148–51.
92. Reymond [1953] 1985, pp. 198 ff.
93. Rolland [1931] 1979, p. 154.
94. Vivekananda, n.d., p. 380. See also Chapter twelve.

95. Reymond [1953] 1985, p. 260.
96. Ibid., p. 261.
97. http://www.vivekananda.org (last accessed on April 9, 2010).

Twelve

Breaking the Wall of Western Contempt

HAD SWAMI VIVEKANANDA listened very carefully to what Jagadish Chandra Bose (1858–1937) actually said at the International Physics Conference in Paris in August 1900 he would have been even more ecstatic than what his memoir reveals.

> From among that white galaxy of geniuses there stepped forth one distinguished hero to proclaim the name of our Motherland, Bengal—it was the world-renowned scientist Dr. J.C. Bose! Alone, the youthful Bengali physicist, with galvanic quickness, charmed the Western audience with his splendid genius…[and] infused pulsations into the half-dead body of the Motherland![1]

To the Indian monk, there was cause for great pleasure in the sight of an Indian holding forth—and holding his own—before a Western audience, in the one realm the West claimed as its very own—modern science. He found this of huge significance. What Vivekananda omitted to mention was the essential substance of Jagadish Chandra's lecture; that he was announcing to the world that there was a similarity between the responsiveness of living and nonliving matter to physical stimuli; that one cannot draw a line separating the 'phenomena of dead matter' from that 'peculiar to living'.[2]

Had he grasped this disarmingly simple sounding (but enormously controversial) idea—what in modern times has been called the 'Boseian thesis'[3]—Vivekananda would have thrilled to it. For here was unexpected evidence from nature itself of unity amidst diversity—nature's monism so to speak. To the monk whose very identity was defined by 'monistic music', Jagadish Chandra's words would have made still sweeter music to his ears.

VIVEKANANDA DID NOT live long enough to savour the full implication of what he witnessed that day in Paris. But another person back in India—he too a Vedantist, he too a nonscientist—would live to enjoy the significance of Jagadish's Paris lecture: that here was evidence, proof positive, of the arrival of modern scientific research in India. That man was Rabindranath Tagore.

In fact, Rabindranath was already aware of Jagadish Chandra's 'thesis'. Earlier, in March 1900, the scientist wrote to the poet that 'from my most recent work I am coming to realize that the boundary between the living [chetan in Bengali] and nonliving [achetan] is increasingly becoming invisible'.[4]

Indeed, like Vivekananda but three years earlier, Rabindranath had also thrilled to the success Jagadish Chandra had enjoyed in England and the Continent. In 1897 the scientist returned to India flushed with the triumph of his European sojourn, and was greeted by the poet with a bouquet of magnolia[5] and a poem on him.[6] Like Vivekananda after him, Rabindranath was struck by the symbolic import of the scientist's achievement. In the poem, the poet saluted the scientist who had crossed the seas to the temple of science in the West. He had returned with a wreath of victory to place on the bowed, shamed head of the poor, lowly motherland. And through the voice of this unknown, obscure poet the motherland was bestowing her tear-filled blessing upon him. (Here, then, is the motif of nationalist pride that marks the final phase of the Bengal Renaissance.)

For both the poet and the monk, the scientist was a saviour: he was the one who could restore pride, dignity, and self-respect to the 'poor, lowly, 'half-dead' motherland. Rammohun Roy's plea to Lord Amherst in 1823 was, in the minds of the poet and the monk, at last bearing glorious, practical fruit.[7]

TO APPRECIATE WHY the poet and the monk were so ecstatic about Jagadish Chandra we must remember the profound *contempt* with which Europeans, the British in particular, held India when it came to rational thought. James Mill, for instance, simply refused to believe that the Indians of antiquity could even produce the kind of astronomy and mathematics the British Orientalists had claimed on their behalf. They must have gleaned their knowledge, Mill insisted, from more advanced cultures such as the Persians.[8] Nor can we forget Lord Macaulay with his contemptuous dismissal of the Indian intellectual tradition.[9]

This Western conviction about Indians was not limited to their more remote past. In the eighteenth century certain European observers, including distinguished scientists (more informed than the likes of Mill and Macaulay), concluded that while the Indians of antiquity had indeed accomplished much in such sciences as astronomy, medicine, and mathematics, the Indians of the recent past had fallen into seriously hard times in the sciences. Indeed, one eminent French astronomer believed that Indians were *incapable* of performing experiments, which made the practice of experimental sciences such as chemistry, botany, and anatomy more or less impossible. Another French astronomer thought that systematic research was beyond the Indians' reach; that they had no interest in the idea of science as a process of the cumulative growth of knowledge. These Frenchmen believed that the Indian mentality was incompatible with scientific inquiry. Even the great Voltaire, an admirer of the civilization of ancient India, was dismayed at the state of disrepair of Indian scientific thinking in his day.[10]

The intellectuals of the Bengal Renaissance were painfully aware of this. Bankimchandra, as we have seen, was willing to 'cheerfully admit' to Europe's superiority in science and philosophy,[11] and it was almost in a desperate attempt to raise a scientific consciousness amongst his Bengali readers that he, and before him Vidyasagar, wrote popular essays on science.[12] Thus, Rabindranath's and Vivekananda's almost identical reactions to Jagadish Chandra's success.

Even in the late nineteenth century British perceptions had scarcely changed. In practical terms this had produced cases of blatant racial discrimination governing the recruitment and appointment of qualified Indians to scientific posts.

In 1880, a young geologist Pramatha Nath Bose (1855–1934) returned to India after graduating with a BSc degree from London University; under his belt were also a fellowship of the Geological Society, brief employment with the Royal School of Mines in London,[13] and publication in Britain's premier geological journal.[14] He was appointed to the Geological Survey of India, the first Indian in the Survey in a 'graded post',[15] but not without opposition from H.B. Mendicott, superintendent of the Survey, who remarked that Pramatha Nath 'is a Bengali and may be physically unfit for our work'.[16] Indians, Mendicott maintained, were 'utterly incapable of any original work in natural science'.[17] He was convinced that the 'scientific chord' had not touched Indians, and wondered whether 'it exists as yet in this variety of the human race'.[18]

Pramatha Nath (who, incidentally, married the daughter of the distinguished scholar Romesh Chandra Dutt, Toru's cousin), went on to work in the Geological Survey for about twenty-three years; yet the prejudice prevailed and eventually, after being passed over for the directorship of the Survey, and the appointment of a man ten years his junior, he resigned in disgust and moved into the private sector. A fortuitous move for the Indian iron and steel industry, as it turned out, for Pramatha Nath's discovery of certain iron ore deposits led to the creation of the famous Tata Iron and Steel Works in Jamshedpur, Bihar.

WELL INTENTIONED THOUGH the efforts were of such writers as Vidyasagar and Bankimchandra, there was a quantum gap between stimulating the interest of the intelligentsia in the science being achieved in distant lands by distant peoples, and creating an environment in which actual scientific *discovery* could be achieved by one's own kind in one's own land under one's own initiative, fundamentally untouched by foreign guidance. Quite a different mindset was required for this to happen.

We detect a gleam of this in at least one Derozian, Radhanath Sikdar (1813–70) who accomplished much in the branch of applied mathematics called geodesy, as a member of the Great Trigonometrical Survey.[19] Geodesy is the science of measuring the earth's three-dimensional surface and projecting it onto the plane of two-dimensional maps. Radhanath Sikdar modified some of the rules of projection that Sir George Everest (1790–1866) had produced.[20] His work was acknowledged by his British superiors including Everest himself, who is on record as saying that the Bengali's mathematical accomplishment was the equal of any in India or in Europe.[21] Yet both Radhanath and Pramatha Nath were constrained by their employment in government surveys, and their work was necessarily dictated by what their bosses approved of.

Experimental science, the science promoted by Francis Bacon and practised by the likes of Galileo, Newton, Robert Boyle, and Christian Huygens, by Joseph Priestley and Michael Faraday, demanded a certain kind of knowledge which is often called, informally, 'know-how' and more formally, 'operational knowledge':[22] knowing how to design an experiment and the apparatus to carry out the experiment; knowing how to operate and manipulate instruments; how to diagnose errors found while performing experiments and how to correct such errors; how to interpret what is observed while doing experiments. Operational knowledge enters into the *practice* of science in the laboratory, in the observatory, out in the 'field' itself.[23]

It means knowing how to get one's hands dirty to elicit nature's secrets.

As early as the late 1830s, there was at least one place in Calcutta where this kind of knowledge could be learnt: Calcutta Medical College, founded in 1835.[24] Yet, even here, the stereotypical Western prejudice prevailed and doubts were voiced whether Indian students could actually master the basic sciences of the medical course: botany, chemistry, and anatomy.[25]

This scepticism was dealt with a serious blow when, on October 28, 1836, Madhusudan Gupta, a former ayurvedic pandit in Sanskrit College, and assistant to Henry Goodeve, professor of anatomy in Medical College, made his incision on a cadaver, thus becoming the first Indian known by name to perform human dissection. Four students of the college followed his lead. Two years later these students passed the first examination conducted by the college, and in 1840, Madhusudan Gupta was awarded a diploma certifying his qualification to practice medicine. The diploma was signed by the senior professors of the college, all (naturally) Europeans. This was the first clear refutation of the Western belief that Indians were incapable of doing experimental science.

SOME TWO DECADES later, Mahendralal Sircar (1833–1904), a student of Calcutta Medical College, received a Licentiate in Medicine and Surgery (LMS) from the University of Calcutta; and three years after that, the far superior degree of Doctor of Medicine (MD), a rare achievement for an Indian at the time.[26]

Mahendralal Sircar turned out to be a medical maverick. He set up a successful medical practice and then, a few years later, abandoned Western (allopathic) medicine for homeopathy, which he had previously denounced.[27]

He was more than a medical practitioner; he was a visionary. In 1869, he wrote an article in the *Calcutta Journal of Medicine*—a journal he had founded the year before[28]—in which he called for the establishment of an institution where lectures in science would be delivered accompanied by illustrative experiments. His 'model' for this institution, as it turned out, was the fabled Royal Institution of Great Britain, created in 1799 by Count von Rumford to instruct the poor in science so that they could better their lot.[29] So, too, Mahendralal's desire was to instruct 'the masses' in science.[30] But he wanted more from his institution.

> Men must continually be at a subject, observing and experimenting, before he can acquire that knowledge of it which will enable him to feel his own deficiencies and the deficiencies in the branch of science which he has made his specialty,— before, indeed he can engage with any hope of success in research which will improve both himself and his science.[31]

Mahendralal, trained in medicine, knew what it was to engage with science; he understood that having a scientific mentality meant not just being dazzled by the latest findings of science or observing, spellbound, the magic of scientific experiment, but possessing operational knowledge, which would enable active scientific *research*. He wanted to create a culture of scientific research amongst his countrymen.

This was Mahendralal's own act of creation and it became the launching pad for his place in this story. And in this context, the word *renaissance* is quite apposite: there had been in remote times in India a culture of scientific inquiry. Mahendralal's dream was to reinvent that culture.

What would Indians gain by this? Why should they do this? What would be the *point* of doing science?

Science, Mahendralal insisted, was the best hope to free the mind of 'prejudice', 'the spirit of intolerance', the 'despotism of traditional opinions'. And 'nowhere is this despotism of traditional opinions more severely felt than in this country'. It was a 'solemn and sacred duty towards ourselves' to cast off such dogmatism. Science was a path to this freedom.[32]

Mahendralal's vision was, thus, driven by a nationalist consciousness. While Bankimchandra's nationalism took a defeatist attitude, acknowledging Indian inferiority in science and turning away from it to eulogize Hindu religion,[33] Mahendralal wanted to 'take on' science itself, to look it squarely in the eye: 'we have inherited a mind not inferior in its endowment to the mind of any nation on earth...'[34]

Who would deliver the lectures and perform the experiments in this institution? The Royal Institution had some mighty people: the chemist and inventor Sir Humphrey Davy (1778–1829) and his protégé, the fabulously creative physicist Michael Faraday (1791–1867), the physicist John Tyndall (1820–93) and the formidable biologist Thomas Henry Huxley (1825–95).

There were no Faradays or Huxleys whom Mahendralal could beckon. There was only himself. And there was his friend, a Belgian priest, Eugene Lafont (1837–1908), who arrived in Calcutta in 1864 to teach at St Xavier's, a 'man of science' as well as a priest.[35]

There was also the practical matter of raising funds to finance the institution. It took a few years to raise money and make the dream a reality. Subscribers were found amongst the elite of Calcutta (as were once found to create Hindu College). Amongst the supporters were some maharajas; Vidyasagar and Dwijendranath Tagore, Rabindranath's eldest brother, were also contributors.[36] There were disagreements about the sort of institution it should be, some desiring a place for technical education and practical training, others supporting Mahendralal's original idea.[37] Eventually, Mahendralal's vision carried the day.

On January 15, 1876, the Indian Association for the Cultivation of Science (IACS) came into being, housed at 210 Bowbazar Street in the heart of the Black Town, with Mahendralal as secretary and Father Lafont as its first lecturer. The name of the institution left no one in doubt of its objective: science would be *cultivated* here; this was its sole objective.

In his beloved institution, Mahendralal would lecture on physics, and to prepare his lectures and the practical demonstrations he was forever performing experiments, repeating work done by the great scientists in the realm of electricity and magnetism. He successfully conducted one of the mighty Michael Faraday's experiments on electricity generation,[38] but failed to see through one of Benjamin Franklin's experiments.[39]

His experimental temper extended into his primary profession as a homeopathic medical practitioner. His 'snakemen' delivered to him two cobras, and he performed experiments on two fowls and a dog to see how much time it took for them to die after the insertion of poison.[40] Another time he extracted the poison—'oily, yellowish, thickish liquid'—from another species of snake, diluted it, and kept a small quantity for titration.[41] He was also an amateur astronomer. Using a telescope purchased from a local British doctor, he observed, as Galileo had first done 350 years before, the four moons of Jupiter and their changes in position relevant to the planet[42] and saw the transit of Venus across the sun.[43]

AT THE TIME IACS was born, Eugene Lafont had been rector of St Xavier's for five years. A Belgian Jesuit, he arrived in Calcutta in 1864 to teach at St Xavier's College. Within six years he was its rector, aged thirty-four.[44] Like Mahendralal, Lafont was not a research scientist. But like Mahendralal again, whom he met and befriended in 1873 or thereabouts,[45] Lafont made a very distinct contribution to the emergence of a scientific consciousness in late nineteenth century Calcutta.

Almost from the time he arrived in the city in 1864, he began to give public demonstrations of scientific phenomena.[46] He established a small laboratory in St Xavier's—the first scientific laboratory in Calcutta—and there he and his colleagues performed experiments for the benefit of their students. He created a meteorological observatory[47] which was later expanded for astronomical studies.[48] He also played a role in persuading the University of Calcutta to establish a BA degree programme in science.[49]

One of the students who would have witnessed Lafont's scientific experiments in St Xavier's was Jagadish Chandra Bose, who attended the institution from age eleven, in 1869, first as a schoolboy and then as an undergraduate, obtaining a BA degree from Calcutta University in 1880.

JAGADISH CHANDRA WAS born into a Brahmo family. His father, Bhagwan Chandra, in his lifetime, would hold various posts in the administrative and magisterial machinery of the Raj, but he was also a nationalist and something of an idealist and philanthropist, who dreamt up educational, agricultural, and industrial projects that could offer opportunities for self-betterment to his poorer countrymen. Behind these efforts, his son would one day say, 'lay a burning love for his country and its noble traditions'.[50] Though many of these projects failed, to Jagadish Chandra, looking back, they were 'not ignoble or altogether futile' for the failure taught him, the son, that 'some defeat was greater than victory'. If his own life had proved to be successful that success 'came through the realization of this lesson'.[51]

Like many of his bhadralok background, Jagadish Chandra was educated up to the age of eleven in a Bengali village school, a pathsala, where he studied alongside 'sons of toilers' and those who belonged to the 'depressed classes'.[52] These were significant and formative years, he would later recall. His love of nature was shaped by his contact with his classmates, 'those who tilled the ground' and 'sons of fisher folk'.[53] In the pathsala he came to learn 'my own language', 'think my own thoughts', and 'receive the heritage of our national culture through the medium of our own literature'.[54] He learnt here to 'consider myself one with the people and never to place myself in an equivocal position of assumed superiority'.[55] In 1869, he was dispatched to Calcutta where, after a brief period in

Hare School—founded by David Hare, by now long dead—he entered St Xavier's.

After graduating from the University of Calcutta with a BA degree in 1880 (these were times when the university still gave an arts degree to students studying the sciences), he proceeded to London to study medicine; this suggests, perhaps, that a career in 'pure' science was not on the books—yet. However, his medical ambitions were thwarted by the recurrence of an old illness, probably the kala azar he had contracted as an undergraduate,[56] a recurrence exacerbated by the odours of the dissecting room in anatomy class.[57] Thus in early 1882, he made the short journey to Cambridge, enrolled as an undergraduate of Christ's College to read for the natural sciences tripos. His subjects were physics, chemistry, and biology.[58]

While still in London in 1882, he played host to a newly arrived student from Calcutta. Prafulla Chandra Ray was en route to Edinburgh on a Gilchrist Scholarship, where he was to enroll in the University of Edinburgh as an undergraduate student of chemistry, physics, zoology, and botany.[59]

PRAFULLA CHANDRA RAY'S (1861–1944) ancestral home was in Jessore (now in Bangladesh). His father, though not formally of the Brahmo faith, had Brahmo leanings.[60] Like some others of the bhadralok class of his generation the father was well-versed in Persian, Arabic, and Sanskrit, and possessed a 'fair knowledge of classical English literature'.[61]

Like Jagadish Chandra, Prafulla Chandra had his first education in a village pathsala. And like Jagadish, he attended Hare School for a short period. In 1874, after a hiatus of two years because of illness and general ill-health, Prafulla Chandra, aged thirteen, entered Albert School, the same year Jagadish Chandra moved up into the college section in St Xavier's.

For college studies, Prafulla Chandra went to Metropolitan Institution (founded by Vidyasagar).[62] About the time Jagadish was learning the mysteries of physics in Eugene Lafont's laboratory in St Xavier's, Prafulla Chandra would make the short trek to Presidency College to attend the chemistry lectures of Alexander Pedler—(later, Sir Alexander), a future fellow of the Royal Society and vice-chancellor of Calcutta University—and admire the professor's skill in chemical experimentation.[63] Whether or not Lafont was responsible for Jagadish Chandra's later attraction to physics, Pedler was certainly Prafulla Chandra's formative influence. 'I began almost unconsciously to be attracted to the science,'[64] he would write later. He also attended, in 1880–1, courses of lectures in physics and chemistry at Mahendralal Sircar's IACS.[65] Like Mahendralal, he too conducted experiments

> Not content with merely seeing the experiments performed in the classroom, myself and a fellow student set up a miniature laboratory in the lodgings of the latter and we took delight in reproducing some of them. Once we improvised an oxy-hydrogen blowpipe out of an ordinary thin tinned sheet of iron with the aid of a tinker.[66]

His 'predilection' was clearly for chemistry though he also admitted to a 'passion for literature'.[67]

HEREUPON, THE TWO young men, one at first ensconced in Cambridge, the other in Edinburgh, embarked on mostly parallel, sometimes intersecting lives in science. Jagadish Chandra obtained a BA from Cambridge University in 1884 (the year in which Rabindranath's *Bhanusingha Padabali* was composed) with a 'respectable' (but not 'brilliant') second class in the natural science tripos.[68] Along the way he obtained an external BSc from London University. He was now the holder of three baccalaureates from three universities. A year later, Prafulla Chandra received his BSc from Edinburgh in 1885.

In Edinburgh, Prafulla Chandra led more than a laboratory life:

> Sometime in 1885 Lord Iddesleigh who...had been Secretary of State for India in 1867–68, as Lord Rector of the University, announced that a prize would be awarded for the best essay on 'India before and after the Mutiny.' Although I was busy working in the laboratory and preparing for the BSc examination, I felt tempted to enter the list of competitors.[69]

And so, for a while his chemical pursuits were interrupted. 'My latent, almost innate love of historical studies now woke up...'[70] He pored over books on India borrowed from the university library, needing to know something of economics to better understand monetary issues, read the relevant authorities on political economy and Indian finance as well as records of parliamentary debates.[71]

The resulting *Essay on India* did not win the prize but was singled out for praise, this despite the comment by one of the examiners that the essay was 'full of diatribe against British rule'.[72]

Prafulla Chandra printed the essay at his own expense, first for private circulation amongst the university students and then for the larger public. The first printed edition included an address to the 'Students of the University' in which he brought their attention to the 'lamentable condition of India at present...due to England's culpable neglect of, and gross apathy to, the affairs of the Empire.' And he went on: 'It is to you, the rising generation of Great Britain and Ireland, that we look for the inauguration of a more just, generous and human policy as to India ... In you are centred all our hopes.'[73]

Here again we find the motif of the latter part of the Bengal Renaissance: the budding chemist was also showing glimpses of a nationalistic consciousness. He dwelt on the 'tendency' of some British writers to unfavourably compare India under the 'worst types of Mahommedan [sic] despots and bigots' with India under the Raj. But:

> It is forgotten that at the time when a Queen of England was flinging into flames and hurling into dungeons those of her own subjects who had the misfortune to differ from her on dogmatic niceties, the great Moghul Akbar had proclaimed the principle of universal toleration, had invited the moulvie, the pandit, the rabbi, and the missionary to his court and had held philosophical disquisitions with them on the merits of their various religions.[74]

Brave words for a twenty-four-year-old Indian undergraduate in a British university. The *Scotsman* found *Essay* 'a most interesting little book...deserving of the utmost notice'.[75]

The *Essay on India* may have been a brief interlude in a scientific life. Yet it was the harbinger of a later Prafulla Chandra Ray: a fluent prose writer in English, and a future man of letters who would go on to write the remarkable *Life and Experiences of a Bengali Chemist* (1932), probably the first autobiography written by an Indian scientist.[76] His 'latent, almost innate, love of historical studies' would also find, as we shall shortly see, lush expression in a few years in his study of the history of Indian chemistry. Finally, his nationalism would lead him to launch the Bengal Chemical and Pharmaceutical Works, a bio-medical factory to be manned by Indians alone.

JAGADISH CHANDRA RETURNED to India, and after some difficulty—resolved by the intervention of no less than Viceroy Lord Ripon, perhaps the only kind of intervention that could overcome British prejudice—he was appointed (the first Indian) professor of physics in Presidency College, in 1885.[77] As Jagadish Chandra recalled some forty years later, his Cambridge and London degrees were not enough to persuade the British educational authorities in Calcutta that he had what it took to be a professor in Presidency College. He was told bluntly by Sir Alfred Croft, then director of public instruction for Bengal that he did not possess the right temperament for the exact sciences[78]—shades of Pramatha Nath Bose's experience a few years earlier.[79]

Prafulla Chandra stayed on in Edinburgh to pursue doctoral studies, and in 1887, was awarded a doctor of science (DSc) degree by the university in inorganic chemistry, for a thesis on 'conjugated sulphates of the copper-magnesium group'.[80]

We must pause on this information: we recall again the British contempt about the Indian's ability to perform scientific research, indeed to even *think* scientifically. If Madhusudan Gupta's dissection of a cadaver and his certification to practise medicine and surgery was a first tentative knock against the wall of Western prejudice, the award of a DSc degree to an Indian from a British university was a veritable assault on this same wall.

Prafulla Chandra himself was surprisingly offhand about his first experience of chemical research.

> After taking my bachelor's degree I had to get ready for the doctorate for which it was necessary to submit a thesis based upon my own original investigation.[81]

> In due course I presented my thesis and I also had to go through a practical examination consisting of a complete analysis of a complex ore. My examiners were satisfied and I was recommended for the Doctorate.[82]

He gave himself a small, wry pat on the back by commenting that in those days, 'Doctorates in science were few and far between.'[83]

Oddly enough, Prafulla Chandra did not publish any papers from his DSc work.[84] If he had done so, his achievement in Edinburgh would have made more of an impact. He remained in Edinburgh for another year on a new scholarship awarded by the university, which he used to strengthen his weakness in organic chemistry.[85] Thereafter, his funds running dangerously low, he returned in August 1888 to India after a six years' absence.

Like Jagadish Chandra, he found it difficult to gain an immediate appropriate teaching appointment.[86] For almost a year he chafed at the bit. 'A chemist *minus* his laboratory... is something like Samson shorn of his locks.'[87] During this time, Jagadish Chandra and his wife Abala offered him the hospitality of their home which he gratefully accepted.[88] Eventually, in June 1889, he was appointed a temporary professor of chemistry in Presidency College. For the next quarter century, Jagadish Chandra and Prafulla Chandra worked cheek by jowl in their respective laboratories and departments in the college.[89]

When Prafulla Chandra joined Presidency College, its chemical laboratory was in a dismal state. 'There were no flues for drawing out the noxious gases and the ventilation arrangement was most rudimentary...the atmosphere, especially in the rainy season, thickly laden with fumes, became suffocating and highly injurious to health.'[90]

He invited the principal of the college, C.H. Tawney, to the laboratory and 'breathe the air for a minute'. As it happened, the principal had weak lungs and within a few minutes 'became terribly agitated and rushed out of the room'. The effect was immediate. Tawney wrote to the director of public instruction threatening to prosecute the college authorities for endangering the health of the students.[91]

Thus a new laboratory building was sanctioned. Prafulla Chandra, already an energetic institution builder in the making, showed the authorities a copy of the plans of Edinburgh University's new chemical building, complete with drawings and diagrams of the layout. Some of this was incorporated into the design of the new laboratory which was opened in July 1894. 'It soon began to attract visitors from different parts of India.'⁹²

IN NOVEMBER 1894, Jagadish Chandra Bose celebrated his thirty-sixth birthday. In the nine years since returning from Cambridge, he had been busy teaching physics—as a professor in Presidency College and, for a briefer three years, as a demonstrator in practical physics in IACS, where his former teacher Eugene Lafont gave lectures in physics.[93]

He was now a married man. Abala Bose, née Das, came from a family which included Chittaranjan Das, later a preeminent barrister and even more preeminent activist in the cause for Indian freedom. Abala Devi was far from commonplace herself. At the time of her marriage, she was a student in Madras Medical College.

Had Jagadish Chandra continued to do what he has been doing he would certainly not have a place in this story. But history decreed otherwise; Jagadish Chandra himself decreed otherwise, for by his own account, he decided, as he completed his thirty-sixth year, to undertake research in physics.[94]

Unlike his chemist colleague, Jagadish Chandra had yet no experience in research. The memory of his Cambridge years and of its great Cavendish Laboratory was all he had to go on. That memory and the scientific journals from overseas that trickled into Calcutta. Otherwise he was all alone so far as physics goes.

Father Lafont was no research physicist; nor was Mahendral Sircar though, as we have seen, like Lafont, he had the experimental temper and was constantly at this experiment and that;[95] nor did Mahendralal's institution have any research laboratories at the time. There were no scientific societies such as the Royal Society. There were no physics journals in India. The nearest to both were the Asiatic Society and its *Journal*—but that was a far cry from *Nature* or the *Philosophical Transactions of the Royal Society* in England, or *Annalen der Physik* in Germany.

In the realm of the natural sciences, the Asiatic Society's interests, at least up to the time of Jagadish Chandra's return to India, were in geology, geography, and natural history—the sciences conducted 'in the field' rather than in the laboratory.[96] So, in 1894, when Jagadish Chandra decided to take up physics research, India was certainly *laboratory* science-deprived. Or, more specifically, it was laboratory science-deprived for *Indians*. (We know, for instance, that a certain Scotsman, Ronald Ross of the Indian Medical Service, was about to begin his remarkable experiments that would lead to his discovery of the role of the mosquito in the transmission of malaria. The final 'proof' of this theory would be discovered in 1898 in Calcutta.)[97]

A research laboratory is a particular rather than a general space. It is 'purpose-built', 'purpose-driven'. One creates a research laboratory for very precise goals; to conduct research on a very particular subject.

In Jagadish Chandra's case he decided to study the properties of radio waves—'electric waves' as they were then called. Physicists had been aware of the idea of such invisible waves for some time, but it was the German scientist and Jagadish's contemporary Heinrich Hertz (1857–94) who demonstrated definitively their physical reality in 1888. In January 1894, Hertz died of blood poisoning, and in June the British physicist Oliver Lodge delivered a lecture in London on Hertz's work which was published soon after in the journals *Nature* and *The Electrician*.[98]

These electric waves excited great interest amongst physicists because they revealed that the universe contained other wave-like entities besides light which were invisible. Much was already known about electric waves (also called 'Hertzian waves'), largely due to Hertz himself, but much remained to be known. Jagadish Chandra decided to study their light-like properties—their 'pseudo-optical' properties. This became his research agenda in 1894. His laboratory was created according to this objective.

That laboratory was 'a small room 20 feet square with an attached bathroom' located in Presidency College.[99] His assistant was a 'tinsmith' whom he trained. Here, Jagadish Chandra designed and built his own apparatus to both generate and detect electric waves, and to manipulate them for his research purposes. He was a technician, instrument maker, experimentalist all rolled into one.[100]

Interestingly, what linked these different facets of the man was his scientific *style*, his way of doing, practising, thinking about science. At the centre of his style was a predilection for drawing analogies. The analogy that was the most daring, the most controversial, and which linked Jagadish Chandra's science with advaita (and, thus, with Vivekananda) was also one that led to his abandonment of physics and the assumption of his second scientific life as a plant physiologist.[101]

In March 1900 (as we have already seen), Jagadish Chandra wrote to Rabindranath Tagore that he was beginning to realize that the boundary between the living and nonliving was far from clear.[102] A few months later, the scientist read a paper at an international physics conference in Paris (the session attended by a rapt Vivekananda) in which he described experiments demonstrating the similarity of the electrical responsiveness of nonliving matter (such as metal) and living matter (such as animal muscle) to various kinds of physical stimuli—to wit, mechanical force, electrical current, heat, and chemical substances. And he concluded that one could not 'draw a line' demarcating the 'phenomenon of dead matter' from that 'peculiar to living'.[103]

This conclusion, which has been named the 'Boseian thesis',[104] was an expression of the monistic idea that 'All is One', as Jagadish Chandra would excitedly write to Rabindranath Tagore.[105] Its genesis in Jagadish Chandra's mind lay in his observation that in the course of his experiments involving the generation and detection of radio waves, his detecting apparatus manifested a behaviour that was similar to the fatigue observed in animal tissue such as muscle: just as animal muscles when overworked do not readily respond to stimulus so also his apparatus; and just as animal tissue recovers its responsiveness after a certain period of rest so also his apparatus. Both, thus, exhibit a kind of fatigue—though, of course, he was using 'fatigue' as a metaphor for his apparatus. There was a continuity in the behaviour of both an inanimate object such as his radio-wave detector and animal matter such as muscle. From this, he generalized that there is a continuity in the responsiveness of nonliving and living matter: the Boseian thesis. This Boseian thesis would lead Jagadish Chandra to abandon physics altogether by 1902. Thereafter, he devoted the rest of his life to showing that ordinary plants, including vegetable, manifest the same kinds of response to stimulus as animals. He would become a plant physiologist and biophysicist.[106]

Jagadish Chandra was most likely drawn to his thesis not on scientific reasoning alone. It is very likely that there was present in him a monistic strain, a belief in the advaita that was perhaps rooted in his Indian philosophical upbringing—a Vedantic advaita common to the Ramakrishna–Vivekananda and Brahmo Samaj belief systems. Indeed, Jagadish Chandra's first book, *Response in the Living and Nonliving* (1902), devoted entirely to the Boseian thesis, began with an epitaph from the *Rig Veda*: 'The real is one: wise men call it variously.'

Jagadish Chandra Bose's science was thus an Indian *response* to Western science; and this is what makes him another extraordinary example of the cross-cultural mind that characterized the Bengal Renaissance.

In the same letter to Rabindranath, written in March 1900, announcing the gist of the Boseian thesis, Bose would write:

> You have often heard me say that thus far, the world's greatest poet and greatest scientist have yet to be born. For until the two kinds of understanding are conjoined in the one and the same person the two will remain incomplete.[107]

For Jagadish Chandra Bose, the scientist and the poet were of a kind; science and literature were of a kind. He denied that there was a schism between the two. Just over a decade after writing this letter, he delivered a lecture at a literary conference in Bengal. There he spoke further of this relationship between the scientist and the poet.

Both strive to express the 'inexpressible', he said. The poet does this by way of his imagination, through rhyme and metre; he sees through his inspiration what others fail to see. But so does the scientist: he too goes beyond the visible into the realm of the invisible, beyond the audible into the realm of the inaudible. Only his path is different. But both have a common goal: 'to find a unity in the bewildering diversity.'[108]

LIKE HIS FRIEND and colleague, Prafulla Chandra was initially hard pressed for time because of teaching duties to think about research, which unlike Bose he had some experience of. He was kept busy but he delighted in his work, and experienced 'almost a romantic sensation'[109] towards it—but then, he was not distracted by such real 'romantic' events as marriage and remained a lifelong bachelor.

The interval between the start of his teaching career and onset of research was much shorter for him than it was for Jagadish Chandra. His first project, began in 1890, two years after returning from Edinburgh, was in applied chemistry and, indeed, it was very much an *Indian* applied chemistry. For the problem he grappled with was a very Indian problem: the adulteration of common foodstuff such as ghee (clarified butter), butter, milk, and mustard oil.[110] His paper, published in the Asiatic Society's *Journal*, appeared in 1894, 'The Fruit of A Labour of Four Years'. It was stolid, solid work, but, as far as our story goes, it takes a backstage.

1895 AND 1896. Anni Mirabilis. Two miraculous years in the history of Indian science. In 1895, Jagadish Chandra published his very first paper on electric waves in the Asiatic

Society's *Journal*.[111] The year after, Prafulla Chandra's paper on mercurous nitrite appeared in the pages of the same journal.[112] The wall of Western contempt finally crumbled.

It would have pleased Sir William Jones that two Indians announced their discoveries in modern experimental sciences in the journal he founded. But the Asiatic Society's *Journal* would not be known to most Western physicists or chemists. Both the Indians recognized this. They, quite naturally, wanted their discoveries to be known in the laboratories of London, Cambridge, Paris, Berlin, Edinburgh, and the like. *Nature*, one of Europe's most prestigious science journals, found Prafulla Chandra's paper 'worthy of note',[113] but this was not enough. So they both sent off a volley of articles, mostly to London, Jagadish Chandra to the *Proceedings of the Royal Society* and *The Electrician*, Prafulla to the *Journal of the Chemical Society* and *Proceedings of the Chemical Society*, thus guaranteeing readership from their Western peers. We do not know whether the editor of *The Electrician* realized the historic significance of an Indian author publishing an article in the pages of his journal. Yet he wrote an editorial upon the 'interesting set of papers by Professor J.C. Bose'.[114] He also recognized the practical potential of this work for sending signals from shore to ship—that is, its potential for what later became wireless telegraphy.

In 1895–8, Jagadish Chandra published a dozen papers in the British journals; in 1896–9, Prafulla Chandra published eleven papers, also all in English journals.

However, neither Jagadish Chandra nor Prafulla Chandra discovered what they are frequently believed to have discovered. Jagadish Chandra did *not* 'discover' electric waves, nor did he 'invent' wireless telegraphy, that is, radio.[115] What he *did* do in these first years of prolific research was design and construct an apparatus that produced and detected radio waves much smaller in wavelength than were produced before, and elucidate some of their properties.[116] And, (as we have seen) he invented the 'Boseian thesis'[117] that established a kind of unification of living and nonliving matter. Of these, it was his work on radio waves that established his international reputation as a scientist—so much so that Sir J.J. Thomson, discoverer of the electron and, at the time as the Cavendish professor of physics in Cambridge, regarded as Britain's 'first' physicist, cited Bose's work on radio waves at length in an article on 'electric waves' in the eleventh edition of *The Encyclopedia Britannica* (1905).[118]

Nor did Prafulla Chandra 'discover' the chemical compound mercurous nitrite as it is still believed.[119] The actual historical record, though rather murky, suggests that chemists had known mercurous nitrite as far back as 1832–3, and it had been discussed several times by chemists since then. So the compound was certainly not unknown when Prafulla Chandra began his experiments in 1896. What he *did* 'discover' was a method of preparing mercurous nitrite in a stable crystalline form. This was certainly a valuable discovery, for having a chemical compound in a stable form meant that chemists could work with the compound and carry out other investigations of its properties. But it was not a seminal discovery in the annals of chemistry.

So their discoveries were not revolutionary as far as *science* is concerned; they caused no *upheaval* in physics or chemistry. Rather, their discoveries entered comfortably into the bodies of accepted knowledge.

Their revolutionary acts were of a different sort: they were the first Indians to add to the paradigms of physics and chemistry; and they together changed Indian self-belief, as also widespread European belief, about Indians and science. If science and the ability to contribute to science ever entered Indian consciousness—especially its nationalist consciousness—then this was almost certainly due to these two men, along with Mahendral Sircar. *This* was their great contribution to the awakening called the Bengal Renaissance.

BUT PRAFULLA CHANDRA'S part in this story is not yet complete. By the end of the nineteenth century he was, in fact, sharing his time between the laboratory and the library. If the laboratory gave him his profession and his living, the library allowed him to indulge his 'favourite hobby': the history of chemistry.[120] He waded into the arcane texts of Hindu alchemy and Ayurvedic medicinal preparation. He read the European authorities and began a correspondence with the distinguished French chemist Marcellin Berthelot who had made French translations of Greek alchemical texts and had written a monumental history of the chemistry of the Middle Ages.

After reading Berthelot's work on Greek alchemy, Prafulla Chandra wrote to the French chemist to draw his attention to Indian alchemy. The French savant replied that he did indeed know of the chemistry of ancient India; but he desired to know more.

> The moral effect, the letter produced on me, was profound. Here was perhaps the then foremost exponent of our science, approaching the allotted span of life, according to the Hebrew

> scriptures, showing youthful unbounded enthusiasm to know all about a new chapter in the history of chemistry, and I, a young man, was progressing rather slowly. I received almost an electric impulse and was stirred to fresh activity.[121]

The history of Indian chemistry was no longer just a hobby for him. It took its place alongside his laboratory researches. Further correspondence with Berthelot followed, and the Frenchman sent him his three-volume work on the alchemy of the Middle Ages. 'I greedily devoured the contents of these, and the idea now firmly took hold of me that I must write a history of Hindu Chemistry modelled upon the examples before me.'[122]

A further stimulus came from the publication of an article by Berthelot in a leading French journal in which Prafulla Chandra was mentioned as a savant.

> A thrill...passed through my body. Here I was, a junior professor...of chemistry almost unknown to fame, and there the foremost chemist and historian of chemistry speaking of me as a *savant*. The idea took possession of my mind that I was destined for some higher production.[123]

Here was another instance of the 'magic wand' from the West that touched and enervated the dormant Indian spirit: a creative encounter between West and India, so characteristic of the nineteenth century. Thus began a formidable, indeed stupendous work of historical scholarship that would span some five years. Its fruit was *A History of Hindu Chemistry* published in 1902. He was just over forty at this time.

In this book Prafulla would acknowledge Berthelot's influence on him:

> The illustrious French savant, the *Doyen* of the chemical world…expressed a strong desire to know all about the contributions of the Hindus, and even went the length of making a personal appeal to me to help him with information on the subject.[124]

Hindu Chemistry was well received in both Europe and India. Berthelot published 'a lengthy and appreciative review'.[125] A second edition was published in 1904. It remains an essential reference to this day on the development of Indian alchemy.[126]

The Bengal Renaissance had come almost full circle: from the Indological studies of the British Orientalists à la Sir William Jones to the Indology of an Indian chemist-historian.

Notes

1. Vivekananda, n.d., pp. 379–80.
2. Bose 1900, p. 258.
3. Dasgupta 2009, pp. 105 ff.
4. J.C. Bose to Rabindranath Tagore, Calcutta, March 16, 1900, p. 18 in J.C. Bose 1994. Freely translated from the Bengali.
5. Geddes 1920, p. 222.
6. Tagore 1957. The poem is on an unnumbered page facing p. 1.

7. See Chapter four.
8. See Chapters one and five.
9. See Chapter five.
10. Adas 1989, pp. 101–5.
11. See Chapter ten.
12. See Chapters seven and ten.
13. Radhakrishna 1997.
14. Bose 1880.
15. Radhakrishna 1997.
16. Quoted in Arnold 2000, p. 139.
17. Ibid.
18. Ibid.
19. See Chapter six.
20. A.K. Chakravarty 1995.
21. Ibid.
22. See Dasgupta 1996, pp. 137–8.
23. For more on the practice of science see, for example, Kuhn 1970; Hanson 1972; Pickering 1992; Latour and Woolgar 1986.
24. Gorman 1988. See also Interlude.
25. Gorman 1988, p. 283.
26. Palit 1991.
27. Ibid., p. 153.
28. Ibid.
29. Berman 1978, p. xxi.
30. Anon 1976, p. 5.
31. Quoted in Anon 1976, p. 6.
32. Ibid.
33. See Chapter ten.
34. Quoted in Palit 1991.

35. Namboodiry 1995, p. 53.
36. Anon 1976, pp. 5 and 8, note.
37. Ibid., pp. 10–13.
38. Mahendralal Sircar, diary entry, August 27, 1879, p. 74 in Biswas 2000. Henceforth cited as 'Sircar, *Diaries*'.
39. Sircar, *Diaries*, March 1, 1879, p. 66.
40. Sircar, *Diaries*, May 31, 1874; June 7, 1874, pp. 20–1.
41. Sircar, *Diaries*, November 9, 1874, p. 26.
42. Sircar, *Diaries*, March 9 and 10, 1874, p. 19.
43. Sircar, *Diaries*, December 9, 1874, p. 27.
44. Namboodiry 1995, p. 53.
45. Sircar, *Diaries*, January 11, 1873, p. 12.
46. Namboodiry 1995, p. 73.
47. Biswas 2000, p. 29, note 10.
48. Namboodiry 1995, pp. 80–2.
49. Basu, 1991.
50. Bose 1917a, p. 32.
51. Ibid., p. 36.
52. Ibid., p. 32.
53. Ibid.
54. J.C. Bose 1917a, p. 33.
55. Ibid.
56. Dasgupta 2009, p. 32.
57. Geddes 1920, p. 28.
58. Dasgupta 2009, p. 34.
59. Ray 1932, p. 59.
60. Ibid., p. 30.
61. Ibid., pp. 8–9.
62. See Chapter seven.
63. Ray 1932, p. 47.

64. Ibid.
65. Ray 1932, p. 149.
66. Ibid.
67. Ray 1932, pp. 47–8.
68. Piele 1913.
69. Ray 1932, p. 61.
70. Ibid.
71. Ray 1932, pp. 61–2.
72. Quoted in Ray 1932, p. 62.
73. Ray 1932, p. 63.
74. Ibid., p. 66.
75. Quoted in P.C. Ray 1932, pp. 66–7.
76. See Dasgupta 1962.
77. Anon 1955, p. 53.
78. J.C. Bose, in an address to the students of Presidency College, January 19, 1925. Reprinted in Sen and Chakraborty 1986, pp. 174–7.
79. See this Chapter, above.
80. Bhattacharya 2004, p. 16.
81. Ray 1932, p. 67.
82. Ibid., p. 68.
83. Ibid.
84. See the bibliography of his publications, Bhattacharya 2004, pp. 797–820.
85. Ray 1932, p. 71.
86. Ibid., pp. 77–82.
87. Ibid., p. 80.
88. Ibid.
89. Anon 1955, p. 55.
90. Ray 1932, p. 112.

91. Ibid., p. 112.
92. Ibid., p. 113.
93. Dasgupta [1999] 2009, p. 44.
94. J.C. Bose 1917b, p. 8. Also, J.C. Bose, 1915.
95. See Sircar, *Diaries*; for a summary of these experiments, see Dasgupta 2007, pp. 142–5.
96. Bose [1885] 1986.
97. Ross 1923, pp. 115 ff.
98. Dasgupta [1999] 2009, p. 46.
99. Bose n.d.
100. Dasgupta [1999] 2009, pp. 52 ff.
101. Ibid., Chapters four and five.
102. J.C. Bose to Rabindranath Tagore, March 16, 1900, p. 18 in J.C. Bose 1994.
103. Bose 1900.
104. Dasgupta 2009, Chapter 4.
105. J.C. Bose to Rabindranath Tagore, August 30, 1901, p. 82 in J.C. Bose 1994.
106. Dasgupta 2009, Chapter 6.
107. J.C. Bose to Rabindranath Tagore, March 16, 1900, p. 18 in J.C. Bose 1994. Freely translated from the Bengali.
108. Bose 1911, pp. 140–1.
109. Ray 1932, p. 84.
110. Ray 1894.
111. Bose 1895.
112. Ray 1896.
113. Ray 1932, p. 114.
114. Anon 1895. *The Electrician*.
115. For an extensive discussion of this myth see Dasgupta [1999] 2009, pp. 76–82, 250–54.

116. Dasgupta [1999] 2009, pp. 49–55.
117. See this chapter.
118. Thomson, 1905.
119. See Dasgupta 2007, pp. 165–8.
120. Ray 1932, p. 115.
121. Ibid., p. 117.
122. Ibid.
123. Ray 1932, p. 118.
124. Ray 1902, pp. 2–3.
125. Ray 1904, p. 6.
126. See for example, Partington [1960] 1999.

Epilogue

The Most Impossibly Gifted of Them All

THE BENGAL RENAISSANCE, as this story has related, is the name some people bestow upon an awakening of the Indian mind in the nineteenth century to new possibilities and new kinds of consciousness. The most visible of these were: a discovery of the Indian past; the creation of Bengali prose and new literary forms; a critical examination and reformation of Hindu society; the battle for the rights of women and the awakening of their self-awareness; the creation of a scientific culture; new ways of interpreting Hinduism—culminating eventually in the rise of a nationalist consciousness.

Arguably, the Bengal Renaissance's richest production was the creation of a cross-cultural mentality, a capability to think, perceive, and create in a manner that involved the melding of two or more traditions seemingly unconnected and even contradictory. In this story, we have seen this largely as a blending of the Indian and the Western cultural traditions: the 'Indo-Western mind', resulting from a constellation of encounters of all sorts between Bengal and the West, beginning in the late eighteenth century and spread across the nineteenth century—encounters that fostered creativity, heightened consciousness, and enlargement of knowledge. We have also seen, as an effect of all this, the beginnings of a Western *reception* of the modern Indian mind: first by way of Rammohun Roy in the 1830s, and then, in the 1890s, by way of Swami Vivekananda and the scientists Prafulla Chandra Ray and Jagadish Chandra Bose.

And this brings us to Rabindranath Tagore (1861–1941).

A RENAISSANCE NEEDS a Renaissance man. The Italians had Leonardo Da Vinci. Bengal had Rabindranath. William Jones had some claims to such a title. So did Rammohun and Bankimchandra. But in the richness and breadth of vision, and sheer productivity in a variety of creative and intellectual fields, Rabindranath exceeded them all. Throughout his long life, he produced a torrent of poems, short stories, novels, operas and dance dramas, plays, songs, literary and critical essays, philosophical works, social and political tracts, and educational ideas. He wrote in Bengali and in English. He founded and nurtured into maturity a school and a university. And near the end of his life he became a serious and prolific painter. He was a writer, poet, composer, philosopher, educationist, social thinker, political thinker, and artist; and his *originality* ranged over each of these activities.

Rabindranath was a contemporary of Vivekananda, Jagadish Chandra, and Prafulla Chandra. Yet he differed from them in an important way. Vivekananda died just after the turn of the nineteenth century. And though Jagadish Chandra and Prafulla Chandra, like Rabindranath, lived long lives, by the beginning of the twentieth century the two scientists had done their most significant deeds.

In contrast, a huge portion of Rabindranath's poetry, fiction, music, drama, life writing, essays, and philosophical work were created in the twentieth century. When the nineteenth century ended, his creativity, and *he himself*, were in the making.

So what better way to end the story of the Bengal Renaissance than with a glance at the man who both epitomized the new awakening of the Indian mind and yet, as a 'work-in-progress', represented the *legacy* of the Bengal Renaissance for the age that followed. It is in this twin sense that Rabindranath's life in the era of the Bengal Renaissance becomes less a chapter and more an epilogue to this story.

RABINDRANATH AND JAGADISH Chandra were contemporaries, the latter three years older. Indeed, for a brief two and a half months, in 1875, Jagadish Chandra and Rabindranath Tagore were schoolmates in St Xavier's. Rabindranath appeared, attended, and disappeared like a brief comet, and we wonder whether Jagadis, then seventeen, ever noticed the fourteen year old? Yet Jagadish Chandra, son of a well-established Brahmo father could hardly have been unaware of the dazzling Tagore family. Which Brahmo of the time would not have heard of Dwarakanath Tagore (1794–1846), Rammohun's friend and fellow signatory of the Brahmo Samaj Trust Deed?[1] Or not know of Dwarakanath's son Debendranath (1817–1905), so prominent in the Brahmo Samaj in the mid-nineteenth century?

Dwarakanath: landowner of massive estates, hugely successful entrepreneur, the original begetter of the family fortune, dubbed 'Prince' for his lordly habits; who went to England when few Bengalis did, and consorted with the likes of Queen Victoria, Prime Minister Robert Peel, and the writer

Charles Dickens; a lover of art and literature.[2] Debendranath, a study in contrast, called 'Maharshi'— 'Great Sage'—for his scholarly and spiritual disposition, shaped by the Upanishads,[3] who fathered a brood of bountifully gifted offspring.

The Tagore siblings. There was the eldest, Dwijendranath (1840–1926), poet, student of Indian philosophy and mathematics, inventor of a Bengali shorthand and the first Bengali musical notation,[4] who served on the planning committee that implemented the Indian Association for the Cultivation of Science.[5]

There was Satyendranath (1842–1923), the first Indian to be admitted, through examination, into the coveted and elite Indian Civil Service; the most westernized of the siblings and a flouter of bhadralok social conventions; and the translator into English of his father's autobiography.[6]

There was Jyotirindranath (1849–1925), the second youngest of the eight brothers, painter, poet, and musician, amongst the most gifted of the siblings and amongst the handsomest.

There was Swarnakumari (1856–1932), the youngest of the five sisters, novelist, dramatist, songwriter, literary journalist, social reformer, and activist, 'a torchbearer in the tradition of women's writing in Bengal',[7] whose novels in her lifetime were said to be as popular as those of Bankimchandra.[8] (Though, in his later life, Rabindranath said rather unkind things about her literary gifts.)[9]

And there was the youngest of the thirteen siblings, the most impossibly gifted of them all, Rabindranath, five years Swarnakumari's junior and twenty-one years younger than Dwijendranath.

BY ANY RECKONING Rabindranath's formal schooling was chaotic. Perhaps it is fortunate that his mind did not veer towards science, for by the last quarter of the nineteenth century it was unlikely that one could hope for a life in science without submitting oneself to the grind of formal learning.

Not for Rabindranth the 'degradation of being a mere pupil'.[10] He was sent to this school and that; and in between these was taught by private tutors at home. His real academy was the lush, artistic, musical, and literary milieu at home in the family mansion in Jorasanko. His mentors, were his older siblings, especially Jyotirindranath.

But there were more than siblings at home: there were the wives, some of whom were scarcely 'ordinary'. Rabindranath greatly admired Satyendranath's wife, Jnanadandini, hostess of an artistic salon in her home and founder-editor of a children's magazine.[11] Then there was Jyotirindranath's wife Kadambari, almost exactly Rabindranath's age, who became his literary companion and soul mate from the time she entered the Tagore household as a young bride, with whom he would enjoy a delicate platonic relationship, and whose suicide at the age of twenty-four left him distraught.[12]

For the child Rabindranath, the Jorasanko abode offered a 'feast of poetry'[13] and no less an abundance of music. Here he would come upon eldest brother Dwijendranath, 'his cushion seat placed in the south verandah, a low desk before him',[14] composing his 'masterpiece' poem, *The Dream Journey*.[15]

Elsewhere he would find Jyotirindranath, 'one of the chief helpers in my literary and emotional training',[16] at his piano, 'engrossed in the creation of new tunes', 'showers of melody' flowing out from his 'dancing fingers'.[17] And when not making music, Jyotirindranath might be seen sketching pencil portraits of friends and family, for he was a gifted artist.[18]

Somewhere else was sister-in-law Kadambari, 'a great lover of literature' and a passionate reader who made Rabindranath a 'partner in her literary enterprises'.[19]

There were also cousins and friends. An older cousin Gunendranath staged a newly-written play in his house.[20] (And later, before the end of the nineteenth century, Gunendranath's son, Abanindranath (1871–1951), painter and writer, Rabindranath's nephew though just ten years his junior, would initiate a new movement in Indian painting known as the 'Bengal School'.)[21] There was Jyotirindranath's friend Akshay Chowdhury, lover of literature, singer of songs, writer of poems; his 'genuine delight in literature' was infectious and awoke the young Rabindranath's own literary sensibilities.[22]

There was one other personal childhood experience that would help shape his creative mind, indeed his very identity. When he was twelve, Rabindranath was taken by his father to the Himalayas. Here the child discovered *freedom*. Debendranath allowed him to explore, by himself, the wilderness.[23] The experience made him greedy for freedom, not just the physical sort but the psychological kind, which urged him to break the chains of school life—hence perhaps his failure as a model schoolchild—and also creative freedom, so that as a poet he was able to experiment with his poetry, break away from the past, and find his own original voice.[24]

Rabindranath absorbed this rich cultural mileu, and it shaped his evolving identity. This was his education.

He was a precocious child. He wrote his first verse at age eight,[25] which of itself is not especially startling, for many children write verse at a young age as they paint pictures, except that Rabindranath never stopped thereafter.

He experienced his first sense of awe at the magic of rhyme in the Bengali lines 'jal pare/pata naré ('the rain patters/the leaf quivers'),[26] and in the children's rhyme 'bristi pare tapar tupur/nadi elo ban' ('the rain falls pitter patter/the river is in flood').[27] The sense of mystery evaporated when someone (clearly aware of his precocity) explained to him the nature of the fourteen-syllable metre in Bengali rhyme known as payar, and he was able to garland together some words and discover that he had created a payar verse. The mist dissipated: 'I felt I had no illusion left about the glories of poetising.'[28] But it had opened the floodgates: 'there was no holding me back.'[29]

When he was sixteen two events happily coincided. Jyotirindranath launched his literary magazine *Bharati* (and young Rabindranath joined its editorial staff)[30] and in its first volume his poem 'Kabikahini' (The Poet's Story) was published. Indeed, the long poem soon after reappeared as a book published by an admiring friend. His first book.[31]

The freedom to break away was also the freedom to experiment. He found some old Vashnavi poems in the Maithili language composed by the fifteenth century poet Vidyapati.[32] He was greatly taken by the sound pattern in this tongue, not least because he did not know the meaning of the words. 'One noon the clouds had gathered thickly. Rejoicing in the grateful shade of the cloudy mid-day rest hour, I lay prone on the bed in my inner room and wrote on a slate the imitation Maithili poem *Gahana kusuma kunja majhé*...'[33]

Thus the first of the 'Bhanu Singha poems' appeared in *Bharati*, in 1877, under his nom de plume Bhanu Singha

('Bhanu' means the sun, as does 'Rabi'). Thus the origins of his collection of songs *Bhanu Singha Thakurer Padabali* (A Song Anthology of Bhanu Singha Thakur; 'Thakur' is, of course, Rabindranath's surname in Bengali, and 'Tagore' is its Anglicization) in which he put the words of the Bhanu Singha poems to music in 1884.[34] The poems launched the adolescent poet, though Rabindranath was both amused and embarrassed at its reception: a friend, not knowing he had written them, reading the poems in manuscript, claimed that they could not have been written even by Vidyapati or Chandidas. After they were published, a Bengali scholar, writing a PhD thesis on Indian lyric poetry in Germany, lauded 'Bhanu Singha' as 'one of the old poets' against whom no modern poet could compare. Reflecting back on this experience, the mature Rabindranath confessed that had the poems fallen into his hands in his later age he would never have been so deceived.[35]

A YEAR AFTER the Bhanu Singha poems, Satyendranath, perhaps in one final exasperated bid to make his seventeen-year-old brother professionally respectable, took him to England (with Debendranath's approval) where they joined Satyendranath's wife Jnanadanandini and their children, Indira (later Rabindranath's confidante and the addressee of many of his delightful letters published as *Chhinapatra*[36] (*Glimpses of Bengal*, in English[37]) and Surendranath (later translator of some of his uncle's Bengali writings into English, in particular, *Reminiscences*).

The idea was that Rabindranath would study for the Bar. At first the days passed 'merrily under the affectionate care of my sister-in-law and in boisterous rompings with the children'.[38]

He attended a school in Brighton, but inevitably that did not work out.[39] In London he stayed alone in lodgings for a while and, quite oddly, discovered a harmonium in his room which he played 'according to my fancy'.[40] He took private lessons in Latin. He travelled through England whenever summoned by his elder brother's wife (boudi) to be with them. He took lodgings once more in London with a kindly English doctor and his family, and enrolled for a while as a student of English literature in University College, London. He began work on a new poem. Eventually, after a sojourn of two years as a quintessential dilettante, he returned to India at the age of nineteen sans barristerial qualifications but chock-full of experience. As he ruefully recalled, it was a period of 'utter disorderliness'.[41]

TWO YEARS LATER he would produce *Sandhya Sangeet* (Evening Song). This was, by his own account, the 'most memorable period' of his poetic career to date, if only because 'for the first time I had come to write what I really meant...'[42] Bankimchandra Chattopadhyay apparently thought highly of these poems. Rabindranath recalled how at a wedding of Romesh Chandra Dutt's daughter (to the geologist Pramatha Nath Bose), the host was about to put a garland of flowers around Bankimchandra's neck. 'As I came up, Bankim Babu eagerly took the garland and placing it round my neck, said, 'The wreath to him, Ramesh; have you not read his Evening Songs?'[43]

Two motifs would run through Rabindranath's poetry. The first was the search for freedom (indeed the very act of writing for him was a means of freedom); the second was a celebration of nature. These twin desires, the need for freedom and the joy in being at one with nature often fused into one in Rabindranath, as in the song 'Amar mukti alaye alaye ei akashé' (My freedom lies in the light of the sky), wherein the poet rejoiced in the freedom that was manifested in the sky above, in the earth and grass below, indeed in all of life.

In 1883, Rabindranath wrote a dramatic poem 'Prakritir Parishad' (Nature's Revenge) which, as he recalled a quarter century later, '...may be looked upon as an introduction to the whole of my future literary work; or rather this has been the subject on which all my writings have dwelt—the joy of attaining the Infinite within the finite.'[44]

'Simar majhé asim tumi, bajao apan sur' (In the midst of the finite you, the infinite, play your own tune), as one of his songs declaimed. This was what he called the 'universal song', the presence of the limitless within the limited, the great that is found in the small, the oneness of the universe.

Like Shelley—whose 'Hymn to Intellectual Beauty' Rabindranath (like Vivekananda)[45] admired in his early years[46]—Rabindranath was a pantheist. 'It is strange,' he told a friend, '...that even when so young I had the idea, which was to grow with my life all along, my realizing the Infinite in the finite and not, as some of our Indian metaphysicians do, eliminating the finite.'[47] In his pursuit of the universal song Rabindranath was a Vedantist.[48] Like Vivekananda, he sought the One-in-the-many.

Something akin to a mystical experience occurred one morning when, standing on the verandah, he observed the sun rising through the 'leafy tops' of trees.

...all of a sudden a covering seemed to fall away from my eyes and I found the world bathed in a wonderful radiance...This radiance pierced in a moment through the folds of sadness and despondency which had accumulated within my heart...and flooded it with this universal light.[49]

Universal light; universal song; the seeking of the One-in-the-many. The result, that very day was a poem, 'The Awakening of the Waterfall', which 'gushed forth and coursed on like a veritable cascade'.[50] The poem was included in the collection called *Prabhat Sangeet* (Morning Song) published in 1883.[51] Rabindranath was then only twenty-two.

THE YEAR 1883 was significant in another, very different way: on December 9, Rabindranath was married to a ten-year-old girl named Bhabatarini, who was promptly renamed Mrinalini after the wedding. Rabindranath was twelve years older than his bride.

Despite the concerns of Vidyasagar and others about the evils of child marriage, despite the fact that Rabindranath's father Debendranath was one of the preeminent Brahmos of the era, in the matter of the marriage of his offspring, Debendranath was paradoxically another conservative Hindu bhadralok. All his sons were married off to child-brides.[52] In his *Reminiscences*, Rabindranath says, laconically, 'Shortly after my return from Karwar, I was married. I was then twenty-two years of age.'[53] There is no further mention of his wife.

A photograph of the couple taken soon after their marriage, shows the tall, almost rakishly handsome groom standing, an embroidered shawl draped carelessly round his shoulders, the hint of a smile in his face. Mrinalini sits in front, not on a chair but almost awkwardly on a balustrade, her head covered by the anchal of her sari, or perhaps a shawl, her feet dangling, a wooden expression on her rather plain face.

They lived apart for more than a year after marriage, in which time Mrinalini lived with her second eldest sister-in-law (ja), Jnanadanandini, and was sent to a prominent Calcutta English-medium convent school, Loreto House, to be educated.[54]

In this time something else occurred. In April 1884, Kadambari Devi, Jyotirindranath's wife and for so long Rabindranath's literary companion and soul mate, committed suicide by poison.[55] He was utterly distraught, indeed in despair. This was his first direct experience with death as an adult. For once, nature betrayed him: they were all there—'the trees, the soil, the water, the sun, the moon, the stars', all 'as immovably true as before'. Yet: '...the person who was as truly there, who through a thousand points of contact with life, mind and heart, was ever so much true for me, had vanished in a moment like a dream.'[56]

Over the years, Rabindranath immemorialized Kadambari—in poems and songs[57]—but most famously perhaps in his novella *Nastanir* (The Broken Nest, 1901).

AT TWENTY-SEVEN Rabindranath was wryly ruminating on what he had achieved—and what others thought he had achieved—thus far: 'Folk are beginning to complain: "where is that which we expected of you—that in hope of which we admired the soft green of the shoot? Are we to put up with immaturity for ever?" ' All he had produced so far, he confessed, was 'a snatch of songs, some tittle-tattle, a little merry fooling'.[58]

But by the time he entered his thirties any of his misgivings would have surely been dispelled. For the final decade of the nineteenth century saw him reach the heights of creativity: in poetry of course, but as much in fiction, drama, essays, and song.

In his poetry, he began to consciously ally himself with the tradition of the greatest Indian poetry. In *Meghaduta* (The Cloud Messenger, 1890), he paid tribute to Kalidasa, the original author of a Sanskrit poem of the same title, and to Jayadeva, author of *Gita Govinda*, and spoke of himself sitting in that part of India watching the Bengal landscape as once Jayadeva had done. Rabindranth's views on Indian literature lies in fascinating contrast to both Bankimchandra's and Michael Madhusudan's views—but we see in him the same nationalist pride in India's cultural heritage that we witness in some of the other Renaissance figures.

A year later, enjoined by his father to help manage the family estates, he moved to Selidah in East Bengal (now in Bangladesh) and ensconced himself in his zamindari duties. Mrinalini and his children—by then he had three, daughters Bela and Renuka, and son Rathindranath—remained in Calcutta and in fact, they along with his two other children born later in the 1890s would join him to live together in Selidah as a family only from 1898.[59]

Rabindranath lived in Selidah for a decade. This period proved to be a wonderfully creative time. As Rabindranath himself wrote, this was 'the most productive period of my literary life, when owing to great good fortune I was young and less known'.[60] This was also the time when a new family magazine, *Sadhana*, was launched, of which he was the main contributor and, later, editor.[61]

Rabindranath spent much of his time during his estate management duties travelling along waterways, mostly the Padma river, and living in the family houseboat (built by his grandfather) and renamed *Padma* by Rabindranath.[62] Then and even before, the riverscape became a rich source of imagery and metaphor, and an observatory for watching nature and humanity, which fed into his writings.

Amongst other things, his zamindari duties gave him the opportunity to observe nature and humanity 'up front', especially in the countryside, which found their way in turn into his short stories. For instance, while residing in one of the family estates, he indulged in 'chats' with the local postmaster.[63] The short story 'Postmaster' (circa 1891), about the relationship between a village postmaster and a small orphan girl who cooks for and waits on him, and tends to him when he is ill, built upon this encounter.[64] Though his first two stories were published in 1884, the remainder of his eighty-four short stories date from his Selidah period.[65]

Before Rabindranath, the short story scarcely existed as a Bengali literary genre. With him it became, in the words of a critic, a 'prestigious literary form'.[66] Through them Rabindranath introduced a realism to Bengali writing eschewing the romantic strain of the Bengali novel which Bankimchandra had pioneered.

But there weren't just poems and stories. His collection of letters, mostly to his niece Indira (Satyendranath's daughter) and published in Bengali as *Chhinapatra* (Torn Leaves, 1912) and in translation as *Glimpses of Bengal*—a representative of the epistle as literary genre—are rich in musings on all that he experienced and observed between 1885 and 1895, mostly in his Selidah period.

APART FROM HIS writing, Rabindranath had also begun to compose music during this period. He would one day say: 'I think that [my songs]…are my very best work… I often feel that if all my poetry is forgotten, my songs will live with my countrymen, and have a permanent place.'[67]

His first musical drama, *Valmiki Pratibha* (Valmiki's Genius, 1881), as an example, contained songs drawn from English and Irish traditional airs. Another musical drama, *Mayar Khela* (The Play of *Maya* or Illusion, 1888) has songs based on the Bengali devotional song genre called kirtan. Later, he composed songs inspired by the songs of the Baul, the mendicant singers of rural Bengal. One of the songs based on the Baul tradition, 'Amar sonar Bangla' (My golden Bengal) would be adopted some thirty years after Rabindranath's death as the national anthem of Bangladesh.

But it would be his rabindra-sangeet (rabindra-music), a genre meandering through more than two thousand songs—music and words both by Rabindranath—that would be his greatest contribution to music.[68]

Music was, of course, in the Jorasanko air; it was part of the Tagore culture, and he absorbed it by osmosis.[69] Perhaps because of this, like so much else of his education, his musical training was haphazard so that 'of what may be called proficiency in music…I acquired none'.[70]

Rabindra-sangeet is a vibrant and remarkable testimony to the fusion of freedom and constraint that formed the epicentre of Rabindranath's creative being. In creating these songs, Rabindranath would draw upon the traditional folk and devotional music of Bengal, Indian classical music, and sometimes Western folk melodies.[71] Sometimes he used a complete tune he had composed in the past to 'fit' to new lyrics, new poems, new words. Sometimes the words already existed, and he concocted the melody to fit it—as in setting Bankimchnadra's 'Vande Mataram' to music.

With rabindra sangeet, Rabindranath created a completely new genre of contemporary, popular music that is still sung and listened to in almost every middle-class Bengali household. Some of these songs—for example 'Ekla chalo ré' (Go your way alone), a favourite of Gandhi's[72]—would become known beyond Bengal, and would even find their way, years later and translated into Hindi, to Bollywood films. He would say, 'They are real songs, songs for all seasons and occasions'[73] and that he would leave them as his legacy.

THE GREATER PART of Rabindranath's creative work would appear in the twentieth century—including the English collection of prose-poems published as *Gitanjali* (1912) which won him the Nobel Prize for literature in 1913, making him India's first modern literary figure to gain worldwide attention. Novels, short stories, poems, songs, plays, musical dramas and operas, philosophical tracts, critical essays, social and political writings would pour forth literally till the eve of his death in 1941. The rebel against the straitjacket of orthodox schooling in his own childhood, he would implement his own ideas on education by founding a school in Santiniketan, a few hundred miles from Calcutta, in 1901, and, in the same place, an international university, Visva-Bharati, in 1921. In 1928 he took up painting and in 1930 an exhibition of his works was held in Paris.[74]

There was, then, far more to come. Yet he had already achieved much when the nineteenth century ended. He had created his own, inimitable lyric poetry and his own form of the musical drama. He had invented the short story as a Bengali literary genre. He had created a completely original contemporary musical style and composed a new, popular Bengali song form. He was already the very epitome of the Renaissance man. The Bengal Renaissance gave the succeeding age in India many legacies. Rabindranath Tagore, himself a work-in-progress when the nineteenth century ended, was probably the richest of that remarkable awakening's legacies.

Notes

1. See Chapter four.
2. Kripalani 1981.
3. Tagore [n.d.] 2002.
4. Dutta and Robinson 1995, p. 37.
5. Anon 1976, p. 8, note.
6. Dutta and Robinson 1995, p. 38.
7. Tharu and Lalita 1991b, p. 235.
8. Ibid., pp. 235–6.
9. Lago 1972, p. 147.
10. Tagore [1917] 2001, p. 40.
11. Ibid., pp. 253–4.
12. Ibid., pp. 268–70.

13. Ibid., p. 132.
14. Ibid., p. 131.
15. Ibid.
16. Ibid., p. 136.
17. Ibid., p. 138.
18. Dutta and Robinson 1995, p. 39.
19. Ibid., p. 140.
20. Ibid., p. 126.
21. Guha-Thakurta 1992, pp. 226 ff.
22. Tagore [1917] 2001, p. 136.
23. Ibid., p. 103.
24. Ibid., pp. 139–40.
25. Ibid., p. 41.
26. Ibid., p. 13.
27. Tagore 1894, p. 101.
28. Tagore [1917] 2001, p. 45.
29. Ibid., p. 46.
30. Ibid., p. 160.
31. Ibid., p. 162.
32. Maithili is a language spoken in Mithila, in northern Bihar. Das 1991, pp. 55, 149.
33. Tagore [1917] 2001, p. 148.
34. Ibid., pp. 753–64, 979–80.
35. Tagore [1917] 2001, pp. 148–9.
36. Tagore [1912] 2004.
37. Tagore [1921] 1997.
38. Tagore [1917] 2001, p. 169.
39. Ibid., pp. 169–70.
40. Ibid., p. 171.
41. Ibid., p. 190.

42. Ibid., pp. 213–14.
43. Ibid., pp. 224–5.
44. Ibid., p. 249.
45. See Chapter eleven.
46. Thompson [1948] 1989, p. 39.
47. Quoted in Thompson [1948] 1989, p. 51.
48. Dasgupta 2003.
49. Tagore [1917] 2001, p. 228.
50. Ibid.
51. Thompson [1948] 1989, p. 43.
52. Dutta and Robinson 1995, p. 85.
53. Tagore [1917] 2001, p. 250.
54. Dutta and Robinson 1995, p. 87.
55. Ibid., p. 88.
56. Tagore [1917] 2001, p. 269.
57. See, for example, the compact disc recording *Kadambari, A Compilation of Songs and Writings on Kadambari Devi*. Rhyme Records, 2000.
58. Tagore, letter, July 1887, pp. 2–4 in Tagore [1921] 1997.
59. Dutta and Robinson 1995, p. 123.
60. Tagore [1921] 1997, p. v.
61. Dutta and Robinson 1995, p. 109.
62. Ibid., p. 110.
63. Tagore, letter, February 1891, in Tagore [1921] 1997, p. 22.
64. Tagore 1959b.
65. Sen 1979, p. 282; Ghosh 2000, p. 10.
66. Das 1991, p. 307.
67. Quoted in Thompson [1948] 1989, p. 61.
68. The lyrics of all rabindra-sangeet are collected in a single volume published by Visva-Bharati Press, titled *Gitabitan*

(1990), first published in three parts in 1931. The tunes for the songs have been published separately under the title *Svarabitan*.
69. Tagore [1917] 2001, pp. 138–9.
70. Ibid., p. 139.
71. Som 2009.
72. Ibid., p. 84.
73. Quoted in Thompson [1948] 1989, p. 61.
74. Dutta and Robinson 1995, p. 288.

Bibliography

Acharya, P. 1990. 'Education in Old Calcutta,' pp. 85–94 in S. Chaudhuri 1990.

Adas, M. 1989. *Machines as the Measure of Man: Science, Technology, and Ideologies of Western Dominance*. Ithaca, NY: Cornell University Press.

Anand, M.R. 1928. 'About *Anandamath*: A Conversation with Rabindranath Tagore,' pp. 9–10 in Chattopadhyay [1882] 1992.

Anderson, L. 2001. *Autobiography*. London: Routledge.

Anon. n.d. *Raja Ram Mohun Roy: His Life, Writings and Speeches*. Madras: GA Natesan & Co.

Anon, 1870. *The Dutt Family Album*. London: Longmans, Green & Co.

Anon. 1895. 'Editorial,' *The Electrician*, vol. 36, p. 3.

Anon. 1955. *Presidency College Calcutta: Centenary Volume 1955*. Calcutta: Government Printing, West Bengal Government Press.

Anon. 1962. *Acharya Prafulla Chandra Ray: Birth Centenary Souvenir Volume*. Calcutta: University of Calcutta.

Anon. 1976. *A Centenary*. Calcutta: Indian Association for the Cultivation of Science.

Anon. [1885] 1986. *Centenary Review of the Asiatic Society, 1784–1884*. Calcutta: The Asiatic Society.

Anon. [1948] 2002. *Sir William Jones. Bicentenary of His Birth. Commemoration Volume 1746–1946*. Kolkata: The Asiatic Society.

Armstrong, K. 1993. *A History of God*. New York: Ballantine Books.

Arnold, D. 2000. *Science, Technology and Medicine in Colonial India*. Cambridge: Cambridge University Press.

Bagal, J.C. (ed.). 1954. *Bankim Rachanabali* [The Collected Works of Bankim Chandra Chattopadhyay], *Volume II: Essays*. Calcutta: Sahitya Samsad.

———.(ed.). 1969a. *Bankim Rachanabali* [The Collected Works of Bankim Chandra Chattopadhyay], *Volume III: English Works*. Calcutta: Sahitya Samsad.

———. 1969b. 'Bankimchandra Chattopadhyay: Life Sketch,' pp. ix–xiii in Bagal 1969a.

Bagchi, J. (ed.), 1995a. *Indian Women: Myth and Reality*. Hyderabad: Sangam Books.

———. 1995b. 'Introduction,' pp. 1–15 in Bagchi 1995a.

———. 1995c. 'Order and Progress: The Reception of Comteian Positivism in Nineteenth Century Bengal,' pp. 150–62 in G.R. Taneja and V. Sena.

Banerjee, S. 1990. 'Marginalization of Women's Popular Culture in Nineteenth Century Bengal,' pp. 127–79 in Sangari and Vaid 1990.

Barua, B.P. (ed.). 1988. *Rammohun Roy and the New Learning*. Calcutta: Orient Longman.

Basu, A. 1991. 'The Indian Response to Scientific and Technical Education in the Colonial Era, 1820–1920,' pp. 126–38 in Kumar 1991.

Bayly, S. 1988. *Caste, Society and Politics in India from the Eighteenth Century to the Modern Age*. Cambridge: Cambridge University Press.

Bentinck, W. 1829. 'Minute on Sati,' pp. 102–15 in Major 2007.

Berenson, B. 1968. *The Italian Painters of the Renaissance*, volumes 1 and 2. London: Phaidon Press.

Berman, M. 1978. *Social Change and Scientific Organization: The Royal Institution, 1799–1944*. Ithaca, NY: Cornell University Press.

Bernstein, J. 2000. *Dawning of the Raj: The Life and Trials of Warren Hastings*. Chicago: Ivan R. Dee.

Bhalla, B.B. 2007. 'Introduction,' in *Bankim Chandra Chatterjee's Durgeshnandini*. (B.B. Bhalla, tr.) New Delhi: Indialog Publications, pp. 9–15.

Bhattacharya, A. (ed.). 2004. *Acharya Prafulla Chandra: Portrait of a Man*, vol. 1. Calcutta: West Bengal College Teachers' Association.

Bhattacharya, S. 1990. 'Traders and Trading in Old Calcutta,' pp. 203–10 in S. Chaudhuri 1990.

Bhattacharya, S. 2003. *Vande Mataram: The Biography of a Song*. New Delhi: Penguin Books.

Biswas, A.K. 2000. *Gleanings of the Past and the Science Movement: In the Diaries of Mahendralal and Amritalal Sircar*. Kolkata: The Asiatic Society.

Biswas, D.K. (ed.). 1992. *The Correspondence of Raja Rammohun Roy, Volume I: 1809–1831*. Calcutta: Saraswat Library.

Biswas, D.K. and P.C. Ganguli. 1988a. 'Supplementary Notes I' to Chapter I, pp. 9–11 in Collet [1900] 1988.

Biswas, D.K. and P.C. Ganguli. 1988b. 'Supplementary Notes I' to Chapter III, pp. 97–8 in Collet [1900] 1988.

———. 1988c. 'Supplementary Notes II' to Chapter I, pp. 15–16 in Collet [1900] 1988.

———. 1988d. 'Supplementary Notes V' to Chapter I, pp. 22–3 in Collet [1900] 1988.

———. 1988e. 'Supplementary Notes VI' to Chapter I, pp. 23–7 in Collet [1900] 1988.

———. 1988f. 'Supplementary Notes VII' to Chapter I, p. 27 in Collet [1900] 1988.

———. 1988g. 'Supplementary Notes II' to Chapter II, pp. 45–50 in Collet [1900] 1988.

———. 1988h. 'Supplementary Notes III' to Chapter II, pp. 50–51 in Collet [1900] 1988.

———. 1988i. 'Supplementary Notes V' to Chapter II, pp. 51–64 in Collet [1900] 1988.

———. 1988j. 'Supplementary Notes V' to Chapter III, pp 102–14 in Collet [1900] 1988.

Bose, J.C. n.d. 'The Uphill Way,' pp. 38–43 in Sen and Chakraborty 1986.

———. 1895. 'On the Polarisation of Electric Rays by Double Refracting Crystals,' *Journal of the Asiatic Society of Bengal*, vol. 64, pp. 291–6.

———. 1900. 'On the Similarity of Effect of Electrical Stimulus on Inorganic and Living Substances,' pp. 253–8 in J.C. Bose 1927.

———. 1911. 'Literature and Science,' pp. 139–53 in Sen and Chakraborty 1986.

———. 1915. 'The History of a Discovery,' pp. 7–20 in Sen and Chakraborty 1986.

———. 1917a. 'The History of a Failure That Was Great,' pp. 30–6 in Sen and Chakraborty 1986.

———. 1917b. 'The Voice of Life,' pp. 7–20 in Sen and Chakraborty 1986.

———. 1927. *Collected Physical Papers*. London: Longmans, Green & Co.

———. 1994. *Patrabali* [Letters to Rabindranath Tagore, in Bengali], D Sen (ed.). Calcutta: The Bose Institute.

Bose, P.N. 1880. 'Undescribed Fossil Carnivora from the Siválik Hills in the Collection of the British Museum,' *Quarterly Journal of the Geological Society*, vol. 36(1–4), pp. 119–36.

———. [1885] 1986. 'Natural Sciences,' Part III in Anon, *Centenary Review of the Asiatic Society*.

Bruner, J.L. 1990. *Acts of Meaning*. Cambridge, MA: Harvard University Press.

Bullock, A. 1985. *The Humanist Tradition in the West*. New York: W.W. Norton.

Burke, P. 1999. *The Italian Renaissance* (second edition). Princeton, NJ: Princeton University Press.

Burkhardt, J. [1829] 1975. *The Civilization of the Renaissance in Italy, Volume II*. New York: Harper Colophone Books.

Cardwell, D.S.L. 1994. *The Fontana History of Technology*. London: Fontana Press/Harper Collins.

Carpenter, M. [1866] 1915. *The Last Days in England of the Rajah Rammohun Roy* (third edition). Calcutta: The Rammohun Roy Library and Free Reading Room.

Chaliha, J. and B. Gupta. 1990. 'The Armenians in Calcutta,' pp. 54–5 in S. Chaudhuri 1990.

Chakravarti, S.C. (ed.). 1933. *The Father of Modern India: Commemoration Volume*. Calcutta: Rammohun Roy Centenary Committee.

Chakravarty, A.K. 1995. 'Three 19th Century Calcutta Astronomers,' *Indian Journal of History of Science*, vol. 30 (2–4), pp. 151–8.

Chakravarty, D. 2002. *Habitations of Modernity*. Chicago: University of Chicago Press.

Chandra, B. 1989. *India's Struggle for Independence*. New Delhi: Penguin Books.

Chandra, S. 2003. 'Two Faces of Prose: Behramji Malabari and Govardhanran Tripathi,' pp. 82–91 in Mehrotra 2003.

Chattopadhyay, B. 1864. *Rajmohan's Wife*, pp. 1–88 in Bagal 1969a.

———. 1870. 'A Popular Literature for Bengal,' pp. 97–102 in Bagal 1969a.

———. 1871. 'Bengali Literature,' pp. 103–24 in Bagal 1969a.

———. 1873. 'The Study of Hindu Philosophy,' pp. 142–8 in Bagal 1969a.

———. 1875. 'Amar Durgotsav' ['My Durga Puja'], pp. 79–80 in Bagal 1954.

———. 1879. 'Bharat Kalanka' ['India's Shame'], pp. 234–41 in Bagal 1954.

———. 1882. 'The Intellectual Superiority of Europe,' pp. 209–18 in Bagal 1969a.

———. 1888. 'Dharmatattva,' pp. 584–679 in Bagal 1954.

———. 1892. 'Krishnacharitra' ['About Krisna'], pp. 407–583 in Bagal 1954.

———. 1892. 'Bangla Sahitye Pyari Chand Mittra' [Pyari Chand Mittra in Bengali Literature], pp. 861–3 in Bagal 1954.

———. [unpublished manuscript in his lifetime] 1940. 'Letters on Hinduism,' pp. 227–67 in Bagal 1969a.

———. [1882] 1992. *Anandamath*. (B.K. Roy, trans.) New Delhi: Orient Paperbacks.

Chattopadhyay, S.K. Bandyopadhyay, and S.K. Das (ed.). 1937. *Vidyasagar Granthabali—Sahitya* [Collected Works of Vidyasagar—Literature]. Calcutta: Ranjan Publishing House.

———. 1938. *Vidyasagar Granthabali—Samaj* [Collected Works of Vidyasagar—Society]. Calcutta: Ranjan Publishing House.

———. 1939. *Vidysagar Granthabali—Siksha o Bibidh* [Collected Works of Vidyasagar—Education and Miscellaneous]. Calcutta: Ranjan Publishing House.

Chatterjee, P. 1993. *The Nations and Its Fragments*. Princeton, NJ: Princeton University Press.

Chaudhuri, A. (ed.). 2001. *The Picador Book of Modern Indian Literature*. London: Picador.

———. 2008. 'The Flute of Modernity: Tagore and the Middle Class,' pp. 69–84 in *Clearing a Space: Reflections on India, Literature and Culture*. Long Hanborough: Peter Lang.

Chaudhuri Lahiri, D.K. 1990. 'Trends in Calcutta Architecture 1690–1903,' pp. 156–75 in S. Chaudhuri 1990.

Chaudhuri, N.C. 1989. *A Passage to England*. London: The Hogarth Press.

Chaudhuri, R. 2003. 'The Dutt Family Album: And Toru Dutt,' pp. 53–69 in Mehrotra 2003.

———. (ed.). 2008a. *Derozio, Poet of India*. New Delhi: Oxford University Press.

———. 2008b. 'Introduction,' in R. Chaudhuri 2008a.

Chaudhuri, S. n.d. 'Defining a Renaissance: Experience Across Cultures.' Unpublished manuscript, Department of English, Jadavpur University, Kolkata.

———. (ed.). 1980. *Proceedings of the Asiatic Society, Volume I. 1784–1800*. Calcutta: The Asiatic Society.

———. (ed.). 1990. *Calcutta: The Living City. Volume I: The Past*. Calcutta: Oxford University Press.

Chowdhury, P. and J. Chaliha. 1990. 'The Jews of Calcutta,' pp. 52–3 in S. Chaudhuri 1990.

Clarke, E. and L.S. Jacyna. 1987. *Nineteenth Century Origins of Neuroscientific Concepts*. Berkeley, CA: University of California Press.

Clive, J. 1975. 'Series Editor's Preface,' pp. vii–x in Mill [1817] 1975.

Cohn, B.S. 1996. *Colonialism and Its Forms of Knowledge*. Princeton, NJ: Princeton University Press.

Colebrooke, H.T. 1795. 'On the Duties of a Faithful Hindu Widow,' *Asiatick Researches*, vol. 4, pp. 209–19. Reprinted, pp. 115–22 in Colebrooke 1837.

———. 1805. 'On the *Vedas* or the Sacred Writings of the Hindus,' *Asiatick Researches*, vol. 8, pp. 369–476. Reprinted, pp. 9–113 in Colebrooke 1837.

———. 1817. 'Introduction to Indian Algebra with Arithmetic and Mensuration.' Reprinted, pp. 623–54 in D.P. Chattopadhyay (ed.) 1982. *Studies in the History of Science in India, Volume 2*. New Delhi: Editorial Enterprises.

———. 1823. 'A Discourse Read at a Meeting of the Royal Asiatic Society of Great Britain and Ireland,' March 15. *Transactions of the Royal Asiatic Society*, vol. 1, pp. xvii–xxii. Reprinted, pp. 1–8 in Colebrooke 1837.

Colebrooke, H.T. 1837. *Miscellaneous Essays, Volume 1*. London: William H. Allen & Co.

Collet, S.D. [1900] 1988. *The Life and Letters of Raja Rammohun Roy* (fourth edition). D.K. Biswas and P.C. Ganguli, (ed.) Calcutta: Sadharan Brahmo Samaj.

Das, S.K. 1966. *Early Bengali Prose: Carey to Vidyasagar*. Calcutta: Bookland.

———. 1974. *The Shadow of the Cross: Christianity and Hinduism in a Colonial Situation*. New Delhi: Munshiram Manoharlal Publishers.

———. 1978. *Sahibs and Munshis: An Account of the College of Fort William*. Calcutta: Papyrus.

———. 1991. *A History of Indian Literature, Volume VIII. 1800–1910. Western Impact: Indian Response*. New Delhi: Sahitya Akademi.

———. 1995. *The Artist in Chains: The Life of Bankimchandra Chatterjee* (second edition). Calcutta: Papyrus.

———. 2001. *Indian Ode to the West Wind*. Delhi: Pencraft International.

Dasgupta, R.K. 1962. 'Acharya Ray as a Man of Letters,' pp. 140–7 in Anon 1962.

———. 1983. 'Bankimchandra Chatterjee's *Anandamath*,' pp. 24–36 in *National Seminar on History and National Development*. Calcutta: Netaji Research Bureau.

———. 1990. 'Old Calcutta as Presented in Literature,' pp. 118–27 in S. Chaudhuri 1990.

———. 1995a. *East-West Literary Relations*. Calcutta: Papyrus.

———. 1995b. *Swami Vivekananda's Vedantic Socialism*. Kolkata: The Ramakrishna Mission Institute of Culture.

Dasgupta, R.K. 1998. 'Poetry of the Mother,' pp. 257–61 in *The Statesman Festival, '98*. Calcutta: The Statesman Press.

———. [1956] 1999. 'Michael o Vidyasagar' [Michael and Vidyasagar], pp. 173–91 in *Oitijya o Parampara: Unish Sataker Bangla* [Cultural Heritage and After: Nineteenth Century Bengali]. Kolkata: Papyrus.

———. 1999. 'Swami Vivekananda's Neo-Vedanta.' Indira Gandhi Memorial Lecture 1998. Calcutta: The Asiatic Society. Reprinted, R.K. Dasgupta 2008.

———. [1948] 2002. 'Sir William Jones as a Poet,' pp. 162–6 in Anon. [1948] 2002.

———. 2003. 'Rabindranath Tagore's Vedantism,' pp. 88–100 in *Vedanta in Bengal*. Kolkata: The Ramakrishna Mission Institute of Culture.

———. 2004. 'Monistic Music,' *The Statesman* (Kolkata), January 12.

———. [1945] 2004. *English Poets on India and Other Essays*. Kolkata: Papyrus.

———. 2008. *Philosophy and Philosophers*. Kolkata: The Ramakrishna Mission Institute of Culture.

Dasgupta, S. 1996. *Technology and Creativity*. New York: Oxford University Press.

———. 2004. 'Cognitive Style in Creative Work: The Case of the Painter George Rodrigue,' in *PsyArt: An Online Journal for the Psychological Study of Art*. http://www.clas.ufl.edu/journal/2005_dasgupta01.shtml (last accessed on July 11, 2010).

———. 2007. *The Bengal Renaissance: Identity and Creativity from Rammohun Roy to Rabindranath Tagore*. New Delhi: Permanent Black.

———. [1999] 2009. *Jagadish Chandra Bose and the Indian Response to Western Science* (Paperback Edition). New Delhi: Permanent Black.

Daston, L. (ed.). 2000. *Biographies of Scientific Objects*. Chicago: University of Chicago Press.

Datta, M.M. 1854. *The Anglo-Saxon and the Hindu*. Excerpted in A. Chaudhuri 2001, pp. 5–7.

De, S.K. 1961. *Bengali Literature in the Nineteenth Century* (second edition). Calcutta: Firma K.L. Mukhopadhyay.

Debi Rassundari. [1906] 1999. *Amar Jiban* [My Life]. (Enakshi Chatterjee, trans) Calcutta: Writers Workshop.

Dennett, D.C. 1991. *Consciousness Explained*. Boston: Little, Brown & Co. Diogenes Laertus, 1950. *Lives of Ancient Philosophers, Book IX*. Cambridge, MA: Harvard University Press/ London: William Heinemann.

Drabble, M. (ed.). 1985. *The Oxford Companion to English Literature* (fifth edition). Oxford: Oxford University Press.

Drummond, D. 1829. *Objections to Phrenology*. Calcutta: Samuel Smith & Co. / William Thacker & Co.

Dutta, K. and A. Robinson. 1995. *Rabindranath Tagore: The Myriad-Minded Man*. New York: St Martin's Press.

Eakin, J.P. 1999. *How Our Lives Become Stories: Making Selves.* Ithaca, NY: Cornell University Press.

Edwards, T. [1884] 1980. *Henry Derozio.* Calcutta: Riddhi-India.

Elliott, K.R.C. 2007. 'Baptist Missions in the British Empire: Jamaica and Serampore in the First Half of the Nineteenth Century.' Unpublished M.A. Thesis, Department of History, Florida State University.

Erikson, E.H. 1975. 'Identity Crisis in Perspective,' pp. 17–47 in *Life History and the Historical Moment.* New York: W.W. Norton.

Everitt, A. 2003. *Cicero.* New York: Random House.

Figueira, D.M. 1991. *Translating the Orient: The Reception of Sakuntala in Nineteenth Century Europe.* Albany, NY: State University of New York Press.

Finch, C. 1850. 'Vital Statistics of Calcutta,' *Journal of the Statistical Society of London*, vol. 13, pp. 168–82.

Fitzpatrick, D. 1999. 'Ireland and the Empire,' pp. 494–521 in A. Porter (ed.), *The Oxford History of the British Empire, Volume III: The Nineteenth Century.* Oxford: Oxford University Press.

Forbes, G. 1975. *Positivism in Bengal.* Calcutta: Minerva.

———. 1996. *Women in Modern India.* Cambridge: Cambridge University Press.

———. 2000. 'Introduction to the Memoirs,' pp. 9–45 in Forbes and Raychaudhuri 2000.

Forbes, G. (ed.) and T. Raychaudhuri, (trans.). 2000. *The Memoirs of Dr. Haimabati Sen: From Child Widow to Lady Doctor.* New Delhi: Roli Books.

Geddes, P. 1920. *The Life and Works of Sir Jagadis C. Bose.* London: Longmans, Green & Co.

Ghose, J.C. (ed.). 1885a. *The English Works of Rammohun Roy, Volume I.* Calcutta: Bhowanipore Oriental Press.

———. 1885b. 'Introduction,' pp. iii–xix in J.C. Ghose 1885a.
———. 1948. *Bengali Literature*. London: Oxford University Press.
Ghosh, T. 2000. 'Introduction,' pp. 1–30 in R. Tagore 2000.
Gleig, G.R. 1841. *Memoirs of the Life of the Right Hon. Warren Hastings*. London: Richard Bentley.
Goleman, D. 1975. 'The Buddha on Meditation and States of Consciousness,' pp. 205–30 in C.T. Tart (ed.), *Transpersonal Psychology*. New York: Harper & Row.
Gombrich, E.H. 1969. *Art and Illusion*. Princeton, NJ: Princeton University Press.
Gorman, M. 1988. 'Introduction of Western Science into Colonial India: Role of the Calcutta Medical College.' *Proceedings of the American Philosophical Society*, vol. 132, (3), pp. 276–98.
Gruber, H.E. 1989. 'The Evolving Systems Approach in Creative Work,' pp. 3–24 in Gruber and Wallace 1989.
Gruber, H.E. and D.B. Wallace. (ed.). 1989. *Creative People at Work*. New York: Oxford University Press.
Guha-Thakurta, T. 1992. *The Making of a New 'Indian' Art*. Cambridge: Cambridge University Press.
Gupta, B. and J. Chaliha. 1990. 'Chitpur,' pp. 27–30 in S Chaudhuri 1990.
Gusdorf, G. 1980. 'Conditions and Limits of Autobiography,' pp. 28–48 in Olney 1980.
Halhed, N. 1776. '"Translator's Preface" to *A Code of Gentoo Laws*.' Reprinted, pp. 140–83, in Marshall 1970.
Halevy, E. [1928] 1955. *The Growth of Philosophical Radicalism*. (M. Morris, tr.) Boston: The Beacon Press.
Hanson, N.R. 1972. *Patterns of Discovery*. Cambridge: Cambridge University Press.

Headrick, D.R. 1988. *The Tentacles of Progress: Technology Transfer in the Age of Imperialism, 1850–1940*. New York: Oxford University Press.

Hobsbawm, E. 1983. 'Introduction: Inventing Traditions,' pp. 1–14 in E. Hobsbawm and T. Ranger (ed.), *The Invention of Tradition*. Cambridge: Cambridge University Press.

Home, A. (ed.). 1933a. *Rammohun Roy: The Man and His Work*. Calcutta: Centenary Publicity Booklet.

———. 1933b. 'Supplementary Notes,' pp. 28–68 in Home 1933a.

———. 1933c. 'A List of the Principal Publications and Other Writings of Raja Rammohun Roy,' Appendix E, pp. 133–47 in Home 1933a.

Humphries, A. 1982. 'The Literary Scene,' pp. 53–100 in B. Ford (ed.), *The New Pelican Guide to English Literature, Volume 4. From Dryden to Johnson*. Harmondsworth: Penguin Books.

Huxley, J. 1964. 'The Humanist Frame,' pp. 72–115 in *Essays of a Humanist*. New York: Harper & Row.

'J.' 1834. 'Reminiscences of the Hindu College,' *Calcutta Literary Gazette*, March 29, p. 189.

Johnson, P. 1991. *The Birth of the Modern: World History 1815–1830*. New York: Harper Collins.

Jones, W. 1784. 'Discourse on the Institution of a Society for Inquiring into the History, Civil and Natural, the Antiquities, Arts, Sciences and Literature of ASIA [sic].' Reprinted, pp. 2–6 in S. Chaudhuri 1980.

———. 1785. 'Second Anniversary Discourse,' February 24. Reprinted, pp. 38–44 in S. Chaudhuri 1980.

———. 1786. 'Third Anniversary Discourse,' February 2. Reprinted, pp. 72–83 in S. Chaudhuri 1980.

———. 1786. 'On the Hindus,' *Asiatick Researches*, vol. 1, Chapter 25. Reprinted, pp. 246–61 in Marshall 1970.

———. 1789. 'On the Gods of Greece, Italy and India,' *Asiatick Researches*, vol. 1, Chapter 9. Reprinted, pp. 196–245 in Marshall 1970.

———. 1794. 'Eleventh Anniversary Discourse,' February 20. Reprinted, pp. 220–30 in S. Chaudhuri 1980.

Jones, W. and Teignmouth (Lord). 1835. *Memoirs of the Life, Writings and Correspondence of Sir William Jones, Volume II*. London: John W. Parker (Kessinger Publishing's Reprint).

Joshi, V.C. (ed.). 1975. *Rammohun Roy and the Modernisation of India*. Delhi: Vikas Publishing House.

Karlekar, M. 1995. 'Reflections on Kulin Polygamy—Nistarini Debi's Sekaler Katha,' *Contributions to Indian Sociology* (new series), vol. 29 (1 and 2).

Kochhar, R.K. 1991. 'Science as a Tool in British India,' *Economic & Political Weekly*, August 17, pp. 1927–33.

Kopf, D. 1969. *British Orientalism and the Bengal Renaissance*. Berkeley, CA: University of California Press.

———. 1979. *The Brahmo Samaj and the Shaping of the Modern Indian Mind*. Princeton, NJ: Princeton University Press.

Kramnick, I. (ed.). 1995. *The Portable Enlightenment Reader*. New York: Penguin Books.

Kripalani, K. 1981. *Dwarakanath Tagore. A Forgotten Pioneer: A Life*. New Delhi: National Book Trust.

———. 1988. 'Rammohun Roy and Mahatma Gandhi,' pp. 4–23 in Barua 1988.

Kripalani Mukherjee, S. 2003. 'The Hindu College: Henry Derozio and Michael Madhusudan Dutt,' pp. 41–52 in Mehrotra 2003.

Kuhn, T.S. 1970. *The Structure of Scientific Revolutions* (second edition). Chicago: University of Chicago Press.

Kumar, D. (ed.). 1991. *Science and Empire: Essays in Indian Context*. New Delhi: Anamika Prakashan.

Kushari Dyson, K. 2004. 'A Tremendous Comet: Michael Madhusudan Dutt.' Parabas.com; http://www.parabas.com/translation/database/ reviews/br1.ured1.html (last accessed on May 18, 2009).

Lago, M.M. (ed.). 1972. *Imperfect Encounters: Letters of William Rothenstein and Rabindranath Tagore, 1911–1941*. Cambridge, MA: Harvard University Press.

Lal, B. [1917] 2001. *A Readable Dictionary of Phrases, Idioms and Colloquialisms*. Calcutta: Writers Workshop.

Latour, B. and S. Woolgar. 1986. *Laboratory Life: The Construction of Scientific Facts* (second edition). Princeton, NJ: Princeton University Press.

Leach, E. and S.N. Mukherjee. (ed.). 1970. *Elites in South Asia*. Cambridge: Cambridge University Press.

Lethbridge, R. 1907. 'Sketches of Some Leading Men in Bengal,' pp. 126–71 in Sastri [1907] 2002.

Lokugé, C. (ed.). 2006a. *Toru Dutt: Collected Prose and Poetry*. New Delhi: Oxford University Press.

———. 2006b. 'A Chronology of Toru Dutt,' p. xi in Lokugé 2006a.

———. 2006c. 'Introduction,' pp. xiii–xlviii in Lokugé 2006a.

Macaulay, T.B. 1835. 'Minute on Education,' in J. Clive and T. Pines (ed.), 1972. *Selected Writings*. Chicago: University of Chicago Press.

Majeed, J. 1992. *Ungoverned Imaginings: James Mill's* The History of British India *and Orientalism*. Oxford: Clarendon Press.

Major, A. (ed.). 2007. *Sati: A Historical Anthology*. New Delhi: Oxford University Press.

Majumdar, R.C. 1960. *Glimpses of Bengal in the Nineteenth Century*. Calcutta: Firma K.L. Mukhopadhyay.

———. 1965. 'English Education,' pp. 31–88 in Majumdar, Majumdar, and Ghose 1965.

Majumdar, R.C., A.K. Majumdar, and D.K. Ghose. (ed.). 1965. *The History and Culture of the Indian People, Part II*. Bombay: Bharatiya Vidya Bhavan.

Mani, L. 1990. 'Contentious Traditions: The Debate on *Sati* in Colonial India,' pp. 88–126 in Sangari and Vaid 1990.

Marshall, P.J. (ed.). 1970. *The British Discovery of Hinduism in the Eighteenth Century*. Cambridge: Cambridge University Press.

Marshman, J.C. 1859. *The Life and Times of Carey, Marshman and Ward: Embracing the History of the Serampore Mission, Volumes I & II*. London: Longman, Brown, Green, Longmans and Roberts.

Mehrotra, A.K. 1990. *Twenty Indian Poems*. New Delhi: Oxford University Press.

———(ed.). 2003. *A History of Indian Literature in English*. London: Hurst & Co.

Metcalfe, T.R. 1995. *Ideologies of the Raj*. Cambridge: Cambridge University Press.

Mill, J. [1817] 1975. *The History of British India*. (Abridgment and Introduction by W. Thomas). Chicago: University of Chicago Press.

Mitra, R.L. 1885. 'History of the Society', pp. 1–195 in Anon [1885] 1986.

Mittra, P.C. 1877. *A Biographical Sketch of David Hare*. Calcutta: W. Newman & Co.

Moore, A. 1947. *Rammohun Roy and America*. Calcutta: Sadharan Brahmo Samaj.

Moorehouse, G. 1974. *Calcutta*. Harmondsworth: Penguin Books.

Mukherjee, M. 2000. *The Perishable Empire: Essays on Indian Writing in English*. New Delhi: Oxford University Press.

Mukherjee, S.N. 1968. *Sir William Jones: A Study in Eighteenth Century Attitudes to India*. Cambridge: Cambridge University Press.

———. 1970. 'Class, Caste and Politics in Calcutta, 1815–1838,' pp. 33–78 in Leach and Mukherjee 1970.

Murshid, G. 2003. *Lured by Hope: A Biography of Michael Madhusudan Dutt*. (G. Majumdar, trans.) New Delhi: Oxford University Press.

———. (ed.). 2004. *The Heart of a Rebel Poet: Letters of Michael Madhusudan Dutt*. New Delhi: Oxford University Press.

Nair, P.T. 1990. 'The Growth and Development of Old Calcutta,' pp. 10–23 in S. Chaudhuri 1990.

Namboodiry, U. 1995. *St. Xavier's: The Making of a Calcutta Institution*. New Delhi: Viking.

Nandy, A. 1983. *The Intimate Enemy*. New Delhi: Oxford University Press.

Newman, J.H. [1852] 1938. *The Idea of a University*. Reprinted in C.W. Eliot (ed.), *Harvard Classics 28: Essays, English and American*. New York: P.F. Collier & Sons.

Nikhilananda (Swami) (trans). n.d. *The Gospel of Sri Ramakrishna*. Madras: Sri Ramakrishna Math.

Olney, J. (ed.). 1980. *Autobiography: Essays Theoretical and Critical*. Princeton, NJ: Princeton University Press.

———. 1988. *Memory & Narrative: The Weave of Life Writing*. Chicago: University of Chicago Press.

Ousby, I. (ed.). 1988. *The Cambridge Guide to Literature in English*. Cambridge: Cambridge University Press.

Palit, C. 1991. 'Mahendralal Sircar (1833–1904): The Quest for National Science,' pp. 152–60 in Kumar 1991.

Partington, J.R. [1960] 1999. *A History of Greek Fire and Gunpowder.* Baltimore, MD: The Johns Hopkins University Press.

Pickering, A. (ed.). 1992. *Science as Practice and Culture.* Chicago: University of Chicago Press.

Piele, J. 1913. *Biographical Register of Christ's College.* Cambridge: Christ's College.

Plumb, J.H. 1964. *The Penguin Book of the Italian Renaissance.* Harmondsworth: Penguin Books.

Poddar, A. 1970. *Renaissance in Bengal: Quests and Confrontations 1800–1860.* Simla: Indian Institute of Advanced Study.

Pyenson, L. and S. Sheets Pyenson. 1999. *Servants of Nature.* New York: W.W. Norton.

Quaisar, A.J. [1982] 1998. *The Indian Response to European Technology and Culture, AD 1498–1700.* New Delhi: Oxford University Press.

Raj, K. 2007. *Relocating Modern Science: Circulation and Construction of Knowledge in South Asia and Europe 1650–1900.* Basingstoke: Palgrave Macmillan.

Radhakrishna, B.P. 1997. 'Pramath Nath Bose (1855–1934),' *Current Science*, vol. 72(3) (February 10), p. 222.

Ray, P.C. 1894. 'On the Chemical Examination of Certain Indian Foodstuffs. Part I, Fats and Oils,' *Journal of the Asiatic Society of Bengal*, vol. 63, Part II, pp. 59–80.

———. 1896. 'On Mercurous Nitrite,' *Journal of the Asiatic Society of Bengal*, vol. 65, Part II, pp. 1–9.

———. 1902. 'Preface to the First Edition,' pp. 1–5 in P.C. Ray [1902] 2002.

———. 1904. 'Preface to the Second Edition,' pp. 6–7 in P.C. Ray [1902] 2002.

———. 1932. *Life and Experiences of a Bengali Chemist*. Calcutta: Chuckervertty, Chatterjee & Co./ London: Kegan Paul, Trench, Trubner & Co.

———.[1902] 2002. *A History of Hindu Chemistry*. Centenary Edition. Kolkata: Shaibya Prakshan Bibhag.

Ray, N.R. and P.C. Gupta. (ed.). 1957. *Hundred Years of the University of Calcutta*. Calcutta: University of Calcutta.

Ray, R.K. 2003. *Exploring Emotional History* (Paperback Edition). New Delhi: Oxford University Press.

Ray, S.N. [1948] 2002. 'Sir William Jones's Poetry,' pp. 152–7 in Anon [1948] 2002.

Raychaudhuri, T. 1999. *Perceptions, Emotions, Sensibilities: Essays in India's Colonial and Postcolonial Experiences*. New Delhi: Oxford University Press.

———. 2002. *Europe Reconsidered: Perceptions of the West in Nineteenth Century Bengal* (second edition). New Delhi: Oxford University Press.

Reymond, L. [1953] 1985. *The Dedicated: A Biography of Nivedita*. Madras: Samata Books.

Robertson, B.C. 1995. *Raja Rammohan Roy: The Father of Modern India*. New Delhi: Oxford University Press.

———. 2003. 'The English Writings of Raja Rammohan Roy,' pp. 1–26 in Mehrotra 2003.

Robinson, E. 1953. 'The Derby Philosophical Society,' *Annals of Science*, vol. 9, pp. 359–67.

Rolland, R. [1931] 1979. *The Life of Vivekananda and the Universal Gospel*. Calcutta: Advaita Ashrama.

———. [1929] 1996. *The Life of Ramakrishna*. Calcutta: Advaita Ashrama.

Ross, R. 1923. *Memoirs*. London: John Murray.

Roy, R. 1818. 'Translation of a Conference Between an Advocate for, and an Opponent of, the Practice of Burning Widows Alive,' pp. 295–310 in J.C. Ghose 1885a.

———. 1820. 'A Second Conference Between an Advocate for, and an Opponent of, the Practice of Burning Widows Alive,' pp. 311–56 in J.C. Ghose 1885a.

———. 1822. 'Brief Remarks Regarding Modern Encroachment on the Ancient Rights of Females According to the Hindu Law of Inheritance,' pp. 357–70 in J.C. Ghose 1885a.

Roy, R. [P.K. Thakoor]. 1823. 'Humble Suggestions to His Countrymen Who Believe in the One True God,' pp. 243–6 in J.C. Ghose 1885a.

———. 1830. 'Address to Lord William Bentinck,' pp. 483–6 in J.C. Ghose 1885a.

———. 1833. 'Autobiographical Sketch,' pp. 22–6 in Carpenter [1866] 1915.

Rushdie, S. and E. West. (ed.). 1987. *Mirrorwork: 50 Years of Indian Writing 1947–1997*. New York: Henry Holt & Company.

Sahlins, M. 2000. '"Sentimental Pessimism" and Ethnographic Experience, or Why Culture is Not a Disappearing "Object"', pp. 158–202 in L. Daston 2000.

Said, E.W. [1978] 1994. *Orientalism* (second edition). New York: Vintage Books.

Sangari, K. and S. Vaid (ed.). 1990. *Recasting Women: Essays in Indian Colonial History*. New Brunswick, NJ: Rutgers University Press.

Sarkar, N. 1990. 'Printing and the Spirit of Calcutta,' pp. 128–36 in S. Chaudhuri 1990.

Sarkar, S. 1983. *Modern India, 1885–1947*. Madras: Macmillan.

———. 1990. 'Calcutta and the Bengal Renaissance,' pp. 95–105 in S. Chaudhuri 1990.

———. 1997. 'Vidyasagar and the Brahminical Society,' pp. 216–81 in *Writing Social History*. New Delhi: Oxford University Press.

Sarkar, T. 2003. *Hindu Wife, Hindu Nation*. New Delhi: Permanent Black.

Sastri, S. [1907] 2002. *A History of the Renaissance in Bengal. Ramtanu Lahiri: Brahman and Reformer*. (R. Lethbridge, trans and ed.) Kolkata: Renaissance Publishers.

———. [1911] 1933. 'Rammohun Roy: The Story of His Life,' pp. 7–27 in A. Home 1933a.

Schofield, R.E. 1963. *The Lunar Society of Birmingham*. Oxford: Clarendon Press.

Schön, D. 1983. *The Reflective Practitioner*. New York: Basic Books.

Seely, C.B. (trans) and M.M. Datta, MM. 2004. *The Slaying of Meghanada: A* Ramayana *from Colonial Bengal*. Chicago: University of Chicago Press.

———. 2004. 'Introduction,' pp. 3–70 in Seely and Datta 2004.

Sen, A. 1977. *Iswar Chandra Vidyasagar and His Elusive Milestones*. Calcutta: Riddhi-India.

———. 1993. *Hindu Revivalism in Bengal*. New Delhi: Oxford University Press.

Sen, A. 2005. *The Argumentative Indian*. London: Allen Lane.

Sen, D. and A.K. Chakraborty (ed.). 1986. *J.C. Bose Speaks*. Calcutta: Puthipatra.

Sen, D.C. n.d. 'About this Book,' pp. 11–17 in Rassundari Debi [1906] 1999.

Sen, S. 1979. *History of Bengali Literature* (third edition). New Delhi: Sahitya Akademi.

Sengupta, S.C. 1955. 'The History of the College,' pp. 1–35 in Anon 1955.

Simon, H.A. 1996. *The Sciences of the Artificial* (third edition). Cambridge, MA: MIT Press.

Sinha, P. 1965. *Nineteenth Century Bengal: Aspects of Social History*. Calcutta: Firma K.L. Mukhopadhyay.

———. 1978. *Calcutta in Urban History*. Calcutta: Firma K.L. Mukhopadhyay.

———. 1990. 'Calcutta and the Currents of History, 1690–1912,' pp. 31–44 in S. Chaudhuri 1990.

Soloman, R.C. and K.M. Higgins. 1996. *A Short History of Philosophy*. New York: Oxford University Press.

Som, R. 2009. *Rabindranath Tagore: The Singer and His Song*. New Delhi: Penguin Books.

Spear, P. [1932] 1998. *The Nabobs*. Delhi: Oxford University Press.

Stephen, L. and S. Lee (ed.). 1917a. *Dictionary of National Biography, Volume IV*. Oxford: Oxford University Press.

———. (ed.). 1917b. *Dictionary of National Biography, Volume VIII*. Oxford: Oxford University Press.

Tagore, D. 1896. 'Reminiscences of Rammohun Roy,' pp. 172–77, 'Rammohun Roy Centenary Celebrations of 1933, Part II,' in S.C. Chakravarti 1933.

———. [n.d.] 2002. *The Autobiography of Maharshi Debendranath Tagore*. S. Tagore and I Debi (trans), New Delhi: Rupa & Co.

Tagore, R. 1894. 'Children's Rhyme' S. Chaudhuri, (trans), pp. 100–27 in R. Tagore 2001.

———. 1957. *Chitipatra* [Collected Letters], vol. 6. Calcutta: Visva Bharati Press.

———. 1959a. *Galpaguchha* [Collected Short Stories]. Calcutta: Visva Bharati Press.

———. 1959b. 'Postmaster,' pp. 19–23 in R. Tagore 1959a.

———. 1959c. 'Ghater Katha' [The Ghat's Story], pp. 1–8 in R. Tagore 1959a.

———. 1990. *Gitabitan* [The Complete Collection of Tagore's Songs]. Calcutta: Visva Bharati Press.

Tagore, R. 1994. *Selected Poems*. W. Radice (trans), Harmondsworth: Penguin Books.

———. [1921] 1997. *Glimpses of Bengal*. New Delhi: Macmillan India.

———. 2000. *Selected Short Stories*. (S. Chaudhuri, ed.) New Delhi: Oxford University Press.

———. [1917] 2001. *Reminiscences*. S. Tagore (trans), New Delhi: Macmillan India.

———. 2001. *Selected Writings on Literature and Language*. S.K. Das and S. Chaudhuri (ed.), New Delhi: Oxford University Press.

———. [1912] 2004. *Chhinapatra* [Torn Letters]. Kolkata: Visva Bharati Press.

Tart, C.T. 1997. 'Transpersonal Psychology—Definition of,' *Journal of Consciousness Studies—Online*. Ics-online@hermes.zynet.net, July 16 (last accessed on June 17, 2010).

Thapar, R. 2002. *Early India*. Berkeley, CA: University of California Press.

Tharu, S. and K. Lalita. (ed.). 1991. *Women Writing in India. 600 BC to the Present. Volume I: 600 BC to the Early Twentieth Century*. New York: The Feminist Press.

———. 1991. 'Swarnakumari Devi (1856–1931),' pp. 235–8 in Tharu and Lalita 1991.

Thomson, J.J. 1905. 'Electric Waves,' pp. 203–8 in *The Encyclopedia Britannica, Volume 9* (eleventh edition). Cambridge: Cambridge University Press.

Thompson, E.J. [1948] 1989. *Rabindranath Tagore: Poet and Dramatist*. New Delhi: Oxford University Press.

Tripathi, A. 2004. *Vidyasagar: The Traditional Moderniser* (second edition). Calcutta: Punascha.

Vidyasagar, I. 1869. 'Bhrantibilas,' pp. 387–452 in S.K. Chattopadhyay, B.N. Bandyopadhyay, and Das 1937.

———. 1855. 'Barnaparichay,' Parts I and II, pp. 257–98 in S.K. Chattopadhyay, B.N. Bandyopadhyay, and S.R. Das 1939.

———. 1850. 'Balyabibhaher Dosh' [The Crime of Child Marriage], pp. 1–10 in S.K. Chattopadhyay, B.N. Bandyopadhyay, and S.R. Das 1938.

———. 1854. *Sakuntala,* pp. 111–66 in S.K. Chattopadhyay, B.N. Bandyopadhyay, and S.R. Das 1937.

———. 1855a. 'Bahu-Bibaha' [Polygamy], Part I, pp. 189–284, Part II, pp. 285–482 in S.K. Chattopadhyay, B.N. Bandyopadhyay, and S.R. Das 1938.

———. I, 1855b. 'Bidhava-Bibaha' [Widow-Remarriage], pp. 11–87 in S.K. Chattopadhyay, B.N. Bandyopadhyay, and S.R. Das 1938.

———. 1860. *Sitar Banabas* [Sita's Banishment to the Forest], pp. 307–68 in S.K. Chattopadhyay, B.N. Bandyopadhyay, and S.R. Das 1937.

———. 1876. 'Jibancharit' [Biographies], pp. 89–152 in S.K. Chattopadhyay, B.N. Bandyopadhyay, and S.R. Das 1939.

———. 1889. 'Bodhodaya' [Enlightenment], pp. 153–92 in S.K. Chattopadhyay, B.N. Bandyopadhyay, and S.R. Das 1939.

———. 1891. 'Vidyasagar Charit' [Autobiographical Fragment], pp. 453–75 in S.K. Chattopadhyay, B.N. Bandyopadhyay, and S.R. Das 1937.

Vivekananda (Swami). n.d. 'Memoirs of European Travel' [translated from the Bengali], pp. 297–406 in Vivekananda 2001e.

———. 1893a. 'Papers on Hinduism,' pp. 6–20 in Vivekananda 2001a.

———. 1893b. 'My Plan of Campaign,' pp. 207–27 in Vivekananda 2001c.

———. 1893c. 'Response to the Welcome at the World's Parliament of Religions,' pp. 3–4 in Vivekananda 2001a.

———. 1896a. 'Practical Vedanta,' pp. 291–358 in Vivekananda 2001b.

———. 1896b. 'India and England' [Interview], pp. 194–201 in Vivekananda 2001d.

———. 1897. 'The Vedanta,' pp. 393–433 in Vivekananda 2001c.

———. 1900. 'My Life and Mission,' pp. 73–91 in Vivekananda 2001f.

———. 2001a. *The Complete Works of Swami Vivekananda, Volume 1*. Calcutta: Advaita Ashrama.

———. 2001b. *The Complete Works of Swami Vivekananda, Volume 2*. Calcutta: Advaita Ashrama.

———. 2001c. *The Complete Works of Swami Vivekananda, Volume 3*. Calcutta: Advaita Ashrama.

———. 2001d. *Complete Works of Swami Vivekananda, Volume 5*. Calcutta: Advaita Ashrama.

———. 2001e. *Complete Works of Swami Vivekananda, Volume 7*. Calcutta: Advaita Ashrama.

———. 2001f. *Complete Works of Swami Vivekananda, Volume 8*. Calcutta: Advaita Ashrama.

Wilkins, C. 1785. '"The Translator's Preface" from *The Bhagavat-Geeta*.' Reprinted, pp. 192–5 in P.J. Marshall 1970.

Index

Amar Jiban, 278-80
Anandamath, 358-61, 367
Anglicist–Orientalist
   controversy, 152–5, 158, 190,
   200, 331
Asiatick Researches, 27–9, 116, 117
Asiatick (Asiatic) Society, 6, 24,
   26–7, 35, 36, 37, 39, 40, 43,
   44, 48, 49, 52, 54, 71, 74, 88,
   92, 93, 116, 117, 128, 155,
   156, 335, 416, 420, 421
Asiatic Society's *Journal*, 420,
   421
Atmiya Sabha, 129, 145
Autobiography, 4, 171, 203,
   220, 278–80, 292, 302, 304,
   317, 412, 434
   in Indian literary scene,
      278–80
   of Rassundari Debi, 278–88,
      291, 292, 294

Baptist Missionary Society in
   India, 67, 68, 71, 99, 108,
   115
Bengali prose, 3, 62–72, 76–7,
   78, 82–8, 93, 94, 113, 146,
   178, 179, 180, 187, 218–220,
   228, 352, 431
   creation of, 84–8
   poverty of, 82–3
Bengal Renaissance and the
   awakening of the Indian
   mind, 2, 132, 172, 431, 433
   bearing of Macaulay's
      contempt on, 154
   contributions of Colebrooke
      to, 36–40
   creation of a new
      consciousness in, 25, 26,
      40, 70
   crossing borders, breaking
      barriers' theme of, 112

Horace Hayman Wilson role in, 116
and impact on women's lives, 292–3
place of Derozio in, 228
primary features and essence of, 26
principal educational 'players' in, 62–3, 238–41
principal protagonists of, 60
role of David Hare in, 146–7
role of William Carey in, 67–84
role of White Townsmen in, 54
Vivekananda's contribution to, 377
the year of its beginning, 9
Bengali bhadralok, 58–60, 62, 64, 86, 104–6, 145, 147, 149–61, 168, 176, 177, 184, 186, 200, 224, 226, 227, 301, 302, 334, 344, 377, 407, 408, 434, 441
Bengali poetry, 85, 236, 260, 266
and the story of the rhymer Madhusudan Datta, 234–67
Bishabriksha, 354, 357

Black Town, 48, 49, 54, 56–8, 60, 62, 64, 104, 108, 148, 165, 176, 215, 256, 267, 405
Blank verse, 236, 253, 256, 257, 259–61
Boseian thesis, 397, 418, 419, 422
Brahmo Samaj, 129–31, 145, 149, 168, 186, 296, 297, 313, 354, 375, 378, 380, 390, 419, 433
creation of, 129
goals and purpose of, 130–2

Calcutta,
cradle of the Bengal Renaissance, 49
city of two towns, 47–65
The Captive Ladie in Two Cantos, 249–51
Child marriage, 221, 278, 309, 441
protests against, 309–10
and the story of Haimabati, 310–6
and the story of Rassundari Debi, 278–91
College of Fort William, 6, 31, 37, 43, 45, 52–4, 57, 59–61, 64, 66, 69, 72–7, 80, 81, 84, 90–6, 114, 116, 117, 190, 220

Oxford of the East, 53, 73
Concept of Mother land, 362–3
Conversion to Christianity,
  56–8, 68, 70, 71, 104, 127,
  129, 200–1, 203, 242, 243–5,
  246–7, 249, 296, 301
  in upper caste Hindus,
    244–5, 301–2
Cross-cultural mentality, 91,
  112, 113, 174, 179, 255, 279,
  344, 419, 431
  Derozio's contribution to,
    169–92

Doctrine of the Trinity, 126, 127
Durgeshnandini, 349, 352, 354–7

Electric waves, 416–7, 420–2
  Jagdish Chandra Bose's work
    on, 416–7, 420–2
English education in India, 60,
  109, 150, 209, 329, 363

Female/women's education,
  123, 149, 151, 157, 181–3,
  191, 194, 221, 222, 237,
  239–44, 253, 260, 292–6,
  298, 309, 318
  missionaries role in, 294

  role of Mary Carpenter in,
    296–8
  and the story of Toru Dutt,
    299–309, 317

Gentoo Laws, 11–4, 26
Geodesy, 179, 401
Ghat killings, 77
Gitanjali, 1, 112, 446
Golden age concept, 39

Humanist reformer Vidyasagar,
  201–29
Hindu College, 6, 62, 64, 128,
  146–50, 153, 154, 158,
  161, 162, 168, 170, 175–7,
  179–81, 183, 185, 186, 189,
  195, 198, 200, 201, 209, 210,
  238, 239, 241, 244–9, 256,
  262, 293, 295, 296, 300, 328,
  329, 332, 333, 405
Hindu law, 11, 13, 27, 36, 53,
  202, 210
Hindu revivalism, 359
Hindu Widow Remarriage Act,
  226, 227
Historical,
  consciousness, 88, 101
  novels, 87, 354, 357, 358

Idolatry (Idol worship), 77, 99, 103, 106, 107, 114–7, 126, 130, 131, 145, 179, 181, 182, 217
Impeachment trial of Warren Hastings, 8–9
Indian Association for the Cultivation of Science (IACS), 405, 406, 409, 415
Indian writing in English, 113, 172, 189
Indo–Western mind, 3, 174, 179, 190, 191, 308, 334, 363, 382, 431
    among Derozians, 190–1
International Physics Conference, 396, 418
address of Jagadish Chandra Bose to, 396

Janus and Ganesa, coherence between, 28–9

La Martiniere, 61–2, 330
    a sahib-para institution, 61

Macaulay's 'Minute' on Education, 158, 160, 190, 238, 331
Meghnadabadh Kabya, 257–61
Memoirs, , 312–6

Missionaries in India, 3, 19, 67, 69, 70, 72, 74, 75, 77, 84, 90, 91, 92, 99, 104, 112, 117, 125, 185, 246, 294, 295, 336, 375, 381, 391
Monotheism, 106, 114, 118, 130, 131
Mosaic law, 27

Nadia poets, 347–8
Nationalist consciousness, 3, 132, 345, 360, 363, 404, 423, 431
Novel writing, 345–6
    contributions of Bankimchandra to, 340–67
    in English-educated Indians, 345–7

Order of Ramakrishna, 376, 388–9, 391
    influence on Vivekananda's life, 388–91
Oriental studies in India, 18–25, 36, 38, 73
Orientalist in India,
    beliefs created by, 27–8
    William Jones, story of, 15–21

Park Street Cemetery, 35, 47, 189
Phrenology, 166, 175
Polygamy, 102, 124, 221–2, 247, 293, 353, 354
  in kulin Brahmins, 102, 124, 221–2, 293
  Vidyasagar's endeavours against, 221–2
Purple prose, 158, 251

Rabindra-sangeet, 445
Rajmohan's Wife, 349–50, 352, 353, 357, 369
  first 'Indian English novel', 349
Rammohun–Hamilton incident, 111–2
Rammohun–Tytler controversy, 128–9, 179
Renaissance man,
  Rammohun Roy, 4
  Rabindranath Tagore as, 432–47

Sanskrit College, 6, 62, 150, 152, 176, 195, 200, 201, 209–12, 214, 216, 226, 238, 330, 402
  established, 150, 200
Sati, 38, 77, 78, 107, 116–25, 134, 142, 149, 185, 186, 202, 223–5, 293, 295
  abolition of, 116, 117, 134, 185, 186, 293
  Rammohun's war against, 115–25, 134, 202, 225, 295
Scientific research in India, 397–425
  contribution of Jagadish Chandra Bose to, 396–8, 407–12, 415–20
  contribution of Mahendralal Sircar's to, 402–6, 409, 415
  contribution of Prafulla Chandra to, 408–14, 420–4
Scottish Enlightenment, 146, 165, 166
Serampore Mission Press, 74, 78–80, 83, 86, 92
Serampore missionaries, 74, 90, 91, 99, 104, 112, 117, 125
Society for the Acquisition of General Knowledge, 190, 191, 238, 240

Universal religion, 375, 379, 382
University of Calcutta, 5–6, 52, 63, 146, 176, 178, 213, 215,

244–5, 260, 268, 270–2, 274, 275, 278, 281, 298, 299, 309, 327, 329–33, 334, 336, 340, 344, 378, 402, 406, 408
  creation of, 327, 329
  symbiosis of East and West, 335
  women candidates in, 298
Vande Mataram, 358, 360, 363, 367, 446
Vedantic movement in America, 384
Vedantic philosophy of Vivekananda, 373–91
  influence on Margaret Noble (Nivedita) of, 385–91
Vedantic socialism, 387, 388

Western education, 92, 149, 150, 229, 377

White Town, 48, 50–2, 54, 56, 61, 63, 64, 99, 104, 165, 267, 330
Widows' remarriage, 57, 191, 221–7, 293, 295, 314, 354
  legalised, 226
  Vidyasagar's support to, 221–7, 295
Widow Remarriage Act of 1856, 226, 227
Women's inheritance rights, 122, 125, 202
Wood's dispatch, 329
World's Parliament of Religions, 373, 382, 384
  Swami Vivekananda's addresses to, 373–4, 382

Young Bengal, 164, 168, 181, 189, 240, 347

A Note on the Author

SUBRATA DASGUPTA IS Director of the Institute of Cognitive Science at the University of Louisiana where he also holds an Eminent Scholar Chair. He has worked for many years on the Bengal Renaissance. He is the author of eleven previous books including a memoir, *Salaam Stanley Matthews*.

A Note on the Type

THIS BOOK WAS set in a modern adaptation of a type designed by the first William Caslon (1692–1766). The Caslon face has enjoyed much popularity in modern times. Its characteristics are remarkable regularity and symmetry, and beauty in the shape and proportion of the letters; its general effect is clear and open but not weak or delicate. For uniformity, clearness, and readability it has perhaps never been surpassed.

In the nineteenth century, Bengal witnessed an extraordinary intellectual flowering. Bengali prose emerged, and with it the novel and modern blank verse; old arguments about religion, society, and the lives of women were overturned; great schools and colleges were created; new ideas surfaced in science. And all these changes were led by a handful of remarkable men and women. For the first time comes a gripping narrative about the Bengal Renaissance recounted through the lives of all its players from Rammohun Roy to Rabindranath Tagore. Immaculately researched, told with colour, drama, and passion, *Awakening* is a stunning achievement.

'Illuminating.' *Telegraph*

'Reading *Awakening* has been an experience…the reader is really transported into that golden era when cultures mingled, barriers broke and benefits flowed both ways.' *Deccan Herald*

'Superbly documented, the book brings to the fore Subrata Dasgupta's skill as a chronicler of events.' *The Hindu*

'[Brings] these characters to life in vivid detail.'
Sunday Guardian

Cover visuals courtesy of V&S Eenterprises Ltd and
Publitek, Inc. dba Fotosearch
Cover design by Rymn Massand
Paperback jacket by Anjora Noronha

ISBN 978-8-184-00183-9

Fiction

MRP ₹599 (incl. of all taxes)

www.penguin.co.in

E-book available